The Liquidation
of Raoul Wallenberg

DEFINITION OF LIQUIDATION

The killing of someone
by violent means.

A term commonly used by the
Russian Intelligence Services.

Raoul Wallenberg was liquidated.

The Liquidation of Raoul Wallenberg

Uncovered: The Missing Evidence
Nikita Khrushchev's secret investigation

By Nigel Bance

Asta Print
Essex, England, 2016

THE LIQUIDATION OF RAOUL WALLENBERG

First published in Great Britain in 2016 by Asta Print
Unit 9, Orwell Court, Hurricane Way, Wickford, Essex SS11 8YJ

ISBN 978-0-9934862-03

Design, typesetting and production: Roger Kohn Designs, Sunningdale
Printed and bound in the UK by Clays Ltd, St Ives plc

Inside front cover: Aerial view of the Lubyanka in Moscow.
The internal prison is identified.

Inside back cover: A typical Lubyanka internal prison cell. This photograph was
taken in the early 1950s. Registration complete in the early hours of February
6, 1945, strip searched and now in prison clothes, Wallenberg was led away to
the fifth floor of the internal jail, like the fourth reserved for 'special prisoners'.
In a typical two-or-three prisoner Lubyanka cell, prisoners slept head-to-head
with raised wooden slatting for the head. The 'paracha', a hole in the floor,
passed as a toilet. 'Special prisoners' often enjoyed better food than the others.

This book is dedicated to Anatoli Sudoplatov, senior economics professor at Moscow State University and KGB officer, who died in 2005, and Colonel Stanley Lekarev, the infamous 'Bluebird', so named by Britain's MI5. This officer, celebrated within the ranks of the SVR and KGB, died suddenly in May 2010.

Friends both.

I would also like to thank the readers for all their support, namely Diana Petersen-Buechse, Shelagh Flower and Stuart Mathieson.

Russian intelligence
– the jargon

KGB: Evolved from the Cheka [1917-1922], GPU [1922-1923], OGPU [1923-1934], NKVD [1934-1943], NKGB [1941, 1943-1946], MGB [1946-1954] and MVD [1946-1954]. The KGB came into being in March 1954 with Ivan Serov its first Chairman. After the collapse of communism, the KGB continued into 1991 and replaced by the FSK. In 1995, the FSK was replaced by the **FSB**.

Smersh: Red Army counterintelligence organisation that grew out of the NKVD in April 1943 and folded into the NKGB in April 1946.

NKVD: Set up in 1934 as the People's Commissariat for Internal Affairs. Within the USSR, it was referred to as the 'secret police'.

MVD: Soviet Ministry of Internal Affairs.

NKGB: People's Commissariat of State Security. It first operated in 1941 and then from 1943 to 1946. The predecessor of the MGB.

MGB: Soviet Ministry of State Security that took over many of the functions of the NKGB including counterintelligence.

GRU: Military intelligence. Often viewed as the competitor to the KGB and SVR, its officers operate under the role of military or defence attaché in embassies and consulates. Highly respected by western intelligence agencies.

SVR: Foreign intelligence service after 1991. It grew out of the NKVD's Fifth Chief Directorate and the KGB's First Chief Directorate (PGU). Officers are recruited from educational establishments such as the Moscow State Institute of International Relations and other top universities. During the NKVD period, the training centre was in Malakhovka, Moscow, with recruits split into foreign language groups. Fully trained officers are posted to embassies and consulates abroad with counsellor (first or second secretary) or attaché roles.

Committee of Information [KI]: A knee-jerk response by Stalin in 1947 to form a clearing-house on foreign intelligence to compete with America's new CIA. Hampered from the outset by inter-service rivalries, the GRU demanded a return to autonomy. Divided into 'Large KI' and 'Small KI'. It folded in 1951.

Rezident: Title given to senior intelligence officers abroad in the embassies and consulates. Also known as head-of-station.

Rezidentura: Intelligence centre within a country.

Back-channels: Lines of unofficial communication between intelligence agencies and governments.

Asset: Another term for an agent.

Controller: Handlers for agents or assets.

Illegal: Undercover intelligence agent working outside the embassy or consulate.

Kommandatura: This is the department that handled the security and logistics for the prisons under the control of the security services. During Wallenberg's incarceration it came under the remit of the MGB. A responsibility was prisoner execution.

At the beginning...

"WHY IS BARKOVSKY talking to *you?*"
I shrugged. Others were also curious. Few had access to this illusive former Russian spymaster, now in his eighties, who still maintained his clearance to the highly-secret operational archive of the SVR, Russia's foreign intelligence service, the KGB and the NKVD. The enquirer was a senior MI5 officer who I often met in her office overlooking the Thames. Occasionally we had lunch in the downstairs bistro in the Tate Gallery. Once we met in The Crown pub in Bray.

Four days a week, Colonel Vladimir Barkovsky took the metro to the vast intelligence complex in Yaseneva to the south of Moscow, just off the city's outer ring road. He had his FSB minders but he usually spurned the use of the car with a driver. The archive is held on two floors below ground level and includes the numerous rolls of film and photographs taken by Barkovsky, when serving as a political attaché in the London embassy during WW2.

Those films had deteriorated badly, according to Barkovsky, and plans were afoot to preserve much of the precious and historic archive. In the embassy it had fallen to Barkovsky to photograph material stolen by Philby, Burgess, Maclean, Blunt, Cairncross and the scientists he personally ran in Oxford, Cambridge, Birmingham and London. This fledgling NKVD officer, employed in the Fifth Chief Directorate – foreign intelligence – was elated when Cairncross had handed over to the embassy's NKVD head of station the details of Britain's plans to build 36 atomic bombs to use on Germany. The original of that Maud Report, prepared in July 1941, needed to be returned to a Whitehall safe by early morning, so

Barkovsky stayed up all night ensuring that Moscow would receive only the most perfect of negatives, accompanied by his translation of the lengthy document. Stalin was to be stunned at the progress of Britain's émigré physicists, compared to Soviet efforts. In the latter years of the war, with Cairncross posted to Bletchley Park, Barkovsky would use his photographic skills to ensure that Moscow had access to the deciphered traffic.

Access into the Lubyanka history room is rarely permitted to a foreigner, but Barkovsky carried the necessary clout. Over a full afternoon, the Lubyanka archivist organised by Barkovsky delightedly guided me around the exhibits, explaining the operational successes against MI5, MI6 and the CIA. Photographs of intelligence officers and foreign agents adorned the walls. A large stone plaque had engraved into it the most celebrated and decorated officers: Barkovsky was one. He had been part of a select NKVD team tasked with stealing the nuclear secrets of Britain and America. As Barkovsky's career developed, he became a legendary spymaster but now in the winter of his life one final challenge needed completion and he was the prime choice to undertake it. With Russia in chaos in the late 1980s, soon set to eschew communism and embrace capitalism, new intelligence masters required Barkovsky to brief them on the most secret events and operations of the past.

My research into nuclear espionage and how Stalin's intelligence services had aided the Soviet rush to build its first bomb – successfully tested in Kazakhstan in 1949 – had led me to Barkovsky. I had put out a feeler on whether the ageing spymaster might be prepared to see me and help with my book.[1] To my surprise he did and we arranged to meet. Rather appropriately for that first meeting, Barkovsky had arranged a private room in the Kurchatov Institute, Russia's former premier nuclear research establishment, and in the 1940s known as Laboratory No. 2. In its grounds is the first nuclear reactor built in the Soviet Union, which was switched on in December 1946 and is identical to the secret US facility that had been constructed in the squash courts of the University of Chicago. Hidden underground, it is now the world's oldest reactor and in dire

---

[1] *Ultimate Deception: How Stalin Stole the Bomb*, Rare Books and Berry, Somerset, 2001

need of decommissioning. I have toured the reactor that in past years was one of the closest guarded sites in the Cold War.[2]

Barkovsky turned up looking very dapper in his suit and the first thing he wanted to talk about was life in London. His English was perfect. Permission had been necessary to meet me, explained Barkovsky: apparently that hadn't been a problem. That meeting went well, lasting three hours. We met several times over the next two years.

Augmenting my research, I needed to fully explore British, US, German and Japanese nuclear efforts. It was important to identity the scientific teams, given I had obtained documents in Moscow confirming that so many scientists had become Russian intelligence assets. Barkovsky, with others, was most useful.

Among the large number of Soviet intelligence documents I obtained, were the scientific reports emanating from an NKVD team of nuclear physicists, led by Georgi Flerov, who travelled to Dresden after the mass Allied air raids in late 1944 and early 1945, to test for radiation. These papers, with many others, were kept under lock and key on the dusty shelves in the basement of the Kurchatov. Before the final German surrender, Flerov needed to locate the secret German nuclear laboratory in a forest outside the flattened city. A complement of 33 German scientists and technicians were subsequently rounded up by the NKVD and transported to the Sukhumi nuclear laboratory in Georgia, to be joined by 60 others found in Berlin and elsewhere. Files on the Dresden bombings in Britain's archives remain firmly sealed, but had the subsequent firestorm deliberately targeted the nuclear facility to obliterate Hitler's final intentions to develop the super weapon?

I had several warnings from Barkovsky to stop seeing some of my sources, advice I chose to ignore. That may have been foolish. I stored documents in Moscow, but before I left the capital I faxed them to the UK and to an address in New York. I had been reliably told that

---

[2] Lavrenty Beria, the notorious security chief, was also in charge of Russia's nuclear efforts and was at the facility when Igor Kurchatov, the chief Soviet nuclear scientist, switched on the reactor. Beria jubilantly phoned Stalin with the news but Stalin made no comment and put down the phone. See photographs of that reactor, including the entrance and the head of the reactor with spent uranium nearby [Moscow-3/4].

the Russian authorities never bothered with monitoring faxes, preferring email. On one trip, I was handed a computer disk listing all NKVD, KGB, GRU and SVR serving officers abroad dating back to the late 1920s: an extraordinary cache. Once I cleaned up the files the printout totalled more than 80 pages.

The Barkovsky meetings unexpectedly terminated. We were due to meet but 10 minutes from his Moscow home, when I called ahead, as I usually did, a gruff unknown voice came on the phone warning me menacingly to stay away. Something was wrong. Barkovsky died several months later. I have never found out why contact had ceased.

MI5 hadn't closed its files on the wartime and Cold War atomic spies, nor had the CIA. Using information I had received in Moscow, I confronted two who still lived in Oxford. When I informed a retired CIA nuclear physicist on who I had unearthed, there was a whoop of elation down the phone. One spy, in particular, had been a wartime physicist employed at Oxford's Clarendon Laboratory and right at the top of a post-war MI5 and CIA list of British-based suspects. With two Clarendon assistants, this scientist had tested uranium separation membranes in a converted theatre on an industrial estate near Birmingham. The apparatus was further secretly developed at a facility in north Wales and later deployed on an industrial scale in America for the building of the Hiroshima bomb.

At a private dinner with several former CIA employees in Reston, Virginia, I was asked how I had paid for some of the most sensitive documents I had obtained in Moscow. It was an entertaining group, including an XO, an executive officer in the agency, who was once thrown out of Moscow by the KGB. I used *The Economist*, I responded, which is easy to fold. The money would be in an envelope inside. 'Times haven't changed', laughed the XO.

And Raoul Wallenberg, what tempted me to delve as deep as I have into his fate? The Swedish diplomat was never part of my research into nuclear espionage. Some readers will quickly understand why, given my source. Quite unexpectedly, one of my Moscow sources – not Barkovsky – had handed over to me the 'smoking gun': irrefutable evidence behind Wallenberg's liquidation, denied to governments and intelligence agencies over seven decades since he disappeared in Budapest, Hungary, in January 1945.

Contents

Stockholm's double-agents, who ordered Wallenberg's liquidation and who was the liquidator

Admission of guilt, the continuing legend and final thoughts

Appendices

Raoul Wallenberg's ashes lie under this mound in the grounds of the Donskoye crematorium, a short drive from the Lubyanka.

1

Here lay the remains of Raoul Wallenberg

BENEATH THIS MOUND in the Donskoye crematorium, a short drive from Moscow's notorious Lubyanka, lay the remains of Raoul Wallenberg.

This much-celebrated Swedish diplomat, with Vilmos Langfelder, his driver, had disappeared in Budapest on January 17, 1945, arrested by Smersh – the wartime Soviet counterintelligence arm of the Red Army. Wallenberg had been promised a meeting with a Red Army general in command of one of two Soviet armies advancing on the Hungarian capital.

Taken to Moscow, they were imprisoned and interrogated. Liquidation would follow in 1947 and their ashes, with those of two foreigners liquidated by association, were unceremoniously dumped into this pit. This one had been newly dug: the existing two open pits in the Donskoye were overflowing.

Only as communism collapsed in 1990 did the Moscow authorities allow a general memorial plaque to those who had perished at the hands of the KGB and its predecessors. Around this mound are dedications to a bare few who were murdered: one is for the 13 victims, mainly doctors, who were executed on August 12, 1952, framed in a fictitious plot to poison Stalin eight months before his death. There is no dedication to Wallenberg.

His disappearance has become the stuff of legend. With a number of other foreign diplomats, Raoul Wallenberg had saved tens of thousands of Budapest's large Jewish community from Eichmann's murder transportations and his death marches. Highly respected researchers, Russian and foreign, have scoured available archives for that illusive 'smoking gun' – a document, memorandum, just a letter that could finally solve the mystery of what had happened to Sweden's 'Lost Hero'. The FSB, the KGB's successor, reported in 2010 that a document had been located referring to 'Prisoner No. 7' who was being held in the internal prison of the Lubyanka in the last days of July 1947. Was that prisoner Wallenberg?

Shock, dismay and then utter disbelief had greeted Andrei Gromyko's unexpected admission in a note to Rolf Söhlman, Sweden's Moscow ambassador, on February 6, 1957, that Wallenberg had died sometime during the night of July 17, 1947 in a Lubyanka cell. Attached to that aide-mémoire from the Soviet deputy foreign minister was a statement from Colonel Smoltsov, the chief of the prison's sanitary ward in the early post-war years. The cause of death, according to Smoltsov, had been heart failure. The international clamour for Wallenberg's release continued unabated.

Released German, Italian, Austrian and Hungarian PoWs, in the mid 1950s, had related to Swedish Foreign Office investigators that they had sighted, heard about, or 'cell-tapped' on water pipes with the diplomat and Langfelder in prisons throughout the USSR. Several had claimed they were cellmates. Claims of sightings were to continue into the 1990s. A supposed veteran KGB officer pitched up at the Swedish embassy in Moscow in April 1992 to reveal that Wallenberg had survived the Lubyanka and in the 1950s was living in Yaroslavl, a city to the north east of the capital, and could still be alive. If that was true, and it wasn't, he would have been well into his eighties.

The Swedish Foreign Office, to its credit, has never swerved from its intention to find the truth but as the years passed, this objective unsurprisingly faded. As one senior Swedish Foreign Office official put it to me, 'there is no official view now and it is almost resigned to the opinion that Wallenberg did die in 1947'. Much of the Swedish Foreign Office's archive on Wallenberg – stretching into thousands of documents – has been moved out of Stockholm to a site 20 km north of the capital. Some valuable records including an extensive card index of PoW interviews have remained.

Collapse of communism brings fresh hopes

As the death-throes of communism convulsed Eastern Europe in

1989, the Swedes hoped there might be a thawing in Soviet intransigence over Wallenberg. A request was made to the Russian Foreign Ministry for a meeting. The positive response was certainly encouraging with even the die-hards at the KGB agreeing to attend. Boris Pankin, the Soviet ambassador to Stockholm, formally handed the invitation to Per Anger, the chairman of the Raoul Wallenberg Association, and colleague of Wallenberg in the Budapest legation, to visit Moscow for specific discussion. Was it a breakthrough? Word was received from Moscow that relevant prison and security agencies had been ordered to search for documents. Anticipation grew in Stockholm and the date was finally set: October 17, in the Russian Foreign Ministry.

Valentin Nikiforov, Russia's deputy foreign minister, and Colonel General Vladimir Pirozhkov, the KGB's deputy chairman, faced the Swedish delegation across the table comprising of Anger, Nina Lagergren, Wallenberg's half-sister, Guy von Dardel, Wallenberg's half-brother and Sonia Sonnefeld, the secretary of the Raoul Wallenberg Association. Hope still lingered that Wallenberg was alive, even if that was an unlikely scenario for a 77-year-old within the brutal Soviet prison and camp system.

Was Wallenberg alive? Any hope in a breakthrough was immediately dashed by Nikiforov's response: there was no repudiation of the line espoused in 1957 by Gromyko. Grim-faced, the visitors viewed the offered original of the Smoltsov document, but that cut no ice. 'Nobody on our part ever believed that document,' stated Per Anger testily to a waiting American journalist from the *New York Times* who had accompanied the party to Moscow.

Pirozhkov did impart some revealing news. An unmarked envelope had been found in the Lubyanka – a fluke 'discovery' reported the KGB deputy chairman. New shelving was replacing the old and documents were being shifted. He placed the envelope on the table and inside was the first irrefutable evidence that Wallenberg had at least been in Soviet hands. Inside was Wallenberg's diplomatic passport, diary and address book for 1944, the registration documents for his car in Budapest, a gold cigarette case, and a Budapest permit to carry a pistol. Currency included Hungarian forints, 1,000 US dollars, 500 Swiss francs, and 30 Swedish crowns, confirming that

Wallenberg had carried large amounts of currency on him. Not included was Wallenberg's second Swedish passport, standard issue for Swedish citizens, which colleagues had known he had carried in Budapest.

Wallenberg's diary demanded close scrutiny. A former official of the Swedish Foreign Office, still in government service, confirmed to me that it contained entries that gave rise to suspicion, given what was known about Wallenberg's movements in Budapest from when he arrived in early July 1944. Names and times of meetings suggested that Wallenberg might have led a double role, aside from his humanitarian efforts on behalf of the Swedish legation and the American War Refugee Board. There was a further conundrum. To his knowledge, revealed the official, several items relating to Wallenberg had been secretly returned in 1957, but as to what they were remained secret even to him, Sweden's acknowledged expert on the disappearance of the diplomat.

Buoyed by what had been found in the Lubyanka, and despite the usual Russian line that Wallenberg had died in 1947, the Swedes pushed further and Moscow agreed to the establishment of a Swedish-Russian working group. It would become a 10-year project concluding in 2001. During these years, much did emerge from a number of Moscow ministries, prison authorities, the KGB and the FSB, but to the group's dismay nothing to confirm that Wallenberg *had* lived after 1947. Throughout this long investigation there were a number of 'closed-room' discussions with the Russian authorities.

There was a major early breakthrough in December 1991 when investigators were given a copy of Wallenberg's arrival registration card for the internal jail in the Lubyanka. It was dated February 6, 1945, nearly three weeks after his arrest in Budapest. There were immediate concerns about authenticity. Other documents emerged, again copies, detailing dates and times of prison interrogations, as well as names of the main interrogators. Revealed for the first time was the date of the death of Langfelder – March 2, 1948, eight months after the death of Wallenberg according to the Smoltsov document. Was *this* believable? A letter had been located, said the KGB, and dated June 12, 1957, after an enquiry from Hungary about Langfelder. Very limited information had also been located relating to the death of Wilhelm Roedel, a cellmate of Wallenberg. Autopsy records for Roedel had been uncovered, said the KGB, stating that he had succumbed to a heart attack on October 14, 1947 whilst being transported from the Lubyanka to Camp 27 in Krasnogorsk, on the north-western boundary of Moscow.

Smoltsov's medical statement was never believed. The medical chief had addressed it to Colonel General Victor Abakumov, the head of Smersh and from 1946–51 the Soviet minister of state security. That statement and a notation had only come to light in 1957, Gromyko had reported in his admission and located only after a search of the Lubyanka's health records for prisoners. It read: [3]

> *I report that the prisoner Wallenberg, who is well known to you, died suddenly in his cell this night, probably as the result of a heart attack. Pursuant to instructions given by you that I personally have Wallenberg under my care, I request approval to make an autopsy with a view to establishing the cause of death.*

> *July 17, 1947*
> **Smoltsov, Chief of the Prison's Sanitary Ward,**
> **Colonel in the Medical Service**

A notation to this report by Smoltsov had also been located, said Gromyko. In Smoltsov's handwriting, it read:

> *I have personally notified the Minister and it has been ordered that the body be cremated without autopsy.*

> *July 17, Smoltsov*

It was too late in 1957 to interview Abakumov or Smoltsov. Abakumov had been executed in December 1954 after an involvement in one of the many political plots that had so characterised Stalin's long and barbarous regime. Gromyko had

---

[3] The full Gromyko statement is in the Appendix.

placed the death of Wallenberg as just one of the many 'gross crimes' committed by Abakumov against the state. Smoltsov had died in May 1953.

Gromyko had concluded to Swedish ambassador, Söhlman:

The Soviet Government presents its sincere regrets because of what has occurred and expresses its profound sympathy to the Swedish Government as well as to Raoul Wallenberg's relatives.

Intriguingly, Aleksandr Yakovlev, the Russian chairman in the late 1990s of the special government committee researching into political persecution during the Stalin era, uncovered evidence that Smoltsov wasn't working in the sanitary services of the Lubyanka in July 1947. He had been dismissed from the service on health grounds in March that year. Smoltsov's surviving son confirmed to Yakovlev that his father had been unexpectedly ordered back to the Lubyanka only to sign Wallenberg's death certificate.

The final report written by the independent consultants to the Swedish–Russian working group[4] concluded that it was impossible to determine whether the Smoltsov document was genuine. The authors of the official report[5] also had doubts. At no time were original documents granted to the investigators only copies, which heightened the suspicion of falsification. Despite continued requests, investigators were never allowed to view the files these copies had originated from or in what context they had actually appeared. The Swedes argued firmly that the original of the Smoltsov document should at least be independently tested. Surprisingly the Russians agreed. In December 1991, a small sample was sent to the Swedish State Forensic Laboratory in Linköping, 200-km to the south of Stockholm, for analysis. The results did confirm that both ink and paper were consistent with materials available in the 1940s. On the handwritten Smoltsov note to Abakumov asking permission to conduct an autopsy, further tests were carried out but given the Russian predilection for forgery, doubts on authenticity remained.

One specific area of the 10-year investigation was exhaustive, the attempt to identify a 'secret prisoner' who had been incarcerated in Vladimir prison, the KGB jail in the medieval city 124-km east of

Moscow. Inmates had included captured Nazis and foreigners rounded up in the wide sweep for collaborators across Central and Eastern Europe at the end of the war. There had been many reports that this prisoner, a foreigner, was Raoul Wallenberg and he was in Vladimir long after 1947.

The researchers conducted a cell occupancy analysis of the Korpus-2 section of the prison[6], especially the solitary confinement cells on the third floor. A database of 8,049 names and 98,030 cell records, from 1947 until 1972, was constructed and analysed. In their final report, the authors of the Vladimir study concluded that Wallenberg had been that 'secret prisoner' occupying several cells before being moved elsewhere in the 1960s, possibly the 1970s.

Not once, however, did Wallenberg's name appear in the card or cell analysis, or had anyone *actually* seen Wallenberg despite interviews with several long-retired prison employees, offered up by the authorities, who believed the prisoner to be the illusive Swede. The major difficulty these researchers encountered in the records was the lack of prisoner names. In institutions such as Vladimir – and the internal jail at the Lubyanka – prisoners were given prisoner numbers and were identified as such.

That Vladimir prisoner was not Raoul Wallenberg and the Russians have never given up his name. There is speculation that he might have been a very senior German officer, very close to Hitler, supposedly killed in the maelstrom that was Berlin in the last weeks of the war. Whoever he was, there was every likelihood he was never released, spending the time he had left in his life in solitary somewhere in the Soviet penal system after he was taken from Vladimir. That must have been hell.

Such was the clamour and concern over Wallenberg, within a year of his disappearance the first biography was published: *Raoul*

---

[4] *Reports by the Independent Consultants to the Swedish-Russian Working Group on the Fate of Raoul Wallenberg,* January 12, 2001.

[5] Raoul Wallenberg, Report of the Swedish-Russian Working Group, Stockholm 2000. This 206-page report was the official conclusion for the working group and published in Swedish and English by the Swedish Ministry for Foreign Affairs.

[6] *Cell Occupancy Analysis of Korpus-2 of the Vladimir Prison,* 2002, Makinen M., Kaplan A., and Berger S.

Wallenberg: Diplomat, Kämpe, Samarit, written by Rudolph Philipp who meticulously researched into why the diplomat had been arrested. Philipp had the immediate benefit of questioning those who had worked with Wallenberg and the family, but he was hampered. Travel in the first years of the Cold War was severely restricted across much of Europe and there was no access to Soviet files or to documents in Hungary.

Suspicions quickly mounted in those early years as to the wartime activities of the Swedish legation and Swedish Red Cross in Budapest. Had some diplomatic staff performed more covert roles?

Henry Thomsen, a Wallenberg colleague, was immediately in the frame. That wasn't his real name but he wasn't available to provide answers on whether he was NKVD. Thomsen, like Wallenberg, was now held within the NKVD prison system in Moscow. The wartime behaviour of Count Michel Golenish Kutuzov-Tolstoy equally raised questions. Russian-born and educated, post-war he never offered more than the barest of detail about his Budapest role working in the shadowy B-department within the legation and for the Swedish Red Cross. As the Red Army moved into Pest, Kutuzov-Tolstoy took it upon himself to act on behalf of the Swedish legation and the large foreign community. Buda was now cut off with the Danube bridges blown as the battle raged. In the archives of the Swedish Foreign Office there is a three-page report, marked secret, written in May 1955, which was an attempt to question Kutuzov-Tolstoy on his role in Budapest. Retiring with his wife to Ireland in 1951 to run an unsuccessful cooking school, Kutuzov-Tolstoy was visited by an Irish military intelligence officer. What transpired can be found in a later chapter.

In an extraordinary twist in the disappearance of Raoul Wallenberg, a Hungarian diplomat working for an intelligence front within the wartime British legation in Stockholm, the Press Reading Bureau, was the first to inform the Swedish authorities that Wallenberg had been taken in Budapest. That is the assertion of Göran Rydeberg,[7] an expert on the disappearance of Wallenberg. From the evidence of my own extensive research in Moscow, the diplomat, Vilmos Böhm, was a double agent.

On January 16, 1945, the day before Wallenberg was last seen in

Budapest, Vladimir Dekanozov,[8] the Soviet deputy foreign minister, had sent a note to Sweden's ambassador in Moscow, Staffan Söderblom, stating that Wallenberg was in custody. That message was transmitted to the Swedish Foreign Office but according to Rydeberg, Söderblom first sent Dekanozov' s statement to Herbert Caird North, who was an attaché in the British legation in Stockholm seconded to the Press Reading Bureau. Why Söderblom relayed this message to Caird North, says Rydeberg, has never been explained nor why Böhm subsequently passed it on before Söderblom's official communication arrived in Stockholm.

✯✯✯

On one of many research trips to Moscow to locate intelligence documents on Soviet nuclear espionage, a bulky envelope was passed to me without comment in the hotel bar. Back in my room I slowly read the letter and the listing of highly sensitive incidents that had involved the NKVD, the KGB and the GRU, during WW2 and the Cold War, including one that referred to 'The Vallenberg Affair'. I eagerly read the 14-page enclosure, an illustration of the depth of material that would be available to me. That enclosure was the 'smoking gun', the actual account of the liquidation of Raoul Wallenberg... and its source was impeccable.

---

[7] Rydeberg presented an illuminating paper in Budapest in September 2003 entitled *'Raoul Wallenberg and Swedish humint actions during WW2'*, that examined the possibility that Wallenberg might have had a double role in Budapest.
[8] **Dekanozov, Vladimir G**: Before becoming deputy foreign minister, he had been appointed head of the foreign department of the NKVD in 1938 and was an ambassador in Berlin in 1941.

2

The trail to the truth

We had discovered that Wallenberg was cremated after his liquidation. The ashes were buried in the grave of unknown remains for the years 1947-1951 in the Donskoye crematorium cemetery.[9] Ashes of the three foreigners were also buried there. As far as I can remember, Wallenberg's driver was liquidated, as were the two cellmates of the driver. They had to be killed because they knew the details on Wallenberg. Abakumov[10] believed that if these men would be freed and returned home, the circumstances of Wallenberg's death would be made public.

Extract from the memoir written in 1987
by former Colonel General Ivan Serov

WALLENBERG *did* die in 1947. I know, because I have the Ivan Serov memoir. As to the precise day and month of his liquidation, Serov does not clarify. Serov was chairman of the KGB between March 1954 and December 1958 and the director of the GRU, military intelligence, from January 1959 to July 1962. His memoir, specifically on Raoul Wallenberg and his liquidation, refers to an investigation into the diplomat's fate, an enquiry ordered in secret by Nikita Khrushchev, the first secretary of the party.

Serov's investigation began in December 1953 and concluded in March 1954, coinciding with the establishment of the KGB, a merger of the MGB (Soviet Ministry of State Security) and the MVD (Soviet Ministry of Internal Affairs). As the Wallenberg investigation had been in progress, Serov had additionally tasked one of his investigation officers with preparing the blueprint for this new security and intelligence organisation.

No one in the 10-year Swedish-Russian study had sight of the memoir nor the material and files used by Serov into the fate of Wallenberg or Langfelder, his driver and engineering graduate from Budapest's university. Requests were made to view what files the KGB, and then its successor, the FSB, held in its archives but they were declined on the basis that all files had been lost or incinerated. What fragments that had remained, reported the Russians, would be made available including interrogation logbooks and prisoner registration cards.

The archives of the Russian Intelligence Services are widely spread. Operational files of the SVR, KGB, MGB and the NKVD are held in the large intelligence complex in the woods near the outer Moscow ring road at Yaseneva. In the mid-1960s, under Vladimir Semichastny's chairmanship,[11] the internal prison in the Lubyanka was closed with the larger rooms converted into staff dining rooms and the cells utilised for storage including archives. The jail is now undergoing a complete modernisation programme including the removal of cell window bars so the archives have been moved. Stalin maintained personal archives, including the daily reports he received from his own intelligence service that was run out of the Kremlin. Omsk is the location of an invaluable cache of documents: the personnel records from 1940-1965 of intelligence operatives. Some years back one of my sources, with special clearance to access sensitive and secret archives, offered to spend three days in Omsk, for a fee, to scan into his computer the profiles of all the officers involved in nuclear espionage. At the time these records were held on two IBM XT desktop computers with floppy-disk backups. In the Moscow apartment of another source, piled on his kitchen table were bound volumes of all Smersh documents.

---

[9] The cemetery is next to the Donskoye monastery in south-west Moscow. There are no official records of the victims dumped in the pits.

[10] **Abakumov, Col. Gen. Viktor Semyonovich**: Head of Smersh, later MGB and minister of state security. He was also given prime responsibility for atomic espionage. Stalin dismissed him in 1951. Jailed and released in March 1953 on Stalin's death, but he was arrested again in the Leningrad Trials. Executed on December 18, 1954. See photograph [Moscow-2].

[11] **Semichastny, Vladimir**: KGB chairman, November 1961 - April 1967.

Many archives are categorised by date so when I received documents, other files were pulled in on the same timeline. They still made for fascinating reading. It was the long-established tradition that KGB archivists added addendums to documents sometimes years later, postscripts on the past including the names and codenames of foreign agents who stole the original material. GRU archives are the most difficult to penetrate. This military rival to the foreign intelligence directorates of the NKVD and KGB is also credited with obtaining Western nuclear secrets during WW2 and the Cold War. Through my research I uncovered two elderly former GRU 'assets'. They had worked in the renowned Clarendon Laboratory in Oxford and had passed nuclear research to their Soviet controllers.

The FSB, the post-communist successor to the KGB, was consistent in its view during the joint Swedish-Russian study that the Wallenberg file would never be found in any archive. If it hadn't been destroyed, it lay in a place where it wouldn't be found unless there was a lead, was the standard response. As that study reached its end in 2001 the final reports were exhaustive, yet still that 'smoking gun' lay uncovered. Apart from viewing the original of the Smoltsov document, confirming the death of Wallenberg in 1947, the researchers saw no conclusive evidence that he was alive after that year. Sightings of 'foreigners' or 'Swedes', fitting the characteristics of the missing diplomat can never be proof.

At this point, I need to digress from Raoul Wallenberg to establish my credentials as an experienced researcher into Soviet archives.

I have the-late Anatoli Sudoplatov, the son of one of Stalin's most notorious security henchman, Lt. General Pavel Sudoplatov, to thank for the unearthing of the Ivan Serov memoir. Anatoli for a period in his own life had been a KGB officer but I knew him as a highly respected member of Moscow's academic elite with excellent contacts. Did I trust Anatoli? Only up to a point.

As part of my investigation into atomic bomb espionage and how British, American, German – even Japanese – nuclear secrets had found their way into the hands of Stalin and his atomic scientists, I frequently travelled to Russia. Often I just visited Anatoli, a professor of economics at Moscow State University, who in his KGB career had been in the Fifth Department dealing with 'ideological' operations, including monitoring dissidents within the universities. One assignment was to recruit and manage the Russian translators who worked at the United Nations in New York. These translators were regularly approached by the foreign intelligence services. At Moscow State, in the inner sanctum of 20 plus professors, he regularly admitted the sons and daughters of senior KGB officers. Anatoli was expected to do favours but there had to be a return. For years he was a major source, introducing me to a wide retinue of fellow KGB, NKVD and SVR officers.

Vladimir Barkovsky – the spy who stole the Bomb

A contact who certainly didn't come through the Sudoplatov network was Colonel Vladimir Barkovsky, one of Russia's greatest spymasters, who I have earlier described as being a major source for me on nuclear espionage. At the time of our Moscow meetings he was struggling with a terminal illness that was relentlessly sucking the energy out of him. Four days a week he slugged his way into Yaseneva, the major intelligence centre. 'I have been given Wednesdays off', he told me once with sarcasm in his voice. At the same time he was undergoing medical treatment at the special facility for intelligence officers.

That tiredness seemed to evaporate as we talked about his past successes and the rings of networks that had been established in the West to steal secrets. We developed interview conventions. He would never bring up a subject, I needed to introduce it, and he would never say a direct 'Yes', using instead the phrase 'I think so'. I would brief him on my ongoing research and if he felt I was going in the wrong direction, he put me right even to the extent of correcting inaccuracies for me in Russian journals and newspapers carrying nuclear stories.

There were several amusing episodes.

It was standard practice for Prokopenko, the KGB representative at the Kurchatov, to organise my visas and in one session with Barkovsky he decided to sit in, much to my annoyance. I was guarded in my conversation, as was Barkovsky. After a few minutes, Prokopenko stood up and jabbed a finger almost in my face accusing me of being a British spy. I was hustled out of the building and

Barkovsky followed behind looking very bemused. On the steps, Prokopenko said I would be reported to his superiors and slung out of the country. I had used him, Prokopenko almost spat out the words, by using the cover of being an energy journalist to conceal my real intention to discuss nuclear espionage. Once Prokopenko had slammed the door behind us no doubt to carry out his threat, Barkovsky and I laughed aloud and we reconvened in the back of my driver's beaten-up Lada for the next hour or so.[12] Eugene, my driver, made himself scarce and sat on a nearby bench working his way through the cigarettes that I always brought him from London. It was always in the back of the car when Barkovsky felt more comfortable in talking. Eugene spoke no English but he knew that Barkovsky was a top KGB officer. I could count on Eugene's silence and I paid him well. That day, as always, we drove Barkovsky home to his apartment.[13] I shook his hand and we discussed a possible month for the next meeting.

The last time I saw Barkovsky was in the coffee room at the National Hotel, near Red Square.[14] I had chosen a time in the late afternoon when it was usually empty and the pianist had taken his hour off. There I sat and awaited the spymaster. Suddenly, a young woman entered and she certainly wasn't one of the hookers that frequented this covered courtyard. She was smartly dressed but carried no bag or briefcase. The place was empty yet she chose the table right next to mine summarily waving away the proffered menu from the attendant waitress.

There she sat, not even glancing in my direction. I smiled: she must have had an inkling that I had guessed who she worked for. A few minutes later her FSB colleague sauntered in, casually dressed and wearing trainers, to join her. The diminutive Barkovsky was suddenly framed in the doorway. He came over and we shook hands, exchanged pleasantries about my chosen location, and we sat down. Another man entered, older than the other two to sit with his colleagues. These were Barkovsky's minders, there because I had broken with our usual convention and chosen somewhere very public. Given Barkovsky's top-security clearance at Yaseneva the meeting needed to be observed. His minders quickly appeared perfectly happy and left me with their important charge. When

Barkovsky and I parted after three hours or so, I escorted him outside to the waiting car to join his minders. Barkovsky had been on top form that day reminiscing how the National had once been a drinking-hole for KGB officers who entertained their young mistresses in communist days, and yes, there had been certain rooms which had bugs and hidden cameras.

Forever the consummate spymaster Barkovsky proved a good listener and he was always courteous, speaking in that soft tone of his. After graduating from the NKVD's foreign intelligence directorate's training centre at Malakhovka, and fluent in English, he had embarked on a trip to London in January 1941. Barkovsky was the new political attaché at the Russian embassy.[15] The journey was long and circuitous via the Middle East given the wartime complications of travel, and he arrived on the quayside in Liverpool in February as the air raid warning sounded for the second of the two attacks that month to hit Merseyside. With another Soviet colleague, also posted to the embassy, they ran for the nearest shelter and after the all-clear was rung they shared several pints of beer in a Liverpool pub much to the delight of other drinkers who had never seen or met a Russian. Britain was a far different place than that painted to Barkovsky in December 1940 as Molotov lectured him for 30 minutes on Soviet foreign policy. In late evening, the new Soviet diplomatic recruits caught the overnight train to Euston station in London and would present their credentials to Ivan Maisky, the Russian ambassador. As an NKVD officer in the Fifth Chief Directorate, Captain Barkovsky used the codename 'Jerry'. On his first day he was given an allowance to buy a suit from the outfitters, Austin Reed in Regent Street: the wearing of a uniform was for formal occasions only.

Liverpool had been Barkovsky's introduction to Britain and many years later he fondly recalled that introduction to a British pub.

---

[12] Barkovsky outside the Kurchatov that day, with his usual folder of information for me. Photograph *[Moscow-5]*.

[13] Barkovsky outside his apartment block on another visit. Photograph *[Moscow-6]*.

[14] Barkovsky and the author at the National Hotel, our final meeting. Photograph *[Moscow-7]*.

[15] Colonel Vladimir Barkovsky became a senior KGB spymaster *[Moscow-8]*.

Trained in Malakhovka to photograph documents, he toiled long nights with his Leica in the embassy always making two sets of negatives of which one would be couriered to Moscow. The NKVD rezident, Colonel Anatoli Gorski, ran the Cambridge spies and Barkovsky copied every document they stole.

Increasingly, Barkovsky took over John Cairncross, the private secretary to Lord Maurice Hankey who headed Churchill's scientific advisory committee – one of the most important and influential committees of the war. In NKVD ciphers to Moscow from the embassy Cairncross was identified as 'Liszt', given his love of Franz Liszt, the Hungarian composer. Hankey was even given his own codename by Barkovsky: appropriately, 'Boss'.[16] Twice a week, Cairncross left his office once Hankey had gone for the day, his briefcase stuffed with papers and nodded through by security at the main entrance. Never once, according to Barkovsky, was Cairncross ever asked to explain the contents in the briefcase. There were times when Barkovsky was overwhelmed by the sheer volume that Cairncross had brought him for photographing. Cairncross needed to have them back before 'Boss' arrived in the morning. Moscow Centre ordered Barkovsky to tell Cairncross to be more selective. That backfired as it soon became clear that Cairncross couldn't discern the good intelligence from the chaff. Barkovsky quickly rescinded the order.

Barkovsky and Cairncross met in London pubs and all-night cinemas, a feature of wartime Britain, which the NKVD particularly favoured given their anonymity and practicality. If they met during the day, Kew Gardens was usually the venue with Barkovsky enjoying his strolls around the capital's landmark garden. When Cairncross needed briefing Barkovsky and Gorski would collect him in the ambassador's car and drive to a 'safe house' in the west of London just off the A40 main road.

Cairncross was the NKVD's most valuable wartime asset providing it access to every War Cabinet scientific secret. Moscow Centre, through Cairncross, received the intelligence that Britain had developed the science to develop a Uranium-235 atomic bomb, delivering 36 within three years to be dropped by parachute from a bomber aircraft. Barkovsky couldn't contain his excitement as he photographed that Maud Report in July 1941. The following day,

Barkovsky's negatives were in the diplomatic bag. Stalin was stunned that Britain, aided by its émigré physicists and chemists, was so far ahead of Soviet nuclear efforts.

The political attaché had made his mark and with other NKVD officers, Barkovsky plundered wartime British secrets. One spy he ran was Engelbert Broda, the Austrian physicist based at the Cavendish Laboratory in Cambridge, who was a member of *Tube Alloys*, the development codename for Britain's atomic efforts. Running agent 'Moor' at the YP Laboratory in Witton, Birmingham, the commandeered and converted staff theatre in the grounds of the ICI Metals' plant, became a shared NKVD and GRU wartime responsibility after the decision was taken in Moscow to combine nuclear intelligence operations. Seconded to this laboratory was a Cambridge-educated physicist from the Clarendon Laboratory in Oxford. With two assistants on this site the uranium separation membrane technology was refined and eventually expanded on an industrial scale in Mold, north Wales. Codenamed 'Moor' because Barkovsky met this physicist in the cafeteria at Moor Street railway station in Birmingham, this physicist was a significant intelligence coup for the Soviet Union. Still alive, I met him twice to confront him with the damning evidence I had located in Moscow. [17]

Promoted to major in 1945, four years later Barkovsky returned

---

[16] Hankey had a long record of public service. An advisor to Lloyd George during WW1 and Secretary to the Committee of Imperial Defence, in 1931 he became Secretary to the Cabinet. The House of Commons on February 7, 1940 debated Hankey's appointment to the Chamberlain government with several MPs vociferously arguing against it. Hankey was continually at odds with the War Cabinet over not viewing all War Cabinet papers. After persistent complaining by himself and Cairncross, that decision was reversed. The real irony lies in a letter dated May 29, 1941 from Hankey to Sir Edward Bridges at the War Cabinet; Marked *Secret*, the second paragraph says *First let me thank you for the documents that I am now receiving, which have already proved of the utmost value.* The final paragraph states *I am keeping these secret papers entirely to myself and returning them immediately I have read them.* Barkovsky had photographed every one of them. Those negatives are held in the Yaseneva operational archives, and as they began to perish over time they were copied to other formats.

[17] MI5 and RAF Intelligence, the two agencies with intelligence responsibility for *Tube Alloys*, maintained a list of scientists thought compromised. 'Moor' was at the very top. He never went to the US as a member of the *Manhattan Project*, held back as a reserve to his annoyance. As at 2002, he lived in Oxford.

to Moscow and was briefed for an imminent posting to Washington. Now Lt. Colonel and using the codename 'Dan', within two weeks of his arrival in the US capital he was urgently transferred to the New York consulate. Moscow Centre was near to panic. Anxiety had been growing since September 1945 when Igor Gouzenko, a GRU cipher clerk, defected in Canada and blew the GRU networks. In particular, he had revealed the names of British and Canadian scientists who had become Soviet assets. Later detection had uncovered the notable British émigré physicist, Klaus Fuchs, a key member of the British team of scientists in the *Manhattan Project* in Los Alamos in New Mexico. By late 1949 with further US decoding of Soviet wartime ciphers emanating from Washington, New York and San Francisco, the final proof emerged that the entire atomic bomb project had been badly compromised. Soviet networks in Britain and the US were to be rolled up.

In New York, Barkovsky urgently attempted damage limitation but it was too late. Facing deportation Barkovsky with Vera his wife, and other intelligence officers with their families, promptly departed to Moscow. Awaiting them was a hostile and unforgiving reception, the intelligence chiefs demanding scapegoats for the loss of the networks. Hauled before countless committees Barkovsky felt lucky to remain in service, even escape with his life. The British arrested Fuchs in February 1950 and the FBI arrested Julius Rosenberg and his wife, atomic intelligence couriers, in July.

Barkovsky was censured. 'I was stuck in the central office here in Moscow', that was his penance he told me. But his travel was soon resumed by returning to the US on short trips, on his diplomatic passport, to advise on the networks replenishment. Given his experience of running agents, Barkovsky eventually secured a Washington posting in 1956 and for the next seven years he ran operations.

Barkovsky rose up the KGB Fifth Chief Directorate ladder to become deputy head of the STI department, the scientific and technical intelligence group that was the second largest operational division within the KGB, a role that ended in 1969. One significant achievement was stealing the plans for the British-French supersonic airliner, the Concorde. These would be incorporated into the design of the short-lived Russian Tupolev-144 that crashed at the Paris air show. In the twilight of his operational career, Barkovsky passed on his expertise as a professor in the KGB's special faculty of intelligence, teaching recruits. Upon the defection of Colonel Oleg Gordievsky to MI6 in 1985, he was asked to return fulltime. Gordievsky had been responsible for researching the history of the KGB and its predecessors, so Barkovsky was eminently qualified to carry it on.

During our Moscow meetings Barkovsky was particularly keen to hear more of my progress in unraveling the truth behind what the Soviet intelligence services had long referred to as the 'atomic notebook'. In one of the strangest episodes of WW2, this notebook was found in the briefcase of a Dutch SS officer on February 23, 1942 after Soviet commandoes stormed German and Rumanian-held Krivaya Kosa, a village on the north side of the Sea of Azov.[18] Located in the snow after the firefight, the briefcase was handed over to the senior commando who could make no sense of the diagrams and formulae in the bulky notebook.[19] Taken to Moscow it was closely studied by Stalin's scientific experts who had to conclude that it contained the most sensitive details of Germany's atomic bomb programme. Why had a Dutch SS officer in Krivaya Kosa had such details? That discovery became the catalyst for Stalin to accelerate Russia's own nuclear efforts that had been almost abandoned since the German invasion. Barkovsky, in London, and NKVD foreign intelligence officers in the US were ordered to redouble their efforts in obtaining nuclear secrets. [20]

Even Barkovsky, many years later, with his access to the most secret of operational files, could never discover what had actually taken place at Krivaya Kosa that had led to the NKVD imposing a blanket of silence over the episode. When the notebook had been brought to Moscow, Beria immediately dismissed it as an ingenuous

---

[18] Little has visibly changed in the village from 1942. Photograph *[Moscow-9]*.
[19] The briefcase with the notebook was located near the schoolhouse where the firefight took place. Photograph *[Moscow-10]*.
[20] Barkovsky in a group of NKVD foreign intelligence veterans tasked with stealing nuclear secrets during WW2. Photograph *[Moscow-11]*.

fake conceived by MI6. By covertly passing Hitler's nuclear secrets to Stalin, the British had wanted to warn the Russians that Moscow, not just London, were targets for the new German super weapon.

Gathered at a US government funded conference in Laxenberg, outside Vienna, in October 1999, were Soviet nuclear physicists, intelligence officers and an invited international audience that included representatives from Los Alamos, Oak Ridge and other American nuclear weapon establishments. Barkovsky was there, as indeed was I, both delegates of the Kurchatov Institute in Moscow. Barkovsky as a speaker carefully described to an enraptured audience the value of stolen Western intelligence in the development of Russia's own bomb. In the second intelligence presentation, the speaker's first slide illustrated the key factors in facilitating that development. The most important had been the discovery of the 'atomic notebook'.

I was happy to brief Barkovsky on my own research and careful not to elaborate too much or divulge other sources. Barkovsky, the wily old spymaster, understood full well that others were speaking to me. Unexpectedly, he warned me off any further contact with Anatoli Sudoplatov, advising that he posed a danger for me. I chose to ignore the advice. Another warning had emanated in London. I was bluntly informed that if I was arrested in Russia in possession of highly sensitive KGB documents 'I would be on my own' with the British embassy ordered to be of no assistance. I took my chances.

Outwardly, Barkovsky was quiet, his conversation thoughtfully delivered, but that demeanour cloaked a ruthlessness hardened by half a century in the spy game. In that career he had appeared several times as a prosecution witness against other KGB officers. Thankfully I never experienced that side of him. Within Yaseneva he commanded the highest respect but in the more convivial confines of the officers' club in Lubyanka-3, there were sniggers behind his back when he proudly wore his medals. In the new Russia, that formality had passed.

The prestigious *Order of the Red Banner* was only bestowed on exceptional agents and officers. Barkovsky had received his award in 1949, the year that Stalin's first bomb was exploded in the testing ground of Semipalatinsk, Kazakhstan. Stalin was indebted to

Barkovsky and other officers for their intelligence efforts. Some decades later, the appreciative Yeltsin had awarded Barkovsky the *Hero of the Russian Federation*. Barkovsky died on July 21, 2003 in Moscow's hospital for KGB and FSB officers. Even his death was shrouded in mystery as veteran colleagues were not immediately informed of his passing and were not invited to his funeral. I had been informed by phone by a former CIA senior officer. Barkovsky's obituary in a Russian newspaper specialising in intelligence matters was not published until October, and only after sanction by the FSB.

The Bluebird

Stanley Lekarev was one of the finest players ever to have graced the KGB tennis team, an exceptional pianist and unlike Barkovsky, an extrovert.[21] His family were theatrical, his father a renowned actor on the stage. MI5 had awarded Stanley the codename 'Bluebird' during his posting as a KGB officer in London in the 1970s to head Sovexportfilm, the Soviet agency that promoted and sold Russian film and operatic productions abroad. Lekarev, working out of a building adjacent to the Russian embassy in Kensington Gardens in west London, was forever the joker playing games with MI5. Knowing he was often followed Lekarev would deliberately take a circuitous trip around the sights of central London, trying to check out the watcher. Often, he ran out of his building towards Notting Hill to shuffle into a bus queue and watch as an out-of-breath MI5 man ran up with the realisation he had been played.

Facing the Russian premises, MI5 electronics experts listened in. What MI5 didn't know was that the KGB had long sussed the devices planted in the embassy lifts and they were left *in situ* to record worthless information. The KGB had also hacked into MI5's listening gear. This is how Lekarev first heard MI5's use of 'Bluebird' to describe him, named after a character in the movie starring Elizabeth Taylor, shot on location in Moscow and Leningrad in 1976.

Under the Sovexportfilm cover, Lekarev obtained the latest

---

[21] Lekarev enjoyed an intelligence career spanning nearly half a century.
The photograph shows him in his Moscow apartment *[Moscow-12]*.

Hollywood releases, well before general public viewing, hosting riotous parties for their showing. One young starlet always keen to attend was Ingrid Pitt, the star in the Hammer vampire movies made at Bray Studios outside Maidenhead. Lekarev was infatuated with Pitt but they never had a relationship much to his regret, or so he said with a glint in his eye. In her autobiography, Pitt made no mention of her relationship with the Russians, or the parties she attended with her mother. Lekarev ran his own KGB cameraman who would be murdered by MI5.[22] When Britain threw out 105 diplomats in 1971 from the Russian embassy and the enclave operating out of the trade centre on Hampstead Heath, accused of spying, Lekarev as the only senior KGB officer remaining temporarily became head of station. It was a surprise that Lekarev hadn't been deported given the number of times he was followed.

Lekarev's KGB career began in 1958 translating English and German medical articles for scientists who worked at the infamous Laboratory X in Moscow [more of this role in a later chapter]. At university he attended the Foreign Languages Institute, a key intelligence-recruiting centre, with the KGB selecting the best graduates to further their languages education abroad. Lekarev had been in a group of 20 postgraduate students sent to England to study English for a higher degree, courtesy of the British Council, which ironically provided the financial grants for study.

Aware that some were fledgling intelligence officers, MI5 wheedled most out: an annual game between MI5 and the KGB. At Leeds, Lekarev was under surveillance by MI5 watchers and he had been warned to carefully avoid a party-loving professor on the KGB payroll as a talent spotter. With Lekarev in its tennis team and captain, Leeds trounced every university it played and on the team coach, he made notes on RAF and US Air Force stations it passed, scribbling on his thigh through a hole in his track suit bottoms. Trained to identify aircraft, each month he passed on his notes and drawings to an embassy officer.

Years later and on assignment in London, Lekarev orchestrated the recruitment of a well-known London dentist with politicians amongst his patients. In another operation he used the celebrated Russian gymnast team, including the diminutive Olga Korbut and the lovely Ludmilla Tourischeva, in a 'fishing' exercise on Edward Heath, the head of the-then Conservative Opposition. Moscow Centre needed to know whether Heath 'preferred men or women', related Lekarev to me. An invitation from the Soviet ambassador was extended to Heath and at a private party in the embassy both girls nestled up to Britain's future prime minister.[23] Heath declined the flirting, which Lekarev duly reported back to Moscow: his sexuality was unknown, and so ended the 'fishing' of Edward Heath.

Lekarev and I would make ourselves comfortable in the deep leather armchairs in the bar at Moscow's Metropol hotel. Anatoli Sudoplatov usually joined us and we laughed, joked, and drank.[24] Lekarev and Anatoli could certainly hold their booze. As I drank Heineken, these two tucked into the brandy: all on my room bill. Once Lekarev recognised a hotel manager as a former KGB employee, and we stopped talking. An old railway carriage converted into an American-style diner was another favoured haunt. Lekarev would insist on entering first, scouting around before calling Sudoplatov and myself in.

With Putin coming to power in 2000, Lekarev's long intelligence career was almost at its end but the SVR insisted he continue his annual training courses for operational intelligence officers from the Central Asian Republics and other friendly countries such as Palestine. The delegates revelled in the experience and quality of the trainers and at the end of each course, Lekarev handed them a diploma and they all had a party. Lekarev also lectured at the GRU headquarters on assassination techniques after the GRU was publicly fingered in several assassinations outside Russia, including one seriously bungled operation in Doha, Qatar, in 2004. Embarrassed, the GRU had called in Lekarev to lend his experience and lecture. The legendary Stanley Lekarev duly obliged.

When Russia had collapsed into near-chaos in 1990, Lekarev

---

[22] Photograph of the murdered cameraman, taking photos in the Russian embassy in London [Moscow-13].

[23] Lekarev used his KGB photographer to record the event, the gymnasts signed a copy. Photograph [Moscow-14].

[24] Two old spies together, Sudoplatov and Lekarev. Photograph [Moscow-15].

received a phone call from MI5 with financial inducements. He declined. Similar offers were made to other officers. I brought Lekarev and two SVR colleagues to London to speak at a conference I had organised. As it was the first time Lekarev had been in London since the 1970s, he was convinced his visa application would be rejected given his past background. I wrote a letter to the authorities that helped and the visa was granted. Over three days he and his Russian mistress, Valentyna, enjoyed the delights of London from an open-top bus revisiting his past. The two SVR colleagues were put up in Kensington Gardens, at the Russian embassy, but Lekarev and Valentyna had a room at the luxurious Churchill Hotel, not I point out on my money.

Eugene always drove for me in and around Moscow. A former lorry driver, Eugene more than once had the skills to avoid deadly accidents on the notorious roads. It was usual for me to give Lekarev a lift. Once I dropped him off at the GRU headquarters. There was a party for George Blake, the MI6 defector, and Lekarev had been chosen to present the *Order of Andropov* to him for services to Soviet intelligence. It was Blake's 80th birthday and some serving and veteran GRU and KGB officers had been invited. Lekarev had showed me the impressive medal, and I handed it back chirpily asking if he could get me in. He laughed. Few are granted an audience with George Blake.

Death came unexpectedly for Stanley Lekarev, the 'Bluebird', in May 2010 through a heart attack at the age of 75, yet he was very fit and still 'in the game'. My name figured in two of the Moscow obituaries.

Archie – the document finder

Vital in my little group of Moscow-based contacts was 'Archie'. Sudoplatov and I used this codename whenever we spoke about him given he had the security clearance at the highest level. I would heave upon entering his flat, the atmosphere stale and thick from chain smoking and the daily consumption of two bottles of vodka. Amongst many documents Archie located for me, two related to the KGB funding for Robert Maxwell, the British publisher. I will elaborate more on Maxwell in the following chapter on Ivan Serov.

With my research into nuclear espionage, Archie's clearance had provided for me secret documents disclosing the names of several eminent scientists that had spied for Russia during WW2 and in the early years of the Cold War. The true allegiance of Professor Robert Oppenheimer, the eminent US physicist, has long been questioned. Archie, some 17 years ago, obtained documentation confirming that Oppenheimer not only spied for the Russians, he had talent spotted for the NKVD other scientists involved in the Manhattan Project.[25] One document addressed to Lavrenty Beria, dated October 2, 1944, a Colonel Kossow described Oppenheimer's value.

> *In 1942 one of the leaders of scientific work on uranium*
> *in the USA, Professor Oppenheimer (secret member of Comrade*
> *Browder's network) informed us about the start of this work. At the*
> *request of Comrade Kheifets, confirmed by Browder, he provided*
> *access to others.*

Earl Browder was head of the US communist party. Gregory Kheifets, an experienced NKVD officer based in the Soviet consulate in San Francisco, was the controller for Oppenheimer and his wife.[26]

I did have other Russian contacts but I trust the reader can now feel satisfied with my research credentials.

Anatoli, the fixer

I return to Anatoli Sudoplatov, the conduit in the unearthing of the Ivan Serov memoir on Wallenberg. His family is steeped in KGB tradition, much of it sinister and bloody. Anatoli's father, Pavel, a Lt. General, ran the most secret departments within the KGB's immediate predecessors.[27] As a 'special tasks' officer, liquidation was a specialty. His officers orchestrated the killing of Leon Trotsky in Mexico.

---

[25] The US codename for work on the Hiroshima and Nagasaki atomic bombs.
[26] The NKVD document on Oppenheimer, with an English translation, is in the appendix.
[27] Lt. General Pavel Sudoplatov. A family photograph [*Moscow-16*].

I have viewed Pavel Sudoplatov's personnel file, and it confirms the faith and responsibility imbued upon him by Stalin. Surprisingly they met only three times. Two Sudoplatov departments are worthy of special mention. From 1944 until its closure in May 1947, he was chief of *Department S*, a shadowy group of experienced officers who amongst other tasks interrogated foreigners suspected of spying for Western intelligence agencies. For a short period *Department S* gathered nuclear intelligence, a task much disputed by Barkovsky who argued that Sudoplatov had never been given any such mandate.

Another Sudoplatov department, *Department F*, functioning from February 1944 until August 1945, moved around the Soviet-liberated German PoW camps in Central and Eastern Europe picking out captured British and American inmates for hard interrogation back in Moscow. Few were ever released.

Post-war, Stalin continued to use Sudoplatov and his people for 'special tasks' but on Stalin's death in March 1953, he knew his days were numbered. Politburo infighting had ratcheted up the tension in Moscow. In the week before Beria's arrest on June 26, Sudoplatov declined two offers of counterintelligence posts in the Ukraine and Berlin. To fight his corner, he preferred to remain in Moscow. The family lived in a luxury block a short walk from the Lubyanka and in the morning of Beria's arrest, Sudoplatov observed the long lines of tanks laid up in the side streets. These were the tanks on alert to block any counter threat of the two MVD divisions who were loyal to Beria. The Khrushchev purge was on. Another concerned resident in the block was Lt. General Pavel Fitin, the NKVD spy chief, who ran the foreign networks. His codename 'Viktor' appeared in countless Soviet wartime cables from Britain and the US. Barkovsky reported to him.

Sudoplatov was duly summoned to the Kremlin, expecting the worst. Khrushchev met him in Stalin's old meeting room and the first secretary bluntly told him that his departments were under investigation for complicity in Stalin's crimes. Sudoplatov left the Kremlin, a worried man. The arrest came on August 21 and he was thrown into Vladimir prison. Five years elapsed before Sudoplatov appeared in court, his military trial held in secret.

Damning was the accusation of being a willing ally to Stalin and

Beria. A further charge was that one of his departments had managed Laboratory X and other Soviet laboratories that researched and manufactured toxins. Sudoplatov denied any such involvement but he couldn't deny that his family had regularly socialised with the family of Dr Grigori Maironovsky, Laboratory X's notorious chief scientist.

A convicted relic of the past, Sudoplatov returned to Vladimir with the tag 'Enemy of the People No. 8' and later he was moved to a privileged prisoner room in the Lubyanka. Conditions were marginally better than for other Lubyanka inmates with regular exercise allowed in the cordoned-off part of the roof in another area. The food was certainly better. Sudoplatov had been lucky not to be executed.

His release in August 1968, upon serving 15 years, was largely due to the tireless campaign mounted by Emma, his wife, herself a retired NKVD colonel with a formidable reputation to match. Pre-war, she had operated in the Ukraine, Rotterdam and Paris hunting down Trotskyites and Russian dissidents who had fled abroad. Before retirement in 1949, Emma lectured in the Malakhovka training academy in Moscow preparing potential officers to run agents in their international postings. The campaign to free her husband included personal pleas to Khrushchev for a pardon or at least a re-opening of the case with a new trial.

Following in the family tradition, Anatoli entered the KGB after university and using the privilege of office he unsuccessfully tried to overturn the charge that his father had run Laboratory X. Such probing opened up old sores and a new KGB chairman in the early 1990s forced him out. What really angered Anatoli was the refusal to return his father's medals – all awarded by Stalin – and confiscated upon his arrest. They were never returned.

As communism faltered and collapsed, a new and more open climate was slowly emerging with journalists lifting the lid of decades-long secrecy without the threat of jail. In the Ukraine, for so long under the thumb of the KGB, the newly installed government had scores to settle with Moscow. Kiev wanted Pavel Sudoplatov dragged back to face trial for the assassinations committed on its soil in the late 1930s. The attempt in 1991 by the Ukrainian state prosecutor to secure an arrest over the killing of Yevhen Konovalets, the OUN nationalist, was successfully resisted. The Moscow media added to the growing clamour and Sudoplatov came into the full glare of the public with revelation after revelation. Pavel Sudoplatov had been a state-sanctioned killer, but he refused to buckle under the weight of the malevolence.

He decided to write a book about his life as Stalin's 'special tasks' officer with Anatoli doing much of the research. Many hours of tapes with his father and his father's old colleagues were recorded. Anatoli also found the American publisher. Archie, the document finder, proved invaluable to Anatoli in locating the complete archive of *Department S.* Entitled *The Memoirs of an Unwanted Witness – a Soviet spymaster,* the book became an intelligence classic when published in 1994. There were glaring inaccuracies, which I later pointed out to Anatoli. Two years later Pavel Sudoplatov died, aged 89.

Anatoli Sudoplatov was the prodigious fixer. He had set up a meeting for me with Colonel Yuri Kolesnikov, a veteran KGB officer who in the 1980s had been deputy chairman of the Anti-Zionist Committee – a KGB front – and a regular conduit for KGB contact with Maxwell.[28] At the last minute, however, Kolesnikov ducked out after he was warned off. On another occasion, Anatoli and I were sitting in his kitchen with the music on quite loud in the background, which we always did when we talked, when in walked Colonel Edward Sharapov, the former deputy director of the German Desk in the 1960s and 1970s. He had been the senior KGB man on duty in Berlin the night that the MI6 spy, George Blake, arrived after his escape from jail in London. We then shared several interesting hours.[29]

With no shortage of contacts, Anatoli was privy to so many secrets. He showed me the typed unpublished memoir purloined for him by a girlfriend who was also the mistress of Rear-Admiral Sokulkin who ran the GRU networks in North America for many years during the Cold War. In it were details of the top GRU agent

---

[28] **Kolesnikov, Colonel Yuri**: Robert Maxwell's final case officer. Photograph *[Moscow-17]*.

[29] **Sharapov, Col. Edward:** Photograph of Sharapov and Anatoli Sudoplatov at our meeting in Moscow *[Moscow-18]*.

in the US Department of State. The agent used a Russian émigré Washington taxi driver as the conduit to his controller in the embassy.

Anatoli fell gravely ill in 2005, dying after a short illness. I did help with some funding for him to travel to Austria for special treatment, but his condition worsened. He had a lingering death, clouded by a suspicion that 'he had been dealt with' because of appearances on Russian television with revelations that were an embarrassment to the state security services.

A warm day in Moscow, June 2002

I return now to 2002, to June, and a trip I made to Moscow mainly to see Vladimir Barkovsky. I had fixed up the time over the phone and the plan was to collect him at the entrance to his apartment block. We had a location in mind to talk. He sounded pleased that I was coming again to Moscow. Enroute to the apartment I called to say that we were on our way but it wasn't Barkovsky who picked up the phone. As Barkovsky's voice usually sounded subdued and soft this voice was aggressive and abrupt, commanding me not to come. I asked for Barkovsky to come to the phone but the phone was put down. We decided to continue and call again when we arrived. The phone just rang. I rang his bell and gazed up to his windows but there was no movement: a disappointing end to my sessions with the spymaster.

That evening over a drink before dinner with Anatoli at the National, I told him what had happened. He shrugged. The Sudoplatov family had little time for Barkovsky. Before we left our table, Anatoli pushed a newspaper in my direction. I knew the form. It was to be read in the confines of my room.

Inside was a package and the accompanying letter, in good English, was from Dr Svetlana Serov, none other than the daughter of the infamous Colonel General Ivan Serov, promoted by Nikita Khrushchev to become the first chairman of the KGB in March 1954. In January 1959, Khrushchev had moved him out to the GRU as its director. That GRU appointment was highly unpopular amongst fellow senior officers. A spy scandal brought Serov down in July 1962.

Serov had maintained confidential diaries during those days as

Russia's intelligence and security chief, keeping many documents and files that may be of use in the future, perhaps even guaranteeing his life.[30] In the mid 1980s, he made the decision to commit to paper the details of many secret operations. Svetlana had assisted.

Ivan Serov died in 1990, amidst crazy days in Russia as Goldman Sachs offered fresh American business school graduates the opportunity to demonstrate their newly acquired skills on a superpower spiralling into terminal decline. As the fissures of political and economic chaos widened, the social fabric in the USSR fell apart. In streets very close to the Kremlin, pensioners stood in the uncleared snow on the pavements offering baubles and personal mementos at any price. On one occasion, I saw an old man frantically begging anyone to buy his faded pair of shoes, held out in front of him. In the National and the Metropol hotels, hookers propositioned foreign visitors in the bars, lifts and on the stairs. Dollar bills were dispensed for services rendered. It was a far different world from outside.

In the Lubyanka, KGB officers couldn't contain their anger as the Berlin Wall was scaled and sledge-hammered apart. The unthinkable had unfolded. Communism that had spanned three quarters of the twentieth century was finished. Some blinkered KGB generals ordered Ministry of Interior troops and tanks onto the Moscow streets to bring reformers to heel but the order was rescinded. Similar confusion reigned in the GRU headquarters, an ugly and brutal building commonly referred to as 'the aquarium' given its layout.

In the meltdown, MI5 and MI6 offered financial inducements to intelligence officers past and present. Some bit. I would also like to admit here that I, too, paid good money for information and documents relating to atomic espionage. In an economy in free fall, foreign currency opened the doors to secrets and there were too many times when I gave a huge sigh of relief when I made the final departure lounge at Moscow's Sheremetyevo airport. On one occasion I had a floppy disc that listed every NKVD, KGB and GRU officer serving abroad back to the early 1930s, with their actual dates of postings and by country. When printed out back in the UK, it came to 87 A4 pages. In later years, I received GRU updates. I was

---

[30] **Serov, Col. Gen. Ivan**: In uniform, see photograph *[Moscow-19]*.

stopped only once at Sheremetyevo and thankfully, just for a currency violation. Feigning ignorance, I apologised profusely and immediately agreed to pay a large fine. Another visitor wasn't as lucky, his luggage was ripped apart and he was taken away for questioning.

Svetlana Serov, an economist, didn't report her father's death to the relevant security authorities, as she should have done. Instead, with a small gathering of family and family friends she buried her father 'on my money without any participation of government agencies', she informed me. Fortuitously, that decision ensured that none of her father's unique archive of secrets was locked away which is the usual requirement for the likes of Ivan Serov. That had happened upon the death of Molotov, who had died in 1986, and Sergei Kruglov, Beria's deputy minister of the interior and Serov's colleague in the MVD.

Anatoli Sudoplatov had met Svetlana Serov before but they weren't close. Such is the closed world of Soviet intelligence that families often prefer to socialise amongst themselves. They had been reacquainted and my name had come up in the conversation.

The day after Anatoli had given me the package he took me to Svetlana's apartment on the south bank and she was pleased to meet me. From his armchair, her husband quietly observed. Over coffee, he did open up. He was a retired Moscow policeman, earning a formidable reputation for chasing gangsters around the capital's metro system. The family cat eyed me suspiciously.

I told Svetlana that I had read her letter and the enclosed memoir written by her father on Wallenberg and needed to know why she had made contact. She smiled in Anatoli's direction, the answer was clear. I enquired what other material would be made available to me aside from the memoir on Wallenberg.

Svetlana left the living room and returned from a bedroom with three bulging holdalls on wheels. Even Anatoli was astonished as we delved into the mass of folders and sheets of typed and handwritten papers. One file had my immediate attention, detailing the secret meetings in London between Serov and his deputy, Lt. General Alec Gribanov, with Victor Rothschild and Robert Maxwell on March 28, 1956. The KGB chiefs had jetted into Heathrow airport with the Aeroflot crew on March 22, onboard the inaugural flight of the

Tupulov-104 aircraft. Serov had actually written 'my secret meetings...'.

I was looking at arguably one of the greatest caches of Soviet intelligence secrets and determined that my next visit must be without Anatoli. After an hour we shook hands and parted. In the morning I called Svetlana and we agreed to meet later in the day. Unfortunately the husband was there and he prompted me to a chair as Svetlana made the coffee. To my surprise the cat jumped on my lap, purred and went to sleep. The husband hurried into the kitchen to tell his wife. Seemingly this cat didn't usually take to strangers, a talking point for the next few minutes.

I laid out to Svetlana the terms of the $25,000 deal that preferably could be paid into a bank account outside the country. She told me she had one and she quizzed me about my publishing plans. I was deliberately vague. The archive would first be categorised and translated, I responded. The cat continued snoozing on my lap.

Svetlana had a concern. These were the papers of her father, she voiced, and despite his reputation she had a reluctance to part with them. There was an alternative, I countered. For the same payment I would roll into her apartment a high-quality photocopier and she would keep the originals. Svetlana said she would consider the options so I left. I didn't want to push too hard.

Storage of the archive wouldn't be a problem as I did have a safe location in Moscow. The risky part of the operation was how best to spirit it out of the country without encountering the authorities. Joining an Intourist guided tour in Moscow and then cruise up the Volga to St. Petersburg was one consideration. These were official tours so suitcases were infrequently searched. Once there, ships to Helsinki sailed frequently.

As a final inducement to Svetlana I doubled the payment to $50,000 but she couldn't give me her decision before I left Moscow. I sensed a genuine frustration but she didn't let on why: maybe she was being influenced by her husband, the retired Moscow cop. Perhaps he didn't trust me, doubting my motives. The feeling was mutual.

Over the following months, and still hopeful, I did put in place a plan on how to bring the archive out. A British intelligence officer came up with one solution, which I rejected. On three further visits to Moscow, I called Svetlana before I left London. She always sounded very positive on the phone yet when I called on my arrival to agree a time to meet, the husband annoyingly answered. Svetlana was either suddenly unwell or outside Moscow was the typical response. Perhaps my instincts about the husband were correct.

Buying the Serov archive proved impossible but at least I had his Wallenberg memoir and family recollections from Svetlana, which she had been prepared to share with me. She had given me a photograph of her father taken at a momentous time in the Third Reich's collapse by an NKVD photographer.[31] The thunderous look on the face of General Eisenhower, in a formal line up with Marshal Zhukov, Serov, Field Marshal Montgomery, and respective military aides heralded the onset of the Cold War.

I didn't begin my research into the Wallenberg memoir until 2008 and I resurrected my small circle of Russian contacts. Unfortunately Anatoli Sudoplatov was dead. Intelligence personnel records were located for most of the names mentioned in the memoir. Stockholm was important and I was allowed to view much of the Wallenberg archive held by the Swedish Foreign Office. I met Göran Rydeberg, considered the foremost authority in Sweden on Wallenberg. In his office were the 'Green Binders' – the collection of the document copies handed over to the Swedes by the KGB, FSB and other Russian agencies during the joint Swedish-Russian 10-year investigation that had concluded in 2001. No one had been privy to the Ivan Serov memoir. I declined to tell Rydeberg what I had in my possession, but he knew I had found something of significant importance.

Using one of my sources, a visit to the internal jail in the Lubyanka was arranged which was to be a very swift and accompanied viewing of the cells that Wallenberg had occupied. Unfortunately, which so often happens in Moscow, 'faces' abruptly changed in the FSB and this experience was indefinitely postponed.

The name of Ivan Serov even now touches raw nerves throughout the former Soviet Union. His rise and fall in the following chapter.

---

[31] That eventful day in Berlin in the first meeting of Allied military leaders. The photograph comes from Serov's archive *[Moscow-20]*.

3

Colonel General Ivan Serov
– His rise and fall

'IVAN THE TERRIBLE' was a play on Russia's historic past headlined in *The Times* in describing Serov's grisly record as he and a fellow KGB officer, Lt. General Oleg Gribanov,[32] arrived in London on March 22, 1956. The British press didn't spare its united revulsion: 'Black Ivan', 'Abominable Serov', the 'Executioner' were worthy attributes to his reputation.[33]

Serov stayed in Britain for a week but such was the public clamour and vitriol he was not included in the entourage of 44 that arrived three months later for the Khrushchev and Bulganin state visit. In his place, Major General N.S. Zakharov accompanied Khrushchev as head of security just as he had done at the heads-of-state meeting in Geneva the previous year. What had been related to the British press by Eastern-bloc defectors and émigré groups was sufficient to encourage an eruption in the House of Commons to the news that Serov was gone and wasn't coming back. To loud cheers and clapping, one MP declared loudly that there had been 'a feeling of deep disgust that this appalling person should ever have been permitted to visit this country.'

Those cheering MPs would have been further outraged if alerted to the private meetings held by Serov and Gribanov in the ambassador's office at the Soviet embassy, the ambassador primed to make himself scarce after initial pleasantries with guests and the corridors cleared of inquisitive employees. 'My secret meetings', Serov had referred to them in his archive.

Robert Maxwell and Victor Rothschild had separately availed themselves of Soviet hospitality in that week in March. Maxwell urgently required the ear of the KGB chairman, as he needed to top up his funding from the KGB for his business ventures. A year later, Serov received a memo marked top secret from his chief deputy, Major General K. Lunyov, and Gribanov regarding one of Maxwell's plans. Financing was necessary to promote the Bolshoi Ballet in Swan Lake productions in Britain, Europe and America, aimed to celebrate the 40th anniversary of the Revolution.[34]

Wrote Colonel Borodin, Maxwell's controller, who had prepared the memo for his bosses:

> *Aiming to maintain business and conspiratorial contacts with*
> *Maxwell, we have identified his broad commercial possibilities.*

Borodin further noted that the money was 'in addition to extra funding and quotas'.

Maxwell's name had been handwritten and underlined, standard operational practice in shielding agent identity from the Lubyanka typing clerks. There is a further revelation in this document, another handwritten and underlined name. Harold Wilson would later become the British prime minister.[35] Serov had agreed to the request.

If further evidence was needed to illustrate that Maxwell had sold his services to the Soviets, I obtained a second document, dated June 24, 1980. Maxwell, pursuing his ambition to become a global media publisher, was the focus of a note written to the Soviet minister of finance, V.F. Garbuzov.[36] It was from the first deputy chairman of the

---

[32] **Gribanov, Lt. Gen. Oleg Mikhailovich**: His name would later appear in an FBI document laid before the Warren Commission into the assassination of President Kennedy. Lt. Colonel Yuri Nosenko, the KGB defector, had named him in an FBI interrogation as having links with the gunman, Lee Harvey Oswald.

[33] How the *Daily Sketch* national newspaper portrayed Serov on his visit to Britain in March 1956. See photograph *[Moscow-21]*.

[34] This KGB memo to Serov is included in the appendix, with an English translation.

[35] **Wilson, Harold**: British prime minister 1964-70, 1974-76. MI5 in the 1970s set up K Branch to investigate Soviet penetration of the Labour Party, including surveillance on Wilson. He had met Konstantin Kukin, the NKVD rezident in London during the latter years of WW2 after being identified as a possible recruit by James Klugmann, the SOE officer who talent spotted for the NKVD.

[36] **Garbuzov V.F**: Minister of Finance, 1960-85.

KGB, General Semyon Tsvigun.[37] Without consulting the KGB, Garbuzov had blocked the Maxwell credit lines. Maxwell had reneged on a repayment of funds extended to him in 1979 via the Swiss subsidiary of Vneshtorgbank, the Soviet foreign trade bank. The $8 million KGB funding had been transferred to a Maxwell private account via Britain's National Westminster Bank (now NatWest).

Tsvigun pulled rank insisting the debt be treated as a special case and rolled into existing KGB channels 'under the funds allocated to us for 1979/1980 by the USSR Council of Ministers for carrying out special measures abroad'. The phrase 'special measures abroad' was underlined in the document. Funding to Maxwell must continue, argued Tsvigun 'to strengthen influence in leading American and British publications'.[38] Presumably that implied Maxwell's influence as he was in the process of acquiring a controlling interest in the British Printing Corporation. In July 1984, those same Maxwell private companies took over the Mirror Group for £113 million.

Maxwell had been 'a walk in', offering himself to the NKVD in Berlin in 1946 when serving as a British army officer.[39] I was told there were further funding documents in the Moscow files and these would be available to me if I needed them. If Maxwell needed Soviet funds to build his burgeoning global empire, Rothschild certainly didn't. His meeting with Serov and Gribanov in March 1956 had a far greater significance. No document has ever surfaced that conclusively pinpoints Rothschild as a Soviet asset, but Serov in his archive did say 'my secret meetings'. In the war, Rothschild had been an MI5 officer with counter espionage skills and post-war Soviet codenames for him included 'Valet', an ironic reference to the high standing of his family and the use of servants, and 'Jack' a high value playing card.

Serov's visit to London had been very productive despite the hostile reception, his well-placed KGB agents disclosing covert MI5 and MI6 plans for the forthcoming Khrushchev and Bulganin state visit. During that visit an underwater operation to sound out the hull structure of the Soviet warship that had brought the leaders to Britain went spectacularly wrong. Sir John Sinclair, the embarrassed MI6 head, was compelled to resign after Khrushchev's people had gone public with the details to the British media. In Moscow, Serov was delighted and he would quietly make another trip to Britain the following year.

Serov's rise

Born in 1905 and in Stalin's personal secretariat in the 1930s, Serov graduated in 1939 from the prestigious Frunze Military Academy. A year later he commanded his first NKVD liquidation operation. After the signing of the Molotov-Ribbentrop Pact in August 1939, Russia occupied the Baltic States and Serov was ordered to clear up the resistance. Thousands were transported into the Russian Gulag. By all accounts he excelled and Stalin was pleased.

Those skills were further honed as the Red Army retreated in disarray from invading German forces in the Ukraine in June 1941. Angered by the spectacle of celebrating pro-German Ukrainians throwing flowers over incoming German tanks and troops, the NKVD exacted reprisals. I saw evidence of such savagery in a unique and unpublished photographic WW2 history taken by Master Sergeant Hans Demleitner of the German Ist Mountain Division.[40] As the regiment advanced into Lemberg (L'vov) in the first week in July, he was called to the Cloister jail to film what had been uncovered. There were piles of bodies, grotesquely tortured, some crucified or beheaded, including a woman with her stomach sliced

---

[37] **Tsvigun, Gen. Semyon K:** In contrast to the usual secrecy surrounding KGB chiefs, he was a public figure in Moscow. It was long believed that he was a relative of Brezhnev. Died January 1982, aged 64.

[38] This second KGB document on Maxwell is also included in the appendix.

[39] Maxwell had several KGB controllers. Mentioned in a previous chapter was Kolesnikov. Others included Colonel Borodin, named in one of the funding documents, the journalist Viktor Louis, who worked for the *London Evening News* and *London Evening Standard* and Nikolay Hlyistov who had studied for a postgraduate degree at the London School of Economics. Hlyistov was well known to MI5, and later banned from entering the UK with the US following suit.

[40] **Demleitner, Master Sergeant Hans:** He boasted to me of personally killing, or executing, 300 Soviet troops while on the Eastern Front. Demleitner ended his life in March 2001, locking his bedroom door and putting his head in the basin before shooting himself in the temple with his military revolver, just weeks after my visit.

open and her unborn foetus extracted and left hanging by tissue. The jail had been an NKVD killing ground. Within days the German Einsatzgruppen requisitioned the prison as its own slaughterhouse, nailing Jewish children to the cell walls.

Serov with Sergei Kruglov,[41] a fellow senior NKVD officer, had orchestrated the wartime systematic emptying of Chechen-Ingush, Kalmyk and Crimean Tatar settlements in the northern Caucasus and the Crimea. Beginning on February 23, 1944, and for eight days, up to 400,000 Chechens and 91,000 Ingush were rounded up and dispersed across the wide expanse of the USSR. For those who refused to go or were too infirm to board the trains, the NKVD simply shot them down. Stalin had demanded retribution for collaboration with the Nazis and the continued refusal to embrace Sovietisation and collectivism. Soldiers from these territories, including even Red Army veterans, were not exempt. Emptying the Crimea of 180,000 Tatars began in May 1944, the majority deported to Uzbekistan.

After his successful ethnic cleansing, Serov accompanied Marshal Georgy Zhukov on the Red Army advance west, into Germany proper and to Berlin. As deputy head of Smersh he ordered the arrest or execution of anyone accused of collaboration. During WW2, Serov was twice awarded *Hero of the Soviet Union*.

With the war at its end, Serov was instrumental in the establishment of the huge Soviet intelligence complex at Karlshorst in East Berlin and according to the documents in his archive he played a major part in the extensive NKVD operation to round up German nuclear and rocket scientists. For a number of years, he ran the Gulag system and his signature adorns countless documents ordering the transportation and imprisonment of millions.

Upon Stalin's death in March 1953, Georgy Malenkov was held up as the likely successor at least through the headlines in *Pravda*, which quoted him incessantly and underlined every mention of his name.[42] But it would be Khrushchev who became party secretary, the supreme leader. A bitter and revengeful Malenkov had to make do with the lesser position of premier. Lavrenty Beria, the security chief, harboured his own leadership ambition, guarded in the capital by two MVD divisions. In the Stalin stronghold of Georgia, Stalin's birthplace and his own, Beria purged the old guard supplanting them with his own people supported by the loyal MVD. He used Serov to purge Byelorussia, run by Nikolay Patolichev, holder of nine *Orders of Lenin*,[43] but with Patolichev enjoying patronage in the Politburo, Serov failed to unseat him.

The downfall of Beria

Widespread social unrest in the DDR erupted in the first two weeks of June 1953. Beria flew to East Berlin to conduct operations against the rioters at a time when he should have remained in Moscow, where his enemies circled and plotted. Never be outside the capital in desperate times is an unwritten rule in Russian politics, but Beria believed that only a phone call was necessary to put his MVD troops on the Moscow streets. Soviet tanks did parade on Berlin's Unter den Linden on June 17 in a show of force as the anti-Moscow revolt gathered apace across the DDR. The power shortages and ongoing economic hardship fuelled the opposition.

Beria was predictably cautious when he arrived at the Kremlin for a Presidium meeting called by Malenkov, its chairman, on June 26. His ever-present MVD bodyguard, alert for any assassination attempt, was nervy and unarmed given the standard regulation that all guns are given up at the Kremlin entrance. Unknown to Beria, Bulganin had waived that restriction for a small number of other visitors, high-ranking military officers, who had been quietly assembled in an adjacent room.

One of those officers, Marshal Kirill Moskalenko, the

---

[41] **Kruglov, Col. Gen. Sergei Nikiforovich**: Stalin promoted him to minister of the interior in December 1945, a position he held until Beria took that role after Stalin's death in March 1953.

[42] **Malenkov, Georgy Maksimilianovich**: Close collaborator of Stalin who served on the State Defence Committee, the GKO, during the war. After Stalin's death, he became Chairman of the Council of Ministers, a post he held only until the appointment of Khrushchev in the following September. Thereafter he was in charge of the Special Commission that reported into the Central Committee.

[43] **Patolichev, Nikolay**: First Secretary of the Central Committee in Byelorussia 1950–56. From 1958 until 1985 he was the Soviet minister for foreign trade.

commander of the Moscow Military District, related in a memoir the events that unfolded. The meeting had convened at 1pm with Malenkov in the chair. Prompted by Khrushchev, Malenkov was to immediately propose a no-confidence vote in Beria and demand he be stripped of all his positions. Moskalenko, Marshal Zhukov, the WW2 military hero, Colonel General Nedelin, head of the artillery, Colonel General Getman, in charge of the tank corps, Colonel General Pronin, member of the Moscow military district and Lt. General Shatilov, the deputy chief of GlavPur, the Chief Political Directorate, awaited the call from Sukhanov, Malenkov's aide.

The plan almost backfired, related Khrushchev in his memoirs, as Malenkov fluffed his cue. Aware of the danger posed by the bodyguard and the possibility that weapons might have been smuggled into the Kremlin, Khrushchev took over, rising to his feet but Malenkov had gathered his wits and pushed the secret buzzer under the table. Sukhanov frantically ushered in the generals with Zhukov at the head, his revolver drawn, followed by Moskalenko.

Zhukov swiftly searched Beria and his briefcase worried he might have a gun. There was no gun, only a note with the words, 'Alert, Alert, Alert' written in large red ink. Clearly Beria sensed that something might be afoot at the Presidium and if given the chance he would wave it at his men. The generals led Beria away to an adjoining cloakroom and the bodyguard was ordered to return to the Lubyanka.

On talking to Svetlana, Serov's daughter, she told me that her mother, who was still alive, related that her husband had returned home that evening flushed with news on Beria's downfall. Serov had said that he had been with Zhukov at the arrest but Moskalenko didn't mention his presence in the Kremlin. A grinning Zhukov had pinned Beria against the wall, his revolver pushed hard into Beria's forehead, Serov reported. Demoted post-war by Stalin and exiled to Odessa, Khrushchev had promised Zhukov the position of deputy defence minister with further promotion to follow.[44]

According to the Moskalenko account, Beria remained in the Kremlin guarded by the generals until darkness fell and then spirited away to the garrison guardhouse at Moskalenko's military base, considered the most secure location in the capital. Rumours were already rife that Beria was shot that very evening. The CIA would later internally circulate a 32-page working paper on events.[45] Western intelligence agencies were convinced a putsch was in progress as tanks had been seen arriving by train at the railway stations. The Red Army was on standby ready to confront Beria's two MVD divisions.

As the new day dawned, with the base on alert to counter any MVD assault, two unexpected visitors arrived at the main gate. Khrushchev had sent Serov and Kruglov, Beria's two MVD henchmen, to interrogate their former boss. Moskalenko was suspicious. Lt. General Pavel Batitskii, his deputy,[46] and Colonel General Getman quickly joined him. Serov demanded immediate access to Beria and without any interference. Moskalenko refused, standing his ground. The situation grew ugly and more than once there was the possibility of weapons being drawn. Serov called Khrushchev to ask for instructions who reluctantly arbitrated that Batitskii and Getman could sit in.

That night the Politburo met at the Bolshoi for a performance of 'The Decembrists' in a visible sense of unity but the absence of Beria, Boris Merkulov,[47] and alternate Politburo members, Bagirov and Melnikov, only heightened the speculation to many in the audience. Melnikov, the strong man of the Ukrainian communist party, had been ousted[48] as had Bagirov, the premier of Azerbaijan, one of Beria's strongest supporters. The absentees had been noted, reported the CIA in a cable to Washington. The tanks remained on the streets until June 30 as the threat from Beria's MVD divisions

---

[44] **Zhukov, Marshal Georgii**: He became defence minister but Khrushchev sacked him in June 1957. He died in June 1974.

[45] *The Beria Purge*, Office of Current Intelligence, Central Intelligence Agency, Caesar-10 archive, prepared August 17, 1954, released June 2007.

[46] **Batitskii, Lt. Gen. Pavel**: Red Army Marshal from 1968.

[47] **Merkulov, Lt. Gen. Vsevold (Boris)**: NKVD chief. If Moscow had been occupied by the Germans, Merkulov would be left behind to control sabotage operations. He was a close ally of Beria in what was referred to as the 'Georgian Mafia'.

[48] **Melnikov L.G**: He was rehabilitated in July 1953, a month after the arrest of Beria and posted to Rumania as Soviet ambassador.

diminished. Still, there was no public announcement on Beria's arrest or fate.

An anonymous article appeared in *Pravda* on July 4, with pointed comments on party unity and discipline claiming that 'the party removes with determination any appearance of petit bourgeois individualism. A leader who neglects theory, who does not raise his ideological-political level inevitably, lags behind life. He is not worthy of being a leader and life will sooner or later strike him off the list'. The US ambassador in Moscow, Bohlen, reported to Washington on July 6 that one of his informants had confirmed that Beria was finished but other sources reported that he was still in the DDR quelling the riots. No one, concluded Bohlen, could confirm that Beria was dead.

The *Pravda* statement on July 10 didn't report the arrest but it did report that Beria was done for, declaring Beria an enemy of the party. His loyal MVD was to be radically purged. Throughout the USSR, *Pravda* reported, meetings had been held with officials invited to demonstrate their solidarity to party and to openly excoriate Comrade Beria. One CIA source described one such event at the Ministry of Defence on July 16 where the 'aktiv', its decision body, had pledged allegiance to the 'collegial' leadership of Khrushchev and Malenkov. Intriguingly, stated the CIA, one senior officer was absent: Marshal Konev.

Pravda, Izvestia and *Tass* fuelled the continued speculation but not one carried any official statement that Beria had even been detained. Foreign journalists conjectured that Beria was in hiding, seeking sanctuary, in whatever country outside the USSR that might shield him. The Supreme Soviet, the highest legislative body in the Soviet Union, added further to that confusing mix by announcing on August 8 that Beria had been removed from post on June 26. No further detail was forthcoming.

Typical Soviet disinformation was how the CIA station in Moscow described the situation to Washington: disguising a Politburo power play with Beria joining a long line of security chiefs to outlive his usefulness. The Americans couldn't fathom why Beria had been in the DDR when allegiance to him in Moscow was crumbling. As to June 26 being the date of the arrest, sources close to the CIA claimed it might even have been earlier, but Beria can be definitely placed in Berlin on June 17.

Beria's death

The news blackout continued until December 16 when the State Prosecutor's Office announced that treachery charges against Beria were complete, adding that it was unacceptable for him to have positioned the MVD above party. Another indictment accused Beria of being in contact with Western intelligence agencies, a reference to the long-standing suspicion that Beria was a British asset. Senior MVD chiefs were also charged: Bogdan Kobulov, deputy minister, Leo Vlodzimirsky, head of special investigations, Pavlo Meshyk, MVD head in the Ukraine, Boris Merkulov and Sergei Goglidze.[49] Vladimir Dekanozov, the former Soviet deputy foreign minister, who had first reported to the Swedish government that Wallenberg was in Soviet custody after being encountered in Budapest, was also indicted.[50] Purges began in the Beria strongholds of Georgia, Azerbaijan and Armenia.

It was December 24 when the Moscow press officially reported that at a special session of the Supreme Court, chaired by Marshal Konev, all the accused had been found guilty and faced execution. Puzzling in the court summary was the statement that the defendants had even been in court. Under an amendment in December 1934, after the assassination of Sergei Kirov, the prominent early Bolshevik leader,[51] such cases could only be heard without the participation of the parties concerned. That same amendment had also stated that death sentences were to be carried out immediately.

Pravda filled page after page on Beria's crimes, not just on subversive activities and the undermining of the state. Under his

---

[49] **Goglidze, Sergei**: In the late 1930s he had been the NKVD chief in charge of the ruthless purges in Georgia. A strong Beria ally, he was arrested in July 1953 in East Germany.

[50] **Dekanozov, Vladimir**: One of the charges laid against him was that he had met German officials in Sweden during 1942-43, attempting to broker peace talks with Russia.

[51] **Kirov, Sergei**: Head of the party in Leningrad. Stalin had ordered his death.

watch, declared *Pravda*, Beria was held fully responsible for the rise in crime throughout the USSR. To celebrate his birthday on April 14 that year, Beria had declared an amnesty for anyone in jail serving five years or less. All could be considered for parole. Hardened criminals now walked the streets and crime in Moscow had surged, reported *Pravda*. In the popular Black Sea resorts, criminals openly targeted holidaymakers and with coast guard patrols relaxed, illegal fishing had proliferated.

The established opinion has Beria's execution on December 23, 1953, the day before the Supreme Court announced its verdicts and death sentences. Moskalenko claimed that he with several other senior officers were present as was Rudenko, the state prosecutor. Supposedly Lt. General Pavel Batitskii had reluctantly fired the bullet at 7.50pm that ended Beria's life. Beria didn't go quietly as a towel had to be stuffed into his mouth to stifle the pleading. Further executions began at 9.20pm, conducted by Colonel General Getman, Lt. General Bakeev and Major General Sopilnik.

The truth? Somewhere in Ivan Serov's archive was the real account, but widely shared amongst veteran KGB officers is the opinion that Beria was taken separately to a location outside the city, maybe even to the killing ground for the security services in Butovo to the south of Moscow. In 1997, a veteran MGB officer added further conspiracy by categorically stating that Batitskii had indeed shot Beria, not in December but on June 26, the day of the arrest, and at the actual Presidium meeting in the Kremlin.

Beria's downfall was to mark a career watershed for Ivan Serov. Khrushchev, with Serov's assistance, was secretly planning a radical overhaul of the security and intelligence services. Serov, with his Wallenberg investigation completed, would become the KGB's first chairman in March 1954, but within months his management style was in serious question.

Serov's own fall

Serov refused to accede to even partial committee governance and fast earned the reputation amongst his senior KGB colleagues as arrogant, complacent and rude. He enveloped himself behind an inner circle of advisers. After three years in post the criticism was withering. Rumours rippled through the Lubyanka and the Kremlin that Khrushchev might abandon his man.

Hostility had extended into the Presidium. Lt. General Nikolay Mironov[52] and Lt. General Alexander Shelepin,[53] finally challenged Serov in June 1958 to demonstrate to members how he might improve the KGB's image. Under Serov, they argued, the KGB was an institutional shambles, publicly perceived as linked to arrest and terror echoing the bad days of Beria.

Serov had met his match with Mironov, the former Leningrad KGB chief, who ran a number of Central Committee departments. Mironov also had a considerable input into the monolithic Administrative Organs Department (AOD), set up by Khrushchev to promote greater economic and political autonomy throughout the USSR. Sharing Khrushchev's reformist ideals, Mironov had little time for the antics of Serov. To Mironov, the KGB had in four short years resembled an outdated dinosaur in dire need of reform. Support for Serov was ebbing away and he fell back on his rapport with Khrushchev.

That friendship wouldn't save him. An unsympathetic Presidium placed the KGB and the Ministry of the Interior under the AOD umbrella, reporting directly to Shelepin. Humiliating was how Serov described the change. Equally livid were Serov's senior colleagues but to them the blame lay squarely with their chairman's rank stupidity and bloody-mindedness. In December 1958, Serov was gone, finished off by Mironov and Shelepin. The obvious candidate to succeed Serov as KGB chairman was Shelepin and Khrushchev duly countenanced the appointment. Seemingly the sacking marked the closure of Serov's intelligence career yet within a month, Khrushchev announced that Serov was to become the new director of the GRU, the highly respected military

---

[52] **Mironov, Gen. Nikolay**: A Ukrainian, he had the ear of Khrushchev and Leonid Brezhnev. He died in October 1964.

[53] **Shelepin, Lt. Gen. Alexander**: Khrushchev promoted him in April 1958 to head of the Administrative Organs Department, a role he held until he replaced Serov as KGB chairman in December that year.

counterintelligence organisation whose reputation transcended the politically riven KGB.

The whispering campaign began again.

With Mironov and Shelepin again at the forefront, the confrontation with Serov degenerated into an all-out dirty personal war. Shelepin mustered support from a number of GRU generals. Khrushchev received a letter from one, Major General Bolshakov. A copy is in the KGB archives and is dated January 8, 1960.

To the Presidium of the CC of the Communist Party

To Comrade KHRUSHCHEV

The decision of the October 1957 Plenum of the Central Committee of the Communist Party called for improving party political efforts in the Soviet Army and Navy. Such action required a more active participation by commanders. However, army general Serov I.A., head of the Chief Intelligence Directorate at HQ, breaches these principles. Comrade Serov does not involve himself at all in the work of the party committee. He refused to stand for election to the party committee. Instead of relying on the party organisation, Comrade Serov uses his own people for administration. Although he does attend the plenums of the party committee, during the last six months he has failed to provide it with either instruction or advice, and reproaches his deputies for following the party committee line. Comrade Serov only creates more difficulties in working with the party organisation and party committee.

Khrushchev had a dilemma, Serov carried his backing but he couldn't ignore the growing outrage that Serov's behaviour had carried over from the KGB into the GRU. He asked Leonid Brezhnev and two other Presidium members to admonish Serov on his aggressive methods. Shrugging off the criticism, Serov merely carried on as before and was usually found improving his tennis on the courts in the Moscow Dynamo stadium reserved for the use of KGB and GRU officers. In the evenings, Serov pitched up unannounced at the Kremlin, regaling anyone who cared to listen with stories of WW2 and his strong friendship with Stalin. Stupidly he began to belittle Khrushchev.

The personal war was to turn even dirtier.

Nikolay Dudorov, the interior minister, pulled no punches in his correspondence with Khrushchev condemning Serov as a rank killer with a track record comparable with the very worst. His own working relationship with Serov had irretrievably soured in November 1956 with Serov in charge of KGB operations in the Hungarian Uprising. Holodkov, Dudorov's deputy, had arrived in the Hungarian city of Mukachevoon on November 6 to meet the head of Soviet forces, Colonel General Komarov, and discuss how best to deal with the growing number of detainees that Serov's snatch squads were strong-arming off the Budapest streets.

Uzhgorod prison in the Ukraine had cells designated for Hungarian detainees but Holodkov doubted it could cope with the numbers. Komarov at least agreed to Holodkov's proposal that Ministry of the Interior units, and not Serov's people, would handle the transportation. Serov called Holodkov to say detainee numbers could swell to 5,000, maybe even go higher. Holodkov objected but Serov was in no mood to listen. Dudorov angrily weighed in and sequestrated cell blocks in other Ukrainian prisons including Stryy, Drogobych, Chernovtsy and Stanislav.

Detainees began arriving on November 15 with 846 Hungarians sent to Uzhgorod, of which 23 were women, another train shifted 400 detainees to Stryy. Holodkov informed Dudorov that the KGB had provided no documentation and he was returning all the youngsters and girls under 17. They were released via the checkpoint at Chop. Dudorov fully supported his deputy. For the detainees in jail, Holodkov ordered food rations be upped to what was called the 'food norm' number two, the same as for the usual Ukrainian inmates. They were also able to trade Hungarian forints for Soviet roubles to purchase essential items in the prison shops.

Holodkov set up a detainee communication system so friends and family could be alerted back in Hungary. In a measured response, Serov upped the number of KGB investigators in the Ukrainian jails to eight with the promise of better documentation, but he baulked at Holodkov's instruction that only Ministry of the

Interior troops would be employed at Chop. Holodkov wanted to ensure that those released would return safely to their homes in Hungary and not be shot by the KGB.

In his accusatory letters to the Presidium in 1960, Dudorov was determined that members be fully informed of the Serov backstory. Argued Dudorov, Serov was Stalin's shameless enforcer in many actions including the exiling of the Chechens, Ingush, and Kalmyks. Using Ministry of Interior records, Dudorov had calculated that huge numbers had been displaced, died or executed.

Sadly, making mischief brought a deadly reprisal as Serov taught him a lesson as a reminder of his muscle. Dudorov's son was found dying in the entrance to the family house, his spine smashed by a severe blow against the staircase railing. Doctors couldn't save him. Serov admitted no culpability, of course, and Dudorov ceased his letters, albeit temporarily. Dudorov had a daughter and he didn't want to lose her.

Penkovsky – the final disgrace

Serov could never survive what happened two years later. His former KGB colleague, Lt. General Gribanov, had organised KGB surveillance on Colonel Oleg Penkovsky, a GRU officer with responsibility for Soviet missile intelligence. Gribanov's officers had tailed Penkovsky around Moscow and in Tsvetnoi Boulevard he was observed meeting Janet Chisholm,[54] the wife of the MI6 head-of-station, Ruari Chisholm. Penkovsky had discretely passed sweets to Chisholm's children and inside the bag was film. Serov was confronted with the photographic KGB evidence that Penkovsky had furnished the British – and ultimately the Americans – with detail on the Soviet arsenal, crucial intelligence to the West during the ensuing Cuban missile crisis.

In his stint as KGB chairman, Serov and Gribanov had worked closely together. They had revelled in the entrapment of the French ambassador in Moscow, Maurice Dejean. A bevy of attractive young ladies had lured the diplomat into a honey trap with a photographer on hand to take the compromising pictures. Dejean had developed into a valuable asset.

During the Penkovsky investigation, the KGB established that when Serov was its chairman, he regularly used Penkovsky for freelance assignments: such a practice was not uncommon, however, as officers in both organisations freelanced for each other to supplement their incomes. Penkovsky often visited the Serov dacha. What Penkovsky couldn't justify to the interrogators was his preference in using closed-KGB communications on GRU assignments. His recent trip to Istanbul was under particular scrutiny. Penkovsky claimed that as he was conducting a covert investigation into GRU rezident Colonel Rubenko, using GRU channels might alert him. The KGB didn't buy it. Investigating Rubenko was just a cover and Penkovsky was seen in conversation with a known MI6 officer. Staff in the Lubyanka jostled at the windows overlooking the internal courtyard to witness the spectacle as the KGB formerly handed Penkovsky over to the GRU.[55]

One KGB officer had witnessed the scene:

We saw a white Volga pick-up drive through the gate of the fifth entrance to House No.2. A tall man in a grey suit, with greying hair, emerged with his guards from the door to the cellar. That cellar housed the case-files, earmarked for destruction. Penkovsky's hair was smoothly combed back. He saw us at the windows but had no emotion in his stare. The guards bundled him into the Volga. Then he was gone.

The GRU is brutal on traitors within its ranks. Penkovsky was reportedly executed by firing squad, but his death may have been more gruesome with reports that the GRU sometimes dealt with traitors by throwing them alive into fired-up furnaces in the crematoria and filming the horror as an example to others who may be contemplating betraying secrets.

There was a handwritten note on Penkovsky in Serov's archive. I had it translated.

---

[54] **Chisholm, Janet**: Upon her death in August 2004, *The Times* obituary alluded to her MI6 activities.
[55] Penkovsky after his arrest. See photograph *[Moscow-22]*.

In April 1962, at the meeting of the members of the Military Council,[56] Guskov[57] acquainted me with information on Penkovsky.

I agreed to help in the investigation. At the end of that month, Rogov, a member of a special commission attached to the Central Committee, put forward the proposal to send Penkovsky to the United States. When I learnt about it I phoned Doluda, the chairman of the commission, asking him to rescind it.

After a few days, Gribanov, the head of the KGB's Second Directorate, rang and asked me to agree that Penkovsky should go. When he was in the US, he said, they would have the possibility of observing him further. I didn't agree. There is no doubt he would have wanted to remain. I then instructed Comrade Smolyakov[58] to transfer Penkovsky to another organisation not connected to intelligence. Penkovsky refused insolently. Then came another telephone call from Gribanov requesting me not to transfer Penkovsky out of the GRU.

Penkovsky had not guessed that he was under observation and they [the KGB] had left any decision on what to do with him with the Central Committee. I was forced to agree. Finally, I asked Gribanov, 'what, is he your agent?' Gribanov went quiet. No, probably not.

An officer, a Major, from a special section, visited me and I forget his name. He informed me that the directors of the KGB were asking me to 'praise' Penkovsky for his work at one of the Party meetings.

I refused and enquired why they needed it. The Major responded saying, 'so he doesn't suspect he is under surveillance'.

This is an illuminating note in Serov's archive and confirms that Serov, despite the reporting to the contrary at the time, did have knowledge of the KGB surveillance on Penkovsky. Gribanov had even sought his opinion on dispatching Penkovsky to the US. Serov's response that Penkovsky would simply defect probably sealed the officer's fate.

Serov's GRU colleagues expressed little sympathy in their director's own going in the general fallout over Penkovsky, ignobly dismissed from the service and reduced by two ranks to Major General. Several deputies went down with him including Colonel General Khadzhi-Umar Mamsurov, in charge of administration,[59] and Colonel General Aleksandr Rogov, his head of operations.[60]

Shelepin still hadn't done. The KGB chairman, in March 1963, accused Serov of collusion with Penkovsky, even an accomplice in the stealing of Soviet missile secrets. Shelepin denounced Serov in the Presidium with the former GRU director formally stripped of his medals, including *Hero of Soviet Union*, for 'lack of vigilance' in managing military intelligence. Mironov, Serov's other nemesis in the Presidium, reportedly beamed with joy. Serov was forced to accept the position of assistant to the chief of staff of Turkestan Military District in charge of tertiary education establishments. Months later he was moved to a similar job in Privolzhsky district, but after two years he was permitted to quit. Dudorov again took to his letter writing with long Serov diatribes but Khrushchev ran out of patience with his interior minister and fired him.

For the next 25 years, Serov 'bravely' took his fall from grace in his stride, it is said by some, spending most of his time in the dacha in the village of Arkhangel'skoe where he tormented the head of the local cooperative. The 11-year Khrushchev leadership would end two years after Serov was thrown out of the GRU and in a telling comment from one of Khrushchev's granddaughters, she

---

[56] Serov is referring to the all-powerful Higher Military Council, established by Khrushchev in 1962 to bypass the Presidium on military decisions. A key military advisor to the Higher Council was Marshal Moskalenko. There were only three Presidium members on this council – Brezhnev, Mikoyan and Kozlov. Given the secrecy of the Higher Military Council, the names of its members were concealed. There were also Lower Military Councils.

[57] **Guskov, Maj. Gen. Anatoly Mikhailovich**: Chief of the KGB special section for the Moscow Military District, and from August 1953 until April 1956, the KGB chief in Azerbaijan. He contributed to a limited-circulation KGB publication, *Military Thought*, the first published in 1962. Published three times year, it ceased in 1970.

[58] **Smolyakov V**: Chief of the political directorate, GRU.

[59] **Mamsurov, Col. Gen. Khadzi-Umar**: Distinguished himself in the Spanish civil war as the legendary Soviet spy. Immortalised by Ernest Hemingway in *'For whom the Bell Tolls'*. He died in 1968, aged 65.

[60] **Rogov, Col. Gen. Aleksandr Semyonovich**: Deputy head of the GRU since 1959, he was the military attaché to Britain from 1954 to 1958 running the GRU networks. He died in 1992, aged 91.

argued that if Serov had continued in post as KGB chairman, the coup of October 1964 would have been prevented given his loyalty to the Khrushchev family. The KGB's dirty hands were all over the plot that led to Leonid Brezhnev becoming first secretary of the party and Alexei Kosygin the premier. Shelepin and the-then KGB chairman, Vladimir Semichastny, had orchestrated it. *The Times* newspaper at the time described Khrushchev as 'the most colourful leader world communism has produced'.

In Khrushchev's memoirs published in the West in 1970, and publicly trashed in Moscow, Khrushchev related that after the Penkovsky business he was left with no choice but to dismiss Serov believing him to be honest and incorruptible. Khrushchev went on to record that 'despite all his faults I respected and trusted him. He was a simple man, naively simple'. That was Khrushchev's opinion, many would strongly disagree.

Serov's term at the GRU had lasted from January 1959 until July 1962, much of this period overshadowed by the withering campaign to unseat him. Under his watch, however, military intelligence enjoyed unparallelled success, as confirmed in his archive. NATO's plans to deal with a Soviet missile attack made its way to Moscow, as did the blueprint of the British Polaris fleet. An agent in the US State Department handed over a CIA document detailing how the US was intercepting Soviet military communications on its rocket testing grounds in Kazakhstan. A very senior British naval officer, a long-standing GRU asset, had enjoyed high-level access to Allied military secrets and had sat on many Washington committees.[61] Stockholm figured highly in Serov's network with an agent purloining a 100-page report on American and British nuclear bombing capacity.

After such an extraordinary intelligence career, reporting first to Stalin and then Khrushchev, Serov spent the rest of his life plotting revenge on the campaigners who had destroyed him. He was riven

---

[61] MI5 knew his identity but he was never prosecuted and was allowed to resign quietly. I brought up his name in certain quarters but my questioning was stonewalled. His name appeared in *Who's Who*. This naval officer was described to me as one of the most productive GRU agents of his generation.

with hatred, said his family. With his passport confiscated on June 25, 1966, Serov wrote in his diary that he now had 'no apartment and no official registration because of one small mistake'. For company, Serov enjoyed an affair with a ballerina from the Bolshoi.

Held in the three holdalls containing Serov's archive were the intelligence secrets of WW2 and the bitter years of the Cold War, up to his sacking from the GRU. Serov made no serious attempt in 'rehabilitation' and Western sources falsely printed reports that shortly after his dismissal in 1962, he became an alcoholic and during one drunken binge he shot himself in a back alley of Moscow's Arbat. His actual death was in 1990, aged 85, with a private family burial.

Before I reveal the details of Serov's investigation into the liquidation of Raoul Wallenberg, the secret enquiry initiated by Nikita Khrushchev, it is worth revisiting the dramatic events in Budapest before and after Wallenberg's arrival.

4

Budapest – the unfolding terror

S EARED INTO THE MEMORY of Frederick Rubin, right up
to his death in 2007, in north London, was the morning of March
19, 1944. Rubin, aged 20, with his father, was enjoying a leisurely
breakfast in the Carlton Hotel in Pest when the noise became a
crescendo. Diners craned their necks from the windows to watch as
the vanguard of SS goose-stepped imperially down the street. Hopes
were now dashed of a peaceful solution with Germany, as Europe's
largest Jewish community feared the worst. Buda and Pest, the two
cities facing each other across the Danube, were occupied.

Droning overhead, aircraft dropped propaganda leaflets, collected
by excited children and the curious. They were unflattering
depictions of a Mongolian, a Negro and a Jew: ethnically
untrustworthy, canted the message. The caricature of the Jew
resembled more an Arab, Rubin recalled. Another leaflet gave the
stark warning that American and British aircraft would soon be
dropping 'gifts' to the people of Budapest... toys, dolls, and fountain
pens with detonators to maim and kill.

Budapest's luxury hotels in Pest were requisitioned. The SS moved
into the Majestic with officers from the Reich Main Security Office,
the RHSA,[62] which was responsible for Jewish transportation to the
Polish death camps. Two days later the RHSA's senior officer,
Obersturmbannführer (Lt. Colonel) Adolf Eichmann, would arrive.[63]
Pest's finest, the Royale, became the headquarters for the officers of
the elite Waffen SS. A short walk away, in Dohány Street, lay Europe's
largest synagogue, a building of great magnificence and the centre of
prayer for Budapest's 184,000 Jews, already assaulted by the Arrow
Cross party, whose head Ferenc Szálasi harboured a ferocious

ambition to accede to government by the gun if necessary.[64] Hotel Astoria, with its glitzy décor,[65] was taken over by the Gestapo. Preferring to be close to the foreign legations in Buda, the SD, the counterintelligence arm of the SS, settled into the Mirabel on the Schwabenberg overlooking the Danube.

Captain Dieter Wisliceny,[66] Eichmann's deputy, was on the triumphant march into Budapest – his mission was to plan the Hungarian actions of the Judenkommando on a far greater scale than his transportation of 60,000 Jews from Greece to 'A', the preferred RHSA reference in documentation to Auschwitz-Birkenau. Eichmann and Wisliceny addressed each other with the informal 'Du'.

The Majestic didn't measure up to Eichmann's eclectic tastes and he repositioned into Apostol Street 13, Buda, a grand villa on the salubrious Rose Hill, sequestrated from Leopold Aschner, a Jewish industrialist.[67] I have been inside and it has an impressive interior with panelling.[68] In what was Eichmann's office on the first floor, he had ordered the immediate painting of a large swastika on the flooring in front of his desk, still *in situ* but covered over by oak parquet.[69] The house had superb views down to the Danube and beautifully manicured lawns ringed with fruit trees, hastily despoiled as Eichmann demanded the turf be dug up and two air raid shelters constructed. At all times, three SS chauffeurs were on call. Eichmann had the choice of an armoured vehicle or the large black limousine parked in the drive.

A Jewish boy working in the house – Solomon – was within days of Eichmann moving in accused of stealing fruit. Slawik, Eichmann's

---

[62] RHSA: The Reichssicherheitshauptamt, reporting directly to Heinrich Himmler.

[63] See photograph of Eichmann in SS uniform [Budapest-1].

[64] With its origins in 1935 as the Party of National Will and imaging Nazi ideology, two years later the party had been outlawed. Reconstituted in 1939 as the Arrow Cross.

[65] Filmmakers now favour the hotel.

[66] Wisliceny's testimony before the International Military Tribunal at Nuremberg on January 3, 1946, provided an illuminating account of the first months of the German occupation in Budapest.

[67] External view of the Apostol Street property. See photograph [Budapest-2].

[68] See photograph [Budapest-3].

[69] These rooms in the villa are presently utilised by a Hungarian company that designs chandeliers. See photograph of Eichmann's office [Budapest-4].

caretaker, some referred to him as a bodyguard, dragged the 16-year-old across the lawn to a shed to await his boss who wanted him thrashed. Solomon's screams were heard by the builders of the air raid shelters as Eichmann and Teitel, the senior chauffeur, set about the boy beating him into a bloody pulp. Satiated, Eichmann returned to the villa for refreshment and to change his bloodstained clothes.[70] That evening Solomon's lifeless body was dumped into the Danube. Indulging in even greater grandeur, Eichmann and his retinue moved within weeks to a bigger villa down the hill, where compliant members of the Hungarian government, who enthusiastically embraced his vision of a Hungary sacked of its Jews, were lavishly entertained.

Interrogation centres on both sides of the Danube were established by the Gestapo and within weeks some 62,000 Budapest inhabitants were newly categorised as Jewish. Hermann Krumey,[71] *in absentia*, described the first days of occupation in his written testimony at Eichmann's 1961 trial in Israel. According to Krumey, thousands were rounded up by the SS and Gestapo. Cold-blooded murder came easy to Krumey. As the SS head of the Lodz[72] office of the RHSA, he had emptied the town's ghetto. After the war Krumey denied any involvement in the murder of 82 children in the Chelmno death camp, taken from the razed Czech village of Lidice on June 10, 1942, even though his name and signature adorned a number of related documents.

Adding to the SS influx was Colonel Kurt Becher, an officer in SS Division Totenkopf – the infamous Deaths Head. Co-opted into the SS Economic Office, given his financial talents, Becher had a different agenda than Eichmann. He commandeered three large detached houses for himself, administrators, clerks and bookkeepers, buildings belonging to the industrialist Manfred Weiss, the majority shareholder of the giant Weiss-Manfred industrial works complex. Becher was to barter the freedom of Jews for convertible currency or valuable commodity to swell SS coffers, and his own. While Becher viewed every Jew as a tradable 'economic unit', Eichmann saw Jews as 'Judenrein', a race to be annihilated. In the coming months SS head, Heinrich Himmler, would arbitrate between the two.

After the war, Admiral Miklós Horthy, the Regent, tried hard to portray Hungary as a reluctant military participant in Germany's territorial ambitions in Eastern Europe and Russia but he couldn't deny that its army bore responsibility for several atrocities. The dismemberment of Yugoslavia in April 1941 saw the Royal Hungarian Army occupy the Banat, Backa and Baranja districts of northern Serbia. Novi Sad, Serbia's second city, fell victim to a three-day pogrom by the Hungarian gendarmerie, an event that still carries shame in Hungary. In January 1942, gendarmes lined up 1,200 Jews on the banks of the Danube and shot them.[73] This practice of using the Danube as a killing ground was later copied in Budapest by the Arrow Cross. In May 1944, some 16,000 Jews held in the Hungarian administered camps were handed over to the Germans for deportation to the General Government in Poland,[74] and extermination.

Hitler mocked his Hungarian ally. Over dinner in the Reich Chancellery on February 26, 1942, with Himmler and the SS Major note-taker, he raged on the inadequacies of Horthy, his government even Hungary's German community – the Volksdeutsche. 'Under Hungarian rule the Volksdeutsche had degenerated and I realised this at Nuremberg, when I saw their delegations march past.'[75] Hitler had grandiose plans for the Danube lands. 'We want to convert the Danube into a German river with 1.5 million German minorities established in the eastern territories. I'll build an autobahn fifteen hundred kilometres long, dotted at intervals of fifty to a hundred kilometres with German agglomerations, including some important

---

[70] This incident was one of many that were used by the prosecution in Eichmann's trial in Israel in 1961. See photograph of the villa's rear garden [Budapest-5].

[71] The Testimony of Hermann Krumey had been a legal submission, signed in Frankfurt, West Germany, on May 27, 1961, to the trial of Adolf Eichmann, in Israel. He refused to travel to Israel for fear of arrest. His full testimony can be found on 'The Nizkor Project', www.nizkor.org/hweb/people/e/Eichmann-adolf/transcripts/Testimony-Abroad/...

[72] This Polish city was renamed Litzmannstadt by the Nazis.

[73] In 2012, the Hungarian authorities opened up a new enquiry into Dr Sandor Kepiro, a police captain who played a major part in the Novi Sad massacre.

[74] Large area in Poland directly under German military control since September 1939, part of Hitler's designated 'Greater Germany'.

[75] Hitler's Table Talk, 1941-1944, His Private Conversations, translated and published in English, 1953, p 338.

towns. We should establish a strong foothold at the Iron Gates… the Danube is also the link with Turkey… and it's only when one's lines of communication are safe that one can build a world empire.'[76]

'The Hungarians have always been poseurs'

Even as losses mounted for the Royal Hungarian Army in the war against Stalin, the disdain never softened. At another dinner in Berlin on August 22, 1942, the note-taker, Heinrich Heim, an officer on Martin Bormann's staff, recorded the contempt. 'The Hungarians have always been poseurs,' Hitler decried. 'In war they are like the British and the Poles; war to them is an affair which concerns the Government and to which they go like oxen to the slaughter. They all wear swords, but none have the earnest chivalry which the bearing of a sword should imply.'[77] Clearly Hitler didn't like Hungarians.

As that German sword was blunted at Stalingrad in February 1943, the once-invincible war machine looked vulnerable, as did the battered Second Royal Hungarian Army that was rolled over on the Stalingrad flank at Voronezh. Before this loss of 120,000 men, Horthy had attempted extrication from the war but was warned bluntly by Berlin that if it did, occupation would follow.

When ordered to the Reich Chancellery in Berlin in April 1943, Hitler bluntly asked the Regent how he was going to eradicate Hungarian Jewry once and for all. The minutes were to be used in Nuremberg at the prosecution of Joachim von Ribbentrop, Germany's foreign minister, who had been present. Von Ribbentrop had stated that 'Jews were either to be exterminated or sent to concentration camps. There was no other solution.' Horthy pragmatically responded that 'he could not, after all, beat the Jews to death.'[78] Von Ribbentrop denied these minutes that had been meticulously recorded by his German Foreign Office aide, Paul Schmidt. At Nuremberg he further disputed Hitler's statement that 'if the Jews there did not want to work they would be shot. If they could not work they would have to perish. They had to be treated like tuberculosis bacilli with which a healthy body may become infected.' There was an admission at Nuremberg that Germany had developed a plan to establish a concentration camp outside Budapest and a ghetto in the Hungarian capital upon occupation.

That occupation of Budapest on March 19, 1944 took place the day after Horthy had again been summoned by Hitler to Berlin, a ruse to lure him out of the country to prevent military opposition. Hitler in preceding months had demanded that the Miklós Kállay government stop advising Horthy to resist German demands for Jewish transportation. On the day of the occupation, Kállay fled for refuge in the Turkish embassy and was replaced by the pro-German lackey Döme Sztójay: an obvious choice given he had been the Hungarian ambassador in Berlin. Sztójay also enjoyed the support of the Arrow Cross. In overall command in Budapest was Dr Edmund Veesenmayer,[79] the Reich SS plenipotentiary, who embraced his new position with gusto by creating on his first day in office the 'Zentralrat der Juden in Ungarn', translated as the Council of Jews in Hungary. Its first edict was to ban all travel for Jews and any change of residence. No servants or domestics were allowed. Veesenmayer had a busy day ordering the arrest of journalists and actors, a Nazi tactic employed in other occupied countries. Within days, the two jails in Budapest were at bursting point and all vehicles, telephones and radio sets were confiscated.

The internment centre, the Schubhaus, was established. Any Jew found at the railway station hoping to escape the turmoil was arrested and taken here for processing and onward escort to Kistarcsa, the camp taken over by the Nazis nine miles north east of Budapest. The huts in Kistarcsa were soon overflowing. Impromptu holding centres sprouted up. The Gestapo used the basements of the Hotel Astoria and the Royal Hungarian Academy of Sciences. Csepel, the large island in the Danube, became a major centre with five camps. Using Budapest as its base, the German authorities now began to set up internment camps around the country. Garany and Nagykanizsa were

---

[76] *Ibid,* p 339.

[77] *Ibid,* p 654.

[78] Owen, J., *Nuremberg – Evil on Trial,* London, 2006, p 181.

[79] **Veesenmayer, Dr Edmund**: Sentenced in 1949 as a war criminal. His 20-year term was reduced to 10 years in 1951 and he was released after US calls for clemency. He died in Germany in December 1977, aged 73. Many argued that Veesenmayer should have been hung, given his record.

amongst the first.

The Jewish population throughout Hungary had swelled from a pre-war Nazi estimate of 747,000[80] to more than one million by March 1944, as refugees had fled from pogroms elsewhere. It now felt abandoned. Through the Jewish Underground came reports of the construction of two new crematoria at Auschwitz-Birkenau and the next big influx would be transported Hungarians. Intelligence regarding the extermination camps at Chelmno, Treblinka and Sobibor had reached Budapest in 1943. The SS would raze Treblinka, codenamed T.11, to the ground after the August 1943 revolt. Up to 900,000 Jews from the General Government area of Poland had been put to death. Sobibor was additionally bulldozed after a similar revolt.

Within a month, Eichmann had agreed the mass deportation plan for the Sub-Carpathia, Transylvania, Upper Hungary and Upper Tisza regions. The capital was to be left until last. Kassa was chosen as the rail hub with four trains a day each carrying 3,000 Jews.[81] Eichmann visited Kassa on April 24 to assess its viability. Willing Hungarian collaborators, including the repellent Andor Jaross, the minister of the interior, and his equally anti-Semitic under-secretaries, László Endre and László Baky, were fully signed up to the mass-extermination operation. [82]

In London, Churchill and his War Cabinet, through the deciphering of German cables in Bletchley Park, monitored the forthcoming pogrom, the biggest yet by the Nazis. There were

---

[80] This figure formed part of the statistical appendix of the Wannsee Protocol, the result of a secret meeting convened under the chairmanship of SS–Obergruppenführer Reinhard Heydrich, the head of the Nazi Security Police and the SD, to effectively rubber-stamp the blueprint to exterminate European Jewry. It was held in a villa on Lake Wannsee in Berlin on January 20, 1942 and attended by 14 people – either key SS officers or senior administrators responsible for the Nazi-occupied territories. Eichmann co-ordinated the event and organized the minutes. A copy of the minutes was discovered after the war. In the minutes was a statistical appendix estimating the Jewish population in every country in Eastern and Western Europe, even non-occupied territories such as England [330,000] and Ireland [4,000]. Of the total Nazi estimate of 11 million, some 5 million were in the USSR and nearly 3 million in the Ukraine, 2.3 million in the area of the General Government in Poland and 747,000 in Hungary.

[81] Pre-1938, Kassa was in Czechoslovakia but it was now part of the Hungarian land-grab after the First Vienna Award. New name is Košice.

[82] All three were rounded up after the war, tried, and executed in March 1946.

demands that Auschwitz-Birkenau be bombed, but they were rejected: a decision that remains hotly debated by Holocaust historians. There was one raid on Auschwitz-3, the sprawling industrial complex at nearby Monowitz, whose German factories, including Siemens, BMW and IG Farben, were fully reliant on slave labour.

Einwaggonieren

The first deportation to Auschwitz-Birkenau began on April 28 when 1,170 internees from Kistarcsa were shipped off by train, along with 400 from the Schubhaus and 214 prominent Jews, who were being held in the rabbi seminary building in Budapest. This first transport consisted of men and women between the ages of 16 and 50. They were to be joined by the 2,000 inmates from the Nagyknanizsa camp. The procedure was referred to by the Nazis as 'Einwaggonieren' or wagon-bound.

The emptying of the rural communities now began in earnest with Eichmann's precise train scheduling via the Kassa rail hub. The free world wrung its collective hands in wretched sympathy, turning away as the genocide unfolded. In Budapest's grand hotels, German units and compliant Hungarian officials partied and toasted the successful implementation of Eichmann's newest 'lightning action' – the liquidation of Jewish communities across occupied Europe in the shortest possible time.

From the outset of the Budapest occupation Frederick Rubin and members of his scattered family wore the obligatory yellow armband. Their homes had been raided for valuables and even the most basic of items confiscated including cutlery and teapots. Jewish emigration out of the country was stopped but that didn't prevent many from trying and dying in the attempt. In short order, two ghettos were established. By June 1944, some 200,000 Jews were incarcerated in the Central Ghetto in Buda, occupying close to 2,000 homes. A smaller number would soon be in the International Ghetto in Pest. Word reached the frantic inmates in the Central Ghetto that it was about to be emptied by the despised Hungarian gendarmerie, the Honved. The occupants were to be handed over to the German Order Police, the units responsible for guarding the Hungarian transportations.[83] The Central Ghetto wasn't emptied.

Wall posters plastered public meeting places in Budapest ordering able-bodied Jewish men, aged 18 to 48, to attend the nearest military centre. Rubin reported for duty at Jaszbere'ny, a small provincial town, manned by the Royal Hungarian Army. Already there was quite a crowd, everyone anxious, worried at the outcome. It would be a long day, including an interrogation by Colonel Zentay, 'a very hard man' remembered Rubin. Trucks took them to a field where they underwent a medical examination by Hungarian doctors. Those rejected were taken away. Rubin was accepted. By nightfall, numbers had been whittled back to 2,000 with groups dispatched to surrounding farms to await job allocation. At Ereszmizsepuszta farm, Rubin was conscripted into a 60-man labour unit attached to the Royal Hungarian Army in northeast Transylvania, felling trees and heaving them onto lorries. Few in the Jewish labour units were destined to survive the war.

The plight of the Jews in Hungary had at last attracted an international response. Henry Morgenthau, the US Treasury Secretary, set up the War Refugee Board. There was sympathy in Britain but Churchill was against mass emigration of European Jewry to Palestine in case it incited an Arab uprising. The neutral legations in Budapest issued letters, passports and safe-conduct passes in a bid to save the city's Jews but they were harried by the Hungarian authorities. No diplomat was allowed to travel outside the city. Pleas were cabled from the Jewish Agency to the chief rabbi in Stockholm, urging intervention from the King of Sweden.

Whether Eichmann or Becher instigated 'Jews for Trucks,'[84] is disputed but Himmler and Heinrich Mueller, the head of the Gestapo, approved it. Joel Brand, a Jewish Budapest businessman, touched down in Istanbul in a German aircraft on May 19, 1944, to start the talks with Jewish Agency representatives. For every 100 Hungarian, Rumanian and Slovakian Jews, the SS wanted one US-made truck. It was prepared to barter one million Jews. Brand's mission failed, and the British held him in Cairo for the remainder of the war.

Becher, the businessman in an SS uniform, had better success in his own deals. The wealthy Choren and Weiss industrialists were quick to bite if their families could flee to America but they had to sell their businesses to the SS Economic Office. A German civilian plane was made ready in Budapest in late June for 32 members of the combined families after US$600,000 and 350,000 Reichsmarks was deposited into a Swiss bank. At the last minute, the devious Becher insisted that the plane couldn't leave unless each family left behind one member in Vienna, as a hostage. Further, he demanded an additional US$170,000. Post-war, Becher was a wealthy businessman in West Germany, the secretive Swiss banking system protecting his lucrative Budapest gains.[85]

Well acquainted with Becher's deals, London publicly condemned them. Several British politicians called for an immediate independent Palestine state to alleviate the risk of SS extermination and financing was sought from well-off Jewish families. Brendan Bracken, Britain's minister of information, in a rousing speech on July 7 at London's Dorchester Hotel raged that 'Hungary was the biggest scandal in the history of human crime.' The Polish government in exile in London issued a statement to the British newspapers that conditions in Auschwitz-Birkenau were far more atrocious than in Dachau, adding that five crematoria were now equipped to gas and incinerate 6,000 Hungarian Jews a day.

Two days after Bracken's stirring speech, Wallenberg arrived in Budapest.

---

[83] The German Order Police, usually comprising retired German policemen, was responsible for many massacres in occupied Eastern Europe. One unit is well described in *Ordinary Men – Reserve Police Battalion 101 and the Final Solution in Poland*, by Christopher Browning.

[84] 'Jews for trucks' – after the war Becher implicated Eichmann, suggesting his own part was minor.

[85] Becher testified as a witness for the prosecution in the trial of Eichmann, but like Krumey refused to attend the trial. See photograph of Becher post-war *[Budapest-6]*.

5

Wallenberg arrives - July 9, 1944

H ORTHY, THE HUNGARIAN REGENT, claimed the credit for stopping the cattle trucks to Birkenau, the industrial-scale killing centre close to Auschwitz. There was some justification in his post-war claim, but the truth lay in Berlin as the Nazis hoped for a positive outcome from the Allies to the 'Jews for Trucks' scheme. On the day the trains ceased, July 9, 1944, Raoul Wallenberg arrived in a city still expecting the worst.

A colleague collected Wallenberg from the railway station and drove him to the legation building in Minerva Street, Buda, halfway up Gellert Hill.[86] The car would have driven past the long line of frantic hopefuls, eager for any form of Swedish documentation to guarantee some measure of safety. Queues were just as long outside the Swiss legation. An apartment had been organized in Tulipan Street 15,[87] a non-descript block constructed in 1941 on Rose Hill, the monied area of Buda. Wallenberg's personal documentation was unlike any other in the legation. In his diplomatic passport – numbered 248 – was inscribed in gold leaf the term 'Kabinetpass', documentation accepted by the Nazi authorities in Berlin that allowed businessmen from neutral countries, such as Sweden, to openly travel around Germany or in occupied territories. With the rank of first secretary Wallenberg headed the new Department C, to specifically handle the rapidly expanding humanitarian efforts, at an annual salary of 2,000 Swedish kronor.

Wallenberg served three masters: the Swedish Foreign Office and the US War Refugee Board in Washington were two. Strict rules of engagement had been imposed by Stockholm enforcing his resignation from Mellaneuropeiska Handels AB, the trading company run by himself and Dr Koloman Lauer, himself a Hungarian Jew. Wallenberg additionally was barred from pursuing any family interests. His third controller was the OSS, the wartime US intelligence service that utilised the War Refugee Board as one of its fronts.

Legation colleagues warmly welcomed the new diplomat and within weeks Wallenberg was in his stride but unease quickly crept in regarding his *modus operandi*, as he sidelined Ivan Danielsson, the legation head, from his Department C activities. Colleagues questioned as to whom Wallenberg did report to. Whatever the criticism, Wallenberg carried the clout to develop connections into key Hungarian government departments and the Nazi administration, which often called for socialising with Eichmann and his ilk.

With lengthening queues on the Gellert Hill, Danielsson did a deal to move Department C into the villa next door, left vacant by the now-departed Finnish delegation.[88] In the months before Wallenberg's arrival, 700 provisional passports had been issued in addition to the large number of protection certificates – the Schutz-Pass – agreed with the Hungarian ministry of the interior.

Danielsson was a diplomat with form, professing Nazi sympathies much to the annoyance of the Swedish Foreign Office. In an earlier posting to Cairo, Danielsson had openly boasted to colleagues that 'it was meaningless for the Allies to fight against Germany.'[89] Within months Wallenberg had established offices in various parts of the city and two Jewish hospitals. The staff under his control in the former Finnish villa and in the main building grew to 400 and he had 30 safe houses in Pest flying the Swedish flag for protection.[90]

Wallenberg arrived too late to witness the scale of the emptying of Jews in rural Hungary. From May 15, 1944, when the transportations began and until they stopped in July, 147 trains had

---

[86] The former Swedish legation is now an apartment block. Inside, in the communal areas little has changed. See photographs *[Budapest-7/8/9/10/11]*.

[87] See photograph *[Budapest-12]*.

[88] Now standing empty, this former Finnish legation building is heavily pockmarked with shellfire from Arrow Cross attacks and the final battle of Buda. See photographs *[Budapest-13/14]*.

[89] The Ivan Danielsson File/UD dossier P.1, Swedish Foreign Office archives.

[90] Two photographs of Raoul Wallenberg, one taken in his office. See photographs *[Budapest 15/16]*.

conveyed Jews to the Polish death camps or to the Polish ghettos. There would have been considerably more if Eichmann had had his way in sacking Budapest. This train total easily surpassed the 87 from France throughout the war, the 63 from Slovakia and 27 from Belgium. From Greece there were 23, Italy 11, Bulgaria seven and Croatia six.[91]

A remarkable document is in the archives of the Swedish Foreign Office, which I unearthed. Someone, and it is unclear who at the Swedish legation in Budapest, had compiled the analysis – in German – of the Birkenau deportations throughout rural Hungary between May 16 and June 10. The numbers could only have been furnished by Eichmann's group or through one of the compliant Hungarian ministries. Town by town, every deportation had been recorded. The total sent to Birkenau had reached 335,000 by June 10: the Sub-Carpathian region accounted for 106,000, followed by 94,000 from Transylvania, 75,000 from upper Tisza, 35,000 from upper Hungary and 25,000 from south Hungary.[92]

Some 437,000 Hungarian Jews had been liquidated by early July in Birkenau, according to statistics compiled for Himmler by Dr Wilhelm Hoettl, a member of Amt. V1, the RHSA's foreign intelligence section. Hoettl, a colleague of Eichmann in Budapest, had provided Himmler with a detailed summary of all Jews exterminated throughout the occupied territories and in Germany. By August 1944, an estimated four million had died in all German concentration camps and another two million had been exterminated by other means, mainly through the Einsatzgruppen during the invasion of the USSR. Hoettl's total of 5,721,000,[93] approximately six million, has become the universally accepted statistic for Holocaust deaths. Birkenau received its last transportation for extermination on November 3, 1944.

Mueller, the Gestapo chief, had instructed Eichmann to temporarily halt the Hungarian transportations with Himmler confirming that it might be permanent. That decision angered Eichmann who fiercely argued that his men could empty Budapest and the entire country of Jews within months. There is a school of thought that Himmler had already resigned himself to a German defeat and the ensuing Allied recriminations. In Himmler's mind, it was vital to steer guilt away from himself to Hitler and Goering, and with Hitler becoming increasingly paranoid he harboured an ambition to take over as Chancellor. Himmler's SS emissaries had already put out feelers in the Allied camp in Stockholm.

London and Washington considered the ending of Hungarian transportations merely an interlude before restarting once the international condemnation had died down. Some trains did run to Auschwitz-3, to the German industrial complex at Monowitz, which necessitated a constant labour turnover. The Swedish legation dramatically extended its citizenship programme. Cordell Hull, the US secretary of state, directly accused the Hungarian Ministry of the Interior of collaboration with the Germans declaring that the 'Hungarian government stands condemned before history.'

Becher exploited further the financial worth of his Jewish 'economic units'. Working with Carl Lutz, the Swiss consul, a train loaded up in Bergen-Belsen, Germany, with 1,684 Jews that had been transported to the camp from Hungary. They were being bartered at $1,000 per head for release in Switzerland. The cash and valuables exchange had been orchestrated through Vaada, the Jewish aid and rescue committee in Budapest, headed by Rezso Kasztner. History remembers this wartime episode as 'Kasztner's train' but for Kasztner at the war's end he was accused of being a Jewish collaborator reporting to Eichmann. A young gunman in Israel ended Kasztner's life in March 1957 but a year later the Israeli Supreme Court posthumously restored Kasztner's humanitarian reputation. His role in Budapest and his relationship with Eichmann, Becher and Hungarian ministers, remains controversial.

Another Nazi plan was hatched in July to allow Jewish transit to Palestine with the German legation in Budapest initiating discussions with the Swedes and the Swiss. Theodor Grell, a German Foreign

---

[91] Source: German railway records and records of the German Order Police who guarded the trains. Browning C., *Ordinary Men – Reserve Police Battalion 101 and the Final Solution in Poland*, London, 1992, p 27.

[92] This unique account of the Hungarian holocaust has been translated and is in the appendix.

[93] Noakes J., Pridham G., *Nazism, 1919-1945, 3: Foreign Policy, War and Racial Extermination*, Exeter, full Willi Hoettl statement, p 1,208.

Office diplomat, was behind it. His department in communications with Berlin always referred to transportations as 'evacuations' and despite protestations after the war, and the written evidence he gave in the Eichmann trial in 1961, his denial of any culpability in the deaths of Jews was rightly treated with contempt.

Under Grell's scheme Jews would leave via Rumania, no longer a German military ally, but only in possession of a special transit visa, issued by the German military authorities in Budapest through its legation. Rightly sceptical, the Swedes and the Swiss placed little trust in this initiative: Grell had already threatened Wallenberg with the warning that at any time the Gestapo might lift him off the street.

The exodus from Budapest was planned to begin on August 25 and Horthy pledged to the International Red Cross that the Germans would honour the commitment given that travel documentation was in order. Children under the age of 11 would not need permits but they were required to have protection documentation from either the Swedish or Swiss legations. Greeted with universal derision that month was the announcement by Andor Jaross. The odious minister of the interior declared that no Jews had been killed on Hungarian soil. He didn't deny the deportations to Poland.

Grell and Jaross modified the evacuation arrangements. The first transport from three holding camps, they said, would now leave on August 27 in two trains each conveying 10,000 Jews with the Honved providing the guards.[94] In subsequent days three trains would run daily but there was a further change of mind with the clearance pushed back to August 28 and the number of camps increased to five. A later modification stated that Palestine was no longer the final destination. Trains would now run 'to the territory of the Reich' with the Jews needed as slave labour.

Stockholm responded immediately by allowing Wallenberg to do whatever was appropriate. That authority included bribing. Eichmann urged Himmler to restart transportations to Birkenau but he was rebuffed. Mueller offered a supportive ear but the Gestapo chief proved typically non-committal. Never a man to share opinions, Mueller was shoring up his value for the inevitable defeat by maintaining regular contact with the NKVD.[95]

Grell's scheme was scrapped but not before some trains did run to the German Ruhr and the Mauthausen concentration camp in Austria. Eichmann now cabled Himmler that his Judenkommando in Budapest had become redundant: a point he would make in his 1961 trial. That could all change, he believed, if his friends in the Arrow Cross took control. Himmler recalled the sulking Eichmann to Berlin.

For Frederick Rubin, life in his Jewish work unit had become perilous. Arguing or stepping out of line was met with the firing squad. Living on his wits, Rubin volunteered for the most arduous of tasks if it meant his life was spared. In July, his unit unexpectedly relocated to Budapest and he seized upon the opportunity to visit his home now clearly marked by a Jewish star. His parents had divorced when he was eight his mother leaving Frederick in the care of his father. To Rubin's delight he found his father had obtained a forged document from the Swiss and had used it to avoid roundups but his mother was less fortunate. She was in the Central Ghetto in Buda with the house at Eva Street 15 crammed to bursting. Arrow Cross and Honved intimidation occurred daily. The stay with his father had been brief as Rubin's work unit regrouped to distribute essential food supplies around the city. In this role he witnessed the utter helplessness of its inhabitants.

Budapest was to sink further into the abyss. Raoul Wallenberg could stomach it no longer, he wanted out. During the third week of September, Raoul contacted Dr Koloman Lauer, his former business partner, to ask him to urgently write to his cousin, Jacob Wallenberg, about possible employment in the family-owned Stockholms Enskilda Bank. Lauer did, urging Jacob that if Raoul didn't leave soon every exit would be closed as the Red Army had penetrated Hungary on three fronts.

---

[94] German Foreign Office document, T/1217, disclosed at the Eichmann trial.

[95] **Mueller, Heinrich**: His post-war whereabouts were unknown. The CIA denied that Mueller had worked for the agency. From my own research in Moscow, there is compelling evidence that he survived the war and lived in the USSR employed by the NKVD and KGB to interview German PoWs. Later he disappeared into South America.

Jacob, although sympathetic, declined. Lauer had even enquired whether Raoul could return to the Huvudsta project on the outskirts of Stockholm, an assignment Raoul had previously advised upon with his architectural qualification. Raoul had political immunity, Jacob had responded, if he was worried for his safety he should use it. The reluctant Raoul remained in Budapest.

Arrow Cross comes to power - Eichmann returns

As Red Army tanks encircled the ancient Hungarian city of Debrecen, Horthy and his son covertly began talks with the Soviets offering the immediate surrender of the Royal Hungarian Army. Hitler responded by sending in a Waffen SS unit commanded by the trusted Lt. Colonel 'Scarface' Otto Skorzeny.[96] Horthy was arrested. The Arrow Cross took over government on October 15 but with most of Hungary in the grip of Soviet occupation its power was concentrated in Budapest and Trans-Danubia in the west, the gateway to Austria. In the mayhem two days later Eichmann returned, re-invigorated and intending to pursue his own new regime of terror.

Arrow Cross militia contemptuously took to the streets as Ferenc Szálasi, its leader, countenanced open executions, not just on Jews. Wallenberg and fellow diplomats from the neutral legations redoubled their efforts in handing out protection documents. Gunfire erupted outside the Swedish and Swiss legation buildings with staff intimidated. In the long queues the savagery was far worse. Throughout the city Arrow Cross militia were photographed standing proudly over rows of dead. The ghettos couldn't cope.

Eichmann's 'foot marches' to Austria began on November 8, with several thousand Jews rounded up by the collaborative Honved and dumped for hours in the Ujlaki brickyards in Buda. With the barest of belongings and in the biting cold, they were forced to walk. The neutral diplomats raced along the lines of people stuffing documents of safe passage into their hands and pulling them out of line, but they could help only a few. Wallenberg and Per Anger, his legation colleague, followed the first march and in the town of Hegyeshalom, their commandeered trucks were quickly filled with

500 fortunates who were then returned under Swedish protection to Budapest. Eichmann was livid.

Desperate appeals were made to Eichmann but by this stage of the war he and his kind were immune to pleas for mercy. There were to be several marches and by the time they ceased at the end of November, up to 76,000 Jews had taken the walk towards the Austrian border and to Mauthausen concentration camp. Many didn't make it.

'That Jewish Dog'

The murderous spectacle on the Danube bridges with the militias herding victims to the execution site on the Pest side of the river near the Chain Bridge continued unabated.[97] On the river's edge they were ordered to take off their shoes and stand in line before being gunned down. Sometimes they were tied together. Those that didn't fall into the Danube were kicked over the edge and for months bloated bodies washed up on the riverbanks. Wallenberg, with Langfelder as his driver, daily moved around his 'safe houses' distributing food and organising security on the buildings as best they could. More often now, he worked out of the International Red Cross building in Benczur Street, Pest.[98] Eichmann had dubbed the Swede 'that Jewish Dog' after Wallenberg purloined SS and Arrow Cross uniforms and formed a small guard of 'Aryan-looking Jews' to protect his buildings.

With the Red Army closing in on Budapest in early December, doubts grew in the ranks of the Arrow Cross whether the Wehrmacht and the still-loyal Royal Hungarian Army could hold the forthcoming onslaught. The Arrow Cross became a rabble with militia units moving west into the Trans-Danubian hoping to reach the comparative safety of the Austrian border. SS units intercepted

---

[96] **Skorzeny, Otto Lt. Col**: Supposedly he was 'De-Nazified' in 1952, dying in July 1975.

[97] This execution site is commemorated with shoes of adults and children made in copper, many adorned with flowers. See photographs *[Budapest-17/18]*.

[98] Now used by the Austrian embassy to issue visas. See photographs *[Budapest-19/20]*.

them to confiscate their weapons. There were numerous firefights.

Adding to the terror enveloping Budapest was the newly formed Liberation Committee of the Hungarian National Uprising, a coalition of the Hungarian Communist Party and the National Peasants' Party. Its militias took on the Germans and the Arrow Cross across the city, even mounting a raid on the city jail to release imprisoned members. One Arrow Cross leader, in particular, was in its sights. Father András Kun[99] was a killer that needed no lessons in the art from the Gestapo. Wearing the robes of a Minorite priest and a gun around his waist, he and his followers were responsible for many of the massacres on the Danube. To his lined up victims he shouted with a crucifix in his hands 'in the name of Jesus Christ, fire!' Kun had other skills. In the torture cells of the Arrow Cross building in Andrássy Street,[100] he gouged out eyes and scalped victims.

With the din of the Red Army artillery inexorably growing closer, a desperate Wallenberg contacted Lauer. Once Budapest had fallen, reported Wallenberg, he would have no option but to remain in the city for months as all escape routes had closed. Any exit would be through Russia or Russian-held territory. Lauer again urged Jacob Wallenberg to think again about a role for Raoul in Stockholms Enskilda Bank.

Frederick Rubin, too, was in despair. Several colleagues in his labour unit had been shot by the SS or transported to Dachau. Some units had been wiped out completely. In his truck, Rubin traversed the Budapest streets distributing munitions to the Hungarian and German military and he knew to survive he had to escape. That decision saved his life, he would recall to me in the winter of his life in Hampstead, northwest London.

Deserters were shot where they were found so Rubin went underground, living in the city cellars before locating his father who through his contacts obtained a forged Swiss protection certificate for him, providing access to a safe house on Jozsef Street in Pest. More than 100 Jews had taken sanctuary in the six-story building which flew the Swiss flag, but that was no guarantee of safety from the Arrow Cross. Defenseless victims were dragged out and beaten senseless or carted off to the Arrow Cross torture cells. A diplomat from the Swiss legation on Castle Hill, Buda, brought news that raised a cheer: tanks of the Red Army were approaching the city, the end of the misery was in sight, or so Rubin thought.

December brings further unimaginable horrors

Eichmann was no fool. To discuss even the possibility of defeat within his earshot incurred the firing squad yet he knew Budapest was doomed, probably the entire Third Reich in a matter of months. He had to have a Soviet price on his head, he believed, given his record of mass extermination of Soviet PoWs across Europe and his reporting into Himmler, Mueller and Ernst Kaltenbrunner, the head of the RHSA. Curiously, Eichmann was mistaken. His name at that time was not yet on the prime list of wanted Nazis to locate and prosecute for war crimes.[101]

Eichmann left Budapest two days before Christmas Eve 1944, travelling west to Austria. In his last weeks in Budapest, Eichmann had ignored orders from Himmler's staff in Berlin: Mueller had become his sole confidant. Eichmann's final order in the city was to liquidate the two ghettos, and only the prompt appeals by Wallenberg and other diplomats prevented the massacre.

Christmas Eve marked the onset of the Arrow Cross offensive against the buildings that flew the flags of the neutrals. One notorious incident was on the Swedish-protected Jewish children's home in Muncaszy Mihaly,[102] a short distance from the Arrow Cross HQ and less than a two-minute walk from the International Red Cross building in Benczur Street where Wallenberg worked. The full frontal assault was driven back by a small detachment of Honved commanded by 44-year-old Gidófalvy Lajos. Lajos was killed the following year and only in 1989, upon the fall of communism, would his courage

---

[99] After the German capitulation Father Kun was charged in the Peoples' Court and executed. See photograph of Kun on a Budapest street [Budapest-21].

[100] See photographs of the former Arrow Cross headquarters and the torture cells [Budapest-22/23].

[101] This interesting fact emerged from his trial.

[102] Post-war the building was a government guesthouse, and is now a hotel. See photograph [Budapest-24].

and the actions of his men be commemorated with a plaque.

The savagery of the massacre on December 29 even surpassed past atrocities. Arrow Cross militia attacked the Jewish hospital in Maros Street, Buda, shooting dead 187 patients and staff and dragging the bodies out into the road, gloating as they did so.[103] Their bodies were buried in the hospital garden but later reinterred.

Queues outside the neutral legations degenerated into a panic-stricken human tide. Legation staffs were threatened and several were taken to the prison in Buda on the Schwabenberg. Many staff remained in their apartments. Anger, attempting to work out of his apartment, in Uri Street, Buda, urgently begged the German and Hungarian military for staff protection. In Pest, Father Kun was hunting down Wallenberg who spent little time in each location for his safety.

The battle for Budapest began in earnest on December 26 with the 3rd Ukrainian Front, under the command of Marshal Tolbukhin, already in the suburbs. If Budapest fell, the Red Army now had a clear road to Austria and Vienna. The city dug in for the siege.

Stalin brings his own brand of terror

Stalin's iron fist was already scourging Soviet-occupied Hungary. NKVD and Smersh units rounded up the intelligentsia, church leaders, political activists, teachers and Hungarian kulaks, the peasant farmers. Rural communities and towns decimated of Jews were now being emptied of anyone considered a threat to the Soviet cause. The Hungarian cattle trains ran again, not to Birkenau, but into the Soviet Union. Hungarian holding camps at Brassó, Temesvár and Maramarossziget Foksanyi now housed tens of thousands and anyone even loosely accused of being a fascist or Nazi collaborator was transported to interrogation camps such as Krasnogorsk, outside Moscow.

Some communities had lost all their menfolk by the end of December 1944. With 300,000 arrested Stalin was carving out a new state apparatus, ridding Hungary of its constitutional past. The communist party, the MKP, which in the 1939 elections barely figured in the voting, demanded full control. Soviet-style people's courts were introduced.

In Budapest, Soviet aircraft daily dropped leaflets targeting the Royal Hungarian Army now deserting in growing numbers. The supposedly conciliatory message recalled Frederick Rubin was *'Soldiers, surrender to the Red Army. Officers can keep their swords. You will all be discharged at the end of hostilities.'* There had been other futile attempts by Marshal Malinovsky, in command of the 2nd Ukrainian Front. Earlier in December, before the massive artillery bombardment had begun, Captain Ostyapenko, an NKVD officer, with two colleagues, approached the Waffen SS frontline in a jeep waving a white flag and yelling surrender terms in German. The SS allowed the jeep to come in close before opening fire. Malinovsky ordered that no German lives be spared: any rules of engagement that did exist were over.

Daily communication between the Swedish legation and Stockholm had now ceased as engineers from the Red Army cleverly neutralised much of the radio traffic emanating from the city. Some 'independent operators' put in place by British and Swedish Intelligence did keep transmitting. Informers were rife with Smersh and the NKVD already in the outskirts. In Moscow, Söderblom, the Swedish ambassador, had prepared a full listing for the Russian Foreign Ministry of the many hundreds of staff in the Swedish legation. Söderblom never did later justify his actions. The Russians particularly wanted to know the names of who worked for Department B, the department for foreign affairs, and Department C, the humanitarian department with Wallenberg as its head.

On New Year's Eve, the Wehrmacht commander, General Pfeffer-Wildenbruch, rejected a final Soviet ultimatum to surrender and in the streets of Pest, hand-to-hand fighting ensued. Staff from the neutral legations tried as best they could to deliver food to their safe houses. Desperate to protect the route to Vienna, Hitler threw in the 4th SS Panzer Corps to help out Pfeffer-Wildenbruch. On January 7, 1945, the Red Army was overwhelmed in Esztergom, to the northwest of the capital. There was hope in Berlin that the tide may have turned.

---

[103] It remains a clinic. See photographs of the massacre *[Budapest-25/26/27a]*.

Anger, the deputy head of the legation, last saw Wallenberg on January 10, in Buda. He had pleaded with him to stay out of Pest. Danielsson had advised Wallenberg to flee the city completely and seek Red Army protection, given he had become a marked man.

Wallenberg and Langfelder left Buda for the last time and returned to Pest, not to the apartment in Harmincad 6[104] or his office in Ullöi Avenue 2,[105] but to comparative shelter afforded by the International Red Cross building in Benczur Street. The Germans let it be known that the bridges to Buda would shortly be blown. In that event, Wallenberg would be isolated from his diplomat colleagues.

First contact with the Russians – January 12, 1945

During a lull in the Soviet bombardment, Wallenberg slipped out of the building on January 12. It is unlikely he used the main entrance on Benczur Street as it was blocked by debris and instead used a side exit on Bajza Street. Across the road, Délibáb Street offered a direct route to Varosliget Park – a short distance away – where he had heard the Red Army had been spotted. The gardens of the mansions in Délibáb Street provided shelter if the bombardment began again, and he didn't want to run up against marauding Arrow Cross militia or the SS.

Varosliget Park, in peacetime, was a popular attraction for the citizens of Budapest, a haven for strollers, dog walkers and tourists who for decades had enjoyed the thermal spas.[106] In the grounds of the grand Szechenyi complex Wallenberg located a Red Army unit. The Swede warily approached waving his Swedish diplomatic passport. It is not known in what language the officer and Wallenberg conversed, but Wallenberg made it very clear that his safe houses and hospitals, identified by the Swedish flag, needed immediate Soviet protection. A meeting with a senior officer in Debrecen, the Red Army headquarters, was necessary, he urged.

What happened until January 17 when Smersh officers finally escorted Wallenberg and Langfelder from the International Red Cross building will be explained in a later chapter but on that day German and Hungarian units blew the Danube bridges leaving only the Elizabeth for the retreat to Buda.[107] Pest had fallen and Buda was now unattached. In the garden of the Swedish legation, in Buda, a German unit dug in for two days but once they fled Anger raised the Swedish flag. The battle for Buda was furious. Red Army troops approached the Swedish legation on January 30 demanding that the building be commandeered as a billet. Anger with his colleague, Yngve Ekmark, confronted them. In the heated discussion, Anger bartered his prized Swiss watch for a guarantee that consular personnel would be located and taken to safety.

With the battle raging, Anger, Ekmark and another colleague, Göte Carlsson, were escorted south of Budapest by Red Army troops to the village of Soroksár. Danielsson later joined up with them with the news that the special relationship between Sweden and the Soviets was terminated and that the Swedish and Swiss legations had been ransacked. The looting troops, related Danielsson, 'had wristwatches up to their elbows'.

The Germans finally capitulated in Buda on February 13, succumbing to overwhelming forces and bombardment. Budapest was finished after a 50-day siege, with 49,000 German dead and 110,000 taken prisoner. The Red Army was triumphant, but its own losses were far higher. Huge portraits of Stalin and Molotov adorned what remained of the bridges. Several members of the Swedish legation were missing, including Wallenberg. One communication to Stockholm had Wallenberg and Langfelder in Debrecen. Hopes ran high that Wallenberg might even be on his way back to Sweden but the treatment meted out to Lars Berg tempered such hopes. He had been hauled in by the NKVD, roughed up, and accused of spying. During that interrogation, the same charge was aimed at the missing Wallenberg.

Anger and others left Budapest on March 20, returning circuitously to Sweden via Bucharest, Odessa, Moscow, Leningrad, Helsinki and Abo, a trip lasting a month. The Swiss, too, were gone, but two of their diplomats could not be contacted and were

---

[104] See photograph *[Budapest-27b]*.
[105] See photograph *[Budapest-27c]*.
[106] Varosliget Park. See photograph *[Budapest-28]*.
[107] The blown Chain Bridge. See photograph *[Budapest-29]*.

presumed to be in Soviet custody. One, Feller, had been badly beaten up by the Arrow Cross militia in late December after his car was stopped and he was dragged out.

Budapest was firmly in the grip of Soviet retribution, with house-to-house searches yielding German stragglers hiding in the ruins. If SS they were swiftly executed. The same fate awaited the Arrow Cross militias. The senior German officer, Pfeffer-Wildenbruch, was found hiding in a Buda cellar by the NKVD. A Moscow cell awaited.

Frederick Rubin recalled one poster that appeared in all the main streets depicting a stern-faced Red Army soldier with a machine gun slung across his broad chest. *'The Red Army did not enter into the territory of your country for the purpose of changing the social, political and economic system. It has only entered to drive out the Germans,'* was the message.

NKVD and Smersh units toured Pest and Buda with lists of people they wanted to arrest. The NKVD turned the Arrow Cross headquarters into its own and expanded the torture cells in the basement for a raft of new incumbents. The term 'The Terror House' would continue but under a new regime. Gabor Péter, a former Budapest tailor, and an informer, became the head of a new and compliant Hungarian Political Security Department, the PRO.[108] Péter had been a member of the Comintern, interned by the Nazis, and was trusted by his new Soviet masters.

A new political mastery stalked the rubble-strewn streets. Friends, neighbours, all Hungarians, viewed each other with suspicion. Vigilantes, including armed Jewish squads, sought out Nazi collaborators. Resistance groups, such as the Anarchist Movement, under Alexei Korsakin and Christ – a young man who at the age of 15 had led an attack on a building occupied by the Gestapo in northern Hungary – demanded a new social order but the Soviet occupiers were in no mood to listen. For the Hungarian gendarmes, the Honved, the regular force recruited from the peasants who had done much of the dirty work for the Germans, they went on the run for their lives.

Péter needed employees for his new organisation, with the only proviso that his officers must share his lust for torture and killing.

Former Arrow Cross militia were hired and they were prepared to utter a new oath on condition that past crimes were quietly forgotten by the communists. Ardent criminals from the notorious jail in Margit Boulevard signed up for the PRO uniform, vengeful on those who had convicted them. Left-wing idealists joined this motley crew slavishly believing that only Stalin's brand of communism could reform the fascist state. In Andrassy Street, the NKVD taught their new PRO charges torture methods such as sleep deprivation and the use of poison. Péter had replaced Adolf Eichmann in Budapest, and this time all citizens were targets, not just Jews.

For the Jews emerging from their cellars the new occupiers offered only more anxiety and concern. The Russians disliked the sight of the neutral country flags that flew imperiously over the protected buildings demanding they be taken down. All protection documentation dispensed by the foreign diplomats was declared invalid. Many Jews were arrested, interrogated, and transported to the Gulag.

Rubin's fake Swiss protection pass cut no ice with his Soviet interrogator who merely shoved it aside when he showed it. What had greater currency was Rubin's experience in his Hungarian army labour unit. Within the hour, he was part of a detail, trucking wounded Red Army troops to the military field hospitals. Rubin had been lucky, surviving the war.

Budapest's heroes

Raoul Wallenberg is rightly commemorated as he and his colleagues issued 30,000 protective passes during the Nazi occupation, but history has tended to have airbrushed over the efforts of many others in saving the lives of the Jews in Budapest.

The War Refugee Board, which had underwritten Wallenberg's efforts, had other agents operating in the city. Roswell McClelland negotiated and bribed German and Hungarian officials in the release

---

[108] In October 1946, its name changed to the AVO.

of 1,700 Hungarian Jews dispatched to Bergen-Belsen. An order for 18,000 Jews in Budapest to be transported to Birkenau was also rescinded through McClelland's pressure. Using political and intelligence contacts with Marshal Tito, the War Refugee Board co-ordinated escape routes for Jews through Yugoslavia.

Another neutral, Spain, had made a major contribution through its embassy in Eötvö Street, almost directly opposite the Arrow Cross HQ. Don Angel Sanz-Briz, the ambassador, issued 750 Spanish passes before he was reluctantly recalled to Madrid. Continuing his work was the Italian, Géorgio 'Jorge' Perlasca, as acting chargé d'affaires. In all, the Spanish legation distributed 5,400 protective passes and had established dozens of safe houses.

Carl Lutz, the Swiss Consul, was credited with being the first neutral diplomat in Budapest to invent the Schutz-Pass, the protective letter, issuing 8,000 of them and persuading the Germans that these letters covered entire families. With the help from his colleagues, and Gertrude, his wife, 76 safe houses were set up and hundreds were rescued from the foot marches.

Monsignor Angelo Rotta, the Papal Nuncio, distributed 15,000 safe-conduct certificates in addition to bogus Catholic baptismal certificates. For many Jews in rural Hungary, due to be transported to Birkenau, he and his aides handed out countless blank such certificates carrying his signature. He, too, had set up numerous protected safe houses.

On behalf of the International Committee of the Red Cross in Switzerland, Friedrich Born issued more than 4,000 Red Cross protective and employment letters. He placed 60 Jewish institutions under Red Cross protection and housed over 7,000 children and orphans. Born is credited with saving up to 15,000 Jews in Budapest.

★★★

Frederick Rubin remained in Budapest. He made a break for freedom to the West in June 1956, just before the uprising, but failed, being caught on the border and jailed for four months in the central prison in Budapest. As in the war he was lucky. Many escapees were executed. His next attempt was a success, catching a train and walking over the border into Austria. His father survived the nightmare of Budapest, eventually immigrating to Israel in 1955. His mother had also survived conditions in the Central Ghetto. I met Frederick in Hampstead, London, in 2002, and we remained in regular contact until his death in 2007. He was a specialist on the Hungarian Secret Service.

6

Sweden's desperate search for news
– The first 10 years

WITHIN DAYS of Wallenberg's disappearance in Budapest, the rumour mill was in overdrive. The diplomat had been invited to Debrecen by the newly installed Hungarian government to receive a decoration for 'all the wonderful work he had done in Hungary during the Nazi occupation', ran one. A car had been sent, with an escort, 'to transport him and his people' but the car had been located, abandoned, between the towns of Gödöllö, with its stunning royal palace, and Aszód, to the northeast of Budapest. 'Pure gossip' was the response from the Swedish Foreign Office (SFO), accusing the Hungarian Ministry of Foreign Affairs as the misleading source.

Wallenberg had been killed, ran another account, with 'Russia too ashamed to admit that such an excellent man could be killed by Russian soldiers'. Gödöllö's holding camp in a converted school, housing arrested Hungarians and foreigners picked up in the NKVD and Smersh sweeps, was the focus of many reports. Sightings of a discarded vehicle outside or nearby were numerous and one witness professed to have seen passengers transferring to another car.

Just days before Wallenberg went missing, the head of the political section of the SFO in Stockholm had written to Ilya Chernyshov, counsellor at the Soviet embassy in the Swedish capital.[109] This cable, dated January 2, 1945, described to the Soviets the strenuous humanitarian efforts being waged by the officials within the Swedish legation in Budapest to save lives: Wallenberg was not mentioned by name. There was no response from Chernyshov, but almost certainly he handed the cable to Colonel

[Budapest-1] Obersturmbannführer (Lt. Colonel) Adolf Eichmann, SS, arrived in Budapest on March 21, 1944, two days after the German occupation of the city. [PD]

[Budapest-2] For his living quarters, Eichmann commandeered this villa at Apostol St. 13, on Rose Hill, Buda, from a Jewish industrialist. A chandelier-design company now uses much of the building.

[Budapest-3] The main reception area of the sequested villa. The quality of the building's interior remains in its original magnificent condition.

[Budapest-4] In what was Eichmann's office on the first floor, he ordered the immediate painting of a large swastika on the flooring in front of his desk, still *in situ* but now covered over by oak parquet.

[Budapest-5] In its grounds, an enraged Eichmann and Teitel, the senior chauffeur, beat the young Jewish worker, Solomon, to a bloody pulp for stealing fruit – his body later dumped into the Danube.

[Budapest-6] Colonel Kurt Becher, an SS officer in SS Division Totenkopf – the infamous Deaths Head, had been co-opted into the SS Economic Office given his financial talents. [PD]

[Budapest-7] The Swedish legation in Minerva St., Buda, halfway up Gellert Hill. With the rank of first secretary Wallenberg headed the new Department C, at an annual salary of 2,000 Swedish kronor. Queues for Swedish protection documentation daily stretched down the hill. The Arrow Cross was a constant threat to those who queued. The building has now been converted to apartments.

[Budapest-8] The main entrance to the former Swedish legation. Wallenberg had maintained a secret cache of documents and notes in a wooden box in the garden, concealed close to the entrance of the underground air raid shelter. The US ambassador in Sweden had hoped it might be recovered before the NKVD stumbled over it during the ransacking of the building.

[Budapest-9] Not much has changed in the main reception area of the former Swedish legation – note the scooter parked outside one of the apartments.

[Budapest-10] The fireplace in the main reception area of the former legation.

[Budapest-11] Sweden quit the building shortly after the war. Ivan Danielsson, the legation head, had this office on the ground floor.

[Budapest-12] On his arrival in Budapest, Wallenberg was given an apartment on Tulipan St. 15, Rose Hill, Buda.

[Budapest-13] Much of Wallenberg's department was moved into the adjacent former Finnish legation building, and it also housed some of the legation's filing system that was either destroyed or removed by the NKVD. Wallenberg's building was attacked on several occasions by the Arrow Cross, later by the oncoming Red Army in the battle for Buda. The now-empty property still shows the pockmarking from the gunfire.

[Budapest-14] Another view of the now dilapidated former Finnish legation building.

[Budapest-15] Raoul Wallenberg at work in his office in the legation. [PD]

[Budapest-16] Wallenberg. [PD]

[Budapest-17] The murderous spectacle of the Arrow Cross executions on the Pest bank of the Danube continued unabated for weeks. Victims, not just Jews, were ordered to remove their shoes, stand in line, and were gunned down toppling into the river. Sometimes they were roped together. For months bloated bodies washed up. Shoes made from copper now commemorate the site.

[Budapest-18] Another view of the Danube memorial looking towards the Chain Bridge.

[Budapest-19] Now used by the Austrian Embassy, as its passport office, during wartime this Pest building housed the International Red Cross. Wallenberg used it as his base during his final weeks in the city. Three Smersh officers escorted him and Langfelder from the building on January 17, 1945. The Russians had long suspected that many of the foreigners who operated from the building worked for a number of foreign intelligence services.

[Budapest-21] Father András Kun, known as the 'Killer Priest'. Wearing the robes of a Minorite priest, with a gun around his waist, he and his followers were responsible for many of the massacres on the Danube. To his lined up victims he shouted with a crucifix in his hands 'in the name of Jesus Christ, fire!' In Wallenberg's last weeks in Pest, Kun sought in vain to hunt him down. [PD]

Left: [Budapest-20] Wallenberg exited the building during a lull in the Soviet bombardment when he heard that the Red Army was in Varosliget Park, which was very close. It is unlikely that Wallenberg used the main entrance on Benczur St given the road outside was blocked. More probable, he used the underground side exit via Bajza St. on the corner of the road intersection. Across the road, Délibáb St. offered a direct route to the park.

Overleaf: [Budapest-22] Kun had other skills. In the torture cells of the Arrow Cross HQ in Andrássy St., Pest, he gouged out eyes and scalped victims. The incoming NKVD expanded the torture cells in the basement.

[Budapest-23] The Arrow Cross building, known as the 'Terror House', is now a museum.

[Budapest-24] Christmas Eve 1944 saw the Arrow Cross launch a series of terror attacks on Jewish safe houses. One was on the Swedish-protected Jewish children's home in Muncaszy Mihaly, a short distance from the Arrow Cross HQ and less than a two-minute walk from the International Red Cross building in Benczur St. where Wallenberg worked. The building is now a hotel.

[Budapest-25] Exterior view of the Maros Clinic, the former Jewish hospital in Buda, where on December 29, 1944, Father Kun and his Arrow Cross militia slaughtered 187 patients and staff. It remains a clinic.

[*Budapest-26*] The bodies of the Maros Clinic were first dumped by the Arrow Cross in the street and then buried in the hospital garden. [PD]

[*Budapest-27a*] After the fall of Budapest to the Soviets, the bodies in the Maros Clinic atrocity were disinterred and reburied. [PD]

Right: [*Budapest-27b*] Wallenberg's last apartment he used in Pest, in Harmincad 6. The building is now used by the British Embassy.

[Budapest-27c] The office Wallenberg used in Pest, in Ullöi Avenue 2. It is the middle block.

[Budapest-28] Varosliget Park is famous for its thermal spas. In the grounds of the grand Szechenyi complex, Wallenberg, reportedly, saw an advance unit of the incoming Red Army into Pest.

[Budapest-29] The blown Chain Bridge. Every bridge was down as the Germans retreated out of Pest into Buda.

[Budapest-30] The typical uniform of the Arrow Cross militia; Wallenberg was always a target.

[Budapest-31] The original front door of the Swedish legation in Budapest.

[Budapest-32] Steps leading to the inner door of the legation; note the exquisite friezes.

Overleaf: [Budapest-33] Some of the many photographs of the Budapest citizens murdered by the Arrow Cross.

Vasily Roschin, the NKVD rezident in the embassy,[110] a spy chief who will figure in a later chapter.

Radio and cipher transmissions between Budapest and Stockholm had been broken as the battle for Budapest reached its expected outcome, forcing the SFO to rely on communication via Soviet channels in Moscow and the illegal radio network set up by Swedish military intelligence in the city. Wallenberg's whereabouts wasn't the only concern, worries mounted for the safety of Ivan Danielsson, the legation head, and other employees sheltering under the incessant Red Army bombardment in the legation cellar or in their apartments.

The first Soviet admission

Vladimir Dekanozov, the Soviet deputy foreign minister, had lightened the apprehension when on January 16 he had informed Staffan Söderblom, Sweden's ambassador to Moscow, that Wallenberg had been encountered by Red Army troops near Benczur Street in Pest. Wallenberg had told them that other members of the Swedish mission were in Buda. Dekanozov had promised that immediate Soviet measures to protect Wallenberg and the Swedish safe houses in Pest had been taken. There were Swedish hopes that given Wallenberg's diplomatic status he would soon be on his way home.

Three weeks had passed before Maj von Dardel, Raoul's mother, received the communication from the Soviet ambassador, Alexandra Kollontay,[111] that her son was in 'safekeeping' in the Soviet Union but that assurance came attached with a disturbing undertone. Further appealing by the SFO to Moscow, warned

---

[109] Many letters to Chernyshov about Wallenberg followed.

[110] Rezident is Russian intelligence jargon for the head of station within either the overseas embassy or legation.

[111] **Kollontay, Ambassador Alexandra**: Brought up in Russia and Finland, she was also a celebrated author in Russia and a long-time campaigner for the rights of working Soviet women. Kollontay was ambassador to Norway (twice), Mexico and Sweden. She pushed a softer communist line and often criticised the Stalin regime. Kollontay died in 1952.

Kollontay, who had known the Wallenberg family for more than a decade, might hinder his return. Molotov recalled the ambassador to Moscow.

The US threw its full diplomatic weight behind the search for Wallenberg. Averell Harriman, the American ambassador in Moscow, offered to intercede with the Russian authorities but Söderblom ungenerously declined. Britain, too, offered all assistance through its MI6 network in Stockholm that monitored news emanating out of Russia. One member of the Press Reading Bureau, a special department based in the British embassy, had already been informed that Wallenberg was in Soviet custody.

Moscow's propaganda radio station beaming into Budapest, *Kossuth Radio*, soon added to the growing despondency in Stockholm. Its broadcast on March 15 reported that the Gestapo in Budapest had probably murdered the missing diplomat. One week later, the news from the Russian Foreign Ministry was marginally better. Moscow informed Stockholm that most of the legation staff was in Bucharest, Rumania, staying in the Athene Palace Hotel. Wallenberg, however, was not in the party. The SFO immediately cabled for information on his whereabouts.

Söderblom met with Dekanozov on April 25 to discuss the growing number of reports that Wallenberg was dead, not to actively push for Soviet news that he might be alive. In a change of attitude in July, Söderblom boasted to colleagues that he would exert more pressure and give the Russian Foreign Ministry photographs of Wallenberg that had recently arrived from Stockholm. Inexplicably, those photographs were never shown. A claim surfaced in Moscow that Wallenberg remained in hiding in Budapest, evading the NKVD who searched for him.

From Switzerland came a report that the diplomat was in Moscow, and alive. With the Hungarian economy in ruins, stalked by rampant hyperinflation and with only gold and foreign currency having any value, the country was desperate to re-establish itself with the international financial and trading community. The Hungarian National Bank sent one of its most respected bankers, Takacsy, to visit Zurich and Berne. During that visit the banker met up with Lauer Mellaneuropeiska Handels AB, the trading company directly linked to Raoul Wallenberg. According to the SFO archives, that meeting in Berne took place on August 28 and Takacsy revealed that Wallenberg was under arrest in Moscow. The Swedish legation in Switzerland urgently cabled the SFO: 'Wallenberg was alive and the Russians had taken him with all his notations and documents, intending to use Wallenberg's information in connection with future proceedings against compromised Hungarians.'[112] Stockholm pushed Moscow for clarification. None was forthcoming.

Sweden's obduracy over Moscow's demands for the return of two defectors added to the intransigence on Wallenberg. Lydia Makarova, the 19-year-old singer, had arrived in Stockholm in 1944, via Estonia, after fleeing Leningrad.[113] Anatoly Granovsky was an NKVD counterintelligence officer.[114] Talks did begin on exchanging Granovsky for Wallenberg but they quickly ended. As 1945 drew to a close, Söderblom felt he should acknowledge to Russian officials that in his opinion Raoul Wallenberg was dead and the family needed to come to terms with its loss.

All but two of the legation's diplomatic staff in Budapest had returned home.[115] The whereabouts of Wallenberg and Herman Grossheim-Krisko remained unknown. Söderblom reported an unexpected development in March 1946. According to the source, three Smersh officers had escorted Wallenberg and Langfelder from the International Red Cross building in Benczur Street. The SFO

---

[112] SFO files dated September 3, 1945.

[113] **Makarova, Lydia**: The Russian demand for her deportation carried on for several years, her case widely reported in newspapers across the world. In 1948, the US government threatened to deport Yakov Lomakin, the Soviet consul general in New York, if the harassment of the Soviet defectors in Sweden continued. The Russians argued that Makarova's father desperately wanted her back in Russia because he had lost his wife in the German siege of Leningrad. The Swedish authorities constantly warned the Russians against any attempt to kidnap her.

[114] **Granovsky, Anatoly**: NKVD officer seconded to the Red Army. In 1942, he defected but his presence in Stockholm was an embarrassment for the Swedes given the on-going Swedish demands over Wallenberg. Granovsky wrote his autobiography in 1962.

[115] Strictly there were three: in the legation was a 'Dutch Department', allowed by Germany to give Holland representation in Axis-occupied territories and its head was missing. More about this in a later chapter.

immediately enquired whether it could speak to the officers but the Russian Foreign Ministry denied that the three had had any involvement.

Totally unprecedented was Stalin's acceptance for a meeting with Söderblom, his first with any Swedish ambassador. It took place on June 15 and an hour was scheduled but it lasted barely five minutes after pleasantries were exchanged.

Wallenberg – was he dead, the fawning Söderblom lamely enquired?

Stalin agreed he was, the victim of either an accident in Budapest or the innocent victim of a criminal. The ambassador cabled that response to Stockholm that evening, further adding that he had the fullest admiration for the Soviet leader, whose foresight and wisdom had led to a speedy conclusion of the World War. Söderblom, purportedly, had written up a fuller report of the five-minute conversation. Curiously, that report has never been located.

The SFO was incensed at Söderblom's ineptitude. Its mood worsened as a further cable from the ambassador stated that the Russian Foreign Ministry now believed that some state agency had hidden Wallenberg in Russia without Stalin's knowledge. Söderblom was immediately instructed to remind Moscow of the Dekanozov note on January 16, 1945, reporting Wallenberg to be in 'safekeeping'.

Sheer incredulity greeted the July 6 missive from Söderblom, suggesting that for the time being the SFO should take no further action on Wallenberg, believing the 'rumour' circulating in Moscow that Wallenberg was in a 'safe' disguise and 'still in Budapest'. The response from Stig Sahlin, a former Swedish envoy to Finland, was dismissive not mincing his words in deriding the ambassador over his attitude and pathetic lack of action. Sahlin was clear: the Russian Foreign Ministry needed to be regularly chased. It took Söderblom a month to respond to Stockholm and when he did he merely stated that 'in the present situation it was hardly appropriate to pursue the matter from Moscow.' The SFO took stock, Söderblom had become a major roadblock.

Yet, it persevered with the ambassador. Further reminders to him followed throughout October and only on November 3 did Söderblom send a note to the Russian Foreign Ministry, with a follow up three weeks later. Abramov, a ministry official, replied. The military authorities had launched an investigation to discover Wallenberg's whereabouts.

The SFO tried another tack. Nazi collaborators from the Baltic States had fled to Sweden in droves to avoid Soviet retribution in the final years of the war. Estimates went as high as 30,000 with many former policemen among them, who had been responsible for several civilian massacres. Moscow had demanded that the worst must stand trial in Moscow for war crimes,[116] which gave Sweden a moral dilemma given its long-held status as a haven for political refugees. On the grounds that deporting some might help in the case of Wallenberg, the Swedes agreed to deport 188, of which 21 successfully appealed on medical grounds.

That initiative failed to shift the Soviet intransigence. Barch-Holst, the Swedish chargé d'affaires in Moscow, orchestrated a ploy that was guaranteed to annoy. Diplomats in the embassy individually enquired about Wallenberg across their collective contacts. That did yield one response. Novikin, another Russian Foreign Ministry official, fed the line that an NKVD investigation had failed to trace the diplomat.

Not before time, Söderblom was replaced and his more dogged successor, Rolf Söhlman, pursued untapped channels. There was a spate of reports during June and July 1947, one an intriguing chance encounter in Moscow between Söhlman's daughter and a released Hungarian PoW, named Litpe. Working in the wartime secretariat in Hungary's Ministry of Finance, Litpe claimed he had known Wallenberg well. Litpe had been arrested in Budapest by the NKVD and transported to the Pushkino interrogation camp in northwest Moscow. In Pushkino, said Litpe, he had personally witnessed

---

[116] Sweden to this day refuses to investigate suspected Holocaust perpetrators despite compelling evidence. Killers such as Oskar Angelus, head of the Estonian department of internal affairs and Karlis Lobe, chief of the Latvian police battalions in Riga, Latvia, were allowed to remain. The Simon Wiesenthal Centre in 1986 prepared a list of the worst 21 war criminals residing in Sweden.

Wallenberg's corpse. When the ambassador later challenged Litpe, the Hungarian was evasive quickly changing his story. Supposedly he now had conclusive proof from another Hungarian PoW that Wallenberg had been stricken by an intestinal illness and perished not in Pushkino but in Gödöllö, the holding camp outside Budapest used by Smersh and the NKVD. The Litpe testimony was worthless.

Sightings and accounts poured into the SFO during 1947. An unconfirmed source in Mexico had Wallenberg being executed in Pest by the Arrow Cross while attempting to cross into Russian lines. That gained some legs within the SFO as the International Red Cross building in Benczur Street, which Wallenberg worked out of in his last weeks in Pest, was close to the Arrow Cross HQ.

Mikhail Vetrov, an influential advisor to Molotov,[117] saw Söhlman on July 16 to report that the Russian Foreign Ministry now seriously believed that Wallenberg did die in the Budapest fighting. That was a real dampener but another report did offer some hope even if the Swedes by now had become leery of the claims. Adolphe Cohen, a Pole who had worked in the wartime Polish legation in L'vov in the Ukraine, claimed that from December 1946 until March 18, 1947, he had shared cell 149 with Wallenberg in the city's NKVD-run Brygidki Cloister prison.

Totally rejected was the note delivered to Söhlman on August 18 by Andrei Vyshinsky. The distrusted deputy foreign minister had reported that after considerable internal investigation, his ministry had concluded that Wallenberg was not in the Soviet Union nor was the diplomat known to the Soviet authorities. Vyshinsky was reminded of the Dekanozov statement of January 16, 1945 stating that the diplomat was in 'safe custody'.

Poisoning the well further was the highly contentious issue of the 'Kiruna Swedes'. In the 1930s, some 300 unemployed iron ore miners from northern Sweden had been recruited to work in the Soviet Union but now their communist dream was over and they wanted to return. Not all were granted exit documentation and those that did return spoke of the hardships, the broken promises and the brutality. During 1947, the SFO campaigned tirelessly to obtain the release of the missing, but like the disappearance of Wallenberg, all requests were batted away. The missing never did return.

Three NKVD holding camps at Krasnogorsk in northwest Moscow appeared on the SFO radar for the first time in April 1951 with 'sightings'. Many Hungarians were held here including Korody-Katona, a released PoW, and Béla Lukács,[118] the Nazi political collaborator, who related that a tall Swede had been encountered just months after the fall of Budapest: more on Krasnogorsk in later chapters.

Between 1947 and 1951, the Soviet silence over Wallenberg had been deafening. The frustrated Swedish public issued a desperate direct petition to Stalin with 1.6 million signatures.

Attention turns to Langfelder

For four days in June 1951, investigation turned again to Budapest but this time to the family and friends of Vilmos Langfelder, Wallenberg's driver. Arne Waldenström, a government officer in the Swedish legation, visited a number under the pretext of distributing food packages courtesy of Sweden. The outcome made for disappointing reading in Stockholm. Gitta, Langfelder's wife, at first was reticent to Waldenström's questioning but she did admit that her husband did visit her just days before he disappeared with Wallenberg.

Probing further, Waldenström asked Gitta to recall whether her husband had said where he was living at this time. Gitta responded that Vilmos had told her that he and Wallenberg daily altered their movements given the worry over their safety. Gitta offered Vilmos money but it was declined. Vilmos had told her that Wallenberg was never short of funds. He did enquire if she had sufficient. Before he left, Vilmos disclosed that they were shortly driving to Debrecen so Wallenberg could discuss Red Army protection for the Swedish safe houses. Vilmos' visit to Gitta must have occurred after Wallenberg's first Soviet encounter in Pest, given the mention of the trip to Debrecen.

That had been the last time Gitta had seen her husband.

---

[117] **Vetrov, Mikhail**: Later the Soviet ambassador to Denmark.
[118] **Lukács, Béla**: There were two factions within the Hungarian Life Party [the MEP] – the Industrialists and the pro-Nazi and anti-Soviet Agrarian Party, headed by Lukács.

Waldenström asked for the whereabouts of Franz Vali, the second cousin of Vilmos, and his best friend, but Gitta couldn't help. She did give Waldenström the address of Stefani Simon, Langfelder's sister and again under the pretext of handing out a food parcel, Waldenström visited her. She, too, was clearly agitated, but she did furnish additional detail on the trip to Debrecen relating that in the car that collected Langfelder and Wallenberg sat two Russian officers. In visits to Clara Miskolcoy and Magda Endrenyi, friends of Simon, these two clammed up altogether even denying any knowledge of Vilmos Langfelder. Waldenström was under instruction from Stockholm to relocate Litpe, the wartime government employee who had spoken to the SFO in June 1947. Lajos Balthazar, the secretary to the finance minister, was asked for Litpe's address but he couldn't or wouldn't help.

The NKVD and the Hungarian secret police had cast a baleful shroud over Hungary, Waldenström informed Stockholm. The tension in Budapest was palpable and people were disappearing. Budapest was a dead end.

An Italian PoW, Dr Claudio de Mohr, a wartime advisor to the Italian legation in Sofia, revealed in December 1951 that from April 28, 1945 until early 1948 in Lefortovo prison, he had pipe-tapped with Wallenberg. In cell 151, the Italian related that Wallenberg was in cell 152 and had been transferred, the Italian didn't know where. Two other released Italians, Ronchi and Moschetti, corroborated de Mohr's account but Sweden's state criminal investigator, Otto Danielsson, who analysed every PoW testimony, had his doubts. The claim, however, was thought important enough to be taken up with Tarabrin, the Soviet ambassador in Stockholm.

More plausible was an episode that emerged in January 1952. A wartime underground Zionist, Alexander Ujvary, had hidden Jewish children in Budapest. He claimed to the SFO that in the city ruins on either February 18 or 19, 1945, he needed to relieve himself and encountered Raoul Wallenberg hiding out in a cellar.[119] The two would have known each other as they had both worked out of the International Red Cross building in Benczur Street but had Ujvary's encounter in the ruins taken place before Wallenberg was arrested and he had forgotten the date?

The shooting down of a Swedish spy plane by a Soviet MIG reduced the rotten relationship with the USSR to a new level. Fitted out with intelligence equipment, the DC3 had been monitoring Soviet naval manoeuvres. Intercepting the Dakota near Gotland, an island between Sweden and the Baltic States, there was an immediate suspicion that a Soviet recovery vessel had reached it and grabbed the equipment. There might have been survivors but the Soviets denied any knowledge of the MIG action. Only in 2005 did the Swedes finally locate the wreck with four skeletons recovered out of the crew of eight.

With more PoW releases in 1952 and 1953, the SFO interviewed any considered to be helpful. Many declined, afraid of compromising those still in the prisons. The testimony of the Rumanian, Stefan Carl, again mentioned Krasnogorsk. He was in the camp during the summer of 1946 and claimed to have seen Wallenberg with two guards.

Lefortovo and the Lubyanka figured in several testimonies referring to Wallenberg's incarceration during 1947. Roland Gottlieb, the German consul in Sofia arrested in 1944, and who had a Swedish wife, had heard from another Lefortovo inmate that Wallenberg was held in the prison. SS General Hilmar Moser, the wartime head of the Lublin District in Poland and whose troops had quelled the Sobibor extermination camp breakout, claimed that Wallenberg was in the Lubyanka. Both those accounts could be factual. What certainly wasn't, was the account from Georg Libik, a Hungarian, that a Lubyanka cellmate had told him of exchanging pipe-tapping messages with the Swede as recently as 1953.

Buoyed by the growing number of PoW testimonies and the unexpected Soviet admission to the Austrian government that Ferdinand Marek, its wartime ambassador in Prague, had died in captivity on May 4, 1947 there was hope that Moscow might at last come clean on Wallenberg. Smersh had arrested Marek on May 23,

---

[119] **Ujvary, Alexander Dr**: Yad Vashem recognised his efforts on behalf of the International Red Cross in Budapest with the award 'The Righteous Among the Nations'. In January 1944, he had escaped from a train enroute to Auschwitz, making his way to Sweden. He arrived in Budapest in October 1944.

1945, and in his nine-year incarceration his very existence had been denied despite sightings in Lefortovo. The SFO felt confident it could prepare a memorandum with irrefutable evidence.

Söhlman, the Moscow ambassador, met Valerian Zorin, Russia's deputy foreign minister, on September 29, 1954, and presented the weighty tome. Zorin was an accomplished diplomat and well known to the Swedes given he had previously served as the Soviet permanent representative at the UN. Great efforts had been made to present the reasons *why* the SFO believed that Russia was still detaining its man, and one-by-one repudiate them.

Spying for Nazi Germany was a charge the SFO did want to nail as incorrect and offensive. Unquestionably the SFO stood by its man and denied any such charge, but in private there had been some misgivings. Wallenberg had increasingly operated independently with little or no recourse to Stockholm. The actual extent of Wallenberg's bartering with the Nazis and compliant Hungarian government officials was the monkey on the SFO's back. There were gaps in what was known. The SFO could only guess how close Wallenberg had become with the likes of Eichmann and Klages, the head of the SD, and what nefarious trades had been instigated. In its memorandum, however, the SFO wanted to portray the image of a diplomat concerned solely with humanitarian duties.

Countering the perceived thought that Moscow had understood Wallenberg to be a US Intelligence agent was equally vital. In the 20 PoW testimonies included in the memorandum, the SFO stressed that none had been aware of each other's statements. That vouchsafing, of course, couldn't be true, as some PoWs had kept in touch after release. Each PoW that had claimed either sighting or communicating with Wallenberg had been questioned on whether Wallenberg had admitted spying for anyone. None had, but in a pipe-tapping the diplomat was unlikely to divulge any dark secrets to someone he would probably never meet.

Another possible accusation against Wallenberg that the SFO wanted to refute was the issuance of Swedish passports and protection documents to collaborators and Nazi officers. The memorandum went to considerable lengths to inform the Soviets that forgery was rife and originals had been stolen but these were exceptional times, reiterated the SFO, not replicated in any other occupied country during wartime. No certification had knowingly been issued.

Failure to safeguard Soviet interests upon the German invasion of Hungary was one accusation that had been publicly aimed at the SFO. Sweden had agreed to take on this responsibility. The memorandum carefully stated that the Swedish legation, through Department B, had acted responsibly in its duties. The monitoring of Soviet PoWs in the German camps was scrupulous and arduous. No Soviet PoWs had been milked for intelligence, which was then relayed to the Nazis. That had been a contentious Moscow accusation. All the PoWs had to identify themselves and provide details of their military units, the SFO argued, but it did admit that profile questioning might have been misinterpreted. Wallenberg had not conducted any PoW interview, said the SFO.

Much store was placed on this memorandum to the Russian Foreign Ministry and it concluded that the American-Jewish financing of much of Wallenberg's humanitarian efforts should not be misconstrued.

'This terrible tragedy has occurred' reported the SFO. 'Wallenberg daily risked being murdered by the Nazis in this courageous personal contribution to rescue people, yet given the circumstances of the time, non-Jewish socialists, communists and fascist terrorists thought him a spy.'

So ended the first 10 years of Wallenberg's disappearance. Immediate optimism had been replaced by a dulled view that the 'Lost Hero' might never return. That 1954 memorandum didn't even yield a response. Ivan Serov, six months in post as KGB chairman, would have studied it, his own investigation still fresh in his mind. Between February 1952 and March 1956, Sweden submitted 15 written reports on Wallenberg and there had been 34 verbal SFO communications. All went unanswered. The SFO had expended considerable efforts in trying to locate its man.

Every Swedish mission worldwide was on the case, ordered to locate any released PoW who might provide a lead. Vivid descriptions had been painted by the PoWs of prison life and the SFO had built a growing dossier of the jails run by the security services and the labour camps where foreigners were known to still remain. The West

German government in Bonn proved helpful in providing copious lists of PoWs and their whereabouts.

Washington's own extensive efforts had also been blocked by the intractable attitude of Moscow. The SFO wrote to the US State Department thanking it for its help, its conclusion devoid of optimism. 'The Foreign Office has no recent information as to whether or not Wallenberg is alive, but feels it must proceed on the basis that he is.'

The extraordinary testimony from a new and unexpected source, a released Gestapo officer, would rejuvenate the search.

7

Gustav Richter, Wallenberg's cellmate and stooge

A RELEASED SS GENERAL PoW, later convicted in West Germany for complicity in the massacre of 11,300 Bulgarian Jews, led Gunnar Lorentzon, the Swedish Foreign Office's chief investigator into the disappearance of Wallenberg, to Major Gustav Richter.

Adolf-Heinz Beckerle had arrived in Sofia, Bulgaria, in June 1941, as ambassador after six months in charge of the police contingent in the Lodz ghetto, the second largest in Poland after Warsaw. In the month Beckerle left Lodz, instructions were in place to deport 10,000 Jews to the Chelmno extermination camp. The NKVD, in September 1944, had rounded up Beckerle in Svilengrad, a small town on Bulgaria's southern border with Greece and Turkey.

Under the second Soviet amnesty law in 1954, allowing 400,000 PoWs to leave, Beckerle returned home but within three years his infamy caught up with him. With some urgency, West Germany had set up a central office to track down Nazi war criminals as the statute of limitations for most WW2 crimes was running out. Beckerle, despite his protestations, was hauled in front of the courts with 1,200 others. Acquittal in his first trial was followed by a conviction in the second, in November 1967, but health grounds ruled out a long sentence. Lorentzon conducted his interviews with Beckerle between 1955-56, before the first trial, and if he had known about Beckerle's wartime crimes, no comment was made in the interview notes. Beckerle often wrote to Lorentzon as the relationship developed.

What Beckerle disclosed proved invaluable to the Swedes especially when the name of the Austrian, Gustav Richter, had emerged. The two were cellmates in cell 164 in Lefortovo, in the

Third Log, in June 1945. A Major Frohman was the third member in the cell. Both Richter and Frohman had worked in the German legation in Bucharest, Rumania. Through pipe-tapping[120] they communicated with cell 165 holding other Bucharest colleagues, namely Bergmann, Rosstel and Helmut Styhler. Later inmates in cell 165 included further members of the legation, Dr Gerhard Steltzer, the chargé d'affaires and Captain Scheller, an Abwehr operative.

While in Lefortovo, Richter had told Beckerle that he had recently been a cellmate of Raoul Wallenberg in the Lubyanka. To the Swedish Foreign Office that was a revelation. Within days of Richter's release, the Swedish Foreign Office made contact.

In Lorentzon's notes of his first interview with Richter, he is described as a police attaché: an officer in the Gestapo. Richter had been posted to Bucharest with the brief to advise the Marshal Ion Antonescu government, in power since September 1940. Rumania would become a fully committed Axis member but the country was factiously split between the Legionnaires and the anti-Semitic Iron Guard with the latter supported by Himmler and his SS. Antonescu decided to take on the Iron Guard by bringing in the army to break it. With the Iron Guard finished, its leaders escaped to Germany under SS protection. To compel Antonescu to begin eradicating Rumanian Jewry, Himmler put Major Richter on the ground. Reporting to Manfred von Killinger, the German ambassador, within three months Richter had a plan in place.

By all accounts, Richter formed a strong partnership with the odious Mihai Antonescu, the deputy prime minister and foreign minister.[121] Rumania established its own version of the German Einsatzgruppen, the Esalon Special, which first tested its strength at Jassy [Iasi] in Bessarabia during the evening of July 29, 1941. The Jewish community was substantial with 112 synagogues and in three days the Esalon Special, aided by the Einsatzgruppen, slaughtered 13,266 inhabitants. Another 25,000 Jews were deported to Moghilev in the Ukraine where 12,000 were shot. The remainder was escorted back to Rumania as the German authorities refused to handle them. Death trains had become a specialty of the RHSA but Richter meted out his own novel method of barbarity on the Rumanian Jews. Cattle trucks left Iasi's main station but not to the Polish death camps.

Starved of air and provisions, some 5,000 suffocated as the trains aimlessly trundled around the country in the stifling summer heat until most of the Jews were dead. Those who did stagger from these pressure cookers were simply shot down.[122]

Happy that his extermination agenda was well underway, Richter returned to Berlin to report. His talents were sorely missed and Richter returned after a request to Himmler by Mihai Antonescu.

The killing continued, but as the Wannsee Conference in Berlin ended in January 1942 with an agreed pan-European approach to eradicate all Jewry, Richter informed Antonescu that Rumania was a key element in that strategy. Richter determined that 300,000 Rumanian Jews must be liquidated by July, a decision ratified by Eichmann, Himmler and Martin Luther, the undersecretary in the German Foreign Ministry. Mihai Antonescu gave his consent to transport the first 250,000 across the border to the Belzec extermination centre in Poland.

Confident, Richter didn't give a jot for secrecy, even penning two articles in a Serbian publication, *Bukarester Tageblatt*, on the need to control Rumanian Jewry but Belzec didn't figure in the content. In desperation, the Centre for Rumanian Jewry put forward to Richter a conciliatory offer termed the 'Rumanian option'. If 3,000 could be granted an exit visa to travel to Palestine, a large sum of currency and valuables would be exchanged. What did eventually evolve is a complex story but the mass emptying of Jews from Bessarabia, Bukovina and the Transnistria never happened. Richter's efforts had been in vain.

Lorentzon first contacted Richter on October 14, 1955, barely days after his release, and it was a hurried affair. Richter was in the middle of the family move to Ludwigshafen-am-Rhein in West Germany but in what time they had, Richter confirmed he had indeed shared a cell in the Lubyanka with Wallenberg. There was a condition to the interview. Richter had primed Lorentzon in advance that he would give up any knowledge he had about

---

[120] A method of cell communication in Soviet prisons.

[121] **Antonescu, Mihai**: Executed by firing squad in June 1946, aged 42.

[122] See photograph of one of the Rumanian train atrocities *[Moscow-23]*.

·Wallenberg, but nothing else. He was not prepared to talk about himself or any other prisoners. There were to be several meetings and in the continuing dialogue that attitude softened.

In that first interview, Richter related that on January 17, 1945, he had been transported from Lefortovo to the Lubyanka. A Stalingrad captive was already in situ in the cell and Raoul Wallenberg became an additional cellmate in early February. The Swede had quickly informed his new cellmates that he was a secretary at the Swedish legation in Budapest. From what Richter could remember, Wallenberg had been interrogated at least once during their time together and accused of espionage.

Wallenberg had been in good spirits: 'sehr lustig' – very cheerful, Lorentzon recorded Richter's actual German phrase in his notes. Even in this brief encounter, Lorentzon considered Richter's testimony to be 'entirely believable'. Further disclosures had followed in the second interview on October 22, which Arne Lundberg, the Swedish Foreign Office secretary, put on paper to Maj von Dardel, Raoul's mother, and marked 'strictly confidential'.

Lorentzon encouraged Richter to elaborate on his arrest and subsequent transportation to Moscow. With others from the Bucharest legation, the Gestapo officer was first interned in a school outside the city before being taken to Teceçi, Moldova, remaining there until September 3, 1944. The following day he was flown to Moscow where he arrived on September 7, following a stopover in Kharkov. Richter was in the third group of captured diplomats and officers from the Bucharest legation. On his aircraft were 15 prisoners including Dr Klotius and Dr Stelzer. Wives had also been part of the NKVD round up: it is unclear what happened to them. On arrival in Moscow, Richter said he was placed in cell 142 at Lefortovo, with Colonel Braun and Dr Fritz Schellhorn, the latter the consul general in the consulate at Czernowitz.[123]

Richter was returned to Lefortovo on June 17, 1945, where he remained for the next six years. In January 1952, Richter would again be escorted to the Lubyanka before he was moved to a cell in Butyrka, another Moscow prison. His final prison before release in early October 1955 was Vladimir, in the Korpus-2 block. A third interview took place between Richter and Lorentzon on October

24, the final one on January 26, 1956.

To verify Richter's story, the Swedish Foreign Office needed a full listing of all diplomats who had worked in the Bucharest legation and through Abwehr contacts they found the helpful Colonel Tarbuk-Sesenhorst, a former Abwehr officer, and himself a newly-released PoW. Tarbuk-Sesenhorst had operated mainly in Italy and had come under suspicion from the Gestapo as being implicated in one of the plots against Hitler. Luckily, all links had proved tenuous at best but he remained under continual surveillance. Captured by the British, Tarbuk-Sesenhorst was later handed over to the NKVD, in one of the many large-scale exchanges that took place, landing up in Lefortovo. Lorentzon contacted Tarbuk-Sesenhorst in Vienna and using his former Abwehr contacts, he was able to help.

The NKVD and Smersh had rounded up the majority of the Bucharest-based officials between August and September 1944 and with the list provided by Tarbuk-Sesenhorst, the Swedish Foreign Office contacted as many as they could locate.

Interviews with these released PoWs now aided the Swedes to track Wallenberg through the Lubyanka and then to Lefortovo. Ernst Ludwig Wallenstein, the legation's scientific attaché, was interviewed in Frankfurt, West Germany, on October 16, 1955, again on December 8 and January 25 the following year. Imprisoned in Lefortovo from September 1944, Wallenstein had been in cells 151, 150 and finally 141 until June 1948. He told Lorentzon that during 1945 he had tapped on the pipes with the cell above his that held Wallenberg and Wallenberg's cellmate, Willy Roedel, who had been the adjutant to the German ambassador in Bucharest. In one episode, Wallenberg had tapped back that he had written a personal plea for freedom to Stalin.

The German cultural attaché in Bucharest, Karl Supprian, who after his release lived in Hamburg, was interviewed on three occasions

---

[123] **Schellhorn, Dr Fritz Gebhard**: It is questionable whether he initiated his claimed actions in Czernowitz to help the Jewish community. As the consulate had moved temporarily to Jassy in 1940, he had witnessed the Jewish pogrom. The consulate was evacuated to the legation in Bucharest. Schellhorn was released in 1955 after incarceration in Lefortovo and Vladimir, and died in 1982.

about his imprisonment in Lefortovo and Vladimir. At Lefortovo, he, too, had been in cell 151 and during April 1945 had also tapped with Wallenberg and Roedel. Supprian had been moved into cell 152 to share with Claudio de Mohr, the Italian diplomat, who had already been interviewed by the Swedes. Heinz-Helmut von Hinckeldey, another mission officer, confirmed that during one of his tapping sessions with Wallenberg in Lefortovo, the Swede had tapped back that he was connected to the Wallenberg family bank in Stockholm. The last tapping from Wallenberg included the fateful message 'We are being taken away.' Von Hinckeldey couldn't remember the date.

Bernhard Rensinghoff, the economic counsellor, interviewed at his home in Gescher, Westphalia, confirmed that he had shared cells 150 and 141 in Lefortovo with Wallenstein and remembered the final Wallenberg tapping and that it was August 1946. Rensinghoff had ended up in Vladimir where he was held in eight different cells. Willy Bergemann, another from the legation, who had returned from the Soviet Union mentally desperate and broken, claimed that he, too, had tapped with Wallenberg.

An informal system of reference communication had operated throughout the Soviet prisons by PoWs, with the sharing of names of previous cellmates and the occupants of other cells. This information was necessary detail if release was ever granted, so relatives back home might be informed.

Two further PoW sources confirmed Richter's imprisonment in the Lubyanka and Lefortovo with additional detail on both Wallenberg and Vilmos Langfelder. Dahm, a Lubyanka inmate, contacted by the Swedish Foreign Office in February 1955, illuminated that not only had he shared a cell with Richter and another PoW, Adolf Schmidt, but he had once received food in his cell with the name slip 'RW, Stockholm' on the tray. Colonel Horst Kitschmann, twice interviewed in the spa resort town of Piding, in Bavaria, confirmed that with Admiral Tillessey, they had been cellmates of Richter in Lefortovo. Kitschmann had been a military attaché in the German legation in Finland and had also served in Stockholm.

With full recall on his imprisonment in Lefortovo, the Lubyanka, again Lefortovo, Butyrka, another spell in the Lubyanka and finally

Vladimir, Kitschmann's testimony was regarded reliable. His testimony had also disclosed that while in cell 105, in his first spell in Lefortovo, Langfelder had been a cellmate. In Vladimir, in the so-called hospital unit in Korpus-2, Kitschmann had again come across Richter.

Richter had already provided Lorentzon with a diagram of Korpus-2, with its 60 cells, and had confirmed that both he and Kitschmann were at one time together in the hospital unit. Richter had had a thyroid disease. Contact between prisoners in Vladimir was banned but that didn't stop news spreading amongst the cells. The death of former Field Marshal Paul von Kleist in Vladimir, in November 1954, spread like wildfire throughout the jail. Extradited to the USSR in 1948, von Kleist was the highest-ranked German military officer to die in Soviet captivity. Throughout his own period in Vladimir, said Richter, he was keen not to be punished and lose his short daily walk that was necessary to prevent further deterioration in his health.

Evidence from Kitschmann had confirmed to the Swedish Foreign Office that Langfelder had been in the Soviet prison system. The Finn, Eino Olavi Pelkonen, arrested in June 1944, offered additional detail. His first cell was in the Lubyanka before being moved to the notorious Sukhanovka prison. Transfer to Lefortovo took place on April 30, 1945 where he shared cell 105 with Langfelder and Rear Admiral Ernst Krafft for a short two weeks. Pelkonen was subsequently moved to Butyrka in Moscow, then Vladimir, before release on July 21, 1955. His testimony card at the Swedish Foreign Office stated that the Finnish police had conducted the two interviews with Pelkonen on its behalf. There was a remark that the Finn had suffered severe facial damage during the war.

The Swedish journalist, Edward Sandeberg, arrested in Berlin in June 1945 and charged with spying, had already added to the growing PoW testimony store. Sandeberg had spent much of the war reporting from the German capital and in the final months before the Third Reich collapsed, he was the sole newspaper representative from the neutral countries. Escorted to Moscow, Sandeberg was jailed for a year in Butyrka where his cellmate was Erhard Hille, a Wehrmacht corporal. According to Sandeberg, Hille had enquired if he had ever met the Swedish diplomat, Raoul Wallenberg. Sandeberg hadn't but he was familiar with the family name, as were all Swedes. Sandeberg informed the authorities that Hille had told him that while in Lefortovo he had shared a cell with Langfelder.

Hille was interviewed ratifying that he did have Langfelder as a cellmate from March 22, 1945. During that time, Langfelder had related to him how he had been arrested in Budapest with Wallenberg and furnished details on their escort to Moscow. That description of the journey, via Rumania, has become the accepted account for Wallenberg and Langfelder. Corroboration of that journey came from another PoW, Ernst Huber, an Abwehr corporal, who had also at one time shared a cell with Wallenberg's driver. In those interviews, Hille had claimed that another of his cellmates was Jan Loyda, who had previously shared a cell with Wallenberg in the Lubyanka.

The interview cards for the released PoWs are extensive and I have viewed many. Testimonies were scrutinised by Otto Danielsson, the state criminal investigator, for discrepancies. Arne Lundberg, the Swedish Foreign Office secretary, also reviewed the material on the chance that anything new and revealing might be presented as evidence to the Soviets. Stig Engfeldt, another Swedish Foreign Office employee, regularly updated what was considered to be the Soviet agenda.

Piecing together the prison movements of Wallenberg and Langfelder, differentiating as best they could the bogus from the real, had been a laborious task for the Swedish Foreign Office. I never saw any reference to the war crimes in the interview notes that many of the PoWs had participated in: perhaps Lorentzon and others figuratively held their noses. Some of the PoWs named by Richter had been executed during their incarceration, such as Lt. General von Pannwitz, the commander of SS Cossack cavalry troops who was accused by the Soviets of massacres in Serbia and Croatia.

Since this extraordinary PoW archive was assembled, there has been internal reflection within the Swedish Foreign Office that key clues at the time may have been overlooked. That's harsh criticism given the difficulties imposed by attempting to track prisoners through the Soviet prison system, with zero assistance from the

Moscow authorities. Detailed hand-drawn layouts of prisons, long lists of PoWs with ticks against those who had been interviewed and numerous letters litter the archive. There are even expense accounts submitted by Lorentzon, for his numerous trips.

Many of his interviews were conducted in secret given the nature of travelling behind the Iron Curtain, especially in and around Vienna that was occupied by the Red Army until troops were withdrawn in October 1955. Lorentzon accepted the risks, averting arrest on several occasions, and one document in the British Foreign Office archives provided an illustrative glimpse on his clandestine activities. At a private dinner in November 1957 with a British embassy official in Stockholm, Lorentzon confided that although he was a secretary in the commercial division of the Swedish Foreign Office, he covertly used the ID of a Swedish representative in the European Free Trade Area organisation, EFTA, when tracking down PoWs. His dinner companion later penned a note to London and it was circulated within the Foreign Office for comments. There were a number.

Norway had had better luck with the Soviets. Einar Gerhardsen, its prime minister, visiting Moscow in 1955 had confronted Khrushchev about the missing Norwegian communist, Osvald Harjo. During the war he had fled to the Soviet Union to escape the occupying Germans, only to be arrested as a Nazi spy. Khrushchev reportedly said to Gerhardsen, 'Do you want to discuss this poor fascist?' Khrushchev did, however, order Harjo's release and he returned to Norway. Encouraged by Norway's success, Sweden pushed ever harder.

Finding and interviewing Gustav Richter was considered a breakthrough but had this Gestapo officer, the architect of mass slaughter in Rumania, been an NKVD cell stooge?

Sandeberg, the arrested journalist, who on his release after his year in Butyrka felt numbed and disoriented after the harrowing experience, believed that Hille, one of his cellmates, was certainly one. There were many in the jails. Cell secrets could be traded with NKVD and Smersh interrogators in exchange for better conditions, even one's life. There is every reason to suspect that Richter, Wallenberg's cellmate, had bartered to save his own skin. Richter would work for a Ludwigshafen firm until his retirement in 1974.

The courts did finally catch up with his infamy, just as they had with Beckerle. Richter was sentenced in January 1982 as a war criminal in Frankenthal, in southwest Germany. The charges were 'inducing Rumania to treat Jews according to Nazi racial laws' and the death of 1,600 Rumanian Jews deported from France to Auschwitz-Birkenau. Like many post-war trials of similar killers the full extent of the slaughter was never part of the charge. The judge gave Richter the derisory sentence of four years, but given he had served 11 years in the Soviet prison system he was allowed to walk out of court a free man.

★★★

Unbeknown to the Swedish authorities, Ivan Serov, one of the MVD (Ministry of the Interior) deputies to the disgraced and executed Lavrenty Beria, was ordered by Nikita Khrushchev to begin his own enquiry into Wallenberg but his terms of reference ran contrary to Sweden's hopes of Wallenberg being alive. Serov started from the factual premise that Wallenberg was dead, liquidated in 1947.

That secret investigation began in December 1953 with Serov determined to uncover the names of the parties behind the liquidation and who was the executioner. Serov's conclusions would prove instrumental in Khrushchev discrediting his political enemies who wanted him gone.

8

The Serov investigation into Wallenberg's liquidation begins – December 1953

… I forgot about Wallenberg until in late 1953 when his name came up in conversation with Fedotov, chief of the MGB's Counterintelligence Directorate. Fedotov related to me that agents of several foreign intelligence services had brought up the matter of Wallenberg in Moscow.

He told me that Wallenberg's registration card was still being held in the Counterintelligence Directorate but more importantly, Wallenberg had a file, which was held in the archive of the Committee of Information and had been there since Fedotov had been the deputy chairman of that department.

Extracts from Ivan Serov's memoir

THE 'BACK CHANNELS' WERE NOISY, communicated Lt. General Peter Fedotov, the MGB's counterintelligence chief, to Serov in December 1953.[124] One issue in particular angered the foreign intelligence agencies. No longer, Fedotov's people had been told, could Moscow conceal the role of Smersh in the lifting of Wallenberg out of Budapest in January 1945.

To the unprincipled and ruthless Serov, no stranger to signing off death warrants, the fate of the Swede was of little consequence. Thousands of foreigners had been rounded up in the closing months of the war, held prisoner and subsequently executed.

In August 1953, Konstantin Rodionov, Russia's ambassador to Stockholm, had delivered a robust note to Lundberg, the Cabinet Secretary, angrily condemning the frequent attempts to connect the

---

[124] Fedotov in uniform. See photograph *[Moscow-24]*.

question of Wallenberg's fate to what Rodionov referred to as 'an alleged stay in the Soviet Union'. Rodionov was further scathing. 'Over a period of several years the question of Raoul Wallenberg has been exploited in the most shameful manner for hostile purposes in relation to the Soviet Union'.

These 'back channels' are unofficial lines of communication between the intelligence agencies, their very existence often denied to respective governments and sometimes for the best of reasons. In the early and bitter years of the Cold War, as the USSR and its former allies locked horns, these channels remained open as vital lines of dialogue. During WW2, SS chief, Heinrich Himmler, used them to initiate discussion in Stockholm first with the Americans and then the Soviets on an SS plan to topple Hitler. Britain's MI6 had kept open a long-established channel into the Abwehr, Germany's much respected intelligence agency, throughout the war.

Fedotov, the wartime head of NKVD counterintelligence and privy to most secrets, let drop to Serov more information on the Swedish diplomat.

> *Wallenberg had been the representative of the Swedish Red Cross in Budapest and had been closely connected with German and American intelligence services. In 1947, he and three other foreigners connected with him were liquidated on the orders of Abakumov.*

There is no admission by Serov that he was already aware of this detail. He did, though, have specific knowledge of clandestine meetings between the Wallenberg family and the German Abwehr.

> *I first heard of the name, Wallenberg, during wartime when I acted as the Special Representative of the Soviet High Command. At that time I had been informed that a member of the Wallenberg family had on several occasions visited the German-occupied Soviet territories, mainly the city of Pskov,[125] where he had contacts with the fascist civil administration and the Abwehr, German military intelligence.*

One Fedotov disclosure was new to Serov: Wallenberg's file still existed in the records of the defunct Committee of Information, known as KI. The creation of the KI was a knee-jerk response by Stalin in 1947 to emulate the birth of the Central Intelligence Agency, born out of America's wartime OSS. Designated to become a clearing-house for all gathered foreign intelligence, the KI was hampered from the outset by inter-service rivalries. The ineffective wartime experiment of combining the espionage strengths of the NKVD and the GRU had hardly been the model to follow. Vyacheslav Molotov,[126] the foreign minister nicknamed 'stone-arse' by the foreign diplomatic community, was put at the KI helm with Fedotov brought in as deputy with full operational responsibility. Fedotov had a known reputation for military-style detail and organisation.

Within a year, the GRU wanted out, demanding that it be allowed to resume its separate existence. Hampering the KI further was Stalin's steadfast refusal to end his own intelligence-gathering capability that operated out of the Kremlin and had its own operational and communications structure. The KI was subsequently split into two with the 'large KI' remaining bogged down in bureaucracy, whereas the 'small KI' enjoyed a more informal and autonomous role that encouraged a more workable relationship between the GRU and the MGB[127]. Stalin finally axed the 'large KI' in February 1952 leaving an angry Molotov discredited. Fedotov's reputation was also sullied as Molotov left him to field all blame.

What instigated Serov to report to Khrushchev the 'back channel' clamour on Wallenberg and the existence of the diplomat's file? Clearly, as the memoir suggests, Serov already had Khrushchev's ear. Opportunism was certainly a factor, given the ongoing chaos in the security and intelligence services after the death of Stalin in March 1953.

To stem a security vacuum, the Politburo had moved quickly to restructure the Ministry of State Security (MGB) and the Ministry

---

[125] Historic city in northwest Russia.
[126] **Molotov, Vyacheslav Mikhailovich**: Generally regarded as Stalin's deputy. See photograph [Moscow-25].
[127] MGB: Soviet Ministry of State Security that took over many of the functions of the NKVD including counterintelligence.

of Internal Affairs (MVD), merging most of their activities, and awarding this new powerbase to Beria as the minister of security. Serov and Kruglov became his deputies and Fedotov was back in favour as the MGB's head of counterintelligence. Three months later Beria was brought down and the reputation of the MVD lay in tatters but Serov was never in peril. Fedotov also survived, but again he was tainted. On the inside, Serov knew of Khrushchev's intention to sweep away Stalinist structures and create his own. That reformist zeal included a new intelligence service, and Serov wanted to be its head.

The Wallenberg file in KI was located and from what Fedotov had confirmed to him, it was clear to Serov that Khrushchev[128] could improve his position against the Politburo plotters who wanted him gone.

From what information I had collected, I briefed Nikita Khrushchev. He became very interested in what I had to say, and ordered me to delve further, but forbade me from talking to Molotov or anyone else in the Ministry of Foreign Affairs about the secret assignment that he had given me.

Keeping the Wallenberg investigation quiet from Molotov was certainly not a problem. There was mutual dislike and had been for years. Khrushchev also wanted to nail some of the blame for Wallenberg's killing on the dead Beria and Victor Abakumov, the former head of Smersh and security minister. The latter now languished in jail, contemplating his own execution.

From my conversation with Khrushchev I had the distinct impression that he wanted me to show clearly that Beria and Abakumov had been responsible for the liquidation of Wallenberg.

During the war Khrushchev was the outsider, sometimes reduced to a drinking partner for Stalin when he wanted an all-night session in the Kremlin or in the Kuntsevo dacha. Khrushchev spent his early political career in the Ukraine masterminding the Moscow-imposed agricultural sanctions that had led to the Great Famine. After 1938 he headed the party apparatus. As the Germans invaded the Ukraine, Khrushchev had called Stalin directly to demand reinforcements. With the Red Army in full retreat in June 1941, Stalin had shut himself away in Kuntsevo for days leaving the Soviet military machine rudderless. Khrushchev pleaded with Molotov to order reinforcements but he was brushed aside. Stalin's deputy was never forgiven for allowing the Ukraine to be overrun.

Serov, too, had been in the Ukraine in 1941 as head of the NKVD and he would have worked closely with Khrushchev. In the Soviet retreat his people had slayed thousands of pro-German Ukrainians. Khrushchev returned to the Ukraine upon liberation and was unforgiving on civilians in the western Ukraine, who he accused of collaboration. Mass transportations took place into the Gulag. There was blood on Khrushchev's hands.[129]

Putting together the investigation team

Serov could fall back on Fedotov for both knowledge and experience and Khrushchev offered the services of his key aide, Vladimir Malin[130], who carried the political clout to open any closed door.

Malin, a former supporter of Malenkov, had changed his allegiance to Khrushchev and the two had developed a relationship similar to that of Stalin and the legendary Aleksandr Poksrebyshev. The minutes of one Central Committee meeting in early 1954, taken by Malin, exemplifies his power. Malin had raised the issue of members' safes after Khrushchev had previously decreed that their contents should not be withheld from other Politburo members. All ministers had surrendered their keys to him, Malin reported, bar one. Kaganovich, the architect of a number of Stalin's worst episodes, bitterly complained that his files were personal documents and couldn't be shared with anyone. Khrushchev had been apoplectic

---

[128] Photograph of Khrushchev taking the salute in Red Square [Moscow-26].

[129] When first secretary of the party, Khrushchev denied that he had been one of the orchestrators of the Great Famine, but he has been linked with the NKVD reprisals in 1941 and 1944.

[130] **Malin, Vladimir**: He was a Khrushchev aide from 1954 until October 15, 1964 when Khrushchev was deposed by Brezhnev and Kosygin.

when Malin told him that Kaganovich wouldn't comply.

The first document that Malin was able to find for Serov was critical. It was the original text written in 1947 by Colonel General Abakumov, the minister of state security.

> *The report that Abakumov had provided for Molotov, on the*
> *suggestion to liquidate Wallenberg, had been given to me personally*
> *by Malin, Khrushchev's assistant in his secretariat, with whom I*
> *was on good terms.*

Given he had to run the investigation in secret, Serov chose carefully and selectively the final members of his investigation team. Locating essential paperwork and documents was to be key in widening its scope, and in Colonel Vasily Dobrohotov[131] there was no one more capable.

> *I now asked Dobrohotov,[132] another MVD officer, to uncover the*
> *operational details of the Wallenberg case. He had recently transferred*
> *from the MGB Secretariat to the foreign intelligence department.*

Colonel Vasily Ivanovich Dobrohotov

Running the Secretariat is a powerful position so Serov already knew his worth. In the intelligence personnel file on Dobrohotov, the name is spelt 'Dobrohoktov' but I have maintained the spelling in the Ivan Serov memoir.

Dobrohotov's background was metalworking, his father's trade. Born in Kirzhach, 125 km to the west of Vladimir, in February 1911, after basic schooling Dobrohotov moved to Kolchugino, famed for its silverware and samovar manufacturing. Enrolling as a factory apprentice Dobrohotov soon found employment in a metal plant in Ordzhonikidze. Gaining experience he moved on to Vladimir in September 1929 to a mechanical vocational college, a tekhnikum. World events then changed his career path.

Japan was expected to invade in 1932, a second front to its invasion of Manchuria the previous October. Leon Trotsky, from his enforced exile in Turkey, argued an alternative view advocating that

Germany posed the greatest threat to Russia with Hitler on the brink of acceding to Chancellor. The Red Army draft in 1933 included the metalworking college lecturer from Vladimir and he was posted to Engels on the right bank of the Volga, a city named after Friedrich Engels. The Japanese invasion failed to materialise and within the year Dobrohotov was out of the army and he moved to Moscow as a design technician in the city's metro system, a position that came with privileges. Hardworking, conscientious and a sound party member, promotion followed and by April 1934 he headed a design bureau in the People's Commissariat of Heavy Industry. Three years later, Dobrohotov had been posted to Plant No. 398 in the People's Commissariat of Ammunition in charge of quality control, a responsibility that carried a heavy penalty if he messed up. That was never a problem for Dobrohotov. In the evenings he studied at the Institute of Defense Industry.

Those studies took Dobrohotov to the Osoaviakhim, the select training organisation for the military and navy and in December 1938, he headed its Sovet, the central board. Another move took him back to Plant No. 398 as the VCP(b) representative in the role of partorg, a full-time organiser. VCP(b) was another name for the Communist Party of the Soviet Union. Encouraged to further pursue his political studies Dobrohotov attended the exclusive Higher Party School from 1940 until 1942. There was no surprise when this loyal apparatchik became an instructor and an authorised organiser within the Communist Party Central Committee. Dobrohotov was now rubbing shoulders with the Politburo.

Even though he hadn't participated in any military actions, Dobrohotov was awarded the *Order of the Patriotic War*, 2nd degree when the Great Patriotic War (WW2) concluded. Within the VCP(b), there were new responsibilities. In the Cadre Directorate, he was assistant secretary of the party committee and a further role in the party's secretariat confirmed that Dobrohotov was moving up.

---

[131] A rare photograph of Dobrohotov *[Moscow-27]*.
[132] **Dobrohotov, Col. Vasily Ivanovich**: MVD, MGB and KGB Secretariat head. During the time of the Wallenberg investigation, Serov tasked him with preparing the blueprint for the establishment of the KGB.

Another promotion from July 1949 saw Dobrohotov as deputy head of the diplomatic and foreign trade agencies of the VCP(b), taking over as head in July 1950.

Well acquainted with working with the Soviet intelligence services. Dobrohotov became the chief of the MGB's Secretariat in September 1951. Invited to join the MGB board – the Collegium – and with the rank of colonel, Dobrohotov and his colleagues needed to operationally confront the worsening relationship with the West. On September 17 that year, the San Francisco Peace Conference was convened to belatedly rubber-stamp the ending of WW2 and terminate Japan's position as an imperial power. As the conference chairman, Dean Acheson, stood up to address the delegates Andrei Gromyko, the Russian delegation leader, loudly interjected demanding an answer as to why Red China hadn't been invited. Gromyko further filibusted protesting that Japan would now be in cahoots with America and the enemy was the Soviet Union. His delegation quit in a huff. Particularly galling for the Soviets was Allied inaction for any return of South Sakhalin and the Kuril Islands, still in Japanese hands.

In January 1952, all foreign intelligence activities of the MGB, which since 1947 had been part of the Committee of Information (KI), returned to the MGB as its First Main Directorate (PGU). Within a month Dobrohotov was shifted into the PGU as deputy to Lt. General Sergei Savchenko,[133] yet given the speed of change in the intelligence services Dobrohotov was posted back to the MGB Secretariat. Dobrohotov's intelligence file shows him as deputy head as at March 11, 1953. Another source has him as acting head of the Second Main Directorate (VGU) of the MVD, handling foreign intelligence, a position confirmed by Serov in his memoir.

Intriguingly, there is a three-month gap in Dobrohotov's file from December 11, 1953 until March 17, 1954, neatly concurring with the timing of Serov's investigation into Wallenberg. So secret did Serov keep it, great efforts must have been employed to conceal Dobrohotov's role and he further reveals in his memoir that during the Wallenberg investigation, Khrushchev had another task. The first secretary of the party needed a full proposal for a new security service. It fell to the experienced Dobrohotov to be the KGB's architect and Serov would reward him in March 1954 with positions as Secretariat head and a seat on the board.

Dobrohotov was promoted to major general in January 1957, to accompany an *'Honorary Officer of the State Security'* award but as Serov was pushed out of the KGB into the GRU in December 1958, many of his acolytes were either demoted or shunted out to the regional offices by the incoming Aleksandr Shelepin. Industrial Ivanovo was the city for Dobrohotov as KGB chief, where he remained until October 1962 as a new job offer unexpectedly emerged. The Central Committee sought his talents.

Its members knew they could rely on the former metalworker. Managing the privileges enjoyed by committee members, such as elite housing, dachas, bespoke tailoring, overseas trips and holidays needed Dobrohotov's tact and discretion. Turning a blind eye to the corruption would be his last state role and he died on July 12, 1971, aged 60.

Colonel Aleksandr Aleksandrovich Kozyrev

Adding to Dobrohotov's experience was an officer with considerable investigation experience, even though he had been involved in a cover-up of an ignominious Soviet WW2 massacre of Polish PoWs that remained controversial for decades.

As well as using Dobrohotov into my investigation over the death of Wallenberg, I ordered Colonel Kozyrev[134] from the Investigation Department of the MVD to look into Likhachev's original investigation.[135]

Kozyrev already reported to Serov and had been investigating Abakumov and other high-ranking intelligence officers. Abakumov, in particular, had an unsavoury backstory that Khrushchev wanted investigating. Stalin's plots were the main focus in the questioning

---

[133] **Savchenko, Lt. Gen. Sergei Romanovich**: MGB foreign intelligence chief from September 19, 1949 until January 5, 1953.

[134] For Kozyrev, no photograph is available.

[135] Likhachev and his role in the Lubyanka interrogation of Wallenberg will be explored in a later chapter.

but the liquidation of Raoul Wallenberg was now a priority. Unfortunately, Serov in his memoir doesn't recall whether Abakumov was co-operative with Kozyrev in his jail cell.

Determining the truth had not always been in Kozyrev's brief. When Russia and Germany were brief allies, Poland had felt the brunt of a twin attack from Germany in the west and Russia in the east. Three camps had been built to hold some 14,500 Polish PoWs captured by the Soviets and in April 1940 the NKVD was ordered to clear them.

The Red Army was beaten out of Smolensk on July 29, 1941, a bare month on from the German invasion of the USSR and for 18 months the murders of the PoWs held in Kozelsk, one of the camps, remained undiscovered until February 28, 1943. The Germans had stumbled upon a mass grave and the Secret Field Police filed a report to Berlin on the discovery. In a bid to deflect any blame, Berlin decided on an exhumation. Pathologists descended on the Katyn site on March 29 but they could only estimate the body count in the 12 layers of corpses in the eight filled in trenches.

What followed was a voluminous 330-page report published by the German Foreign Office, with extensive documentary evidence, accusing the Soviets of a war crime.[136] Substantiating its claim, American and British PoW officers had been escorted to the exhumation site and they would later submit their observations through German channels to London. From Moscow came a flat denial of culpability. The measured response from the Allies and the Russian and Polish émigré community in Britain, with first-hand experience of living under Stalin's security services, added to the doubt on who was ultimately responsible for the killing of Kozelsk's 4,500 inmates.

With the tide of the war turning by September 15, 1943 the Red Army had encircled Smolensk. Surrender came 10 days later and in Moscow a deafening barrage of 244 guns, each firing 20 shells, saluted the victory. That revelry, however, was somewhat muted within the Kremlin and the Lubyanka as a plan was hastily conceived to invalidate the German war crime accusation. The task fell to Lt. General Vsevolod Merkulov, the very same NKVD chief who had been responsible for the massacre in 1940. Nikolay Bourdenko, the

Red Army Surgeon General, headed the medical commission to exhume the corpses, reburied by the Germans in its investigation.

Working closely with Sergei Kruglov, a deputy commissar in the Ministry of Internal Affairs, Merkulov put an NKVD team on the ground under Lt. General Leonid Raikhman, the deputy head of the counterespionage department, just days after the German surrender. Immediately the whole site was fenced off to avoid prying eyes. Bourdenko's people and the large NKVD contingent remained on site until late December 1943. Eight investigators, headed by Colonel Yuli Mathusov, and including Kozyrev, then with the rank of captain, had pulled in local witnesses for hard interrogations. Bogus testimonies were hatched accompanied by threats of reprisals. Supposed witnesses were brought in from outside the area to add further credibility. Bourdenko and his doctors falsified the autopsies.

In the first week of January 1944, Merkulov was ready and the foreign correspondents in Moscow and officers from the Allied Military Commission, also based in the capital, were invited to travel to Smolensk and inspect the now uncovered death pits. Under strict supervision, they talked to the provided witnesses but it was quickly clear the statements had been rehearsed. Foreign journalists had to agree in advance that copy could only be submitted to their editors after first passing it through the Soviet censor in Moscow.

Tass, the Soviet news agency, released a statement on January 17 that the official report on German guilt would be released in a matter of days. When it was, the chronological errors were glaring but given wartime conditions the disclosed facts couldn't be verified. As in the response to the earlier German report, London and Washington remained non-committal. Nazi Germany still needed to be beaten and without the Red Army a victory seemed impossible.

Later promoted to a senior interrogator, Major Kozyrev honed his investigation talents on captured foreign PoWs and arrested local officials caught up in the Red Army sweep westwards. In the first years of the Cold War, Kozyrev became a deputy head within the

---

[136] Its full title from the German: The official statement concerning the Mass Murder at Katyn, collected and prepared by the German Information Bureau on the basis of documentary evidence by order of the German Foreign Office.

vast Gulag network and responsible for investigations. Documents bearing his name were tough to locate but one, dated March 1948, illustrated the perks that accompanied the status as a member of the Gulag's central committee. Replacement cars were to be awarded. Dobrynin, the Gulag chief, was allocated a Packard, Kozyrev and another deputy a Mercedes, another deputy a Chevrolet. The head of the Gulgmp, the chief directorate for camp mining and metallurgical industries, had a Horch and the officer in charge of the Gullp, the chief directorate for camp forestry, a Lincoln. A Russian-manufactured Gaz M-20 Pobeda was driven by the head of Glavpromstroy, the chief directorate for construction, and at Glavspets-tsvetmet, the directorate for the production of non-ferrous metals in the camps, its head was to have a Buick. The ZIS-101, a large eight-cylindered vehicle favoured by Stalin, was driven by the chief of Glavgidrostroy, the chief camp directorate for construction of hydraulic facilities.

Another document has Lt. Colonel Kozyrev as acting head of the investigation department in the MGB's Fourth Directorate in 1951. Upon the death of Stalin in March 1953, Serov moved him under his wing into the MVD and in December the Wallenberg investigation began. As it ended in March 1954, Serov tasked him with a Central Committee initiative to reinvestigate many of the guilty verdicts imposed during the Stalin era.

That reappraisal programme was scheduled to take eight months but it lasted for several years. Lev Sheinin, the former head of the investigations division in the Procurator General's office and who had prepared the Soviet documentation for the Nuremberg trials, was acquitted thanks to Kozyrev. One charge Kozyrev discredited was attempted arson in the Kremlin. Also set free was L.B. Berlin, the former department head of the Moscow clinic of diet therapy. For some, rehabilitation came too late. Alexander Fadeev, writer and chairman of the Union of Soviet Writers, had committed suicide just weeks before Kozyrev would authorise a release.

There is evidence that Kozyrev tried to protect Vasily Iosifovich Stalin, the dictator's son arrested on anti-Soviet charges after his father's death, from a cold and lingering death in the Gulag. The Party Control Committee reporting into the Central Committee, wanted to lose the son but Kozyrev argued that similar harsh conditions could be replicated in Vladimir prison. In Kozyrev's top-secret note to Colonel Bulanov, head of the KGB's prison section, dated June 12, 1956, he ordered urgent preparations be made at Vladimir for the arrival of a 'special prisoner'. To preserve Stalin's anonymity, Kozyrev demanded he could work with no more than seven other prisoners and only those with exceptionally long sentences. No other contact was permitted and Stalin had to remain in solitary confinement. Bulanov responded that the identity precondition at Vladimir was impossible. Kozyrev ignored him and sent Stalin anyway.

Kozyrev had incurred enemies within the KGB with his reappraisal programme and eventually he was posted out to Rostov-on-Don as assistant head of the KGB's office, later becoming its chief. That tenure ended in July 1959 with a discharge. According to the report to the Central Committee in July 1961 on the results of that programme, a staggering 387 cases had been investigated of which 40 had their party membership restored.

Kozyrev would die young in 1974, aged 58. The role that he and Dobrohotov played in Serov's investigation into Wallenberg has remained hidden and will never be disclosed.

9

The investigation – Arrest

At first the plan was to hand Wallenberg back to the Swedes but the NKGB's First Directorate[137] had received a memorandum on his ties with Hitler and the US Intelligence agencies.
Stalin ordered Abakumov to issue a warrant to arrest Wallenberg and bring him to Moscow for interrogation. Wallenberg's driver in Budapest was also to be interrogated in Moscow.

Extracts from Ivan Serov's memoir

A FLURRY OF CODED COMMUNICATIONS between Nikolai Bulganin, Russia's deputy defence minister in Moscow, and Lt. General Gennady Kupriyanov in Debrecen, followed Raoul Wallenberg's surprise contact in Pest on January 12, 1945. Bulganin instructed Kupriyanov to maintain the dialogue with the diplomat and maybe even isolate him from other foreigners, as a course of action was determined. Wallenberg was to be fed the line that his request to meet Marshal Malinovsky in Debrecen was under consideration. Stalin had been informed.

In pre-war days Debrecen was one of the richest and influential of Hungarian cities, famous since the Middle Ages for its livestock and horse fairs. As the German army had retreated westward this provincial centre had become the seat of the interim Hungarian government. When the Red Army reached Debrecen, the city became the Red Army headquarters for the push onto Budapest.

Kupriyanov handed the Wallenberg responsibility to Major General Ivan Afonin who brought in a Smersh unit, attached to the 15th Infantry Division of the 7th Army Guard in the 2nd Ukrainian

Front, to maintain the necessary contact. Wallenberg with Langfelder, his driver, continued to tour the Pest safe houses and hospitals but nowhere was secure. According to a Lefortovo cellmate of Langfelder, their vehicle was constantly harried at Red Army roadblocks and in one incident the tyres were slashed. One report had Wallenberg checking on patients in the Tatra Street hospital.[138] Wallenberg was isolated with no help from his colleagues stuck on the other side of the Danube.

The day before Smersh officers lifted Wallenberg out of the city on January 17, Söderblom, the Swedish ambassador in Moscow, had been handed an unambiguous note from Vladimir Dekanozov, the Russian deputy foreign minister. Wallenberg had been located and was in safe Soviet custody, Dekanozov had reported. This note was to be the only official Soviet notification up to 1957 – with Gromyko's statement – that Wallenberg had been in its hands. Serov confirms that Wallenberg had made the initial contact.

Bulganin finally gave the order to bring him in and Major Dmitry Demchenko, Captain Nikolai Zenkov and First Lt. A.L.Ruzhentsov, arrived at the International Red Cross building in Benczur Street where Wallenberg now worked and lived. Malinovsky had agreed to meet him, Demchenko told the diplomat. Transport was an immediate problem as Wallenberg's car had been badly damaged by road damage but Demchenko offered the use of a military vehicle: Langfelder should also come. Wallenberg agreed, grateful for the company of his friend and colleague.

On the pavement outside the building Wallenberg said his goodbyes, expecting a swift return. László Petö, a Hungarian friend, offered to go with Wallenberg but he changed his mind at the last minute, a decision that probably saved his life. Wallenberg slung his rucksack over his shoulder. Packed inside were two Swedish passports: his diplomatic one that had extricated him from many scrapes, the other a standard passport for all Swedish citizens. He had

---

[137] NKGB: People's Commissariat of State Security – it operated in 1941 and then 1943-1946. Its successor was the MGB.
[138] *Lost Hero, The Mystery of Raoul Wallenberg*, by F.E.Werbell and T. Clarke, McGraw-Hill Book Company, New York, 1982.

his notebook, diary, some mixed currency and other personal items. Wallenberg reportedly made his legendary statement, 'I go to Debrecen but I am not sure if I am a prisoner or a guest'.

With a sidecar escort, Demchenko's party set off almost certainly to the Gödöllö holding camp outside Budapest. On their arrival at this converted school, now in use by the NKVD and Smersh, Wallenberg would have starkly realised that he had been played. In Gödöllö the two might have endured their first separate interrogations with their interrogators demanding the names of other diplomats and foreigners they knew or had encountered in Hungary. Wallenberg might have refused: Langfelder, a Hungarian, might have cooperated.

Intriguingly, Serov states that the first thought in Moscow was to simply hand Wallenberg back to the Swedish authorities. He doesn't mention Langfelder. A communication from Abakumov, the Smersh chief, ultimately sealed Wallenberg's fate. Serov stated that the NKGB had disclosed that the diplomat and members of his family had intelligence connections that needed explaining.

The journey to Moscow

The train left for Moscow on January 25, eight days after the lifting. Captain Zenkov and four Smersh guards provided the escort for the trip that would take 12 days. Iasi, Transylvania, was the first main stop, a detail that Langfelder had shared with one of his Moscow cellmates, Ernst Huber, the Abwehr corporal.

Wallenberg would have witnessed the 'City on Seven Hills' in ruin. In May 1944, Iasi had seen a ferocious battle between the Red Army and German-Rumanian forces. Only in July had the Red Army broken through, and the savagery of the battle was gruesome. Three years earlier Iasi had experienced the notorious Jewish pogrom co-ordinated by Mihai Antonescu, the Rumanian foreign minister and his Gestapo advisor, Major Gustav Richter. Wallenberg might have been familiar with the Iasi atrocities when he was in Budapest. The Zenkov party was met at Iasi's main railway station and they were taken to the restaurant 'Luther' for a meal, another detail furnished by Huber.

Moscow came into sight in the late evening of February 5 and not long after midnight the two captives and their escort arrived outside the gate to the rear of the Lubyanka, the entrance for prisoners. A sergeant of the Border Guards, the military unit that provided guard duties for Russian state security and its jails, greeted Zenkov. He had been expected. Directed into the courtyard, Zenkov's charges would have only seen a silhouette of the infamous internal jail in the dark. Langfelder was ordered to remain in the vehicle.

Wallenberg was hauled inside where Zenkov officially handed him over with documentation. A Lubyanka internal prison registration card was completed.[139] Raoul Gustaf Wallenberg is entered as the full name with 1912 for year of birth. The Budapest address of Utca Donau, 5 is recorded as is Wallenberg's diplomatic passport, nationality and employment at the Swedish legation. The arrest date is January 12, 1945, the day he first made contact with a Red Army unit in Pest. The final handwritten entry on the card stated 'Prisoner of War transferred from Budapest February 6, 1945, to be controlled by GUKR Smersh'.

His possessions confiscated Wallenberg loudly complained. He had made copious notes on the long train journey to Moscow. In his mind, despite his predicament he still entertained some hope that he and Langfelder might be immediately released. Demanding to see the commandant of the jail and Söderblom, the Swedish ambassador, his anger only increased when his protest was roughly waved aside.

Stripped and searched, Wallenberg was led away in his prison clothes to the fifth floor of the internal jail, like the fourth reserved for 'special prisoners'. In a typical two-or-three prisoner Lubyanka cell, prisoners slept head-to-head with raised wooden slatting for the head.[140] The paracha – a hole in the floor – passed as a toilet. 'Special prisoners' did, however, enjoy better food.

In early 1945 all the cells on the fifth and fourth floors in the

---

[139] A copy of Wallenberg's registration card was relinquished by the KGB in 1991 and is in the appendix.

[140] See photograph of a typical Lubyanka cell taken in the early 1950s *[Moscow-28]*. See further photograph of the entrance to Lubyanka-3 *[Moscow-29]*. The author used this entrance to visit the Lubyanka's history room of past operations. Under Lubyanka-3 is a tunnel leading to the underground killing chamber.

internal jail were occupied, and with the high turnover prisoners were moved on to Butyrka[141] and Lefortovo.[142] Outside the capital, Smersh and the NKVD used Aleksandrovsk Central Prison, a former distillery 64-km south of Irkutsk and notorious for its hard-labour regime[143] and Vladimir,[144] 200-km to the east of Moscow. To the northwest of Moscow, the expanding Camp 27 in Krasnogorsk was the holding centre for thousands of captured foreigners.

Gustav Richter, the Gestapo officer from the Bucharest legation, had been moved from Lefortovo to the Lubyanka on January 17, 1945. He was placed in cell 123 with an existing occupant, Lt. Otto Schlitter, also known as Scheuer,[145] a fellow Austrian who had been captured at Stalingrad. Wallenberg joined them. In Lorentzon's interview notes with Richter there is a discrepancy on Wallenberg's arrival in the cell. Recorded is January 31 but that is clearly incorrect given the February 6 date on the Lubyanka registration card. Assuming the registration document is not false, Richter was wrong in his recollection. Lorentzon does later refer to an early February date for the beginning of Wallenberg's incarceration with Richter and Schlitter.

'We passed the time playing chess,' Richter had told the investigator from the Swedish Foreign Office. Wallenberg had related to Richter that he was dispatched to Budapest to help the Hungarian Jews by issuing Swedish protective certificates and passports, but the German authorities in the city had obstructed his efforts. When the Red Army was close to the city centre, said Wallenberg, he had made contact but was sent from one location to the next, until finally he was arrested. One must only conjecture whether Richter imparted to his Swedish cellmate his role in the RHSA programme to eradicate the Jewry from Rumania.

Wallenberg had drafted a strong letter to the prison director, conveyed Richter, explaining his position in the Swedish legation and protesting against his incarceration. During the October 22, 1955 interview with Richter, Lorentzon had concluded the session by showing the former Gestapo officer photographs of six men. 'We had only just put the photos down when Richter picked up one photograph and said that this was Wallenberg,' reported the investigator in his notes. At another interview two days later, Richter had added further detail. What Lorentzon found disturbing was the answer to his question on whether Richter knew if Wallenberg had been imprisoned in any other jail apart from the Lubyanka, or any other cell. Richter didn't know, a surprising response given prisoners always traded information with cellmates in case of release so people could be informed. Had Wallenberg suspected Richter of being a stool pigeon, a cell informer?

Richter did impart that Wallenberg had brought with him into the cell some tins that were subsequently opened by the prison director and confiscated. Wallenberg was allowed to keep the contents. Usually, prisoners were not allowed tins in any shape or form but given Wallenberg had special prisoner status he must have been allowed them before his move to cell 123. Wallenberg was a disruptive, said Richter, continually hassling prison guards with demands to see the Swedish ambassador and forever putting pen to paper to complain about prison conditions. Richter advised him to tone down the criticism. In their long cell conversations about Budapest, Wallenberg was intensely resentful that the Soviets had not immediately protected the safe houses. In his interviews with Lorentzon, Richter does not record the bitterness that Wallenberg must have felt when his contact with the Red Army had cost him his freedom.

Sleeping drafts, mixed into prisoners' drinks, was a regular feature of Lubyanka prison life as was the 6am general reveille. In each cell, a 500-candle bulb never went out and when sleeping or lying on the bed it was forbidden to lie on one's stomach. Prisoners were subjected to humiliation and provocation, all elements in the psychological process to invoke a confession. Cell 123, as in all occupied cells, would be roughly turned over, often several times a day adding to the anxiety. As informers, Richter and Schlitter would

[141] Butyrka prison, Moscow. See photographs *[Moscow-30/31]*.

[142] Lefortovo prison, Moscow. See photographs *[Moscow-32/33/34]*.

[143] Aleksandrovsk Central Prison. See photograph *[Moscow-35]*.

[144] Vladimir prison, Vladimir. See photograph *[Moscow-36]*.

[145] **Schlitter, Otto [also Scheuer]**: After his time in the Lubyanka he was moved around the prison system, including the notorious Aleksandrovsk Central Prison. He survived, released in 1955, and lived in Vienna where he was contacted by Lorentzon.

be individually taken away for debriefing and encouraged to delve deeper with Wallenberg.

Given Wallenberg's special prisoner status he was never to be left alone in his cell. During the few weeks he was a cellmate of Wallenberg, Richter had remembered, Wallenberg was interrogated the once, lasting for one and a half hours. Wallenberg had told him that the interrogator spoke German, and said, 'Sie sind ja uns bekannt. Sie gehören einer Hochkapitalistischen Familie in Schweden an', which translates as 'Of course we know you. You belong to a prominent industrial family in Sweden'. Wallenberg had been accused of being a spy for the Americans. Richter had given no indication to Lorentzon of his own interrogations at the Lubyanka during this time.

Richter was transferred out of cell 123 on March 1, 1945, to cell 91 where he remained until June 17 until his transfer back to Lefortovo. Wallenberg and Schlitter remained. Richter stayed in Lefortovo until July 1951, when he was escorted back to the Lubyanka, staying until January 1952. Thereafter, Richter was held in Vladimir until his release in October 1955.

Wallenberg was moved to the adjacent cell 121, and his new cellmates would be first Jan Loyda[146] and then Willy Roedel, the adjutant to the wartime German ambassador in Bucharest and colleague of Richter. According to NKVD prison records, Wallenberg remained in the Lubyanka until May 29, 1945, when he and Roedel were transferred to Lefortovo. A Lefortovo card for Wallenberg was completed with a number of official signatures including the 'store-keeper'. Wallenberg had arrived at Lefortovo with a 'sack, single'.

After depositing Wallenberg at the Lubyanka, Captain Zenkov escorted Langfelder to Butyrka, an equally dark and sinister place that in pre-war times housed the very worst of Russia's criminals and killers. Now, an entire wing was crammed with foreign PoWs.

---

[146] **Loyda, Jan (Hans)**: German-Czech. After his release in the mid 1950s he lived in East Germany. The Swedish Foreign Office interviewed him twice. Loyda also stated that he had shared a cell with Langfelder in Lefortovo. It is unclear whether he had been a cell informer like Richter.

He had arrived with a suitcase. The date on his prison registration card is also February 6 and his full name of Vilmos Karlovich Langfelder is recorded. Perversely it was customary at Butyrka for the inmate to make a financial contribution for his stay, but for Langfelder that condition was waived. In the coming days, he would be roughly interrogated.

Wallenberg and Langfelder were now separated in Moscow.

10

The investigation - Interrogation

The officer in charge of the investigation and interrogation was Likhachev (who was later shot). Likhachev, the deputy head of the Investigation Department of Smersh, always handled the high profile cases.

Extract from Ivan Serov's memoir

WALLENBERG HAD THE MISFORTUNE to be grilled by a brutal Smersh interrogator, specialising in exerting mental torture. Likhachev took great pleasure in forcing his victims to personally address their fabricated confessions to Stalin. Wrote Serov, Likhachev *'always handed the high profile cases'*. Smersh and the NKVD had their own interrogators in the Lubyanka and as Wallenberg was in Smersh custody, he came under Likhachev's remit. Stalin was kept in the loop. Likhachev[147] has no mention in the 10-year Swedish-Russian study that concluded in 2001.

What the KGB did hand over to the researchers in 1991 were copies of entries in the interrogation logbooks for the Lubyanka and Lefortovo. Several interrogators were identified including a Major Kuzmishin, who interviewed Wallenberg on March 11, 1947, the year of his liquidation. Another was Colonel Sergei Kartashov who died before he could be interviewed but to the delight of the researchers, Lt. Colonel Daniil Kopelyansky, was still alive.

Fluent in German, Senior Major Kopelyansky, his wartime rank, had interrogated a large number of captured German officers transported to Moscow and increasingly his prime focus had been to undercover the whereabouts of prized Nazi loot. In the months after the end of WW2, he helped in the preparation of captured

German documents for use in the forthcoming Nuremberg trials. Kopelyansky had interrogated Lt. General Reiner Stagel of the Wehrmacht who had been captured around the same time as Wallenberg in Warsaw.[148]

A purge of Jewish intelligence officers, ordered by Stalin and orchestrated by Serov and others, led to Kopelyansky's dismissal in the early 1950s. He proved reticent in being interviewed so what he did relate was deemed to be of little value, denying he had interrogated Wallenberg and questioning the validity of what the researchers had been given by the KGB. Kopelyansky did concede, however, that on one occasion he had sat in as translator with a more senior officer conducting the session. That officer was probably Abakumov, the head of Smersh, was the conclusion in one of the final working group reports published in Stockholm. More likely, that officer was Likhachev as Wallenberg was his direct responsibility. Kopelyansky is not mentioned in the Serov memoir.

Why didn't the KGB give up Likhachev's name to the Swedish-Russian researchers? The KGB never had the slightest intention in divulging the real truth by disclosing Likhachev's involvement.

There has been a long misconception that the interrogation rooms were in the internal jail but they were on a floor in the Lubyanka used by administrative and senior officers. Lavrenty Beria and Peter Fedotov, his counterintelligence chief, were on this floor and their two offices were interconnected through a concealed door in a cupboard. Beria was known to frequently use it. A lift from the fourth and fifth floors of the jail opened into the corridor.

In the lift prisoners were handcuffed to the solid metal rail. Lights always burned in the corridor and prisoner movement to and from the interrogation rooms was a regular sight. In the 1940s, to limit prisoner contact, an alert system had been devised. Semi-open wooden 'doggy booths', referred to as 'sobachnik', were built in so

---

[147] **Likhachev, Gen. M.T:** With Smersh absorbed in 1946, he became deputy head of investigations for the MGB from 1946 to 1951. Executed in December 1954, sentenced by the military board of the Supreme Court for crimes against the state.

[148] **Stagel, Lt. Gen. Reiner:** Renowned as the butcher of Warsaw, he was sentenced to 25 years in jail but amnestied under the collective PoW releases. Held in a transit camp, he was never released, the Soviets did issue a burial certificate.

prisoners could be pushed into them to avoid staff identification. The booths are long removed but in 2000 a couple still remained stored in the basement. Installed in the 1950s throughout the Lubyanka buildings was a corridor lighting system with red ordering staff to remain in their offices and yellow to freely move around. Often a loud click of fingers by the guards was the signal to immediately stay away. It was commonplace to see prisoners dragged back to the lift if the interrogation beatings were severe.

According to the KGB, Wallenberg's first Smersh interrogation was on February 8, 1945, just two days after he had arrived. It began at 1.05am and lasted until 4.35am. Such a lengthy session would have been exhausting. Interrogation in the early hours was a favoured technique, a time when the prisoner was at his lowest ebb. Back in his cell, Wallenberg would have barely an hour of sleep before the general reveille throughout the jail at 6am.

It was general practice during interrogations that prisoners were left alone to write down key dates, names of friends and contacts. Drugs or beatings usually induced acquiescence. Wallenberg would have endured pressure to recall meeting with top Nazis and Hungarian collaborators, and account for his movements within Germany and Nazi-occupied Europe before taking up the position in Budapest. The interrogator, using Wallenberg's diary and address book, would have probed any Wallenberg family connection with the Abwehr, the SD (the counterintelligence arm of the SS) and Western intelligence agencies.

Amongst the cache of document copies passed over by the KGB in two batches on October 30 and 31, 1991, included the following:

*KGB document numbered **A17** by the Swedes: Dated May 29, 1945, this is a note from the registry of Lefortovo, confirming that Wallenberg had arrived from the Lubyanka.*

A22: *Interrogation record: Wallenberg was interrogated by Senior Major Daniil Kopelyansky in Lefortovo on July 17, 1946 and the interrogation lasted from 10.30am to 13.00pm – a two and a half hour session.*

A23: *Interrogation record: It asserted that Langfelder was brought into*

the Lefortovo interrogation room on July 17, 1946 at the very time
that Wallenberg was being interrogated by Kopelyansky. Langfelder had
joined Wallenberg and Kopelyansky at 12.20pm and remained until
the end. Both men were then led away to their respective cells. It was
the first time they had seen each other since they were separated on
February 6, 1945.

A27: Dated February 27, 1947, this record stated that Wallenberg was
to be transported back from Lefortovo to the Lubyanka.

A29: The date of transportation from Lefortovo to the Lubyanka for
Wallenberg is now March 1, 1947. One can only surmise that the
transfer timing was changed at the last moment and the original record
wasn't amended. Usually a return to the Lubyanka implied that further
intensive interrogation was to take place, and maybe execution.

A30: This note, dated March 2, 1947, says that Wallenberg's personal
belongings had been registered in the Lubyanka after his move from
Lefortovo. These possessions were the items handed over to the Swedes
at the Moscow meeting in October 1989.

A31: Interrogation record: Dated March 11, 1947, it stated that
Wallenberg was interrogated in the Lubyanka in the afternoon. This is
the last notice that Wallenberg was still alive. That interrogation took
place at 2.15pm and ended at 4pm. Major Kuzmishin was the
interrogator.

On December 5, 1991, the KGB handed over copies of documents
referring solely to Langfelder.

A12: Receipt from the Lefortovo registry of all of Langfelder's
belongings and dated July 1947.

A36: This note, dated July 22, 1947, stated that Langfelder had been
interrogated that day in Lefortovo.

A37: 'Have received all items' was the Lefortovo note on July 23, 1947.

D59: Dated June 13, 1957, this was an instruction given to the
Ministry of Foreign Affairs on how to answer an enquiry by the
Hungarian government into the fate of Langfelder. The Russians
privately told the Hungarians that Langfelder had died on March 2,
1948 but there is no mention of where he had died or the cause of
death.

Serov's memoir does not give any actual date in 1947 for Wallenberg's execution nor the dates for Langfelder and the two Langfelder cellmates liquidated by association. Did all the killings take place on the same day? Intriguing is **A31**, the reference to Wallenberg and his interrogation in the Lubyanka on March 11, 1947. Might Wallenberg have been executed shortly afterwards? It is worth remembering that the head of the Lubyanka's medical services, Colonel Smoltsov, had retired that month and his son disclosed that his father had been recalled several months later to the Lubyanka purportedly to sign Wallenberg's death certificate. As most of the prisoners executed in the Lubyanka and Lefortovo ended up as ashes in the unmarked trough in the Donskoye crematorium, a precise date didn't actually matter to the record keepers.

The copies of the documents handed over to the Swedes by the KGB were revelatory, despite doubts on their legitimacy. A letter, dated February 24, 1947, from Colonel Kartashov, formerly of Smersh and later interrogation head at the MGB, did shed further light. Kartashov's note to respective prison directors was an instruction that Wallenberg and Willy Roedel, sharing cell 203 in Lefortovo, were to be transferred to the Lubyanka.

That transfer was delayed. Roedel left first, on February 26 and Wallenberg shortly later as confirmed in KGB document **A29**. Wallenberg's belongings were recorded as being received at the Lubyanka on March 2, 1947, as stated in **A30**. Wallenberg would have another five months to live, if Gromyko's statement to the Swedes in 1957 is to be believed.

Langfelder was moved from Butyrka to Lefortovo on March 18, 1945, and there are records of several interrogations, including one on April 10 that year timed at starting at 2pm and ending an hour later. His interrogation officer was Major Yendovitsky. Smersh would have wasted no time in working over Wallenberg's chauffeur in Butyrka after arrival in Moscow from Budapest. Two further interrogations were recorded: one on August 16, 1945 and another, the following December. The interrogators, according to the records were Lt. Oleg Bubnov[149] and Lt. Livchak.

What had been the purpose of interrogating Wallenberg and Langfelder together on July 17, 1946 in Lefortovo? According to

KGB record **A23**, Langfelder was brought into the interrogation room as an interrogation of Wallenberg was in progress. Were either Langfelder or Wallenberg, perhaps both, displaying visible effects of physical violence or drugs, which might induce a confession?

Gustav Richter had told Lorentzon, the investigator from the Swedish Foreign Office, about one of his own interrogations on July 27, 1947, during his second spell in Lefortovo. It was a rough interrogation, related Richter. The officer was an awkward NKVD colonel who demanded that he recall the names of every cellmate he had shared with in Lefortovo and the Lubyanka.

The very mention of Wallenberg had stirred an immediate response from the colonel. Who else had known he had shared a Lubyanka cell with the Swede, the interrogator had demanded? Richter named three, Willy Roedel, Dr von Ley and Franz Langer, despite the figure being much higher given the constant shifting of PoWs within the prison system. The interrogation lasted an hour before Richter was taken away to a solitary confinement cell where he remained for 14 days. The letter that Arne Lundberg of the Swedish Foreign Office wrote to Maj von Dardel, Wallenberg's mother, on November 4, 1955, included significant detail of the first interviews with Richter and this Lefortovo interrogation was mentioned. In Richter's response to Lorentzon's questioning, Lundberg had written (deceased) after Roedel's name and (probably shot) after the name of von Ley. Had Richter told Lorentzon that both Roedel and von Ley were dead or had Lorentzon obtained that information from another source? Langer, the third name given up to the NKVD colonel by Richter was, however, very much alive. Richter had provided Lorentzon with an address in Duisberg-Hamborn. Why was Langer allowed to live, had he been another stool pigeon?

Serov in his memoir had written that two cellmates of Langfelder had been executed at the same time as Langfelder. Could Serov's memory have failed him when he wrote his memoir in 1987, and were these prisoners Roedel, Wallenberg's cellmate, and von Ley, the

---

[149] **Bubnov, Lt. Oleg**: Interviewed by researchers in the 10-year Swedish-Russian study, Bubnov denied any knowledge of interrogating Langfelder.

two mentioned by Richter? That scenario is unlikely, as Serov, in writing his memoir on Wallenberg, would have referred to his archive of documents and diaries.

Likhachev – Stalin's brutal interrogator

With Likhachev in charge of Wallenberg's interrogations once he arrived in the Lubyanka in February 1945, it is very likely that the diplomat would have been badly worked over. Likhachev would not have held back if the answers to his questions were not forthcoming. At times, he sat in and observed as other interrogators took over.

Wallenberg might also have experienced the notorious Dr Maironovsky, the chief scientist of Laboratory X, the toxins establishment run by the security services. No records are available of what Wallenberg did endure. Some detail, however, does exist of Likhachev's interrogation methods. In July 1946, he badly beat up several air force senior officers charged with incompetency over the shortage of front-line aircraft. General Shakhurin, the air force chief, was so severely beaten he wasn't expected to survive. Only after Stalin's death was Shakhurin released.

Years later, Czechoslovakia sought justice over one Likhachev episode. His name was raised in April 1968 by the short-lived reformist Dubcek government, which had conducted reviews into a number of assassinations of prominent Czechs in the early post-war years. The Czech state prosecutor, Kotlar, directly laid the blame on Likhachev for the murder of Jan Masaryk, the Czech foreign minister, in March 1948, in Prague's Cherninsky Palace. Masaryk's body had been found one morning directly under the windows from his bedroom. Kotlar stated that General Likhachev and his colleague, General Makarov, had been in a group of Soviet 'advisors' in Prague led by the head of the MGB's *illegal* intelligence directorate Lt. General Aleksandr Korotkov[150] at the time when the communist party in Czechoslovakia took full control of the country.

A terrible accident was the opinion of compliant Czech and Russian officials despite strong doubts to the contrary and the evidence of Zdenek Borkovets, an officer in Czech Intelligence, who had found the bedroom littered with broken glass and pillows strewn on the floor in the bathroom, indicating a major struggle. Kotlar didn't mince his words: he blamed Likhachev and Makarov.

Likhachev had aided Abakumov in the 'Leningrad Affair' in 1948, a plot instigated by Malenkov and Beria, in moving against the Leningrad power base of party boss Andrey Zhdanov.[151] He also had an involvement in the infamous 'Doctors Plot', framing a group of mainly Jewish doctors and accusing them of attempting to poison Stalin.[152] In the weeks after Stalin's death, Serov had Abakumov, Likhachev, and a clutch of NKVD generals arrested and put in front of Roman Rudenko, Russia's chief prosecutor.

Locating Likhachev's interrogation notes on Wallenberg had proved a tough ask for Colonel Kozyrev, Serov's investigator, who reluctantly had to report that little had remained. However, all was not lost. Kozyrev was additionally investigating the Stalin plots and with Likhachev and Abakumov languishing in jail, awaiting sentence, they could be interviewed. Serov doesn't comment how those interviews progressed and what was discovered. Rudenko never lost his cases and the firing squad was busy in December 1954, nine months after Serov concluded his Wallenberg investigation. Likhachev, Wallenberg's brutal Smersh interrogator, was dead. If Kozyrev had located any Wallenberg confession, sadly, Serov doesn't elaborate.

---

[150] **Korotkov, Lt. Gen. Aleksandr**: Careerist intelligence officer. During the 1930s he was behind the murder of several Trotskyites who had fled to France. Up to June 1941, Korotkov was Berlin deputy rezident and a controller of the Red Orchestra intelligence network. He was forced to divorce his wife in 1948 because she was Jewish. In the mid-1950s Serov promoted him to first deputy director of the KGB. He collapsed and died of a heart attack on a Moscow tennis court in August 1961, playing against Serov who by then was GRU director.

[151] **Zhdanov, Andrey**: Long-standing member of the Politburo and confidant of Stalin. Zhdanov's son had married Stalin's daughter in 1949, a marriage that lasted barely a year. He died of 'heart failure' in August 1948, with suspicions that he had been dealt with.

[152] In the final Stalin years, there were a number of plots against prominent Jews. In 1952, 25 Jewish writers were executed in the Lubyanka.

11

The investigation
– The accusation of spying

*Dobrohotov now had more details for me regarding Wallenberg's
special wartime mission in our territories occupied by the Germans.
He informed me that at the time we had received details about
Wallenberg's mission from America and Sweden. The intelligence
we had received from America had been of particular importance.
One of our sources working in American Intelligence during the war,
a prominent agent for the NKVD, had related to us that Wallenberg
was a US Intelligence agent with established contacts in the Gestapo.
We also had reliable information that the Swedish Embassy in
Budapest had provided diplomatic passports and other documents
to officers of Hitler's secret services involved in covert operations.*

Extracts from Ivan Serov's memoir

ANY FOREIGN DIPLOMAT who had chosen to remain in
Budapest during the final chaotic weeks of the battle was
considered by the Soviets to be a spy. Those who operated out of the
International Red Cross building in Benczur Street were especially
under suspicion. The capture of a member of Sweden's premier family
was considered a prize indeed.

With the Red Army taking over Budapest, the NKVD and Smersh
began sweeping up foreigners, clearing the ground for a future
communist regime. In a Smersh arrest account dated January 23, 1945,
a list of 48 individuals already in custody and accused of spying had
been compiled by a Major Petrovsky.[153] Two names on this list were
from the Swedish legation. Wallenberg was taken on January 17, six
days before Petrovsky's report, and presumed to be one. In an update

134

a week later, Petrovsky included a listing of all the diplomatic addresses in the city: the source, according to Petrovsky, had been the now-detained Wallenberg.

The resourceful Colonel Dobrohotov, a member of Serov's investigation team, had located the intelligence files on Wallenberg. Damning at the time of Wallenberg's arrest was the evidence that a valuable NKVD agent within US Intelligence confirmed the diplomat to have intelligence connections. Moreover, upon Wallenberg's arrival in the Lubyanka, the Smersh interrogators would quickly have corroborated Wallenberg's contacts with the likes of Eichmann, Clages, the SD chief, Veesenmayer, the Reich plenipotentiary for Hungary, and the collaborative Hungarian authorities through his diary. Very likely, Wallenberg would have admitted that those Nazi relationships were necessary in his humanitarian bartering.

Since Wallenberg's arrest by Smersh, accusations of spying have accelerated. If Wallenberg had used his position as a Budapest representative for the American War Refugee Board to covertly work for the OSS, was he also a source for Swedish military intelligence, the C Bureau, or Britain's MI6? Does the factual evidence of his relationship in Budapest with the Abwehr or Sicherheitsdienst, the SD, stand up to inquiry? Is it such a ludicrous assertion that Wallenberg might have agreed to become an informer for the NKVD, an idea promoted by one senior Soviet intelligence officer who had operated in Sweden?

Separating reality from speculation and downright nonsense is difficult. Good spies cover their tracks, they fabricate: it becomes an art. What isn't in doubt is the level of Russian surveillance and monitoring of the Wallenberg family well before Raoul Wallenberg arrived in Budapest in July 1944, carrying Swedish diplomatic documentation. Russian Intelligence had built up an extensive file on both him and other members of this illustrious family, which had the political clout and economic muscle spanning continents. The Wallenbergs' were bankers, industrialists, traders and very good at it,

---

[153] Smersh document entitled *'Agents arrested by Smersh department at the 2nd Ukrainian Front 1-20th January 1945.'*

too. During the war, they had channels into several intelligence agencies: it would have been unusual if they hadn't. As a neutral, Sweden maintained its legation in Berlin and that was an invaluable third-party toehold for the British.

The charge of Nazi collaborator

Post-war the Wallenberg family cloaked itself behind a perceived blanket of invincibility, brushing away all accusations of Nazi collusion. The family had enjoyed a profitable war, burning the industrial candle from both ends trading with the Allied and Axis powers. In Berlin, the Swedish legation was a regular meeting place for trade negotiations with the Nazi regime, with the Wallenberg family frequent visitors to the German capital. Raoul was in Berlin in November 1942 and on that trip conveyed a private letter from the legation to Jacob, his uncle in Stockholm.

Before Raoul Wallenberg arrived in Budapest in July 1944 to work for the War Refugee Board, he would not have been aware that he had left traces around occupied Russia.

> ... I had been informed that a member of the Wallenberg family had on several occasions visited the German-occupied Soviet territories, mainly the city of Pskov, where he had contacts with the fascist civil administration and the Abwehr, German military intelligence.

Later in Serov's memoire, he confirmed that this Wallenberg-family member was Raoul. The Pskov trips were a factor in him being accused by the NKVD and Smersh of 'being a double agent and a Nazi spy' – an agent for both America and Germany.

Travelling to Pskov from Sweden would have been through Estonia, also occupied. The city was strategic for Germany's Army Group North, whose eventual aim was to lay waste to Leningrad, the prime munitions manufacturing base. Occupied on July 9, 1941, the Germans had embarked on a mass killing programme in Pskov and its environs. By the time it was liberated by the Red Army on July 23, 1944, some 290,000 inhabitants had been slaughtered according to Soviet records. Only 250 Jews were left alive. There had been a significant SD and SS contingent. Amongst it was Colonel Kurt Becher of SS Division, Totenkopf, an experienced officer seconded to the SS economic management office. This is the same Kurt Becher who arrived in Budapest in March 1944 to fill SS coffers, and his own, by bartering Jews for money.

Had Wallenberg, according to the Soviets, abused his position at the Budapest legation by issuing Swedish diplomatic passports to Third Reich intelligence officers? Such a document would be very valuable if these individuals needed to disappear through the rat-lines to countries willing to take in war criminals. On a practical level, however, could Wallenberg have issued diplomatic passports without authorisation from Danielsson, the head of the legation? Serov's accusation is quite specific.

We also had reliable information that the Swedish Embassy in Budapest had provided diplomatic passports and other documents to officers of Hitler's secret services involved in covert operations.

Per Anger, deputy head of the Budapest legation, did argue after the war that document forgeries had widely circulated, but he was referring to the Schutz-Pass, the document given to Budapest's Jews to provide some measure of safety.

Wallenberg's links to the Abwehr had prompted the Soviet accusation. Across occupied Europe, if the longer-established Abwehr was professional and well managed under Admiral Canaris, the SD operated with far fewer principles. Both operated in Budapest and Raoul Wallenberg's diary seized by Smersh would have recorded any contact with the notorious Lt. Colonel Gerhard Clages,[154] the head of the SD office. Hitler had operationally truncated much of the Abwehr network after the July 1944 attempt on his life. With Canaris and other Abwehr officers suspected, the SD took over the Abwehr

---

[154] **Clages, Lt. Col. Gerhard**: Sometimes referred to as Otto Klages. Before Budapest, he was Gestapo chief in Pardubice, Czechoslovakia, and responsible for the Lezaky village massacre in June 1942. This massacre and the larger one in Lidice was SS retribution for the assassination of Heydrich in Prague. He died in Budapest in October 1944, during the SS mission to kidnap the Regent's son.

operations in many cities including Budapest.

It didn't help Raoul Wallenberg's case during his Lubyanka interrogations that the NKVD had knowledge of Jacob Wallenberg's association with top Nazis, including aides of SS Reichsführer Heinrich Himmler. The Americans had cloaked the clandestine activities of the OSS behind non-military institutions such as the US Commercial Company. Abram Hewitt, masquerading as an employee, opened dialogue in Stockholm in August 1943 with two Himmler emissaries, Felix Kersten, Himmler's personal doctor, and General Walter Schellenberg, the Berlin head of SD counterintelligence. Operating in Sweden was not a new assignment to Hewitt. He had first met Jacob Wallenberg in 1932 and that relationship was rekindled when Wallenberg had confided to him that Himmler wanted to secretly broker a peace deal with the US and elevate himself as the new German chancellor.

Himmler's proposal soon unravelled. The resourceful Kersten reluctantly conceded to Hewitt that the Soviets had found out about the Himmler proposal and a counter proposition had been presented to the German ambassador and the SS office in Stockholm. If Germany capitulated, said the Soviets, it could keep half of the Baltic States area and Poland would be divided along 1939 lines. On its own demands the Soviets wanted the whole coastline of the Black Sea, including the mouth of the Danube, an area extending as far as Istanbul and Salonika, and a port on the Adriatic Sea. Berlin was split over the Soviet proposal, Kersten informed Hewitt. Ribbentrop and Goebbels were in favour but Himmler and Hitler were steadfastly against.

Hewitt described developments to General William Donovan, the OSS chief, who passed on the report to Roosevelt. Nothing would come of the Himmler or the Soviet proposals. Hershel Johnson, the US minister in Stockholm, had railed against the discussions with Kersten and Schellenberg[155] from the outset, angered further that Hewitt was operating independently of any US official jurisdiction. Johnson made it clear that this SS pitch was merely another German ruse to create a catastrophic rift between the Allies and the naïve Hewitt had fallen for the ploy.[156]

These German peace overtures with the Americans, orchestrated through Stockholm, had been a factor in the pre-trial 'Red Lines' bargaining between Russia and the US at Nuremberg, Serov stated.[157]

The Swedish connection

Sweden's C Bureau, headed by Major Carl Petersen and his deputy, Captain Helmut Ternberg, maintained links with intelligence agencies throughout the war with both sides. Ternberg ran the networks in Berlin, Slovakia, Switzerland, Finland and Hungary and he would surely have added the high-profile Wallenberg to his list of Budapest sources. The Swedish authorities have acknowledged that Ternberg visited Budapest at least twice, in 1943 and 1944, and established regular contact with the MFM, the largest of the resistance groups in Hungary. C Bureau ran an illegal radio ring that continued to operate well into the early days of the Soviet occupation. Whether Ternberg shared those communications with the British or the Americans is unclear.

It is standard practice for intelligence agencies to function under the diplomatic guise and the Swedes in Budapest were no exception. Almost certainly there were legation sources that reported back to C Bureau as gathering intelligence was an expected function for diplomats in a war zone. Anger had begun his diplomatic career in Berlin in January 1940 working in the trade department but he quickly became involved in ferrying intelligence to Stockholm on Nazi intentions towards Norway and Denmark. Several of Wallenberg's colleagues had openly speculated who Raoul did ultimately report to.

Working for the OSS

The Smersh interrogators would have tried every method to extract a confession. A reminder of Serov's statement:

---

[155] In the last days of the Third Reich, Schellenberg had prompted Himmler to contact Count Folke Bernadotte of Sweden about surrendering German armies in the West.
[156] The full report of Hewitt's Stockholm operation, with the involvement of Jacob Wallenberg, is now available in the CIA archives, written by John Waller, a wartime OSS agent.
[157] More on the 'Red Lines' bartering at Nuremberg in a later chapter.

One of our sources working in American Intelligence during the war, a prominent agent for the NKVD, had related to us that Wallenberg was a US Intelligence agent with established contacts in the Gestapo.

Who was this source? Serov doesn't provide a name but that embedded agent might have been based in London, in the FBI.

The FBI had maintained a small but specific intelligence presence in London since June 1940, under the guise of the Legal Attaché Programme, focusing primarily on penetrating German networks operating within the US. Similar offices were established in Ottawa and Mexico City but London was its hub. Arthur Thurston, the legal attaché, was the head with John Cimperman his deputy. As the war progressed, Churchill succumbed to US pressure to share intelligence gathered at Bletchley Park. In January 1943, MI6 showed the FBI the decrypted German communications identifying German agents, an operation codenamed by the British as 'Operation Ostrich'. FBI officers regularly visited the MI6 office in Ryder Street in London's West End.

Some years ago, via Archie, my best Moscow source for obtaining secret documents, I received an NKVD cipher that had emanated from the Soviet embassy in London in April 1945. It reported to Moscow on the state of the war in Italy. That was of little importance to me regarding my research into nuclear espionage but the cipher did identify the codenames and positions of two prime NKVD agents in London. One was 'Agent D', a senior MI5 officer with direct access to Guy Liddell, the head of counterintelligence.[158] The other, a sub-source for 'Agent D', was an FBI officer, a woman codenamed 'Lemon'. She may have confirmed to her NKVD handler that Wallenberg was an OSS asset.

That OSS connection was certainly alluded to in an internal CIA report, written in January 1981 and timed to coincide with the 'Wallenberg Hearing' convened in Stockholm.[159] Two years earlier, said its author, the US State Department had privately disclosed to the Soviet chargé d'affaires to Washington that it had funded the wartime programme to save Hungarian Jews. The writer of the CIA report found it curious that the US hadn't admitted the relationship between Wallenberg and Iver Olsen, the OSS bureau chief in

Stockholm who also operated as the chief representative of the War Refugee Board in Europe.[160]

The OSS had been set up in 1942 with the US now embroiled in both European and Pacific wars. No longer were Americans able to travel at will throughout occupied Europe as they were between 1939 and 1941, and a covert organisation was essential. London was the operational hub with Stockholm the key to its operation. Olsen was a frequent traveller to London to visit the Secret Intelligence Branch [SI] of the OSS, based at 72, Grosvenor Street in London's Mayfair. Its head, William Casey, put several hundred agents into Nazi-occupied Europe. Wallenberg reported to Olsen.

Given the late entry of the US into the war there was no time for a coherent vetting system for recruits. Just being a lawyer was a positive selective criterion given the large number in the organisation. High on the recruitment lists were foreigners with language skills and local knowledge. Loyalty could not be guaranteed nor backgrounds checked. The NKVD and GRU benefited.

Raoul Wallenberg was well connected in the US, even personally acquainted with Roosevelt, stated the CIA. In Stockholm, briefings with Wallenberg by Olsen and Herschel Johnson, the US legation minister, had confirmed the remit in Budapest, the levels of authority and extent of financial support. In a cable sent to Washington by Johnson in June 1944, the minister reported that the Swedish Foreign Office was fully onboard. Wallenberg had been instructed how to contact his American controllers in Stockholm

---

[158] Archive of the First Chief Directorate, NKVD. Numbered 244, sheet 257. 'Lemon' had heard from an OSS operative, just arrived in London from Italy, reporting that two senior officers on the staff of General Kesselring had discussed with British officers the capitulation of all German forces in Italy. 'Agent D' had passed on 'Lemon's' information to Moscow. 'Agent D' was one of the best placed Soviet sources in Britain during WW2, compromising many War Cabinet secrets.

[159] Declassified in 2007.

[160] **Olsen, Iver C**: His role at the US legation in Stockholm lasted from 1940 until 1950. Thereafter, Olsen worked for the US Treasury in Thailand and Turkey. Outside government service, Olsen became the Washington representative for Wall Street brokers, Tritt & Co. Born in Oslo, Olsen graduated from Boston University and the Georgetown University School of Foreign Service. He died in Arlington, Virginia, on November 6, 1960, aged 56.

and how to secretly transit Jews out of Budapest. The cables between all parties, including the Swedish Foreign Office, make clear reference to Olsen and the intended lines of communication from Budapest.

Such was the OSS and SI presence in Stockholm that by mid-1944, there were 35 operatives in the Swedish capital. The CIA, in its 1981 paper, debated that Olsen's intelligence function had probably been known to the Soviets. It most certainly was. Russia ran an even larger contingent in Stockholm with 44 NKVD and GRU agents working out of its own legation, *Tass* and *Pravda* and other agencies.[161]

Koloman Lauer, Wallenberg's chief partner in the European operations of the foodstuffs trader, Mellaneuropeiska Handels AB, might have been aware of Raoul's secondary role in Budapest. In a letter dated April 20, 1945, three months after Wallenberg's arrest, Lauer had written to Marcus Wallenberg at the Stockholms Enskilda Bank explaining Raoul's function. There was no mention of the OSS connection, as there wouldn't be.

Before Raoul's departure in June for the long trip to Budapest, Olsen had handed him 10,000 Swedish kroner soon to be followed by 50,000 kroner, which Lauer had organised through a new account at the family bank. More payments were made, probably higher than 100,000 kroner in total. Account statements were additionally circulated to the Swedish Foreign Office. This funding came via the US legation in Stockholm, directly from US state sources. In his letter to Marcus Wallenberg, Lauer informed him that other Swedes had been saving the Jews including Professor Marcus Ehrenpreis, the chief rabbi in Stockholm[162] and within six months of Raoul's arrival in Budapest, Wallenberg's department had grown exponentially to 335 employees, to include 40 doctors and two hospitals with a combined total of 150 beds. The number of Swedish safe houses proliferated to 30.

The War Refugee Board couldn't have been more pleased with Wallenberg's immediate impact but according to the CIA internal report, Olsen had written to John Perle, the director of the humanitarian organisation, that the Swedish Foreign Office had become 'somewhat uneasy about Wallenberg's activities in Budapest

... and feels that he has jumped in with too big a splash'. Wallenberg and his colleagues had deemed 9,000 to be eligible for settling in Sweden. Also reported to Perle was that Wallenberg 'had left Stockholm in a hurry with little or no instructions and few funds'. Transmitting and couriering funds to Wallenberg had been fraught with difficulty, and what funds he had been given needed urgent replenishment after acquiring properties and paying bribes to Nazis and local officials. From the US legation in Stockholm, Johnson provided updated reports to Washington.

Serov in his memoir pinpointed US Intelligence links with Berlin, further worsening the spying accusations against Wallenberg.

Under the cover of negotiating the fate of the Jews in the occupied territories, there existed secret and informal channels of communication between German and American intelligence.

Those inferred channels were the 'back channels', communications that have long existed between even warring parties. Towards the end of the war, the Abwehr and the British communicated given the Abwehr's growing concern to Hitler's increased paranoia and the state of the war. The CIA has never admitted the extent of the US relationship with the Abwehr.

The Vatican discussions in July and August 1944 illustrated how 'back channels' had prompted secret discussion on a proposed peace agreement between the Allies and Germany, but with the Soviets excluded.

The first took place on July 24 in the private quarters of Pope Pius XII. In the room waiting for the Pope's guests were Hitler's Vatican ambassador, Ernst von Weizsäcker and two top German military officers, Field Marshal Wilhelm Keitel,[163] and General

---

[161] See listing of names, including some codenames, in the appendix, obtained by the author from a reputable KGB source.

[162] **Ehrenpreis, Professor Marcus**: Lauer had arranged a number of meetings between Ehrenpreis and Wallenberg in the weeks leading up to Raoul's departure over the funding issue. Ehrenpreis was keen to allow Hungarian and Rumanian Jews to settle in Sweden. He died February 27, 1951, aged 82.

[163] **Keitel, Field Marshal Wilhelm**: Tried at Nuremberg and executed in October 1946.

Walther von Brauchitsch.[164] To join them were Cardinal Francis Spellman, the head of the American Episcopacy, and Myron Taylor, an American catholic and president of United Steel. They were Roosevelt's personal envoys. Von Weizsäcker had covertly worked with Keitel and von Brauchitsch to engineer a ceasefire with America and Britain and assimilate the remaining German military strength to collectively take on the Soviet Union.

Hitler's ambassador proposed that the Rhineland be returned to French and British control, as under the Weimar regime, Austria to be independent and Poland should revert to its pre-war borders with the Danzig corridor. A new military government in Germany needed to be established from generals not compromised by Nazism. Above all, insisted von Weizsäcker, the integrity of Germany must be preserved. Spellman and Taylor duly reported back to the White House. Unbeknown to the Americans, the full details of the Vatican meeting were spirited to an NKVD agent in Rome for transmission to Moscow.

The NKVD quickly confirmed to Moscow another Vatican discussion but this time with Churchill on August 27. Strangely, Eden, the foreign secretary, didn't accompany him. Instead Churchill brought his private secretary. On von Weizsäcker's agenda was the eradication of the growing threat of the Red Army in Europe.

It is worth reporting the text of the NKVD report on Churchill's discussion:

Message of the rezidency of the Soviet NKGB in Rome on the talks of German representative with Churchill in the Vatican concerning the conditions of a separate peace.

27th August 1944

Churchill was received by the Pope not on Friday, as the newspapers have reported, but on Wednesday. Churchill came without his entourage, only with one personal secretary. After his talk with the Pope, he visited the state secretariat of the Vatican where Weizsäcker was expecting him. Von Weizsäcker heads the German delegation,

---

[164] **Brauchitsch, General Walther von**: Condemned for war crimes he died in 1948, in Hamburg, before he could be prosecuted.

which has arrived for talks with the English. Churchill's talk with von Weizsäcker was not long.
The English put forward the following conditions:

1. Complete German capitulation and speedy occupation of Germany.
2. Detailed negotiations concerning territory will be conducted after the occupation, the Germans have objections.
3. To revive the Christian Democrat party and farmers who have to make up the majority in the government.
4. Provisional administration has to be in Anglo-American hands.
5. Immediate return of territories annexed by Germany.
6. Germans have to co-operate in eliminating the danger of communism.
7. As far as the Vatican is concerned it insists on a speedy formation of the German government in order to avoid any pro-Soviet government during the occupation of Germany.

This document was one of a series I obtained from the Moscow archives of the First Chief Directorate of the NKVD. In total there are 14 that refer to the Vatican proposals.

A smile must have come across Stalin's face as he read the stolen minutes of the Vatican discussions, barely a month after D-Day with his allies bogged down in Normandy. It was clear to him that the Soviet Union was the new enemy. In contrast, his Red Army was rolling over the Wehrmacht notching up the victories. On the very day that the Americans were at the Vatican – July 24 – the Red Army had been poised to retake six more German strongholds, including L'vov and Bialystok. By the end of the month, the Soviet front line stretched well into Poland and the Baltic States.

Betrayed by Hitler in 1941, Stalin was in no mood for a second perfidy given his war with Hitler was on a far greater scale. The Vatican documents only further convinced Stalin that his allies were militarily prepared to thwart his own post-war European ambitions.

On the MI6 radar

Britain's MI6 has never disclosed that Wallenberg was an asset and if he was, no admission would ever be forthcoming given the publicity it would globally generate. The Stockholm station monitored the activities of the Wallenberg family and maintained contact: it was probably aware of the connection to Olsen.

The Swedish legation in Budapest was a valuable source for the British before the arrival of Wallenberg in July 1944. Attached to B-department was the secretive 'Dutch Department', known as such as it was staffed by Dutchmen. These departments were replicated in Swedish legations throughout Axis-controlled territories with Germany allowing Holland international representation through the neutral Swedes. Lt Gerrit van der Waals ran the Dutch Department in Budapest and was arrested by the NKVD, accused of running a front for British Intelligence.

Expert in producing false Swedish IDs for Wallenberg to distribute, van der Waals disappeared on December 8, 1944, as the Red Army began its encirclement, and a month before Wallenberg and Langfelder were escorted out of Pest. Supposedly, according to the Soviets, van der Waals had been 'found' with documents purporting to show the extent of intended subversive action once the Red Army controlled Budapest. Being 'found' is a euphemism that he was arrested after an intelligence trade went badly wrong. Van der Waals was never released, and probably executed in Moscow. Wallenberg was assumed by the Russians to be complicit in the van der Waal operation.

Very close to the legation on Gellert Hill was the house where MI6 ran one network. Karoly Schandl, a Hungarian, with others, was rounded up by the Soviets once Buda was overrun. Schandl was released in 1956 but never heard from again was the RAF Warrant Officer, Reginald Barratt, operating under the name of George Godden.

Flak had brought down Barratt's Wellington bomber over Zeebrugge, Belgium, in June 1941. A front gunner, he bailed out with the rest of the crew only to be quickly captured. Barratt was taken to Camp 8B on the banks of the Oder near the Czech border and typically RAF, he was desperate to escape. When he did escape in May the following year it was an extraordinary episode. The real George Godden, who had served in the Rifle Brigade, and captured in Calais in 1940, was in the army compound of the camp where security wasn't as tight and inmates were allowed outside in working parties to till the Sudetenland farms. The camp escape committee arranged for Godden and Barratt to swap identities and in a dental parade the two men switched uniforms, the guards none the wiser. Both men marched off to their new respective compounds. For the remainder of the war as a PoW, Godden was RAF Warrant Office Reginald Barratt while the real Barratt made good his escape some weeks later. During the period up to the escape they occasionally saw each other and silently nodded in greeting. After the real Godden's account was published in *The Times* after the war, a follow-up from another camp inmate who had read the article verified the story.

Barratt's circuitous escape route did not lead back in Britain, but ended in Budapest where he met Evelyn Gore-Symes, a 24-year-old English girl who surprisingly hadn't been interned by the Hungarian authorities. By all accounts Gore-Symes,[165] a linguist from Twickenham, south of London, was an excellent operative for MI6 and MI9, the department that helped British servicemen on the escape run. Gore-Symes had been in Budapest since 1938 and had helped to establish the network. After the war she would be awarded the King's Commendation for Brave Conduct, a well-earned decoration.

The risk she took in Budapest was even greater with her apartment next door to Gestapo headquarters, and it was here that she first met Barratt, still masquerading as Godden. Gore-Symes reported after the war that the last time she saw Barratt was in December 1944. London had instructed him to make contact with incoming Soviet forces and share military intelligence. The NKVD arrested Barratt at Szarvas in southeastern Hungary on Christmas Eve and there were several uncorroborated sightings of him in the following months. In April 1945, Barratt was seen in a holding camp at Cserkesz near Bratislava and in June, there was a report that he was seen at Marshal Tolbukhin's headquarters at Szombathely, in western Hungary. The British Military Mission in Moscow demanded an

---

[165] **Gore-Symes, Miss Evelyn**: She died in 1998, aged 80.

investigation but to no avail. Barratt was taken to Moscow for further interrogation.[166]

Barratt had disappeared, similar to Wallenberg and Van der Waals. Ernest Bevin, the new British foreign secretary, demanded angrily to Molotov that the RAF man be found. Kathleen, Barratt's wife, wrote a letter to Stalin in January 1946, personally delivering it to the Soviet embassy in London and the response was typical: 'in spite of a careful search, the authorities have been unable to trace him'. Evelyn Gore-Symes had been rounded up in the NKVD sweep of foreigners in Budapest and with some Americans was taken to Bucharest, Rumania, for further interrogation. She was later released.

A further twist in the Barratt story occurred in May 1947, an episode buried away in *The Times*. His parents in Britain had received a belated Christmas card, dated December 1946, postmarked Vienna and supposedly sent by an R. Rupert, the name of Dr Raphael Rupert, a Hungarian lawyer. Barratt had stayed with him for a while in Budapest, but his parents instantly recognised the handwriting on the card as their son's. Furthermore, there was a reference in the message to 'Tim', a nickname for the son used by his parents. Gore-Symes provided authenticity to the Christmas message and the British authorities attempted to investigate that Barratt somehow had survived his arrest and was in Soviet-occupied Vienna. The card was more likely an orchestrated Russian disinformation exercise, and Barratt might well have been amongst the large number of foreigners held in Soviet prisons that were liquidated in 1947 on the orders of Molotov, the foreign minister. Serov, in his memoir, specifically refers to Molotov's demand for the executions: Wallenberg amongst them.

Wallenberg had worked closely with van der Waals in the legation and as the foreign community was closely knit, there was every likelihood that he knew Gore-Symes.

An unlikely Soviet asset

If Wallenberg had been a Soviet spy, Serov certainly never alluded to it in his memoir yet according to a retired KGB officer, Colonel Elisei Sinitsyn,[167] recruitment was certainly a possibility. Sinitsyn had been posted to Stockholm as the NKVD rezident in late 1944, with the cover of first secretary. Moscow had informed him that Wallenberg had been arrested so he hurriedly cabled Abakumov, the head of Smersh, and Molotov. Raoul Wallenberg would be extremely valuable, suggested Sinitsyn, if he could be brought onside. Such Soviet practice had proved successful in a number of cases in the latter months of the war. Kollontay, the ambassador, had long cultivated the Soviet relationship with the Wallenberg family, reported Sinitsyn. Luring in Wallenberg would be an exceptional bonus.

A far more plausible scenario was the Soviet penetration in the Budapest legation.

The Swedes urgently conduct an enquiry

Some 300-plus additional staff had been taken on by the legation in the last six months in 1944, mainly in Wallenberg's department. Few were vetted given the chaos of war. In the weeks after Wallenberg had disappeared, the Swedish Foreign Office undertook an urgent enquiry on what actually had occurred in the legation during the German occupation. It had suspicions that needed careful investigation.

Under immediate scrutiny was Hermann Grossheim-Krisko, an employee in B-department who had worked under the name of Henry Thomsen, but he too was missing. To any enquiry from a legation colleague about his nationality, Grossheim-Krisko had responded that he was Norwegian-born. Only on release in 1953 after imprisonment in the Lubyanka, Lefortovo, Butyrka and Vladimir did he admit his birthplace as Rostov-on-Don in southern Russia. Grossheim-Krisko would tantalisingly relate that in one Moscow jail he had seen Wallenberg, and they had nodded their heads in recognition. Verification of that claim was impossible.

During his Moscow interrogations, Grossheim-Krisko further

---

[166] **Barratt, RAF Warrant Officer Reginald**: In *MI9: Escape and Evasion*, by M.R.D. Foot and J.M.Langley, 1979, there is a very limited report of his clandestine activities in Budapest. Both authors had been PoWs. Barratt would probably have reported back to London the effectiveness of the Allied bombing of Budapest.

[167] **Sinitsyn, Col. Elisei Tikhonovich**: Later promoted to general, he died in 1995.

claimed on his release that he had disclosed the details of subversive activities carried out by a number of diplomats within the Swedish legation and how these had threatened a post-war communist regime. Grossheim-Krisko directly accused Wallenberg of dishing out Swedish documentation to top Nazis and Hungarian businessmen.

Thomsen first appeared in legation reports in October 1944 and why he was taken on has never been clarified, but his fluency in Russian was important for his role. The Swedish cabinet had responded to a Soviet request on June 25, 1941 to take over Russia's interests in Hungary. That involved disposing of property and assets, crediting Moscow with the proceeds but by 1943 with many thousands of Red Army PoWs being held in German holding camps in Hungary, B-department took on a more exacting responsibility. Each PoW needed to be regularly inspected but it is unclear whether Thomsen accompanied Lt. Colonel Wester, the military attaché, on the trips. The Swedes set up a military hospital for injured and sick Russians.

Destroyed in the battle for Budapest was the filing system of B-department based in the adjacent Finnish legation building taken over by the Swedish legation in mid 1944, the same building in which Wallenberg and his group worked. A few documents did survive. One cable sent to Stockholm did reveal that even then doubts existed over Thomsen, the supposed Norwegian. Lars Berg had cabled that between October 18 and December 1, 1944, Thomsen had issued the Schutz-Pass, the Swedish protection order, to 14 Soviet PoWs without any legation authority. There was no back-up paperwork, reported Berg and to make matters worse, Thomsen, again without permission, had even taken on a deputy. He was a Russian, named Gleb Joukowsky-Volinsky, also known as Zsukovszky. Confidential B-department documents had leaked to the Soviets, to the Soviet legation in Stockholm, including a comprehensive listing of all Soviet PoWs who had died in Hungary. The leak was Thomsen. Curiously no legation member later questioned by the Swedish Foreign Office could recall any correspondence or document bearing his signature.

Concern now mounted that the NKVD had assets inside the

legation. Count Michel Golenish Kutuzov-Tolstoy was another suspect. This Russian, like Thomsen, had inveigled himself into B-department. Born in 1896 in Tsarskoie, in the Russian town of Selo, Kutuzov-Tolstoy had been educated in St. Petersburg and served in WW1 in the Russian horse guards. Moving to Belgium in 1933, he married a monied countess and WW2 was spent in Hungary. The couple had retired to Ireland in 1951 to run a poorly attended cooking school.

An Irish military intelligence officer surprised Kutuzov-Tolstoy in May 1955 and his secret report of what transpired was made available to the Swedish authorities. There is no explanation which intelligence agency had initiated the interview.

Stonewalling, Kutuzov-Tolstoy failed to elaborate on much of his past. As to why the couple had settled in Hungary in 1940, he would only admit that they had received a commission to teach languages to the children of a Hungarian baron. The Irish officer refused to buy it and he probed harder, questioning the Russian on the couple's activities in Budapest where they had moved to in 1944: vague and evasive, wrote the officer in his report as to the responses. Kutuzov-Tolstoy did relate that he was put in charge of the Swedish Red Cross working out of the Swedish legation and that Danielsson, the head of the legation, had awarded him full power of attorney to act for Swedish interests in Pest once the battle for Budapest had begun. That authority had been fully recognised by the incoming Soviets, he stated, as was another duty to act as a liaison for the foreign community.

If Kutuzov-Tolstoy had been NKVD, wrote the intelligence officer, he had yielded nothing that might condemn him.

Kutuzov-Tolstoy dealt only with superficialities and avoided the details of his personal life under the Russians – or in association with them – and with the Communist Partisans in Transylvania, but all indications point towards an unsavoury record on his part during that critical period.

Concluding, the officer offered a clear warning:

It is possible that he may now be both anxious and thankful to forget that part of his life so that he can live a tranquil existence in this country. He is, however, a person who definitely cannot be trusted. The circumstances under which he came here [Ireland] *seem reasonably genuine, but in the light of his previous history he has continued to be regarded with suspicion and has been kept under discreet observation.*

There is evidence that Kutuzov-Tolstoy did fulfill some of his claimed B-department duties. In the Swedish Foreign Office files are several reports filed to Stockholm from Wester, the military attaché, concerning the Russian. Kutuzov-Tolstoy and his wife had unexpectedly pitched up at the Soviet PoW hospital to see the inmates. Further hospital visits by the couple followed and in one they distributed musical instruments. In November 1944, 150 seriously wounded PoWs were transferred to a military hospital in Budapest, an arrangement that angered the German administration who demanded they be forcibly evacuated out. The resourceful Kutuzov-Tolstoy, on behalf of B-department, quickly set up a temporary Swedish legation office within the hospital as a protective shield. All this was done without any authorisation from Danielsson who post-war denied he had delegated any legation responsibilities to Kutuzov-Tolstoy. The PoWs in the military hospital were eventually moved out without Danielsson's knowledge.

B-department, reported Wester, had become a law unto itself with Danielsson rarely in the loop and Stockholm kept in the dark. No authority was ever given by the legation to begin a programme to search for disappeared Hungarian Jews. Kutuzov-Tolstoy, Langlet, the representative from the Swedish Red Cross, and an English married couple[168] were involved. Employee nationalities had been a focus in the Swedish Foreign Office enquiry as it struggled to get a grip on what had occurred in its legation. Langlet in one of his reports to Stockholm had stated that Kutuzov-Tolstoy was Belgian yet in ciphers emanating from other staff he is acknowledged as a Russian.

As the Red Army rolled into Pest in mid January, Kutuzov-

---

[168] The document in the Swedish Foreign Office archive simply stated 'unnamed'.

Tolstoy had immediately distanced himself from any further involvement in legation affairs. The Soviets had required him to head the newly created City Commandant's Aliens' Office to monitor the movements of every foreigner: a role he readily accepted.

If Kutuzov-Tolstoy and Thomsen were NKVD, Wallenberg had been under observation.

Budapest was rife with double agents. There is a further intriguing possibility. Kutuzov-Tolstoy, with his wife, would have been ideal recruits for the OSS with their command of several languages and well-placed connections. With his Russian background, might Kutuzov-Tolstoy have been a double, reporting into NKVD and OSS controllers but with a main allegiance to Moscow? Did the CIA prompt the interview in Ireland? Kutuzov-Tolstoy ended his days in Ireland, dying in County Louth in 1980, the cooking school a financial disaster.

Serov's evidence

Through the eyes of the NKVD and Smersh, Wallenberg's trips to Nazi-occupied Soviet territory to meet the Abwehr were compelling: Wallenberg had to be a double agent. Further damning was the NKVD report that one of its agents, well-embedded in US Intelligence, had confirmed Wallenberg to be an American asset.

Serov and Colonel Kozyrev, his MVD investigator, tried to determine whether Wallenberg had indeed been a spy, but they were hampered.

> *Kozyrev reported to me that no details of the original investigation remained but of what there was, no direct evidence implicated Wallenberg with espionage. However, during the interrogation Wallenberg did not deny that he maintained regular contacts with prominent Nazis and persons who had been confirmed by the MGB as American Intelligence officers.*

There is no knowing now what Wallenberg had disclosed during his Smersh interrogations. Those original investigation records had been lost – probably destroyed – so without the factual evidence

Kozyrev couldn't definitely conclude to Serov that Wallenberg had been OSS.

The CIA in its internal 1981 report did admit that Wallenberg's 'modus operandi certainly exceeded standard diplomatic practice'. As Buda had fallen, the Allied Control Commission was installed in Debrecen. Brigadier General Bonner Key represented the US and when he arrived in Debrecen on February 18, he found the Russians in a belligerent mood. Moscow had demanded that Hungary immediately supply commodities and materials to the tune of US$60 million, a down payment on the US$200 million in reparations demanded in the hastily arranged armistice agreement with the new Hungarian authorities. Hungary was bust, like the rest of occupied Europe, its economy in ruins. All gold and currency in the Hungarian central bank had been transferred to the German Reichsbank upon occupation. The Soviets had demanded the reparations be paid in full by 1951, an unfeasible challenge.

As the senior OSS officer in the area, Key reported into Alexander Kirk, the political adviser to General Eisenhower. Uppermost in his mind in Debrecen was to determine the whereabouts of Wallenberg and the two missing Swiss diplomats, Max Meier and Harald Feller. The brusque Soviet rejoinder to Key's questioning about the three prompted an urgent cable to Kirk expressing the fear that the Russians had conclusive proof of pro-Nazi collaboration. The 'Department should be concerned', Key reported. The use of 'Department' likely refers to the OSS.

Had Wallenberg been a US spy, or had he merely reported back to Olsen in Stockholm as an employee of the War Refugee Board? Serov couldn't definitely determine from the documents that were available. Sadly, Serov, in his memoir, omitted to mention if he and Kozyrev had been able to explore the diplomat's connections to the Abwehr that had taken him to Pskov and other occupied Soviet cities.

Wallenberg had left a legacy in Budapest that might have shone more light. Wallenberg had kept a secret cache of documents and notes in a wooden box in the garden of the Budapest legation, concealed close to the entrance of the underground air raid shelter. In Stockholm, an apprehensive Herschel Johnson, the US minister, wanted the box recovered before the NKVD stumbled over it. Six months had elapsed since Wallenberg had been lifted out of Budapest before the despondent Johnson sent a note to Edward Stettinius, the US secretary of state, accepting that recovery hopes for the box were dashed. The NKVD had systematically ransacked the legation after the staff was forcibly turned out after the fall of Buda, so sadly we will never know what Wallenberg had left behind, hidden even from his legation colleagues.

12

Covert Stockholm

IN THE SECOND WEEK of September 1942, there was growing apprehension within the British legation in Stockholm. A message was urgently dispatched to the Foreign Office that two small sealed metal tins would be couriered to London. 'We think it advisable in the event of emergency,' was the communication.

Given its neutrality Sweden thought it could step aside from the war that had seen the occupation of two of its Nordic neighbours, Denmark and Norway, but by allowing German military transit traffic to Norway – where a military garrison of 300,000 needed to be maintained – that status appeared to the Allies a myth. The Allied pressure on Sweden to ban the traffic was met with intransigence, not helped by the public utterances of some politicians. Allan Vougt, the Social Democrat and former journalist, wrote in one Swedish newspaper that the regular convoys of German military across its territory was of little consequence to the Swedish public and should be ignored. Upon the ending of the wartime Swedish coalition in July 1945, with Vougt now defence minister, the legation filed to London a review of all members of the new government. Whilst the foreign minister, Östen Undén, was regarded as being strongly pro-British during the war, Vougt was labelled a 'defeatist'.

Vougt's wartime opinions and pro-German sympathies gained some currency amongst the Swedish population. Circulating freely throughout Stockholm and in other cities was the *Dagsposten*, a daily Norwegian-based newspaper taken to supporting Nazi ideology.[169] Outwardly, the British government respected Sweden's neutrality but inwardly it seethed as Swedish industry propped up Hitler's war machine, even accepting payments plundered from the central banks of occupied Europe. To make matters worse, Sweden insisted that British imports of essential Swedish manufactures, such as ball bearings, would only be delivered on payment of physical gold.[170] The Allies relentlessly pursued an ending to the German war transit and in response Berlin drew up invasion plans using the troops in Norway if the Swedes acquiesced to the pressure. Publicity films were shown to the large foreign press corps in the pressroom in Stockholm's Grand Hotel demonstrating the defence capabilities of the Swedish military and air force in training. Dive-bombing a railway and troops was pure bravado as the military could never resist the Wehrmacht.

As tension mounted the British legation copied all sensitive documents. Using in-house photographic capabilities each negative was categorised 'white', 'buff' or 'blue' depending on importance. These rolled negatives were inside the two metal tins sent to the Foreign Office in London.

Stockholm had become a listening and whispering city, with spies masking their covert activities behind the guise of diplomats and foreign correspondents. Abwehr, SS and SD agents monitored the Allies and the Norwegian partisan émigrés. Axis allies, including the Hungarians, also mixed freely participating in the city's culture and drinking in the same bars as their enemies. Himmler favoured this febrile atmosphere to engineer secret peace talks with the Americans and Russians. The Allied intelligence agencies built up a significant presence.

From the war's onset, the Swedes distilled a semblance of diplomatic discipline and to a degree it was maintained. Some fell foul of the authorities. Henry Threlfall, a Special Operations Executive (SOE) operative and formerly a British civilian who had lived in Berlin from 1936 until 1939, was kicked out. In May 1984, Threlfall recorded an interview for Imperial War Museum archives

---

[169] Closed down at the end of the war.

[170] Payments in gold continued post-war. In October 1947, the British legation requested to London that it upgrade to a more central Stockholm location copying the Americans. The US had successfully bartered surplus military equipment but the Swedes declined a similar British request. The UK Treasury stopped any property purchase given its scarce gold deposits.

elaborating on his espionage operations in Norway, all orchestrated in Stockholm, and his final wartime months in Italy organising mayhem behind German lines.[171] Two NKVD officers, Nikolay Vasileyev and Mikhail Onyukhov, clandestinely working out of the Soviet legation were also expelled. During the war, Russian Intelligence had 44 operatives in Stockholm, more-or-less the same number that operated in America and double the number in Britain. Even today Sweden ranks closely behind Britain as a vital intelligence centre for Russia's SVR.

Even military allies spied on each other. Major General Makoto Onodera, the military attaché in Japan's legation, headed his country's intelligence capability with a big budget to buy both agents and information. When serving in Riga, Latvia, Onodera had met Admiral Canaris, the Abwehr chief, who wanted to be helpful. An introduction was made with Colonel Hans Wagner, the senior Abwehr officer in Stockholm[172] but Wagner took an instant dislike to him and refused to share any intelligence with this particular ally. Not put off, Onodera hatched a botched plan to penetrate Wagner's office and even bribe the maids in his house to eavesdrop.

Onodera had better success with one of the most successful Abwehr operators in Stockholm, Karl Heinz Kraemer. Other contributors to Japanese Intelligence included Colonel von Uthelmann, the German military attaché, and Major von Rosenblatt, a German engineer with access to the technical details of the German rocket programme. Kraemer met Onodera once a week, either in the Japanese legation or in a safe house. In October 1944, Kraemer handed over arguably the greatest secret of the war: details of the atomic bomb. It is unclear if this referred to German or Allied nuclear efforts. Information provided by Von Uthelmann, who exploited his contacts in Swedish military intelligence, was also well received in Tokyo.

US interrogators in 1946 explored the Japanese relationship with the supposedly neutral Swedes in their grilling of Onodera and intelligence officers who had served under him in Stockholm. They were languishing in Tokyo's Sugamo prison awaiting trial.[173] Major Petersen, in charge of espionage activities in Swedish military intelligence, admitted Onodera was amongst his sources. This is the same Petersen who ran the Swedish networks in Budapest and who was probably known to Raoul Wallenberg. Onodera told his interrogators that Petersen enjoyed excellent contacts within the British and US Intelligence community. Amongst the intelligence handed over was detailed information on the British convoys to Murmansk and Archangel, and Allied troop movements across all fronts. Had this intelligence sharing with the Japanese been countenanced?

Onodera part funded one extraordinary Petersen operation. With Finland's capitulation in 1944, some 1,000 military specialists had fled into Sweden including a special services parachute battalion of 400 men. Using the technical experience of some of the Finns, Petersen set up a crypto-analytical section outside Stockholm with four monitoring stations to monitor Russian activity in Finland. One Finnish officer, Colonel Stewen, had been a Petersen asset for several years. Friendly with Sweden's Crown Prince, Stewen had been an invaluable source in Helsinki with Petersen paying him Skr 1,000 for every report. Was this intelligence shared with the Allies?

Apart from Petersen, Onodera fingered other senior Swedish military intelligence officers including Colonel Bjorn Jorna, Colonel Kaemp and Major Boude. The head of the Swedish air force, General Bengt Nordenskiöld, had been another source with updates on Allied aircraft strength. At a cocktail party in the Swedish capital in 1943, Nordenskiöld had 'inadvertently' disclosed to Onodera the dates and concentrations for the impending mass bombing offensives against German cities. That 'inadvertently' was probably intentional. Three chiefs on the Swedish general staff, too, were on Onodera's radar. Colonel Aldercreutz, a member of an illustrious military family, was a personal friend of Canaris; Commander Lindquist was never discreet about his contacts with the German military; and Colonel

---

[171] **Threlfall, Col. Henry**: In the Italian campaign, Threlfall was a member of the joint British/US liaison committee. He participated in the US investigation into the massacre of US troops by the SS at Bolzano.

[172] **Wagner, Dr (Colonel) Hans Georg**: He took over the Swedish station in 1942 but was one of the many Abwehr officers compromised in July 1944, accused by the SD of involvement with the assassination attempt that month on Hitler.

[173] The CIA report on these interrogators was declassified in 2005.

Juehlin-Dannfeld regularly travelled to Berlin with Wagner, the Abwehr chief.

Stockholm's wartime dark side needed to be further explored, especially the covert activities of the Hungarian, Vilmos Böhm, who the British employed in the Press Reading Bureau within its legation – a front for MI6 and the SOE.

This former Hungarian diplomat was crucial to the British in the secret discussions that took place during 1943 and early 1944, to attempt a Hungarian withdrawal from the war, discussion that would end abruptly with the German invasion and occupation of Budapest. Böhm also had a part in the Raoul Wallenberg story.

Böhm's political past

Born in Budapest on January 6, 1880 into a Jewish family, Böhm[174] had trained as a metalworker in the typewriter industry after his school years. Marrying Maria Steiner in December 1905, Böhm shortly afterwards became an activist in the Metal Workers Union (Vasasszakszervezet) and elected its secretary. Politics was certainly his forte and in 1913 he sat on the executive committee of the Hungarian Social Democratic Party (MSzDP), adhering to a centrist position.

Drafted into the Austro-Hungarian army during WW1, Böhm fought as a first lieutenant on the Serbian front. Sent home in 1917, Böhm again took an active part in the Metal Workers Union and the MSzDP and in the following spring he drafted a position paper advocating a nationwide professional organisation to protest against the worsening economic situation in Hungary. Böhm was arrested in the resulting general strike later that year.

The Hungarian Revolution of October 1918 catapulted Böhm to the political forefront. With his war experience he became deputy minister of war reorganizing the army and demilitarisation. After Count Mihály Karolyi's appointment as president of the republic on January 11, 1919, Böhm was one of five social democrats to hold posts in the new government. He became the commissar of a new ministry to handle nationalisation despite bitter personal objections from the communists.

Post-WW1 Hungary was in economic and political upheaval

exacerbated by the victorious Entente dismantling of the Austro-Hungarian Empire. Rumania grabbed the opportunity to invade and Böhm assumed the more urgent post as commissar of war and commander-in-chief of the Hungarian Red Army. Factory workers in Budapest were mobilised and with Rumania now the common enemy, the tense relationship between the communists, socialists and unions softened. Böhm's army enjoyed immediate military success pushing the Romanians back to beyond their starting point by June 1919, before the Entente ordered an immediate Hungarian retreat. In disgust, Böhm[175] and his general staff resigned.

Böhm wasn't finished politically and he accepted the role of Hungarian ambassador to Austria, giving him a seat at the Vienna negotiating table on the breakup of empire. Siding with the trade unionists and social democrats, he loudly rejected any occupation by foreign troops. Eventually the Vienna horse-trading would see the expulsion of all communists from Hungary's governing council and the formation of a caretaker government under the leadership of the trade unions. Böhm had effectively sold the communists down the river, and again there was bitter personal hatred towards him.

Remaining in Vienna after the ambassadorship ended, Böhm with his social democratic friends founded the weekly magazine, *Világosság* (Clarity), and participated in the Vienna International (the so-called 2½ International). *Világosság* took aim at the semi-dictatorial Horthy regime in Hungary and the MSzDP leadership. By the early 1930s, however, Böhm had decided to mend fences in Budapest with conciliatory articles in the *Népszava* (Peoples' Voice) and *Szocializmus* (Socialism) publications using the pseudonym, Molnár. Civil war in Austria was never far away and in February 1934 it violently erupted. The Schutzbund, the paramilitary socialist group, took on the army, police and the Heimwehr, the armed wing of the Christian Social Party. Vienna was a bloodbath.

Böhm fled to the comparative safety of Bratislava, in Czechoslovakia, to write a lengthy analysis on the reasons behind the

---

[174] I am indebted to the Russian researcher, Svetlana Chervonnaya, for her considerable research into his political career.
[175] See photograph of Böhm *[Moscow-37]*.

civil war,[176] published in *Szocializmus*. The paramilitaries in Schutzbund had been soundly beaten, its leaders executed and 10,000 of its members and supporters were in jail. That publication prompted Böhm and his cousin, Eugen Prager, to establish the Prager publishing house that published a series of books on post-WW1 socialism and the ever-growing menace of fascism.

An intelligence centre for the British

That fascism threat grew louder and before the Germans occupied Czechoslovakia, Böhm sought refuge in Stockholm, settling in well with the growing Hungarian émigré circle that included his good friend Mihály Károlyi. He forged links with the British Labour Party when its members visited Stockholm on trade or fact-finding missions. The British Foreign Office saw his value and Böhm was hired to work in the Press Reading Bureau in the Stockholm legation that was intended to become a major intelligence gathering operation.

Heading the Press Reading Bureau was Cecil Parrott,[177] a former schoolmaster at Christ's Hospital and the Edinburgh Academy, who with other members of the Norwegian legation had relocated to Stockholm as the Germans invaded. Before Norway, Parrott spent five years in Belgrade privately tutoring King Peter of Yugoslavia. As the war began, the Foreign Office called on his language skills. Herbert Caird North was his deputy[178] and together they ran the combined linguistic talents in the Press Reading Bureau, providing reports and analysis into the Foreign Office's fledgling Foreign Research and Press Service (FRPS). Substantial resources had been thrown at the FRPS, which monitored developments in 65 countries and it was a vital source for the War Cabinet. Its London office was relocated to Balliol College in Oxford during the London bombing, working closely with British Intelligence that had taken over Blenheim Palace.

Frank Roberts,[179] the top diplomat in the Foreign Office, ordered Böhm to London in March 1943. Wielding considerable influence within the War Cabinet, Roberts also kept a handle on MI6 operations. In Berlin before the outbreak of war, Colonel General Ludwig Beck,[180] had confided in him that a group of senior German officers believed Hitler to be a psychopath. Roberts had further brokered the meetings with Birger Dahlerus, the charismatic Swedish businessman who personally attempted to convince Herman Goering in the summer of 1939 that any German move on the strategic and Free City of Danzig would risk war.[181]

Böhm was needed by Roberts to help develop a strategy to extricate Hungary and work with Carlile Macartney,[182] who had lectured in Budapest for three months in early 1940. On his return, Macartney, an academic, had joined the FRPS. He had authored a controversial report for the Foreign Office on European minorities and how to treat them after the war.[183] Owen O'Malley, the head of Hungarian affairs in the Foreign Office, disliked the proposal that

---

[176] In July 1934 there was an attempted coup by the Austrian National Socialist Party, the Nazis, as the federal chancellery in Vienna was attacked leading to the shooting of the chancellor, Engelbert Dollfuss. Defeated insurgents fled to the Altreich, the German Reich, to return in March 1938 after the Anschluss.

[177] **Parrott, Sir Cecil Cuthbert**: Foreign Office. He served as head of the Press Research Bureau for the duration of the war. From 1945-48 he was posted to Prague. Various UN positions followed until he moved to the Moscow embassy in 1954 as minister. Returning to London in 1957, he became director of research and acting librarian in the Foreign Office. Ambassador to Prague 1960-1969, later head of Soviet studies at the University of Lancaster. Died June 1984, aged 75.

[178] **North, Herbert Caird**: Foreign Office, seconded to the Press Reading Bureau. Little is known after his term in Stockholm. He died September 6, 2008, aged 97.

[179] **Roberts, Sir Frank Kenyon**: Posted to Moscow at the end of the war, Roberts, when introduced to Stalin, was startled. Stalin began 'I know you, you are my enemy and what is more you are a member of the British Intelligence Services'. In 1948, as an aide to Ernest Bevin, the British foreign secretary, Roberts confronted Stalin and Molotov demanding the lifting of the Berlin blockade. In 1960, Roberts was again posted to Moscow, this time as ambassador. Born in Argentina, Roberts died in January 1998, aged 91.

[180] **Beck, Col. Gen. Ludwig**: In the unsuccessful July 1944 attempt to kill Hitler, he was a central figure and committed suicide before the SS could arrest him.

[181] **Dahlerus, Birger**: As a witness at Nuremberg, called by Dr Stahmer, Goering's counsel, Dahlerus recalled those meetings. In June 1939, Dahlerus had met with Lord Halifax, the UK foreign secretary, who told him that no British official would attend. Goering, with Hitler's sanction, met with Dahlerus on August 7, 1939, in Schleswig Holstein and Dahlerus handed over a personal note from Halifax.

[182] **Macartney, Carlile Aylmer**: Resigned from the Foreign Office in May 1946 after six years of government services as an advisor, writing 143 memoranda and conducting 186 BBC broadcasts (the last in 1943). He returned to academia in Oxford, dying in 1978, aged 83.

[183] Entitled *'Minority Regimes and the Transfer of Populations in Central Europe after the War'*.

Hungarian lands lost post-WW1 should be returned on ethnic lines at the end of WW2. Britain had no stomach to be party to compulsory mass movements of populations.

The opinionated Macartney had broadcast regularly on the BBC to Hungarian listeners but these ceased in August 1942 after he was accused in Britain of being a pro-Nazi propagandist.[184] Anthony Eden, the foreign secretary, further restricted Macartney's access to sensitive documents and ciphers. That bar was rescinded as the FRPS merged with the Political Intelligence Department (PID) in April 1943, to form the Foreign Office Research Department (FORD). Böhm stressed to Roberts and Macartney that Hungary, at all costs, should not fall under the influence of the Soviet Union when the war ended.

What was discussed in London on Böhm's trip has never been disclosed but Colonel Evgeny Popov, a retired GRU officer,[185] had access to documents in Moscow, as it appeared that the Soviets had a direct line into the secret discussions. Böhm had also met exiled Czech political leaders including Edvard Benes who had agreed with Macartney's ideas on European minorities. To the anger of the British, when Molotov invited Benes to Moscow in December 1943, the Soviet foreign minister handed the former Czech president a copy of the contentious FRPS report. Molotov backed Benes, to British embarrassment, on the proposed mass expulsion of 3.3 million Sudeten Germans from the Czech lands.

Britain's Stockholm legation, by 1942, had grown to become the most important of all Britain's listening posts, operating networks in Russia, Germany, occupied Europe, the Baltics and the Balkans. Cyril Cheshire,[186] fluent in German and Russian, ran the MI6 desk whose cover was the well-trodden MI6 position of senior passport officer. Harry Carr[187] together with fellow MI6 officers from the Helsinki station had relocated to Stockholm to manage operations in Russia. Another key officer was Victor Hampton who controlled networks in Hamburg, Bonn, Konigsberg, Berlin and Vienna.

Whether MI6 shared intelligence with the SOE officers in the legation is unclear, given both organisations usually acted independently of each other. Peter Tennant masqueraded as the legation press attaché,[188] and had been one of the first recruits into

SOE, posted to Stockholm in 1939. His first marriage was to a Swede and he spoke the language perfectly. Tennant was becoming expert in the black arts of espionage running an agent inside the German legation to steal military codes. That insider was never discovered and in gratitude, after the war, Tennant secured British nationality for him and a new life in Britain. Like his opposite MI6 number, Tennant would serve in Stockholm throughout the war.

Using his cover of press attaché, Tennant circulated seamlessly around the capital mixing with foreign journalists and diplomats. Tennant's contacts included the Hungarian journalist, Andor (Pandy) Gellért, himself an intelligence officer, Alexandra Kollontay, the Russian ambassador, and Vladimir Semenov, the Soviet chargé d'affaires. Kollontay was the Soviet link to the Wallenberg family in the days and first weeks after Raoul Wallenberg's disappearance in Budapest. The ambassador informed Raoul's mother that her son was in 'safekeeping' in the Soviet Union but had warned her that further appealing by the Swedish Foreign Office to Moscow would not be in the best interests of Raoul. A colleague of Tennant's in the legation was the colourful and idiosyncratic William Montagu-Pollock.[189] His dress was never formal, and to the amusement of the

[184] Macartney's BBC broadcasts were restarted later in the year.

[185] **Popov, Col. Evgeny Vladimirovich**: *The GRU's Hungarian Rhapsody,* Moscow, 2010. As a young GRU officer, fluent in Hungarian, he acted as translator at the secret negotiations in Moscow with Hungarian representatives in late 1944. In his retirement he was privy to secret documentation and ciphers regarding Hungary.

[186] **Cheshire, Cyril**: MI6 operative in Berlin before Stockholm.

[187] **Carr, Harry**: MI6 chief in Helsinki before being posted to Stockholm in 1942. Post-war, he was the MI6 controller of Northern European Area operations, based in London, but many of his Latvia and Estonia operations in late 1945 and 1946 failed after the rings were infiltrated by the NKGB/MGB. Carr also ran operations into the USSR. Philby in his book, *My Silent War,* referred to a trip Carr made to Washington, for meetings in which Philby sat in, to discuss with the CIA why the Russian operations were such a failure.

[188] **Tennant, Sir Peter Frank Dalrymple**: Posted to the Paris embassy in 1945 as information counsellor, again an intelligence cover. He moved to Berlin in 1950 as deputy commandant of the British sector. Left the Foreign Service in 1952 to become the overseas director of the Federation of British Industry. A long and distinguished commercial career followed. He died in 1996, aged 86.

[189] **Montagu-Pollock, Sir William 'Bill'**: Post-war ambassador in Damascus, Lima, Berne and Copenhagen. He died in October 1993, aged 90.

legation staff Montagu-Pollock with military precision would prepare his lunch of gravadlax on the lid of the legation's piano.

By March 1944, the number working in the legation had grown to 200, with more than half in 'propaganda' or 'cultural' duties: a camouflage for intelligence operations. Tennant had four SOE officers supporting him: Lamming, Leadbitter, Eyre and Leonard. The Press Reading Bureau was a listening post for Churchill, for all European theatres of the war. Berlin whispers were being reported back to Stockholm and in a city where Allies and Axis diplomats could move freely.

Transmissions were received by the Press Reading Bureau from occupied Yugoslavia on the activities of the two rival partisan groups. In January 1944, according to SOE documents sourced from the bureau, there was open disagreement between Churchill and the Foreign Office over General Dragoljab 'Draza' Mihailovic[190] and Tito.[191] Churchill favoured Tito and his communists but the Foreign Office saw more long-term political mileage in Mihailovic, the Yugoslav Serb and royalist, who commanded the Chetniks that had as its emblem, a skull and bones. The Soviets had made no secret of their suspicions that the Chetniks were collaborating with the Nazis. With the Soviets on their backs Churchill and his War Cabinet needed to decide.

One Press Reading Bureau cable illustrated the problem: 'SOE here is most anxious that the decision regarding the break with Mihailovic should be taken before the Soviet mission arrives in Yugoslavia. Partisans will be concerned that we have only acted under Soviet pressure and we will consequently lose all credit for it'. Moscow was well aware of the internal British dilemma. In the ranks of the Yugoslav department of SOE in London was James Klugmann, arguably amongst the most treacherous of the Britons who spied for Russia during the war. Klugmann was an NKVD talent spotter, identifying individuals in the British Labour Party that could be recruited, including Harold Wilson.

Germany, too, had established a significant press corps to work closely with the Abwehr, SS and SD. Some 75 of its 220 staff in the legation performed media duties. Heading its press corps was Dr Theodor Böttiger, who represented the Nazi-newspaper mouthpiece, the *Völkischer Beobachter*. He and his deputy heads, Dr Rudolf Rösel, Dr Werner Knorre and Dr Helmut Lindemann, gathered intelligence picked up in the Stockholm Grand Hotel's pressroom. In addition there were two official German press attachés: Dr Paul Grassmann, a journalist for *Leipziger Neuste Nachrichten*, and Walter Standacher. In October 1944, Grassmann, with the naval attaché and the legation's cultural attaché, received a direct order from Himmler to return to Berlin. The SS was still rounding up diplomats and intelligence officers after the failed assassination attempt on Hitler in July. Fearing the worst, Grassmann defected to the Swedes.

The Russians emulate the British

Kollontay, now in her seventies, needed no convincing that her own Stockholm legation must establish its own press department to shield covert pursuits. The ambassador cabled Moscow and one of its most seasoned husband-and-wife NKVD couples arrived: Zoya Rybkina and her husband Boris. Rybkina had been the overall controller of the German desk in the Lubyanka,[192] which included directing the operations of the Red Orchestra, the network that had supplied intelligence on Hitler's plans for European domination. One celebrated agent was in the Gestapo. She had charmed Count von der Schulenburg, Germany's wartime ambassador to Moscow, and bugged his office. This NKVD couple had travelled to Stockholm under the passport surname of Yartseva. Enroute, they stopped in London, for embassy briefings. The Russian ambassador, Ivan Maisky, had introduced them to David Lloyd George, the former prime minister, whose son took them on a private visit to the House

---

[190] **Mihailovic, General Dragoljab 'Draza'**: Branded a war criminal, he was executed by firing squad on July 17, 1946.

[191] **Tito, Josip Broz Marshal**: Later used his own communist brand of 'Titoism' to run the country. Died May 1980, aged 88.

[192] **Rybkina, Col. Zoya**: Rybkina alone knew all the names of the Red Orchestra operatives keeping a diary of her activities. After the war she was purged by Stalin and sent to Vorkuta as chief of operations running informants in the camps. Allowed to return to Moscow, she became an author writing a biography of Lenin's mother and another on Lenin's stay in Finland. MI6 defector, Philby, befriended Rybkina after his defection to Moscow. See photograph *[Moscow-38]*.

of Commons.

Boris, codenamed 'Kin', was to be Stockholm's NKVD rezident with the cover of counsellor. Zoya Rybkina, codenamed 'Irina', and using the first name of Alexandra, was press attaché and she quickly set about preparing and launching a press bulletin to shock the Swedish public, the foreign diplomatic staff and the foreign press corps with graphic detail of Germany's murderous invasion of the Soviet Union. When the press bulletin was ready, Kollontay persuaded the Swedish Foreign Office to host a social event in the Grand Hotel to celebrate the inaugural edition.

That first bulletin produced by Rybkina was launched with a fanfare in the banqueting hall in January 1942. A press officer from the Swedish Foreign Office guided Rybkina down the line of journalists and in her later years, Rybkina would describe this line waiting to greet her. 'Among them there were two women – one from the United States and the other from Norway. A Swedish diplomat arranged the men as if on a parade, with the women at the head, and began the introduction', she wrote. The American woman greeted Rybkina with an enthusiastic smile. A Soviet correspondent was the last in the line.

From its legation the Germans howled in protest demanding that Rybkina's bulletin be immediately pulled. It was upheld, a strange decision given the Swedes had hosted the launch reception. Undaunted, Kollontay complained. The Swedish Foreign Office rescinded, but only if the Soviets met the postal and distribution costs. According to Russian records, the print run of that first bulletin was 200,000, an incredible circulation by Swedish standards. The Russian press bureau, headed by Madam Yartseva, had cut its publishing teeth.

Flushed with that success, Rybkina rented a basement in Stockholm for her next venture, the showing of Soviet films. The foreign press corps lapped up the typical conviviality and ample drink. There was further German railing against the bi-weekly journal pumped out by Jens Schive, the press attaché in the Norwegian legation. *Handslag* ran from June 1942 for three years vividly reporting the terrors of the Norwegian occupation. Copies clandestinely circulated throughout Norway but there was a wide readership in Sweden where 50,000 Norwegians had fled. From the

Norwegian legation, the XU organisation ran espionage operations. The Germans were powerless to intervene despite the angry objections to the Swedish government.

The Yartsevas left Stockholm in July 1943 after a successful 21 months that included shoring up continued Soviet trade arrangements with the Wallenberg family. Hard pressed for quality steel, the Soviets bartered with platinum and other precious materials. Moscow sent in another highly experienced NKVD foreign intelligence officer, the resourceful Vasily Petrovich Roschin, whose real name was Yakov Fedorovich Tischenko.[193]

Roschin had cut his intelligence teeth in China with a posting to the Russian consulate in Harbin in 1925. By the time he left in November 1930, he was its INO OGPU resident[194] and Harbin was the hub of a major intelligence network. Roschin had run the successful infiltration of the 'White Sector' ring of Japanese agents and saboteurs that penetrated USSR territory. Disillusioned by failure the Japanese disbanded the network.

One significant achievement in Harbin was the running of 'Brown', the codename for a colonel in the Chinese army who penetrated the White émigré group, Bratstvo Russkoi Pravdy (the Fraternity of the Russian Truth). 'Brown' also infiltrated similar groups such as the Russian Falcons Armed Force and the Russian Common-to-all-arms Union. When the legendary General Arthur Artuzov recalled Roschin to Moscow,[195] 'Brown' went with him.

Years later, when Roschin wrote his unpublished memoir, typically a lengthy statement in which intelligence officers record their careers in depth, Roschin proudly described how he and his agents had obtained the Japanese plans for military conquest

---

[193] **Tischenko, Col. Yakov Fedorovich**: Born August 22, 1903 in the village of Zharikovo, Nickolo-Ussury district of the maritime province in the Russian Far East, into a family of Cossacks. In 1920, he joined a guerrilla regiment in Spassk fighting the Japanese and later engaged in the Russian civil war. In 1921, his guerrilla unit was incorporated into the regular army. A colleague was Ivan Konev, the future Marshal of the Red Army.

[194] INO OGPU: INO referred to the foreign department of OGPU, the predecessor of the NKVD.

[195] **Artuzov, Gen. Arthur**: Chief of INO OGPU, later the NKVD. He was a disinformation expert. Arrested in August 1937 in the 'Plot of the Generals' and executed.

throughout China. A highlight was in mid–1928 when he led a group of Chinese delegates to the sixth Congress of the Comintern that opened in Moscow in July, crossing the Chinese-Soviet border, which carried enormous risk for the large party.

Artuzov posted Roschin to Berlin in the summer of 1932, under the name of Vasily Toumanov, to open what the Russians referred to as a 'shoemaking shop', a cover for the production of forged IDs, mainly passports. With the rise and then election of the Nazis, Artuzov expanded the OGPU rezidency to 10 officers and Roschin was its head. Roschin recruited Reinhold Wulle, the former Reichstag deputy of the Deutsche Völkische Freedom Party, the DVFP, and in the spring of 1935 Wulle disclosed to his controller how Hitler could be assassinated. Wulle's intentions were reported back to Moscow but orders came from the Centre to discontinue any further contact. Artuzov moved Roschin the following year to Vienna. Within months, Roschin had penetrated the Austrian Foreign Service and obtained for Moscow the details of the forthcoming Anschluss.

As fascism geared up across Europe, Stalin's paranoia and his Great Terror convulsed Russia. The intelligence services were decimated. Roschin had been recalled to Moscow where he was arrested, dismissed from the service, deprived of military rank and his awards stripped. Unexpectedly reinstated in March 1941, Roschin was moved into the Fourth Directorate of the NKVD and with the German invasion in June he ran a group operating behind the German lines. He was posted to besieged Leningrad but two months later Roschin was ordered to Stalingrad, given his fluency in German, to interrogate captured high-ranking German officers. One, Colonel Schieldknecht, before Stalingrad, was on the Berlin general staff and had drawn up invasion plans for Sweden.

The Edinburgh encounter with Böhm

Roschin's hazardous and circuitous trip to take over Stockholm's NKVD station had begun in Stalingrad. He travelled via Baku, Teheran and Cairo and a ship took him to Gibraltar from where he awaited further passage to Britain. Once in London, he spent time in the London embassy, awaiting further briefings from Moscow Centre and enjoyed the wartime social life of the city despite the bombing. It was late October 1943.

A berth was found on a cargo ship to Stockholm departing from Edinburgh so he took a train from London and booked into a hotel. He travelled on a Russian passport bearing the name Vasily Fedorovich Razin. Roschin's codename was 'Valerian'.

Edinburgh rooms were scarce and guests were informed they must share even with complete strangers. Roschin found his roommate for several days was Vilmos Böhm who was returning to Stockholm after his trip that had lasted eight months. Böhm's introduction shocked the seasoned NKVD agent.

In a cipher Roschin sent to Moscow, dated November 24, 1943,[196] a month after his arrival in Stockholm, Roschin reported the circumstances of his chance encounter in Edinburgh with Böhm. He used Böhm's codename 'Orestes' in the cipher. The recipient was 'Victor', otherwise Lt. General Pavel Fitin, the intelligence chief who ran all NKVD foreign intelligence agents abroad.[197]

Roschin had introduced himself as a Russian diplomatic officer and Böhm responded whether he had been posted to Stockholm to replace Boris Yartseva, who had left in July. What shocked Roschin, he reported to Fitin, was Böhm's reference to 'Kin', the NKVD codename for Yartseva. Does that imply that Yartseva had been the controller of Böhm and for some reason Roschin hadn't been informed?

Fitin made no comment. The relationship with Böhm developed

---

[196] Venona decrypted cipher, No 3,118 – Venona was the secret US operation set up after the war to read Russian wartime ciphers.

[197] **Fitin, Lt. Gen. Pavel Mikhailovich**: Chief of the NKVD's Fifth Directorate. He was a journalist and photographer by profession. Pre-war, he ran a department that monitored Trotskyites. Post-war, Fitin was deputy chief of the MGB in Germany but later exiled to Siberia as MGB head in Sverdlovsk. In 1951, he was posted to Kazakhstan in the Ministry of Security but two years later, after the execution of Beria, Fitin was dismissed and stripped of his pension. His last job was chief of photography of the All-Union Institute for Cultural Ties with Foreign Countries. Fitin died in 1971, aged 64.

and in further ciphers to Moscow, the codename 'Orestes' was used. Böhm had discussed with him establishing a line of contact with another Hungarian, named Gorets. Roschin agreed even giving Gorets a codename, 'Mountaineer', but he needed Moscow's approval for the recruitment.

Little of Böhm's intelligence career is straightforward, and to Roschin's surprise Moscow declined contact with Gorets and gave no reason. Roschin now had a problem as Böhm had already given him intelligence from Gorets. Roschin and Böhm met to discuss the position and Böhm suggested that contact with Gorets should continue. Roschin disagreed and communicated with Moscow.

Smelling a possible plant, Fitin filled in Roschin on what was known. Gorets was a Hungarian intelligence officer using the cover of a press attaché in the Hungarian legation. His real name was Andor Gellért, nicknamed Pandy.[198] Aware that Britain's Press Reading Bureau, where Böhm worked, was an intelligence front, Fitin was not prepared to countenance the recruitment of an agent offered up by him.

Further ciphers, however, indicated that Gellért was ultimately recruited and he regularly provided high-quality intelligence on Hungary, Finland, the German military in Czechoslovakia, partisans in Slovakia and the communist groups in Yugoslavia. Gellért had clearly become a major NKVD source. Before his posting to the Stockholm legation in 1942, Gellért had served in Berlin as a journalist for the Hungarian Telegraph Agency (MTI) and had been the contact man between Paul Teleki, the-then Hungarian prime minister and the Third Reich. Per Anger, Wallenberg's colleague in Budapest, after the war confirmed that he had got to know Gellért in Stockholm.

In Sweden, the Hungarians had needed Gellért as the conduit in the Hungarian withdrawal discussions with Britain but had Gellért taken it upon himself to also share intelligence with Russia or was that determined by Budapest to sound out Moscow's intentions for a post-war Hungary? Did MI6 know that Böhm had become a Soviet asset or was he run as a double agent to deliberately feed disinformation to Moscow? Gellért obviously knew that his fellow Hungarian provided material to the NKVD. One memo sent to

London from the British minister in Stockholm, Victor Mallett,[199] particularly points to the value of Böhm and the high quality intelligence he was receiving.

Journalists make first-rate spies

Intelligence agencies – on all sides – have long used the umbrella of journalism. Journalists infiltrate where government ministers cannot and they can sup and drink with the devil as they often do. The history of intelligence is littered with the names of unsung journalists who provided editors with great copy but also satisfied darker masters.

By March 1944, there were 125 registered foreign correspondents in Stockholm and with the right documentation the intelligence services could place as many agents as they needed. With a permit granted by the Swedish Foreign Office, and with a required police pass, names were added to the listing of all nominated correspondents in the pressroom in the Grand Hotel. Meeting the shapely Miss Gullevi Westelius, the government's press attaché, was a delight for many. She dispensed a double set of ration cards, a courtesy accorded to correspondents, the precious 'motbok', a passbook to purchase ample quantities of booze from government monopoly stores, and other perks such as theatre tickets. Stockholm was a tough assignment.

Westelius also helped out with accommodation and expenses were no problem for Edwin Shanke, representing Associated Press, who moved into a room in the Grand. Often boastful of churning

---

[198] **Gellért, Andor (Pandy):** After the war, he worked as a correspondent in Hungary and in the late 1940s he moved to New York serving on the staff of Radio Free Europe (RFE). From September 1954 to June 1957, he was RFE's bureau chief at the Hungarian desk in Munich. Moving back to New York he became an active member of the numerous Hungarian associations and societies that abounded in the US. Gellért died in Budapest in November 1990, aged 83.

[199] **Mallett, Sir Victor Alexander Louis:** Stockholm minister for the duration of the war, and then chargé d'affaires in Washington. Later he was ambassador to Spain and Italy. He wrote *Life with Queen Victoria*, drawing on his mother's employment with Victoria. Died May 1969, aged 76.

out 4,000 words a day in some dispatches, Shanke[200] protested bitterly if his copy was not transmitted swiftly via the agency made available by the Swedish Foreign Office. There were suspicions that the Swedes gave priority over traffic to the large German press contingent and both Shanke and Gordon Young of the *Daily Express* were vocal in the loud protest.

Lavishing food and drink on foreign correspondents had yielded positive results for the NKVD and GRU. Gellért, according to Roschin, not only cultivated other correspondents but diplomats from other legations. Roschin knew Hugh Prenois Cunningham well, the first secretary at the American legation. There is no mention in Roschin's ciphers on whether Cunningham had become another asset. From his Berlin days, Gellért had known Shanke and his name appeared as an important source in Roschin's ciphers to Moscow.

Included in Roschin's network in Stockholm was the American journalist, John Scott.[201] Studying engineering at university, Scott had quit his course in 1932 and after taking advice from his father, an ardent communist, he tried his luck in Russia. Using his skills, he obtained a job as a welder in the Urals, at Magnitogorsk, the largest steel plant in the world. Gaining a fluency in Russian, he began to study in his spare time. Five years on and now with a young family, Scott developed his talent for writing. He took the family to Moscow and became a freelancer but the tone of his journalism didn't always satisfy the censors. Covering the announcement of the Molotov-Ribbentrop Pact in Berlin for a British newspaper Scott was temporarily barred re-entry. With the German invasion of the Soviet Union imminent, he and his family were granted exit visas and they fled to the US. Money was tight as he struggled to find a job so Scott took to writing a memoir about his hard life in Magnitogorsk.[202] It isn't clear when Scott became an NKVD operative.

For the next two years he earned a living from freelancing but in October 1943, Scott won assignments for *Life* and *Time* magazines in Stockholm. It was an obvious move by the OSS to try and recruit him given his fluency in Russian and his contacts. Scott, codenamed 'Ivanov' by the NKVD, rejected the American overtures, yet there remains the possibility that he was successfully planted inside the OSS as a double agent.

In Stockholm, Scott, with Roschin as his controller, quickly delivered. The former Magnitogorsk welder nurtured high-level contacts in Helsinki. On one trip Scott interviewed several ministers in the Jukka Rangell government that proved insightful for Roschin and Kollontay in developing the Soviet position for concluding the armistice with Finland in 1944.

Equally productive, first for Rybkina and then Roschin, was the Austrian-born American journalist, Augustina Stridsberg, who went under two codenames, 'Klara' and 'Annette'. Her daughter, Marietta Voge, lived in Berkeley, California, and had the cover name of 'Doch' – the Russian for daughter. Voge knew Grigory Kheifets, the Soviet vice-consul in San Francisco, the NKVD controller who ran a network of nuclear scientists in the University of California laboratories. In Stockholm, using her press credentials, Stridsberg[203] was able to travel to Germany and Austria to meet underground Soviet sympathisers and communist groups. Her talents were also spotted by MI6 in Stockholm but she resisted recruitment attempts.

The *Tass* correspondent in Stockholm, Mikhail Kossov, codenamed 'Raoul',[204] was a hardened intelligence officer and trained by Soviet naval intelligence after graduating from the Leningrad Institute in Foreign Languages. His brief was to infiltrate the large corps of foreign journalists. Able to mix freely in the city, Kossov regularly attended press gatherings where Scott and Shanke were also present.

Who was Edmond Demaitre's ultimate intelligence controller will forever remain a mystery. Originally the Stockholm correspondent

---

[200] **Shanke, Edwin**: AP staffer since joining the company in Milwaukee in the late 1930s. Fluent in German he was posted to Berlin and later embedded into the German advance into Poland and France. After US journalists were expelled from Germany in 1942, he was posted to Stockholm as bureau chief. He made frequent trips to Finland to cover the Finnish-Russia war. Post-war, he covered the Nuremberg trials and later returned to Stockholm for AP. Died December 2004, aged 94.

[201] **Scott, John**: Died 1976, aged 64.

[202] *Behind the Urals: an American Worker in Russia's City of Steel*, Houghton Mifflin, Boston, 1941.

[203] Stridsberg had a sub-source, codenamed 'Cylinder', who reported to her on Finnish matters.

[204] **Kossov, Mikhail**: Intelligence careerist, his real name was Rahmiel Kosoy. He returned to Stockholm, in 1971, now KGB, where he remained until 1973. In 1989, Kosoy emigrated to Israel where he died in 2008, aged 86.

for the *Petit Parisien*, Demaitre later reported for the London-based *Daily Express* and the *Sunday Express*. Demaitre cultivated Vladimir Semenov, the Soviet chargé d'affaires. When Demaitre wasn't in the pressroom in the Grand Hotel, he worked from his flat in the newly built block in Strindbergsgaten. For those meetings outside Stockholm, he frequented a summer-restaurant in the popular Baltic-side locality of Saltsjobaden.

Demaitre featured in NKVD cipher traffic from Stockholm to Moscow and he was a major figure in the discussion with the British over Hungarian withdrawal from the war. He organised a group that included Gellért, Böhm and Aladar Szegedy-Maszak, the Hungarian diplomat sent from Budapest to help move along the talks.[205] Records confirm in Moscow that in early 1943, Demaitre had fixed up a venue outside Stockholm to discuss Böhm's impending trip to London to see Frank Roberts at the Foreign Office. Böhm was given approval to tell Roberts that Hungarian military forces would not resist if the Allies moved into the country. When Böhm returned from London in late October, Hungary had added to its firepower in Stockholm by sending in the arch propagandist and experienced Antal Ullein-Reviczky.[206] Running the press and cultural ministry in Budapest, Ullein-Reviczky was a slippery propagandist with Nazi connections believing that Germany had a moral right to win the war in Europe. Now in Stockholm, Ullein-Reviczky insisted that all discussions with the British be channelled through himself, not Böhm.

In the final months of 1943 there was a real urgency to conclude the Hungarian withdrawal. Otto Hatz, Hungary's military attaché in Stockholm, travelled to Istanbul for secret talks with the British and Americans. Stupidly, George Gibson, the former president of the Trades Union Council (TUC) was to blow Böhm's secret trip to London in an interview to the Stockholm correspondent of the *Daily Telegraph*.[207] Gibson had met up with Böhm in London but they had met before in Sweden in 1940. Gibson disclosed to the *Daily Telegraph* that no discussions could take place with Hungary until its troops were pulled out of Russia.

That Gibson newspaper interview precipitated a furious exchange between Molotov and Archibald Kerr, the British ambassador in Moscow. Outraged, Molotov issued a formal protest complaining bitterly that the British had been acting unilaterally. In his note, Molotov specifically brought up the role played by Böhm in the Press Reading Bureau, and even acknowledged that he knew that Böhm travelled on a Czech passport. A bemused Kerr was staggered to hear Molotov's detailed account of Böhm's meetings while in London. On the back foot, Roberts decided that the Soviets had to be brought onside and given details of what had been happening for the best part of the year. Böhm and Gellért had already done that covertly through Roschin.

Kerr reported back to Britain's War Cabinet that Moscow would never countenance any British attempt to assist the Hungarian government, or any effort by Hungary to avoid its full share of blame for the invasion of the Soviet Union. At the meeting of the Allied foreign ministers in Moscow lasting from October 18 to November 11, 1943, Molotov moved that in future any approach by a German ally would be discussed between Britain, the US and Russia.

Did Böhm compromise Wallenberg?

Lev Bezymensky,[208] the Russian historian with impressive sources including former KGB chairmen, was adamant that Raoul Wallenberg and Böhm knew each other in Stockholm. Evgeny

---

[205] **Szegedy-Maszak, Aladar**: Diplomat and broadcaster. After Stockholm he was arrested by the Gestapo and sent to Dachau. At the end of the war, he became Hungarian ambassador to Washington in 1945, resigning in 1947 when the communists gained power in the country. Broadcasting stints followed at Radio Free Europe, a front for the CIA, and Voice of America. Died March 1988, aged 84.

[206] **Ullein-Reviczky, Antal**: He studied in Vienna and in the 1920s and 1930s worked as a diplomat in the ministry of foreign affairs, serving in Paris, Geneva, Ankara and Zagreb. By the end of the 1930s he was head of the press and cultural ministry in Budapest. After the Hungarian entry into the war, publicly he espoused pro-German opinions.

[207] **Gibson, George**: After the war, he held a number of positions including a directorship of the Bank of England. He resigned all public posts after being implicated in the Lynskey Tribunal in 1947 held to assess the activities of the Polish businessman, Sidney Stanley, who had bribed members of Parliament. Died 1953, aged 68.

[208] **Bezymensky, Lev Alexandrovich**: During WW2, he served as a military translator in intelligence on the Don Front and after the Soviet victory at Stalingrad he was one of the team of interrogators of Marshal von Paulus and other senior German officers. At the end of the war he was on the staff of Marshal Zhukov.

Pitovranov,[209] the wartime military attaché at the Soviet legation in Stockholm, understood that before Wallenberg left for Budapest, Böhm had handed Wallenberg a list of 18 names that might be useful in his mission. On the list was Anna Kéthley,[210] a well-connected member of the Social Democratic Party in parliament who had fled from Budapest after the German occupation in March 1944 and was in hiding.

It would be absurd to believe that Böhm and Wallenberg didn't meet, or even socialise in Stockholm. Legation members, especially those in intelligence and trade, would have been in contact with the Wallenberg family. In the Stockholm archives there is a report that Böhm had been privy to cables sent by Wallenberg, beginning just weeks after he arrived in Budapest in July 1944. One cable was to Dr Lauer, Wallenberg's business partner in the foodstuffs import-export company, Mellaneuropeiska, requesting him to pass on to Iver Olsen, the OSS bureau chief in Stockholm and the War Refugee Board representative, the rumour circulating in Budapest that Germany sought peace talks with Russia.

Böhm had access to the most secret of cables sent by Wallenberg and there is evidence that the Swede had even sent material to him directly from Budapest. Montagu-Pollock in the British legation in Stockholm had cabled London that confidential information emanating from Wallenberg had flowed through Böhm.

There is every possibility that Wallenberg had also met with Ullein-Reviczky, the Hungarian diplomat later posted to Stockholm, on a business trip to Budapest in 1943, the year before he joined the legation. The Hungarian authorities have released Wallenberg's visa application. In a meeting in 2011 between two Wallenberg researchers[211] and Ullein-Reviczky's daughter, documentation was revealed that Wallenberg met and socialised with Hungarian business heads and government officials on that trip.

If Wallenberg was compromised to the Russians, Böhm and his fellow Hungarian, Gellért, are in the frame as is Demaitre, the *Daily Express* correspondent, whose allegiances have never been clarified. However, the Soviets had prior knowledge about Wallenberg's involvement with the OSS as Serov confirmed in his memoir. The NKVD had a well-placed agent embedded in the organisation.

Böhm left Stockholm as the war ended to be greeted warmly in Budapest by the social democrats with immediate election to the MSzDP board. In December, Böhm gladly accepted the position to return to Sweden as Hungary's ambassador. Working again with his British connections, he advised Clement Atlee's Labour government on the post-war chaos that was Hungary. After the Treaty of Paris in February 1947, Hungary had to pay a high financial price for being a German ally as the Soviets demanded immediate reparations of $200 million with additional compensation to Czechoslovakia and Yugoslavia. Territory was also acceded.

Two months later, Böhm returned to Budapest and as the éminence grise of Hungarian politics, he played a discreet role in the unfolding political crisis that saw the MSzDP accepting the inevitable, that the Hungarian Communist Party had tightened its iron grip. The communists did win in 1947, with fraud tainting the election. Böhm viewed it as the final chapter for his social democratic party, fleeing to Stockholm, for the second time an émigré, where he wrote a memoir about the unfolding events in Hungary.[212] As the final act in his life drama, on June 3, 1949, Böhm's Hungarian citizenship was revoked and he died in Stockholm on October 28, that year.

Who was Böhm's ultimate controller in wartime Stockholm, MI6 or the NKVD? Such is the exigent nature of war that intelligence boundaries become blurred, and sympathies confused. Perhaps in his mind, Böhm had played both sides against each other in an attempt to save his country from the ruination that he had personally witnessed in the aftermath of 1918 and the forced disintegration of

---

[209] **Pitovranov, Lt. Gen. Evgeny**: He later had a long career in the KGB and wrote *Budapeshtskaja missija, Raoul Vallenberg, Sekretno,* Moskva, Sovershenno, 2001 (*The Budapest Mission. Raoul Wallenberg, Top Secret,* Moscow, 2001).

[210] **Kéthley, Anna**: In 1954, arrested in Hungary, she was accused of spying by the government and given a life sentence. Anna was released only after significant international pressure. She died in 1996, aged 87.

[211] Susanne Berger, Dr Vadim Birstein. More detail on this material can be found in the Raoul Wallenberg Committee of the United States.

[212] Besides his post-war memoir, Böhm published an in-depth analysis of the years 1918-1919, *Im Kreuzfeuer zweier Revolution (Munich 1924)* in 1947 was published by the MSzDP. Selected correspondence was published in Budapest in 1997.

the Austro-Hungarian Empire.

Roschin,[213] in his unpublished memoir, had illustrated clearly that Böhm had been a spy, as was Gellért. Both men had supplied him with invaluable intelligence. Members of the foreign press corps, including Scott and Shanke, had also been part of his Stockholm network. Roschin did confess that he always had the suspicion than one or several might be double agents. Roschin had been part of the secret peace overtures that had taken place between the Russians and the SS, but Moscow Centre had advised caution as the real motives of all concerned on the German side could never be trusted. In his memoir, Roschin admitted that he had contacts in the German legation and had been involved in the secret deals to bring out wealthy Jews from Nazi-occupied Europe in exchange for cash.

The British, a past master in playing the double game, had elevated Stockholm to its prime centre for gathering intelligence in all theatres of the European war. In an earlier chapter, I described the transmission path on how the Swedish Foreign Office first received the definitive news that Wallenberg had been taken in Budapest, and it is worth repeating given the part played by the Press Reading Bureau.

On January 16, 1945, the day before Wallenberg was last seen in Budapest, Vladimir Dekanozov, the Soviet deputy foreign minister, had sent a note to Sweden's ambassador in Moscow, Staffan Söderblom, stating that Wallenberg was in custody. There is a twist to that official record. Göran Rydeberg, the Swedish expert on Wallenberg's disappearance, has reported that Söderblom had first confirmed that news to Caird North, the Press Reading Bureau's deputy head. Böhm had then relayed this news to the Swedish authorities, before Söderblom's official message from Moscow had arrived.

Stockholm lived up to its wartime role as the listening and whispering city, full of spies and double agents.

---

[213] Roschin (aka Tischenko) died in 1988, aged 85.

13

The Investigation
– Why Wallenberg had to die

From the reports of Dobrohotov and Fedotov, it became clear that Stalin and Molotov had planned to use evidence extracted from the interrogation of Wallenberg for secret negotiations with the Americans on issues not to be raised at the Nuremberg trials. Fedotov had been responsible from the Soviet end for the preparation of these trials and he told me that the Americans had met our request not to raise the issue of the secret Ribbentrop-Molotov protocols. In exchange, we could not raise the issue of the financial ties that existed between the United States and Hitler's industrialists arranged with the help of the Wallenberg family, and the secret contacts that had taken place on negotiating a separate peace treaty with the Germans.

At the ending of the Nuremberg trials Raoul Wallenberg had lost his validity and his usefulness to us. On the orders of Molotov and Abakumov, the Soviet Ministry of Foreign Affairs hinted to the Swedes that Wallenberg could be exchanged for the return of Soviet traitors who had escaped to Sweden. These proposals yielded no results.

Molotov then raised the issue of liquidating Wallenberg as well as American, German, Japanese and other foreign citizens detained by us after the war.

Extracts from Ivan Serov's memoir

WALLENBERG had been languishing in his Moscow cells for 10 months as the first military tribunal at Nuremberg of top Nazis began in November 20, 1945. Serov's memoir explains what happened in October 1946 when they were sentenced.

At the ending of the Nuremberg trials Raoul Wallenberg had lost his validity and his usefulness to us.

Before the tribunal had begun the relationship between the Soviet Union and its former military allies was soured. Stalin's NKVD and GRU agents had provided valuable intelligence insights as to how Britain and America had planned their own peace, even before Hitler was beaten. One agent had obtained the details of what was to become the Washington Agreement, a post-war strategy to carve up the world's oil resources. Funding would be found to buy the loyalty of South American governments, allowing US and British oil companies preferential rights to develop existing fields and explore new territories. The oil-rich Middle East was to become another Western fiefdom on similar financing arrangements, to ensure global oil supremacy for the long term. The Soviets could only monitor through their excellent intelligence networks how this new world economic order was envisaged. Every time Major General Stewart Menzies,[214] the head of Britain's MI6, sent a memo to his heads of department the contents were compromised. One directive in August 1944 had revealed MI6's post-war plans to infiltrate Russian Intelligence across Europe.[215] Stalin, thanks to his agents, for almost the entire war metaphorically had a seat on Churchill's War Cabinet[216] and a position in the White House.

The arguments on how the Nuremberg trials should be conducted were bitter. Fedotov, Serov's MVD counterintelligence chief, had filled in for him the precise detail on the horse-trading. Sensitive and embarrassing wartime episodes would be barred from the military legal counsels representing both defence and prosecution. All parties had their 'Red Lines'.

Fedotov had been responsible from the Soviet end for the preparation of these trials…

If the 23 Nazis on trial believed that in their defence they could accuse the Soviets of equal culpability in committing war crimes, they were sorely mistaken. Stalin was adamant that his dirty linen would not be aired in the Nuremberg courtroom, with its rapt worldwide audience. Murderous retribution by the Red Army and NKVD on German populations in the sweep westwards towards Berlin; the massacre of a near 15,000 Polish PoWs in 1940;[217] and atrocities committed on the civilian population in the city jail in L'vov, in the Ukraine, in July 1941 were some of the barbarities that Stalin and Molotov insisted had to be stifled even if any defence counsel raised them. Likewise, the new Truman administration was determined to suppress the American dealings with the Third Reich from the time Hitler became chancellor in 1932.

The Secret Protocols

Nuremberg was a trial, not just for the accused. Raoul Wallenberg, too, was on trial for his life, a political pawn in the horse-trading. Wrote Serov:

The Americans had met our request not to raise the issue of the secret Ribbentrop-Molotov protocols.

After the Wehrmacht had rolled into Czechoslovakia in May 1939, Britain and France had guaranteed to safeguard the sovereignty of Poland. An Anglo-French delegation arrived in Moscow on August 23 to discuss with the Soviets how best to engineer an arrangement, whereby Poland might allow the passage of Red Army troops across

---

[214] **Menzies, Maj. Gen. Stewart**: Head of MI6, 1939-1952.

[215] I obtained a copy from my Moscow sources.

[216] As to the identity of a key source in the War Cabinet, one name, in particular, came up several times in my research in Moscow on WW2 spies. In later years, he became Conservative prime minister.

[217] To counter the previous Nazi accusation of blame, the NKVD had published its own report in January 1944 into the shooting of the Polish PoWs from the Kozelsk camp near Smolensk. In London, Owen O'Malley, the Foreign Office official who held the brief on Poland, submitted his own conclusions to Anthony Eden, the British foreign secretary. O'Malley concluded 'let us think of these things always and speak of them never. To speak of them never is the advice, which I have been giving to the Polish Government.' Eden agreed, and O'Malley's conclusions were never circulated. Churchill in a 'Personal Minute' to Eden had written: 'I think that Sir Owen O'Malley be asked very secretly to express his opinion on the Katyn Wood enquiry', concluding 'we should none of us ever speak a word about it.'

its territory to counter the growing threat from the Wehrmacht. That was a Soviet blind. In another gathering in Stalin's meeting room in the Kremlin, at the same time, Molotov with von Ribbentrop, his German opposite number, pursued a far different agenda.

Attached to the Ribbentrop-Molotov Nonaggression Pact were several addenda, the Secret Protocols, which, because of their intended outcome, were to remain confidential. Signed by the foreign ministers in Moscow was a joint land grab across Eastern Europe and the Baltics. Poland was to be divided up with Russia moving in from the east and the German military from the west. Hitler had agreed to Latvia, Estonia, Lithuania and Finland coming under Soviet control. Britain's prime minister, Neville Chamberlain, had again been hoodwinked, and this time by Stalin. The Emergency Powers (Defence) Act was urgently pushed through the British Parliament, and a week later war was declared on Germany.

There were further agreements. The German-Soviet Boundaries and Friendship Treaty was signed September 28 and another on January 10, 1941 relating to the so-called Suwalki Strip, a narrow strip of land on the Lithuanian/German border. For the land, Stalin had agreed to compensate Germany the sum of $7.5 million or Reichsmark 31.5 million in a staged payment of non-ferrous metal and gold equivalent. In telegrams marked 'most urgent' from Ribbentrop to German ministers in Kaunas, Tallinn, Riga and Helsinki, the foreign minister urged strict secrecy over the actual delineation of spheres of interest in Eastern Europe.[218]

For decades after the war, copies of the Secret Protocols that did emerge were denounced as fakes by the Soviets. Only in 1988 as communism collapsed throughout Eastern Europe did Moscow even acknowledge their existence. The originals of the Molotov-Ribbentrop Pact and further agreements, with the protocols, have never been located in the Russian archives. That is the official line. On the German side, much of the Foreign Ministry archives fell into Allied hands in the closing stages of the war and in the months thereafter. A specialised British and American team of investigators was tasked with the capture and filming of all Third Reich documents.[219] Originals of the pacts between the Soviet Union and Germany were not among them.

Before its imminent defeat, Germany took steps to protect its secrets including the signed pacts with Molotov. Government buildings were systematically ransacked in Berlin and transported to Czechoslovakia with Prague still under SS and Gestapo control. One such episode is worth recalling, as it has never been made public.

A convoy of 11 trucks from Berlin reached the Czech capital on May 2, 1945, and was met by an 18-man SS technical unit under the command of General Heinrich Klein. Another Berlin consignment was expected the next day, this time by plane.

Two Junkers 52 transports and the single Messerschmitt 109 escort were amongst the last aircraft to take off from Gatow airfield in the German capital. Initially the crews were briefed that Madrid, the main routing for cargoes for Argentina, was the destination but deteriorating weather and enemy attacks over Berlin delayed the departure and orders were amended.

Loaded aboard were crates from the Berlin ministries, including the foreign ministry, and the Kaiser Wilhelm institutes in the Dahlem suburb that before the war was so favoured by ambassadors. Through haste, the crates were left unsealed. Included in the Kaiser Wilhelm Institute for Biology crates were details of the medical experiments conducted by the infamous SS doctors at Auschwitz and other camps. Safes and archives from the Kaiser Wilhelm Institute for Chemistry and Kaiser Wilhelm Institute for Physics German were

---

[218] The Molotov-Ribbentrop Pact: Copies of the agreements, the secret protocols and Ribbentrop's telegrams, with some English translation from the German and Russian, are available in the *Lithuanian Quarterly Journal of Arts and Sciences*, vol. 35, No.1, Spring 1989.

[219] In June 1946, the British Foreign Office and the US State Department agreed to jointly publish the captured documents located in the Reich Chancellery and the German Foreign Ministry. The French joined the project in April 1947. The archives of the Foreign Ministry came into Anglo-US custody chiefly through the incomplete execution of Nazi orders to destroy the most important documents. In April 1945, the Americans discovered more than 300 tons of papers in storage jars in the Harz Mountains. Other archives were located in Thuringia. All captured documents and archives were first assembled in Marburg Castle, then moved to Berlin and in the summer of 1948 were removed to Britain. The dispersal of German Foreign Ministry archives had begun in 1943 given the increasing intensity of Allied air attacks. As well as the Harz and Thuringia archives, other documents were found in Kkrummhubel, a resort in the Riesengebirge, and Lake Constance.

emptied. Chemical warfare research dating back to WW1 was packed away as were documents relating to nuclear fission. Some personnel records of nuclear physicists involved in atomic bomb development were missed and I was allowed to view them.

The three aircraft flew low and penetrated the Czech border, but Soviet fighters picked them up and the ME-109 was hit and it crashed. An anxious Klein and his SS unit waited at the airfield. Circling twice over the bumpy airstrip the Junkers' landed safely. During the night the aircraft were dismantled and buried in pits dug out by commandeered tractors. Ever the perfectionist, Klein left behind no evidence.

By morning Klein's men had loaded the 400 crates from the two Berlin deliveries onto trucks, but he told no one of the final destination apart from his driver and trusted SS sergeant, Hans Lauber. The convoy moved off to the south of Prague, to the heavily wooded area of Stelhovic, a two-hour drive, and unloaded in a clearing. A platform was constructed with quick-setting cement and large drums were heated up to melt tar for the sealing of the crates.

That smell of molten tar wafted through the woods and a curious young Czech girl hid in the undergrowth observing the activity. It was only when shots rang out that she ran home, terrified, and told her mother who banned the girl from ever mentioning what she had witnessed. After the war she would settle down in Bavaria in southern Germany, abiding to the wishes of her mother and wary that the long arm of the Nazis could still harm her.

For what seemed like hours she had watched Klein and his unit struggle to manhandle the heavy crates into a tunnel dug out of the rock by SS engineers some weeks earlier. The task completed, Lauber, Klein and his driver mercilessly turned their guns on their SS colleagues, their bodies left inside the tunnel that was sealed.

Red Army tanks entered Prague on May 9 and with no escape all captured SS were interrogated by the NKGB.[220] Rumours abounded about stashes of Reichsbank gold outside Prague and special teams scoured potential sites but nothing was found. Klein never broke under interrogation, despite the torture; nor did Lauber. A young Czech intelligence officer, Helmut Gaensel, was covertly placed into Klein's cell in an attempt to induce the location. Klein was deeply suspicious of his new cellmate. Over the weeks they did bond, yet Klein never disclosed the location of his tunnel in Stelhovic.

Most German and other Axis PoWs imprisoned throughout the USSR were repatriated between 1952 and 1955 but the Russians and the Czechs held onto the survivors of the SS technical group held in Valdice jail, the former monastery 100-km north of Prague. Gaensel[221] remained involved but it was eventually decided that Czech Intelligence – the StB – would barter the SS men for money. Effectively a demand for ransom, Gaensel travelled to West Germany to arrange the transactions clandestinely, meeting up with several groups that organised both cover and a safe refuge for those evading capture by the Allies. Klein was the last to be bartered but not without final attempts made by the Czechs and the KGB to persuade him to reveal the locations of Berlin's last two consignments, which included the originals of the Molotov-Ribbentrop Pact.[222] Remaining in Valdice jail until 1968, Klein was eventually bartered for DM 250,000 and he left for Germany still concealing his secret. Gaensel arranged the transaction.

The US deflects blame onto the neutrals

Moscow bartered non-disclosure of the Secret Protocols at Nuremberg by agreeing not to raise US corporate activity with the Third Reich regime and the role of the Wallenberg family. Wrote Serov:

---

[220] By this stage of the war, the NKVD had changed its name to NKGB.

[221] **Gaensel, Helmut**: Leaving the Czech Intelligence Service and through his German contacts, he funded a mining company in Bolivia, with Klaus Barbie as his partner. Gaensel was eventually wanted by the US authorities and barred entry. In the 1990s he was wanted by the South African authorities over an operation to smuggle uranium out of the country. I met him several times.

[222] Gaensel was convinced the two consignments had been buried in the woods in Stelhovic outside Prague. The KGB ran several investigations in the area post-war, all unsuccessful. There were hopes that the lost Amber Room had been crated in these last consignments. In Gaensel's excavation at Stelhovic in 1990, a large concrete slab was uncovered that bore tar marks, but the sealed tunnel entrance wasn't discovered.

In exchange, we could not raise the issue of the financial ties that existed between the United States and Hitler's industrialists arranged with the help of the Wallenberg family, and the secret contacts that had taken place on negotiating a separate peace treaty with the Germans.

In the early years of the Cold War, the US used all its resources to keep a lid on that collaboration by conveniently deflecting any accusation onto the wartime activities of the European neutrals: Sweden, Switzerland, Portugal, Spain and Turkey. These five, argued Dean Acheson, the US assistant secretary of state from 1941 until 1945, had scuppered American and British economic warfare efforts against the enemy.

Allied relations with Sweden and Switzerland had been tricky. Pilots were briefed that if downed, they should try and head for occupied Denmark where resistance groups were primed to spirit them to Sweden, where British Mosquito aircraft regularly flew low-level missions to return aircrew. Switzerland provided an alternative escape route if aircrew could get to its borders.

That compliancy was overshadowed by Allied anger that Sweden and Switzerland actively traded with the Nazis. The Wallenberg family owned SKF, the largest ball bearing manufacturing company in Europe, and discussions on ending the supply to the Nazis had come to nothing. There was further resentment with the Swiss, which supplied industrial diamonds that were vital components in proximity fuses for missiles.

To shore up Britain's own military requirements for ball bearings, in the early years of the war fast British motor torpedo boats (MTBs) shipped cargoes between Sweden and Britain. With the advent of the Mosquito aircraft, a squadron owned by the British Overseas Airways Corporation replaced the MTBs. The Mosquito bomb bays were adapted for both ball bearing cargo and passengers.

Outside its Swedish facilities, SKF had factories in Schweinfurt, Germany, Norway and a plant in Philadelphia in the US. Stockholms Enskilda Banken was naturally the house-bank for the company. An American bombing raid on Schweinfurt resulted in the loss of 60 Flying Fortress aircraft, one of the USAAF's largest operational losses during the war. That news went down badly in the US as newspapers channelled the increasing irritation that the Allies hadn't brought the European neutrals to heel.

The Allied diatribe with SKF and the Wallenberg family had been in secret but Moscow, too, had an interest. Serov in his memoir disclosed the ongoing NKVD surveillance, specifically mentioning that one of Raoul Wallenberg's uncles had been observed in Pskov, in occupied Russia, meeting the Abwehr. The long-entrenched Wallenberg link with holding entities in Switzerland cloaked much of the family's trade with the Axis powers.

Oil shipments to Sweden from the US were reduced to a trickle by September 1942 given the persistent suspicion that some of this fuel was being re-exported to Germany for cash and subsequently utilised by the Third Reich to pay for Swedish ore and ball bearings. The Swedish government bitterly protested to Washington complaining that as its own military was so starved of fuel it could never defend itself against a German invasion.

Despite being in the forefront of shale oil and lubricant technology, Sweden's shale oil plant at Kvantorp proved insufficient to satisfy demand. US oil imports filled the imbalance. Sweden invested in a new plant at Kinnekulle that produced high-quality lubricants and transformer oils after research had confirmed that the addition of stabilisers enabled shale gasoline to be stored for long periods. The further innovation of coating the steel storage containers with synthetic resin to reduce the level of corrosion was another technological advance. Kvantorp and Kinnekulle regularly hosted visits for German scientists and fuel technicians.

Washington eventually caved in to the relentless Swedish political clamour, with the sanctions reversed and two oil tankers returned to ply the route. There was a condition: Sweden had to immediately end German troop movements across its territory to Norway. It took almost a year for the recalcitrant Swedes to sign up to those terms in October 1943 but in practice that condition was ignored and the transit persisted.

Swedish exports of charcoal and iron ore to the Third Reich created further hostility. Charcoal output in Sweden had doubled in less than five years as producer-gas vehicles proliferated around Europe, given the wartime conditions. With RAF and USAAF bombing of the German synthetic fuel plants the shortfall in oil grades grew more chronic. The Luftwaffe was often grounded by the lack of high octane. The withdrawal of Rumania from the war with the resulting loss of the Ploesti oil fields worsened the German position. Swedish charcoal had become even more vital.

With the Allies encountering stiff opposition in France in August 1944, Washington and London refused to accept further Swedish excuses over the SKF trade. SKF mitigated that it had already restricted ball bearing sales to Germany by a quarter of the contracted orders, but no one believed a word. In a desperate ploy to placate the Allies, Sweden declared it would close the Bothnian transit route to Finland, all insurance would be withdrawn on Swedish ships that entered German ports and its Baltic Sea ports would be closed to German shipping. The Wallenberg-family trade with the Third Reich persisted as usual.

Allied negotiations fared no better with Spain and Portugal, two other neutral traders with Germany. Oil sanctions were threatened. The Iberian peninsular held 95% of Europe's annual output of wolfram – a tungsten ore – with Portugal the major producer and despite it being a long-term ally of the British its government capitalised on the European war. Wolfram prices were capped to all buyers but competitive German buyers used plundered funds held in Swiss bank accounts to bulk-buy at any price.

In the early years of the war the British had taken a soft approach towards Spain and its wolfram trade, given the vulnerability of Gibraltar and Franco's links with Germany. As the probability of a land-based attack on the peninsula lessened, the US took a more positive tack by banning all oil shipments. Franco subsequently proved responsive, as did the Turks who exported chromium to the munitions industries in the German Ruhr.

Switzerland had no intention of buckling to Allied pressure as German traders dealt openly for diamonds and Swiss-made precision instruments and munitions. Arm-twisting did have limited success in August 1944 with the Swiss imposing a ceiling on some of the trades. The Simplon Pass was prohibited to German transit traffic but volume was merely stepped up through the Gotthard. Only in April 1945 did the Swiss ban all trade with Germany, a mere gesture as within weeks the Third Reich was finished.

Sweden, Switzerland, Spain, Portugal and Turkey had enjoyed a profitable war.

Safehaven reveals America's dirty hands

A researcher from the World Jewish Congress in 1996 prized open the doors to what had been kept secret in *Operation Safehaven* for five decades. Not only did this extraordinary archive cast more detail on the business dealings of the neutrals, it shed further light on corporate America's collaboration. The disclosures were a national embarrassment.

Safehaven had its genesis in May 1944 as the US Department of State and the Treasury decided that an interagency unit should track down and block the transit of German assets in neutral and Nazi-sympathetic countries in Europe to South America. With an expected Allied victory, Henry Morgenthau, the Treasury secretary, wanted to dismember the German state, destroy any remaining industry and render the country feudal and agrarian. The Foreign Economic Administration (FEA) established the mechanics for *Safehaven* and in August secret directives were dispatched to relevant US embassies and legations on implementation.

From the outset, stated the CIA in a report written years later,[223] *Safehaven* was poorly conceived. Between the FEA, the State Department and the Treasury there were interminable rows on which government department should control it and stupidly, the OSS was excluded. As a bystander, the bemused OSS shook its collective head in disbelief, as it alone was the only capable agency with effective intelligence resources. Reality only prevailed in November 1944 with the OSS confirmed as lead agency for *Safehaven* with its specialist X-2 and SI (Special Intelligence) units in control, which already monitored the flow of Third Reich assets to countries abroad. Adding to the general rancour was the State Department's objection

---

[223] *The OSS and Project Safehaven: Tracking Nazi Gold*, Central Intelligence Agency. Donald P. Steury, a Californian-based CIA officer, wrote a major report on the documents based on the OSS reports in its archives.

to Morgenthau's plan that the German economy should be plunged back into the Stone Age, arguing that Germany must be propped up politically, economically and militarily as a post-war buffer against the Soviet Union.

Safehaven material flowed by early 1945 but not without dogged interference. Carlton Hayes, the US ambassador in Spain, prohibited X-2 agents from operating out of the building. The agents went ahead anyway, documenting currency transfers and compiling weekly Spanish export statistics to Germany of everything from orange juice, wolfram to steel rails. Photographs were obtained of German aircraft using Spanish airfields and U-boats in the ports. Spain, reported X-2, was a major German hideout with 50 Spanish firms covertly in league with German companies and 3,000 German agents operating throughout the country. In November 1940, Franco's foreign minister, Ramon Serano Suner, had signed a secret protocol becoming an 'adherent' to the Tripartite Pact signed on September 27, 1940 by Germany, Italy and Japan, agreeing to enter the war at a later date.

Across the border, in Portugal, one joint Allied covert operation was a spectacular success with Britain's MI6 gaining access to enemy safe-deposit boxes in every bank in the country. By the end of the war, MI6 and X-2 had details on 1,900 enemy agents in the country and 200 state officials who collaborated.

Most *Safehaven* resources were allocated to Sweden and one covert operation monitored the Stockholm-based trade in looted diamonds from Antwerp, run by a ring of German traders that the Swedish government appeared reluctant to ban. Other operations maintained surveillance on the Wallenbergs' and X-2 hacked into Stockholms Enskilda Banken that revealed that between May 1940 and June 1941, transactions between the bank and the German Reichsbank totalled $4.5 million. Stockholms Enskilda Banken had also acted on behalf of the Reichsbank in purchasing German bonds and securities in New York, transactions hidden by using a US relationship bank and nominee names.

The *Safehaven* files further nailed the myth of Swiss neutrality. X-2, working closely with Britain's MI6, estimated that the value of German gold moved into the Swiss banking system was $785 million at the-then price value. Of that total, $579 million had been looted. Intercepted cipher traffic confirmed that on one occasion the Swiss had received a looted gold deposit worth Sfr378 million from the Belgian central bank. This consignment had first been deposited by the Belgians with the Bank of France for safekeeping before the May 1939 invasion by Germany but after the French surrender, the compliant Vichy government had turned it over to the Reichsbank.

Complementing the work of *Safehaven* was the Harley Kilgore commission in the US that had begun its own work in June 1945. The senator for Virginia, with his small team, gathered overwhelming evidence of Swiss bank culpability in the German deposit of confiscated assets from Europe's Jewry.

The western Allies took the view that despite Switzerland's support of a regime that had slaughtered millions in the death camps, a blanket of secrecy should be drawn over its wartime dealings. That amnesia came with a hefty price, financial compensation. The Swiss government baulked and renegotiated but in May 1946 the Allies settled for $58 million, plus a half share in the liquidation of all German assets held in Switzerland. Compensating the victims of the Holocaust only came in 1996 after the release of the *Safehaven* documents. Within a year, a $1.25 billion total settlement had been agreed but victims or victim families had to jump through the legal hoops imposed by the Swiss authorities and provide definitive evidence of theft of assets to stake a claim. In many cases ownership couldn't be proved, and the thieved assets remained in the Swiss banking system.

Wall Street names were in the frame. Chase Manhattan Bank and JP Morgan had arranged correspondent banking transactions in the US for the Reichsbank, Deutsche Bank, Dresdner Bank and others. Dresdner had a significant wartime role by taking over and managing key banks in the occupied territories.

Corporate America felt the heat of exposure. Ford and General Motors, whose German subsidiaries, Ford Werke and Opel, had adapted their manufacturing lines to accommodate military vehicle production, resorted to the courts to attempt to show they hadn't profited from their links to the Third Reich. Other household names such as IBM, through its Dehomag subsidiary, had leased accounting equipment to German ministries, and conveniently disguised its ultimate ownership behind a holding company based in Switzerland. International Telephone and Telegraph (ITT), the giant Standard Oil, and DuPont feebly declared that their respective subsidiaries had not aided the war effort. DuPont could never hide its relationship with the notorious IG Farben, the manufacturer of the poison gas used in the death camps.

Further charges accused corporate America of entering into a multitude of patent agreements with German firms on processes such as synthetic rubber, beryllium, tungsten carbide, optical glass and plastics. With the war in Europe nearing its conclusion, the US had been desperate to enhance its global industrial supremacy. Britain, too, had skeletons in the corporate cupboard: had several international subsidiaries of two major household names operated against the country's wartime interest?

Condemnation was aimed at two US lawyers, brothers, who had built lucrative reputations on establishing pre-war European interests for corporate America with a well-trodden legal framework of Swiss-based ownership. John Foster Dulles after the war became the secretary of state in the Eisenhower administration and his brother, Allen Welsh Dulles,[224] a partner in the US law firm Sullivan & Cromwell, moved into intelligence, to head the Central Intelligence Agency. Sullivan & Cromwell has never admitted any responsibility for its Swiss dealings.

A further embarrassment was Thomas McKittrick's role as president of the disgraced Swiss-based Bank for International Settlements (BIS). His links with Germany stretched back to 1931 when he served on the German Credits Arbitration Committee. Upon the outbreak of war, the meetings of BIS governors were suspended but it continued to operate under Swiss law with executives from both Allied and Axis powers. The German Reichsbank, however, dominated the bank's day-to-day operations.

Founded in 1930 to regulate and monitor Germany's WW1 reparations – a futile exercise given it persistently refused to pay – the BIS had openly colluded with the Swiss financial system to shield Nazi gold and currency loot. In July 1944, at the Bretton Woods Conference to formalise the establishment of a post-war UN, there were calls to liquidate the bank but it remained to carry a permanent stain on its past. Only in the 1990s did the BIS begrudgingly divulge, that during the war, the bank had melted down looted gold shipped to it by German intermediaries. It would only admit, however, to receiving bullion from the Belgian and Dutch central banks and restamping it with pre-war markings to disguise the origins. The Union Bank of Switzerland and Credit Suisse admitted their role in the receipt of stolen loot.

The US has never disclosed whether McKittrick might have been a back-channel source for Nazi Germany.

When the trial concluded

What had Wallenberg disclosed to Likhachev and the other members of the Smersh team of Lubyanka interrogators? Sadly, Serov doesn't enlarge but *'evidence extracted'* might have proved damning for the Wallenberg family and the US on collaboration with the Third Reich.

> *From the reports of Dobrohotov and Fedotov, it became clear that Stalin and Molotov had planned to use evidence extracted from the interrogation of Wallenberg for secret negotiations with the Americans on issues not to be raised at the Nuremberg trials.*

The horse-trading on the 'Red Lines' had been bitter. Stalin's secret protocols and his war crimes were left unsaid as agreed with the Americans. It would take another 50 years before Boris Yeltsin admitted state culpability for the slaying of Polish PoWs, an admission that surprised very few. On its part, the Soviet Union had accepted that corporate America could bury its Nazi collaboration. At the end of the war, the Truman administration could never have survived the scandal. That, too, would take a half-century before disclosure with the American authorities reluctantly allowing access to the sensitive files. Sweden's connivance with the Axis powers had also avoided

---

[224] **Dulles, Allen Welsh**: CIA director February 1953 to November 1961.

scrutiny, as had the Swiss banking system. There was to be no admission that it had willingly accepted deposits looted from the occupied central banks of Europe and dispossessed Jews. Those Swiss banks fully deserved the wrath when it came in 1996.

Raoul Wallenberg had a political value at Nuremberg, as a leveraged pawn. Serov explained what triggered his liquidation once the trial concluded.

> At the ending of the Nuremberg trials Raoul Wallenberg had lost his validity and his usefulness to us. On the orders of Molotov and Abakumov, the Soviet Ministry of Foreign Affairs hinted to the Swedes that Wallenberg could be exchanged for the return of Soviet traitors who had escaped to Sweden. These proposals yielded no results.

According to Serov, Sweden could have successfully had its man returned if it traded like the Swiss whose two diplomats, Max Meier and Harald Feller, were released in January 1946 in Berlin. They had been taken in Budapest in February 1945 and held first in the Lubyanka and then Lefortovo. At first the Soviets wanted to barter them for six defectors living in Switzerland, but after that exchange was rejected a financial proposal was agreed. For Wallenberg, Molotov demanded an exchange for Soviet defectors living in Sweden and policemen from the Baltic States who had been willing collaborators in the German killing machine. The Swedish government declined to co-operate.

Fedotov had been Serov's prime source on Nuremberg with his first-hand knowledge. He had first ingratiated himself with Stalin and Molotov when his NKVD agents had thwarted an audacious Abwehr operation to wipe out the Allied leaders during the Teheran conference in November–December 1943. For that action, Fedotov was awarded the *Order of Kutuzov 1st Class* and the prestigious *Order of the Red Banner*. Promotion soon followed as Fedotov replaced Fitin as the head of NKVD foreign intelligence, a position he held until becoming deputy minister for state security.[225] Serov never discloses

---

[225] Fedotov was replaced in September 1946 by Sergei Savchenko, the wartime head of the NKVD in the Ukraine.

whether Fedotov might have been party to the decision to liquidate Wallenberg.

Not just Wallenberg was deemed dispensable, according to Serov.

Molotov then raised the issue of liquidating Wallenberg as well as American, German, Japanese and other foreign citizens detained by us after the war.

In his cell in Lefortovo in Moscow, Wallenberg had been abandoned by his government, maybe even by his family whose reputation had been left intact by the Nuremberg bartering. With the onset of the Truman Doctrine and US approval in March 1947 to grant $400 million in military aid to Greece and Turkey to combat communist-led insurgencies, the Cold War suddenly grew colder.

Stalin endorsed Molotov's proposal, believing that there was no reason now to return Wallenberg to Sweden.

Wallenberg's fate was sealed.

14

The investigation
– Identifying the liquidator

The documents in the Wallenberg file included the report by the prison doctor, the statement signed by the head of the internal prison, Mironov, and the commandant of the Kommandatura of the MGB, Blokhin.

It confirmed Wallenberg's death in 1947.

My officers subsequently questioned Blokhin. He stated that neither he nor any of his officers had a connection with Wallenberg's liquidation. He didn't even recall the episode.

We then questioned members of the special department within the MGB that had dealt with toxins and the use of such poisons at that time, including its head, Zhelezov, and his officers, Naumov and Smiakov on the events of 1946-47. They had liquidated a number of foreign citizens in the Lubyanka, Vladimir prison and in the PoW camp in Krasnogorsk.[226] However, all three men were unaware of the names of their victims.

Extracts from Ivan Serov's memoir

ANY DEATH OF AN INMATE in the Lubyanka's internal prison required certification. The head of its medical services signed off the death certificate, the prison director, Colonel Aleksandr Mironov, and the head of the Kommandatura, Lt. General Vasily Blokhin, had completed another. When Serov began his investigation in December 1953, both Mironov and Blokhin were still in post. Blokhin was an obvious candidate as Wallenberg's liquidator, but the scientists from Laboratory X, an establishment that researched into toxins and under the remit of the MGB, may equally have been culpable. Serov had first-hand knowledge of both.

Mironov, the prison director, had for 30 years served in the prison service. Privy to many of the darkest secrets of the Stalin regime, Mironov was a thug. Wallenberg probably experienced the sharp end of his methods.

Eschewing the family tradition of farm labouring, Mironov had joined the VChK,[227] Russia's fledgling security service, in 1921, with civil war raging across the new Bolshevik state. He became a warder in the internal prison of the Lubyanka, part of the growing security complex that was now expanding into adjoining properties. Notoriety and terror stalked the prison corridors, now crammed with White Army officers. As the VChk later reformed into the OGPU and then the NKVD, Mironov, now a senior warder, was fast gaining a reputation for his brutality.

The cells bulged again as the Great Terror unfolded, orchestrated by NKVD chief, Nikolai Yezhov, enveloping every political and social class. Promoted to second lieutenant, the reliable Mironov became a duty assistant to the prison director and he began what would develop into his time-honoured custom of personally escorting prisoners to their trials, including those prosecuted in the show trials. The first was in in August 1936 when Grigory Zinoviev[228] and Lev Kamenev, two original members of Lenin's Politburo, were sentenced and duly shot. The second, the following year, saw the defendants accused of scheming with Leon Trotsky against the state.

The internal prison director had two deputies and four duty assistants. Prison guards totalled 175. Other staff comprised of five handling admin and admissions, two worked in accounts, 11 in the medical section and five were involved in prison maintenance. Given the arduous hours, a nearby apartment block in Bolshoi

---

[226] Camp No. 27, Krasnogorsk, was essentially a group of three camps on the northwest border of Moscow. The NKVD ran it from 1942 to hold PoWs. It closed down in 1950.

[227] VChK: All-Russian Special Commission for Combating Counter-revolution and Sabotage.

[228] **Zinoviev, Grigory**: He was attributed as author of what became known as the 'Zinoviev Letter', encouraging a revolution in Britain – now widely regarded as a fake.

Komsomolsky Pereulok was requisitioned for senior staff, known as House No.5.

As Russia and Germany colluded over the dismemberment of Poland, followed by invasion from both east and west, an NKVD reception centre for Polish PoWs was established in the Orekhovo-Zuevo camp, some 50 km east of Moscow. In September 1939, Mironov, now a Captain, was made its head in the sifting of prisoners and transport to Moscow for interrogation. According to NKVD reports, Mironov excelled and two years later he returned to the Lubyanka as its prison director. The cell capacity expanded to 570 inmates and Mironov grew the staff count to 308.

During WW2, and in following years, the Lubyanka ran out of sufficient interrogation rooms so Mironov arranged a room in Lefortovo where Office No. 65 soon gained notoriety. Mironov hadn't held back here in the interrogation, in 1951, of Lt. General Mikhail Belkin, the MGB deputy chief. He was so badly thrashed that there was a genuine worry he wouldn't survive.[229] In the fictitious 'Doctors' Plot' in late 1952, just months before Stalin died, Mironov handed out similar beatings to the innocent defendants before their executions. The unfortunate director of Lefortovo, Lt. Colonel Durinov, two years later, also felt the brunt of Mironov's truncheon in Office No. 65 upon his own arrest. Mikhail Ryumin, the deputy head of the MGB, had led the interrogation, accompanied by two of his officers and Mironov. All four had waded in. Serov would have been very familiar with Mironov's methods.

Nearly two years after Serov completed his Wallenberg investigation, Mironov found himself under arrest and the charges were unclear. Serov, now head of the KGB, might well have issued the order. During his own interrogation, Mironov had to record his operational procedure in the Lubyanka. Under his watch, prisoners were shifted around the cells to prevent settling and to heighten anxiety. Cell informers were encouraged with the promise of better conditions. Some prisoners endured being handcuffed at all times and at night, they were ordered to sleep on their backs with their hands cuffed in the front. Mironov escaped execution and was pushed into an administrator job in a measuring equipment laboratory connected to the Russian Academy of Sciences. For the rest of his life he was remembered for his brutal regime as prison director.[230]

Killing in the Lubyanka

The steep concrete stairwell, known in the Lubyanka as the 'steps', led to the underground execution chamber. Stanley Lekarev, the KGB officer, who I knew well, shed some light on its use after an unexpected encounter. As a young intelligence officer, he had been tasked with the ongoing debriefing of the British spy, Kim Philby, who had defected to the Soviet Union in January 1963. Suspicion still remained that MI6 had engineered Philby's flight from Beirut. The job was tedious as several times a week, for four years, Lekarev visited Philby in his Moscow apartment to deliver questions and collect typed responses. Each answer had to be analysed and verified if possible from Lubyanka records before they were passed upwards, to the Central Committee and to relevant KGB heads of station. Lekarev picked over Philby's answers searching for inconsistences.

The questions were a mixture of the broad, such as British foreign policy, to the more defined with Philby instructed to name former colleagues and friends. Lekarev recalled to me that he had particularly probed into MI6's famed 'dead drop' operations and what he learned would stand him in good stead for his own intelligence career ahead.

Philby constantly asked for English-language books and British newspapers, which Lekarev provided as he did the supply of Red Label Johnnie Walker whisky, a rare commodity in Moscow. Whisky helped him to think, Philby had lamely explained. When the defector complained that his windows were draughty, Lekarev had them replaced.

That heavy drinking began to weigh on Philby's performance and for a week his typewriter became redundant. Philby demanded

---

[229] **Belkin, Lt General Mikhail Ilyich:** Wartime Smersh officer and head of counterintelligence in the Soviet Control Commission in Hungary 1945-1946, and deputy MGB head 1950-1951. Arrested in 1951, he was released in 1953. Died in 1956, aged 55.

[230] **Mironov, Col. Aleksandr Nikolayevich:** Born in the Volga region in 1896, he died in 1968, aged 72.

a holiday, in Czechoslovakia. Lekarev took advice and the request was refused. Any trip outside Russian borders offered danger, the KGB very mindful that a revengeful MI6 or the CIA might mount a hit. Philby wasn't to be put off and his request went higher. The entourage that did eventually tour Prague was almost comedic, Lekarev recalled to me. Philby acted the part of a senior Moscow official, chaperoned by Lekarev, three retired Czech intelligence officers and a photographer hired by the KGB to record the trip. In the hotel they stayed in, the staff fawned over such an important guest who was obviously British. The entourage visited the city's zoo and its churches, Philby professing to an interest in wood-crafted altars. That unique cine film of Philby's only venture outside Russian borders is now in my possession. Back in Moscow, Philby's spirit and humour improved immeasurably. Lekarev would later edit Philby's manuscript for *My Silent War*, published in 1968, much to Philby's annoyance.

To debrief efficiently, Lekarev had regular access to the operational files of the KGB's British desk, which with other archives were securely held in the Lubyanka basement. Each time he needed a file Lekarev completed a request, passing it through the tiny hatch to the surly woman behind. Some time later, the hatch would open and the file was pushed through, before it was slammed shut.

It was to locate a file that Lekarev took a wrong turn in the underground labyrinth and he found himself at the entrance to the Lubyanka's boiler room. What should have been an apologetic and brief greeting turned into a 30-minute illuminating conversation. The boiler man revealed that he was once a prison guard and often he was called upon to execute. That usually involved shooting a prisoner on the 'steps', in the nape of the neck, the victim toppling down the stairwell onto the concrete floor. A second bullet was often necessary, explained the boiler man. Lekarev left.

The butcher of Butovo and Kommunarka

Serov expected the name of Blokhin[231] to be on one of the death certificates in the Wallenberg file. Lt. General Vasily Blokhin still remained in post as the chief of the Kommandatura, the unit that arranged the logistics and internal security for all prisons managed by the security services. For 31 years, Blokhin's infamy as a state-sanctioned executioner had shielded him from the purges. His name was spoken only in whispers, even the Politburo feared him. Blokhin was also the scourge of the intelligence services and the Red Army.

That specialty for killing began in an OGPU spetsnaz (special forces) unit in 1923 and Blokhin's tally grew exponentially in Butovo, to the south of Moscow, as the Great Terror took its toll from 1936. Concealed behind rows of trees, the NKVD never did convince the local residents that the rifle range was just a mere training centre for the security services.

The Butovo body count piled up. In February 1938, there were 3,165 executions that month with 429 on February 21 alone. Victims were lined up on the banks of the long pits. Captain Blokhin, amongst others, moved along emptying their revolvers in a systematic slaughter.[232] The worst ever day at Butovo was August 17, that same year, with 502 victims shot. Eager to prevent messy brain parts from splattering his uniform, the NKVD's engineering workshop had manufactured for Blokhin a tailored killing wardrobe, a near copy of what was worn by Malyuta Skuratov, the mass murderer in the time of Ivan the Terrible. Arguably, Blokhin by the time his guns finally ceased spitting bullets in 1953, may have surpassed Skuratov in the number of victims. Blokhin resembled a butcher with his leather apron, cap, flared gloves extending up to his elbows and rubber boots.

He openly boasted that he always killed with an ordinary soldier's revolver that never misfired: a claim far divorced from reality. Two German-manufactured Walther pistols were Blokhin's preferred weapons and with his predilection for speed, he shot with both hands: a rapidity that caused the Walthers to overheat and jam.

An underground tunnel led from the front of the Lubyanka, across the large square to Nikolskaya Ulitsa 23, a building that housed the Military Collegium of the Supreme Court. Immediately after sentencing, the guilty were taken downstairs for immediate execution. Blokhin shot Yezhov and his NKVD deputy, Mikhail

---

[231] Vasily Blokhin in the latter part of his career. See photograph *[Moscow-39]*.
[232] Butovo killing ground. See photographs of the pits *[Moscow-40/41]*.

Frinovsky, in this basement on February 4, 1940. Frinovsky, the accomplished chess player and mountaineer, the leader of numerous NKVD team ascents, was the first and he brazenly faced off Blokhin before being forced to kneel. Reportedly, Blokhin grinned broadly as Yezhov was made to strip and grovel for mercy. No record exists of how many died here but estimates suggest as many as 40,000. Today, the building is retained by the FSB with Muscovites referring to it as Rasstrelny Dom, the 'Shooting House'. In the basement of No. 8, almost opposite No. 23, the skeletons of 34 victims were discovered during renovation in October 2007.

Another mass execution ground, this one nearby the modern high-rise headquarters of Gazprom, the oil and gas giant, in southwest Moscow, may have consumed 14,000 bodies into its soil. Kommunarka, in the 1930s, was a sprawling collective farm with its wooden dacha once used by Genrikh Yagoda, the notorious security chief. Ironically, Yagoda became the first to be shot and buried in Kommunarka in March 1938, executed on the orders of Stalin. Blokhin would have been responsible for some of the death count.

There is no execution record as to what had occurred in Sukhanovka. Today, this Gothic monastery in south Moscow is beautifully restored but when the NKVD converted it in 1938 to accommodate the Lubyanka and Lefortovo overflow, inmates were subjected to terrifying conditions. The NKVD referred to Sukhanovka as 'Special Object'.

Blokhin had excelled in the basement of the NKVD headquarters in Kalinin, now Tver, northwest of Moscow. The Smolensk office had coordinated the slaughter over six weeks between April and May in 1940. Blokhin, with two Kommandatura colleagues, arrived in Kalinin on April 4 with two suitcases, one containing his Walther pistols and rounds, the other had in it his killing garb and ear-protectors. The Central Committee, notably Stalin, Molotov and Kaganovich, had instructed Lt. General Vsevolod Merkulov to eradicate the very existence of three camps that held Polish PoWs. I have referred to the clearing of the Kozelsk camp in an early chapter as Colonel Kozyrev, Serov's investigator, had been involved in the Soviet cover up.

Ostashkov was the largest, with some 6,570 PoWs held in the

disused Nilov monastery[233] on the island of Stolobny, in Seliger Lake, to the north of the town that bore the camp's name. Every available transport was daily requisitioned to convey the Ostashkov PoWs to Kalinin. Batches were forced at gunpoint into the NKVD basement where a fully garbed Blokhin, with his colleagues, awaited in what would become the 'Red Corner' given the volume of blood slopping around the floor. On Blokhin's first day, 300 were dispatched with the bodies taken away to a forest in Yamok, north of Mednoye, where three excavators were on standby to dig the required 15-metre-wide trenches. Each night, with the guns silent, Blokhin and his colleagues retired to the well-provisioned NKVD dacha outside Kalinin to get drunk. At first light, the transports would come again. The killing ended on May 12: only 100 Ostashkov inmates had survived.

Three years after the Ostashkov butchery, Blokhin was promoted head of the Kommandatura, whose staff had now grown to 870. As the war ended, Blokhin liquidated many foreign prisoners held in the Moscow prisons, the greatest number in 1947.

Under Stalin, Blokhin was secure,[234] but on Stalin's death in March 1953 and the subsequent political scramble for power, this feared executioner was moved aside. Beria, the minister of state security, rolled the Kommandatura into the MVD, his power base. Forced retirement came in November 1954 and on Blokhin's exit from the Lubyanka, the relief felt was palpable with one officer sardonically commenting that 'he had murdered impeccably'.

Less than a year into drawing his pension, Blokhin committed suicide.[235] That was the official explanation. He knew he was living on borrowed time, a blood-soaked dinosaur in a new age with Khrushchev keen to publicly wash the country's hands of its past. Frequently drunk, Blokhin often shouted 'God, I am covered in so much blood!' Over his years in the Lubyanka there was a standing gibe amongst staff that many of Blokhin's victims lay in the pits at the Donskoye near 'the intersection of the two roads'. Yezhov, the

---

[233] Nilov monastery is again a religious centre.

[234] His many awards from Stalin had included the *Order of Lenin* and the *Red Banner of Labour.*

[235] Blokhin died February 3, 1955.

NKVD chief who Blokhin had dispatched, had declared in January 1937 that no burials at the Donskoye could ever be indicated and at the time of Blokhin's death that edict was still in force.

Sometime between December 1953 and March 1954, during the Serov investigation, Colonel Kozyrev interviewed Blokhin on the circumstances of Wallenberg's death. The outcome was unsatisfactory.

My officers subsequently questioned Blokhin. He stated that neither he nor any of his officers had a connection with Wallenberg's liquidation. He didn't even recall the episode.

The toxic killers

It is worth exploring the genesis of the 'Special Office', as Laboratory X was referred to after its birth in the fledgling Bolshevik state, and the facility's modern day development. Established by Lenin, the new Russian leader dispatched opponents that hadn't bought into his reformist vision. Stalin, within a year of his taking office after Lenin's death, ordered the death of Mikhail Frunze, the head of the Revolutionary Military Council, who died on the operating table after digesting poison. Vladimir Bekhterev, Stalin's eminent neurologist and medical advisor, was poisoned in 1927 after unwisely advising Stalin that he displayed classic symptoms of paranoia. Pyotr Wrangel, the exiled popular commander of the anti-Bolshevik White Army, was murdered the same year.

The intelligence service, the OGPU, lost several top officers. Vyacheslav Menzhiusky, its Polish chairman, died in agony in 1934. Friends of Stalin went the same way including Maxim Gorky, who often rounded on the harshness of the state. Fatally, he had returned from Italy in 1936: Stalin and Molotov were in the funeral procession. Regional leaders fell victim. Nestor Lakoba, the Abkhazian communist leader, ingested something toxic as he dined with Lavrenty Beria in Tbilisi, Georgia.

Further resources flowed into the 'Special Office' in 1938 and the odious Dr Grigori Maironovsky was recruited as chief scientist.[236] His early victims in Lefortovo included Marshal Vasily Blyukher, one of the most senior officers in the Red Army, and Lenin's widow,

Nadezhda Krupskaya. Almost certainly, Wallenberg encountered Dr Maironovsky on his arrival in the Lubyanka in early 1945. Maironovsky maintained meticulous records.

Jewish, Maironovsky was born in 1899 in the city of Batumi, in Kutaisi province, Georgia, his family running a restaurant. At school he showed academic promise earning income for the family by tutoring other pupils. Graduating in 1917 from high school, Maironovsky was admitted into the medical faculty at the university in Tbilisi, where he joined the Jewish revolutionary movement. Maironovsky became a member of the nationalistic Bund organisation before joining the communist party in 1920. That same year he moved to Baku as the head of an artisan's co-operative in the Azerbaijani Sovnarkhoz (Economic Council).

A medical position was offered in 1923 at the MGU Clinic No 2, with additional work in a sanatorium in Zheleznovodsk. Three years later, Maironovsky requested a transfer to Moscow and took up the position as manager in the outpatient medical department at the Livers factory. Furthering his interest in toxicology he grabbed the opportunity of a research position in the Bach Biochemical Institute in 1931, quickly moving on to the toxicology section at the eminent All-Union Institute of Experimental Medicine (VIEM).

Willfully trashing apparatus and research in his laboratory should have brought this budding toxicology career to an end during one crazy day in 1936. Maironovsky was fired and dismissed from the party in disgrace but after a short stint in the People's Commissariat for Health, the Chief Directorate of State Security (the GUGB) required his obvious talents.

As Laboratory X was then rolled into the NKVD's Fourth Directorate, Maironovsky worked closely with Lt. General Pavel Sudoplatov and Colonel Mikhail Filimonov, the latter wheedling out dissenters within the NKVD and handing them over to Maironovsky to medically torture. If Maironovsky didn't finish them off, Blokhin did.

After six years in post, Maironovsky was awarded his doctorate in

---

[236] **Maironovsky, Dr Grigori Moiseyvich**: See photograph *[Moscow-42]*.

February 1943, no one doubting any inability to defend his thesis: 'Interaction between pyrite and skin tissues'. Arsenic is a derivative from pyrite and the laboratory director had subjected Lubyanka prisoners to his experiments. A professorship followed that November with pathophysiology as his specialism – the change in physical and biochemical bodily functions. As a further reward, Maironovsky was promoted to Colonel in the Medical Service.

With foreign PoWs being rounded up by the NKVD and Smersh, Laboratory X subjected many to drug experimentation during interrogation, administering lethal doses when required. As Smersh was rolled into the NKGB in May 1946, Abakumov, its former chief, and now the minister of state security, shifted Maironovsky out to Laboratory No.1 in December as the engineer responsible for operational technology.

In December 1951, the MGB, whose ranks had suffered terribly at the hands of Maironovsky, finally nailed him with wide-ranging charges including spying for the Japanese, embezzlement, and the illegal storage at home of highly toxic substances. Thrown into Butyrka, other charges followed involving terrorism and murder. Surprisingly, the prosecutor would only hand down a 10-year jail sentence. After the arrest of Beria in June 1953, the MVD and MGB provided evidence to the prosecutor's office that Maironovsky had colluded with the disgraced security chief. The original sentence, however, stood. Maironovsky was now stripped of his degrees: the ultimate humiliation for a Russian scientist.

After three years in Butyrka and the Lubyanka, Maironovsky was moved on in July 1956 to Vladimir and further deprived of his Honoured Employee of the NKVD award. Vladimir is where he remained until his release in December 1961 but in March 1962 he was deprived of all remaining awards and medals.[237] There were conditions attached to his freedom. Maironovsky couldn't live in Moscow, or even close, and a position was found for him in the resort town of Makhachkala, in Dagestan, on the Caspian, as a scientist in the city's toxicology research institute. Travel outside Makhachkala was barred and it was here that a cardiac arrest ended his days, not a dissimilar death to many of Maironovsky's victims.

Khrushchev, on taking office shortly after Stalin's death in 1953, believed that Laboratory X must compete with the West on toxin development and stepped up the funding. Stefan Bandera, the Ukrainian nationalist whose relationship with the Nazi regime remains controversial to this day, fell dying in a Munich street in October 1959 after the KGB assassin, Bogdan Stashinsky, sprayed cyanide gas into his face. Stashinsky would later defect. With Serov in charge of the KGB, his officers in Mokryye Dela – Liquid Affairs – perfected their assassination techniques and had the choice of curare, cyanide, fentanyl and ricin in many forms. Russia's toxins technology was exported. The KGB's Ninth Directorate, the elite protection squad known as the 'Devyatka' was specifically trained in toxin detection. The Devyatka guarded government officials, visiting foreign politicians and dignitaries. One unit helped protect Egypt's President Nasser.

Hugh Gaitskell's sudden death in January 1963 bore all the hallmarks of a Soviet hit. This well-respected and ambitious head of the British Labour Party had the previous month accepted the London embassy's offer to personally collect his travel documents for a forthcoming trip to Moscow, at the invitation of Khrushchev. The Opposition leader never did make the trip as within days of that visit to the embassy he fell ill with a bad bout of flu. With his conditioning worsening, Gaitskell was admitted to hospital where a team of specialists failed to prevent the deterioration of his heart, lungs and kidneys.

In Moscow, *Pravda* reported the death and Khrushchev's reaction to being 'particularly grieved', despite Gaitskell's strident criticism of Soviet foreign policy. Harold Wilson, the shadow foreign secretary, was selected as the new party leader and Labour would win the General Election in October 1964. An autopsy had failed to determine how flu had devastated Gaitskell's organs to the extent they did. In the Porton Down laboratory, further tests led to the

---

[237] **Maironovsky, Dr Grigori**: Full listing of his awards and medals. Order of the Red Star (1944), Patriotic War Order 1st degree (1946), Badge of Honour (1943), For the Defence of Moscow (1944), Partisan of the Patriotic War 1st degree (1946), Honoured employee of NKVD (1940), Brigade Doctor (1940) and Colonel in the Medical Service (1943).

discovery that the flu symptoms had cloaked the more serious systemic variant *lupus erythematosus*, a disease rarely seen in Britain and then usually in women. British intelligence agencies made enquiries through its networks to determine whether Gaitskell had become another Laboratory X victim. The NKVD had first groomed Wilson during an official visit to Moscow in WW2 when he was the director of economics and statistics at the Ministry of Fuel and Power. As the president of the Board of Trade in the Atlee Labour government, in 1947 he had led the discussions with the Soviets in attempting to negotiate a settlement over the vexed and outstanding ownership question of the Ukrainian gold lying in the vault of a London bank.[238]

Suspicion of poisoning led to the exhumation of Yasser Arafat's remains in 2013 and polonium was subsequently discovered in the bones of the former Palestinian leader, who had died of a stroke resulting from organ failure in a French hospital in November 2004. Blame immediately fell on Israel's Mossad but a Russian hit shouldn't be ruled out. As the young chief of the PLO terrorist organization, which committed many outrages including the shooting of Israeli athletes at the Munich Olympic Games in 1972, Arafat was a KGB asset. According to my sources, his controller was Major Vasily Samoylenko and they met frequently.

A minute ricin pellet ejected from the tip of a specially manufactured umbrella did for Georgi Markov, the Bulgarian defector and BBC World Service broadcaster, on London's busy Waterloo Bridge in September 1978. Laboratory X had tested that umbrella for several months on Lubyanka prisoners awaiting execution with none lasting longer than two days. The umbrella was conveyed to the Bulgarian embassy in London. After the hit, the Bulgarian assassin left Britain within hours.

Alexander Litvinenko, the FSB defector, died in agony in a London hospital in 2006 through ingested polonium and his poisoning continues to test Anglo-Russian relations. His organs had deteriorated into an uncontrollable pulp. The assassin escaped back to Moscow but he left a chemical signature for Porton Down to uncover. Moscow is unforgiving on intelligence defectors and if they are tracked down, their days are numbered. Litvinenko never fully appreciated the danger of moving freely around London. He consulted for the research arm of a medium-size security firm that had several lucrative military contracts, including oil facility guarding in Iraq. Boris Berezovsky, who openly opposed the Putin regime, was an acquaintance. This Russian oligarch was found dead on a bathroom floor in the Ascot mansion belonging to his former wife. Berezovsky supposedly had tied one end of a cashmere scarf to the shower rail, the other around his neck. He jumped off the edge of the bath. At the Windsor inquest a year later, the Police believed that the cause of death in March 2013 was suicide by strangulation. The Coroner, however, felt he had no option but to declare an open verdict given the strength of the evidence against.

Since Russia embraced capitalism, businessmen and journalists have succumbed to the poisoners. On Moscow hotel staircases, sprays, concealed in newspapers, silently envelop the passing victim. Flu-like conditions develop and if the target is a foreign visitor only a visit to a cardiologist back home confirms a swollen pericardium, the membrane that surrounds the heart. Death follows within a week. Sitting in hotel armchairs offers further opportunity, with the chair arms sprayed. Toxins quickly pass into the palms of the hands. Once the target has gone, the assassin wipes all traces away. Spraying curtains in a hotel bedroom, so the target inhales the toxin during the night, is equally deadly. By morning the substance loses its venom but the damage is conclusive.

A curious report emerged from a GRU source into the fatal events at Moscow's Dubrovka Theatre in October 2002, as 50 Chechens held 850 theatregoers hostage. As the siege entered its second day, an aircraft landed at one of the airports and its plain-clothed British occupants were whisked away. Within hours, the

---

[238] A Ukrainian family, involved in an investment in the East India Company, deposited the gold at the Bank of England in 1858. Negotiations over ownership began with the Soviets in 1922 and the NKVD took over the case in 1937. The Russians never got the gold in 1947. Essentially, the British kept it as a part payment for wartime military aid. The British further received 750,000 tons of Soviet wheat at an abysmally low price. The Russians raised the question again in the 1950s and in 1967 with Wilson as prime minister. Margaret Thatcher in July 1986 was asked by Moscow to review the 1947 settlement. The gold remained in London.

nerve gas to temporarily overcome all in the theatre was pumped into the theatre's ventilation system. The Russian commander on the scene had mistakenly trebled the necessary dosage, leading to 180 deaths and television stations ran harrowing pictures of buses conveying rescued hostages to hospital, their eyes bulging and heads back in seizure. Frantic doctors demanded an antidote, or even the name of the gas, but from the security services no answers were forthcoming. According to the GRU source, the British slipped away home and the Russian media could only guess that fentanyl had been used. To this day, no details of the toxin have been admitted. Had the drug been of British manufacture?

In the final years of his career in Russian Intelligence, my good friend Stanley Lekarev ran annual KGB–FSB training courses for recently graduated intelligence officers from the central Asian republics and Palestine, and the day always given over to assassination techniques was a highlight for the delegates. The GRU invited Lekarev to lecture its officers after the bungling of the car-bomb assassination of Zelimkhan Yanderbiyev, a former president of Chechnya, in February 2004. Yanderbiyev died but the operation in Qatar had left clues that led to the arrest of three GRU officers still in the country.

Naumov, Smiakov and Zhelezov

Three members of Laboratory X, including the senior scientist, were most certainly in the frame for Serov in his Wallenberg investigation.

We then questioned members of the special department within the MGB that had dealt with toxins and the use of such poisons at that time, including its head, Zhelezov, and his officers, Naumov and Smiakov on the events of 1946-47. They had liquidated a number of foreign citizens in the Lubyanka, Vladimir prison and in the PoW camp in Krasnogorsk. However, all three men were unaware of the names of their victims.

Not knowing their victims was a collective lie, as Serov knew full well. Maironovsky from his cell in Butyrka had admitted that

Laboratory X had always maintained records. Dr Vasily Naumov had been the obvious choice to succeed Maironovsky as scientific director at Laboratory X and he was to be in post for many years. Stanley Lekarev, in his first intelligence assignment, after returning from Britain following a postgraduate year at Leeds University, studying English, had unexpectedly discovered Naumov was to be his new boss.

Under Serov, the KGB grew the number of scientific research centres under its control to 15 and Lekarev was none the wiser as to the activities of the building at 26, Gilyarovskogo – Scientific Research Laboratory No. 12 – when the unexpected assignment came through.[239] Lekarev had been tasked to use his language abilities at Laboratory X to translate English and German scientific papers and journals.

On his first day, Lekarev was introduced to Naumov who had a formidable reputation. To his staff, Naumov was courteous bordering on the shy, but in meetings in the Lubyanka and the Kremlin he fiercely resented any interference in the laboratory's day-to-day scientific management. Given his rank, Naumov had full use of a chauffeur-driven car enjoying every privilege befitting his status.

Women comprised more than half the scientific staff at the laboratory, the well-qualified daughters of the top apparatchiks and senior KGB officers, the majority educated at Schools 1-6, the reserved academies for the great and the good. Moscow State University then took only the very best. Mainly female scientists worked on perfecting what the KGB jokingly referred to as the 'Devil's Bullet', the term given to toxin camouflage that characterises many assassinations. If possible, the victims of MI6 assassinations in Eastern Europe – and there were several during the Cold War – were brought to Moscow for autopsy to discover how Britain's Porton Down laboratory was refining its techniques.

Scientific Research Laboratory No.12 experimented on purebred animals brought in from its farm, also under KGB control, in the southern outskirts of the city. Known simply as 'The Farm', animals

---

[239] The front gate of 26, Gilyarovskogo – Scientific Research Laboratory No. 12. See photograph [Moscow-43].

were also prepared for Scientific Research Laboratory No. 13 – the 'Virus Centre' – where scientists developed antidotes to viruses that Russia knew were available in the West. From his office overlooking the main gate of Laboratory X, Lekarev observed the almost daily arrival of animals. Both front and rear exits of the laboratory were guarded, and the scientists underwent security searches.

One floor was given over to the manufacture of specialised toxin-dispensing equipment. Lekarev recalled Vladimir, an engineer, a large man with ginger hair and awkward in his manner, yet an ingenious inventor in perfecting gadgets to silently inject toxins into targets. Vladimir enjoyed a long career in Laboratory X and is attributed with some of the best devices.

Still remaining hidden behind large rusting sliding gates and tall walls in Varsonof'evskiy Pereulok,[240] a street not far from the Lubyanka-3 building, is the medical room that was in use at the time of Wallenberg's incarceration in the Lubyanka and Lefortovo, and for some years afterwards. The entire building is now used by FSB counterintelligence.

Curious passers-by are encouraged to move on but beyond these gates is a large parking area and to the left, a ramp descends to an underground garage. Above this ramp is a room with a small window.[241] This was the 'Spetsialnie Laboratotornaya Kamera', the cell used by the scientists of Laboratory X that was strictly off limits to everyone without a special pass. Procedure required that all prisoners must first be submitted to a stringent medical examination and records were kept. Tellingly, this room was chosen over the garage so engine noise deadened the screams. In this cell, many foreign PoWs met their end by being given a lethal toxin. Was Wallenberg eliminated here in 1947? Maironovsky had already been transferred out of Laboratory X in December 1946, so Naumov or his deputy, Smiakov, would have administered the lethal dose.

Serov also interviewed Colonel Zhelezov, the administrator head of Scientific Research Laboratory No. 12. In Solzhenitsyn's memoirs there is a mention of an MGB colonel with that name. From my own research, Zhelezov had a range of MGB responsibilities, which included interrogation. He never believed in innocence, as he proved in 1945 when nine scientists and inventors arrived in Butyrka from prisons in Kazan and Sverdlovsk. Their charges were trumped up, of course, but to Zhelezov that was of no consequence.

The scientists included L.S. Termen, the renowned inventor who perfected a 50x50 cm television in the 1920s, which was way ahead in its time of anything in the West. Soviet intelligence had sent Termen to New York, where he worked as an engineer and in the 1930s, patented a device known as a 'Termenvox' and manufactured it. Recalled in 1939, he was arrested. In prison he worked as a prisoner-specialist, and he continued to invent. One device was a multi-wave band radio hidden in a table lamp, which became standard use for the NKVD. Litvinsky, the head of a Leningrad institute, engaged in working on radio-controlled devices for the NKVD was also worked over by Zhelezov, as was Berkalov, a former Lieutenant Colonel in the Tsarist army, and a specialist in artillery. Berkalov had railed against pre-war inaction in not increasing the production of anti-tank guns. Work did begin in 1937 but all members of his manufacturing and design team had been arrested and imprisoned.

As the administrative head of Laboratory X in 1947, Zhelezov would have been in the decision loop if his scientists had eliminated Wallenberg.

Timing of the liquidation

Two documents in the Committee of Information file, located by Serov, certified Wallenberg's death in 1947. Apart from the statement completed by Mironov and Blokhin, the medical certificate carried the signature of the head of the Lubyanka's medical services. Gromyko in his momentous announcement to the Swedes and the world in February 1957, had reported the death as July 17, 1947 and

---

[240] The fortified sliding gate of the former Scientific Research Laboratory No. 12 location in Varsonof'evskiy Pereulok, behind which is a large parking area and the killing room. See photograph *[Moscow-44]*.

[241] The ramp down to the underground garage with the small window above. That room was the killing room. A guard tried to prevent me from taking photographs. See photograph *[Moscow-45]*.

he named that Lubyanka doctor as Colonel Smoltsov.

Was the date in Wallenberg's file the same date as that announced by Gromyko? Frustratingly, Serov never spells out the day and month.

Gromyko had included two notes from Smoltsov, referring to the heart attack as the cause of death and an Abakumov instruction not to conduct an autopsy. Serov doesn't name the prison doctor in his memoir: was it Smoltsov? The son had recalled that his father had been dismissed as prison doctor in March 1947 on the grounds of poor health and was later recalled to the Lubyanka to sign Wallenberg's death certificate.

That surely poses the question on why Smoltov's replacement hadn't signed the certificate in July. Does this imply that Wallenberg was dealt with between January and March 1947 when Smoltsov was still in post, but for some reason the paperwork hadn't been completed at the time? Smoltsov died in May 1953, seven months before Serov and his people began their investigation.

It is worth repeating what Serov wrote over the timing as the military tribunal to prosecute the top Nazis had ended in October 1946.

> At the ending of the Nuremberg trials Raoul Wallenberg had lost his validity and his usefulness to us. On the orders of Molotov and Abakumov, the Soviet Ministry of Foreign Affairs hinted to the Swedes that Wallenberg could be exchanged for the return of Soviet traitors who had escaped to Sweden. These proposals yielded no results.
>
> Molotov then raised the issue of liquidating Wallenberg as well as American, German, Japanese and other foreign citizens detained by us after the war.
>
> Stalin endorsed Molotov's proposal, believing that there was no reason to return Wallenberg to Sweden.

Those 'hints' on an exchange by the Soviet Foreign Ministry would have extended several months and certainly into 1947 until they unsuccessfully concluded.

It is probably safe to assume that Serov had vetted the Gromyko statement given he was now chairman of the KGB and had his own unique knowledge of Wallenberg's death. If the Gromyko date had been fudged, what would have been the Soviet purpose? Unfortunately, the account recanted by Smoltsov's son on the timing of his father's dismissal must remain a loose end.

Three foreigners in Lefortovo had also been liquidated, disclosed Serov. One was Langfelder, the other two were the driver's cellmates who by association also had to die. The impression given in Serov's memoir is that they, with Wallenberg, had been dealt with at the same time. Moscow did admit to the Hungarian authorities that Langfelder had died in prison on March 2, 1948 – eight months after Wallenberg's death. That date can no longer be safe. Why would the Lefortovo victims be allowed an extension on their lives?

Serov couldn't ultimately nail the blame on any of the four contenders interviewed – Blokhin, Naumov, Smiakov and Zhelezov – no one fessed up. Serov was further hampered by the loss of Laboratory X records concerning Lubyanka prisoners. They had been lifted by an aide of Molotov and were probably destroyed in the cover up.

We could not establish in our investigation the precise details of Wallenberg's liquidation as well as the liquidation of three other foreigners who were connected to him. One was his driver, an Austrian or German, and the other two were cellmates of the driver.

Not disclosed in the memoir is whether Mironov, the director of the internal prison, had been interviewed as part of the investigation. Surely he would have known how Wallenberg had met his end? Evidence of Blokhin's possible culpability surfaced in December 2000 when the Russian State Prosecutor's Office, in a two-page statement, revealed that Vladimir Kryuchkov, the disgraced former chairman of the KGB,[242] had privately told colleagues that Wallenberg had been executed in the Lubyanka by shooting. Inevitable questions followed but back came the standard response

---

[242] **Kryuchkov, Vladimir Alexandrovich**: Appointed KGB chairman in 1988, he was dismissed in 1991 for leading the coup attempt against Gorbachev and publicly denouncing Perestroika. Jailed, he was released in 1994 and died November 26, 2007, aged 83.

that all records concerning Wallenberg had been lost or destroyed. Was this statement deliberately misleading? Blokhin may have been the culprit: one of the most prolific state-executioners in Russian history can never be discounted yet equally, Laboratory X had its own long dark history.

During my own investigation, I have been drawn to Krasnogorsk the PoW camp in the northwest of Moscow as Serov disclosed that he had prior knowledge that the scientists had killed here, as well as in the Lubyanka and Vladimir. In the files of the Swedish Foreign Office, there were reports of Wallenberg sightings in Krasnogorsk even if the dates don't tally with what we now know from the Serov memoir. It is telling, however, that in Mironov's death certificate for Willy Roedel, a cellmate of Wallenberg in the Lubyanka and Lefortovo, his death was supposedly during transit to Krasnogorsk in October 1947. He may have been executed because of his cell association and that date may well be false. Was there also an association between Wallenberg and Krasnogorsk in the Swede's final days?

There can be no certainties on who or what killed Wallenberg apart from the confirmation that Wallenberg did die sometime in 1947. In my belief, the scientists did for Wallenberg maybe in the 'Spetsialnie Laboratotornaya Kamera', the cell in Varsonof'evskiy Pereulok, a street not far from Lubyanka-3. In Lefortovo, Blokhin, or a fellow Kommandatura officer, shot Langfelder and his two cellmates, the names of whom we will never know. They were loose ends that needed tidying up. All four bodies were taken to the Donskoye for cremation, their ashes dumped into the pit. Blokhin, Mironov and the Lubyanka's doctor duly completed the necessary paperwork recording Wallenberg's death as a heart attack.

Chapter 15

The investigation –
Aftermath

*'Those scoundrels Stalin, Molotov and Vyshinsky stirred this dirty
soup and now we must drink and eat up this shit'.*

Extract from Ivan Serov's memoir

COLOURFUL WORDS from Serov, but this blistering
paroxysm is attributed to Nikita Khrushchev. A sense of
morality to learn the truth hadn't been the driver behind his
instruction to Ivan Serov to launch a secret investigation into who
ordered the liquidation of Raoul Wallenberg. Khrushchev, now
armed with Serov's conclusions, saw a window to exploit some sorely
needed political capital. Molotov, in particular, had long thwarted the
first secretary's economic ambitions and an accommodation with the
West. Wrote Serov:

> *Khrushchev wanted me to go into detail on the involvement of Molotov
> and Vyshinsky in Wallenberg's liquidation and he instructed me not to
> charge Abakumov or Abakumov's associates with his death. Khrushchev
> also wanted me to speak to Molotov and tell him that people in the
> West had serious intentions to bring up the disappearance of Wallenberg.*

This revelation by Serov utterly contradicted what he and his KGB
colleagues, in February 1957, would contrive for Andrei Gromyko,
the Soviet deputy foreign minister. Gromyko publicly heaped the
blame on Victor Abakumov, the minister of state security in 1947
and the Smersh chief when Wallenberg was lifted from Budapest in
January 1945. Abakumov could not answer for this particular crime.

At the time of Serov's investigation, Abakumov was languishing in jail, being investigated by Colonel Kozyrev, one of Serov's officers.

The aftermath – Vyshinsky

Vyshinsky's guilt is indubitable. The Foreign Ministry had been behind the initiative in 1947 to eliminate Wallenberg with other foreign PoWs held in the jails. Less than a month after Wallenberg was dealt with – if Gromyko's July date is to be believed – Vyshinsky, the deputy to Molotov in the Foreign Ministry contrived the note to Söhlman, the Swedish ambassador, denying that the diplomat was being held in the Soviet Union nor had any Soviet authority even heard of him.

Incredulity, shock, followed by downright anger had greeted the Vyshinsky statement that had completely contradicted the announcement to the Swedish Foreign Office on January 16, 1945 by Vladimir Dekanozov, the-then deputy foreign minister, that Wallenberg was in Soviet military custody after being encountered in Budapest. There had been a further assurance in February from Alexandra Kollontay, the Soviet ambassador in Stockholm, to Maj von Dardel, Wallenberg's mother, that her son was alive in the Soviet Union and being well treated.

Within days of Vyshinsky's delivery, the Wallenberg Committee in Stockholm had convened and the wretched Unden, the Swedish foreign minister, asked of the committee, 'Do you think Vyshinsky is lying?' An indignant *Dagens Nyheter* reminded its readers of Unden's miserable record in his handling of the Wallenberg affair with Vyshinsky and Molotov.

Lying and intimidation came easy for Vyshinsky, who had honed his legal skills as chief prosecutor in the show trials in the Great Purges between 1934 and 1938. He successfully prosecuted Stalin's political enemies including Grigory Zinoviev and Lev Kamenev, in what became known as the Trial of the Sixteen, in July 1936 on trumped up charges of acting against the state. In the gallery of the Military Collegium of the Supreme Court sat foreign observers and journalists, many impressed by Vyshinsky's biting interrogation and oratory, tempered by the sham moments of compassion and leniency. The long and deliberate lapses before each question were designed to draw in his audience, with the foreign press lapping up the drama. Closing speeches lasted hours and Vyshinsky was never short on invective, dotted with phrases such as 'mad dogs' and 'despicable rotten dregs of humanity', usually culminating in a demand for the death penalty. Each trial became a command performance.

In the trial of The 21 Communist Leaders in March 1938, Vyshinsky's courtroom mastery was again on full display. Nikolai Krestinsky, an old Bolshevik, member of the very first Soviet Politburo with Stalin, Trotsky and Kamenev, former ambassador to Berlin and an assistant minister in the Foreign Ministry, unexpectedly reversed his previous innocent plea to guilty. The court hushed at the implication. Vyshinsky had engineered the change, the previous evening. Now in the questioning of Christian Rakovsky, founder of *Pravda* and ambassador to France, this fellow defendant strongly denounced Krestinsky to be a Trotskyite, admitting to the existence of a letter Krestinsky had written to him.

Vyshinsky now waved that letter at the accused relishing the moment, and read it out aloud. Palpable, reported *The Times*, on the tension in court. Krestinsky had, of course, been worked over in his cell and he now solemnly confessed that the contents of the letter to Rakovsky were genuine. 'It was the letter of a Trotskyist written in the Trotskyist interest. I retracted my innocent plea under the influence of a painful feeling of shock at hearing the Act of Indictment being read. I said I was not guilty almost mechanically because I hadn't the strength to face world public opinion, but now I ask the court to understand my weakness, and I admit myself wholly guilty'. That retraction wouldn't be sufficient to save his life and he was shot on May 15. Rakovsky and two others would be spared, but jailed with hard labour. Rakovsky would finally have his date with an NKVD executioner, probably Blokhin, in 1941.

Having served as deputy to Molotov from 1940, Vyshinsky was promoted to foreign minister in March 1949 just months before Russia exploded its first atomic bomb at Semipalatinsk, in Kazakhstan. A medical problem in 1952 was a setback and he relinquished the post back to Molotov but after a short recovery he returned as Molotov's deputy and appointed the permanent UN representative for the USSR, so earning a formidable reputation.

Vyshinsky's death at the age of 71 through a heart attack was unexpected, despite evidence of a previous heart condition. On the evening of November 21, 1954, in New York, he had attended a cocktail party hosted by the French delegation, reportedly in fine form, drinking and making toasts. The following day he was to address the General Assembly and detail the Soviet position on the US nuclear initiative entitled 'Atoms for Peace'. After the party he declined to take his official car to Long Island to join his wife and daughter at the official Soviet residence, preferring instead to spend the night at the embassy in Park Avenue. Sometime that night 'his heart failed and he died the following morning,' according to the official Soviet statement. When the news reached the General Assembly every meeting that day adjourned in sympathy. Tribute came from 30 countries, including the UK and the US, the latter in its statement saying that 'We, who vigorously disagreed with him, respected his forensic talent'.

Born in 1883, in Odessa, into a Polish Catholic family, Vyshinsky's political career had spanned the Bolshevik Revolution in 1917 to just over a year after Stalin's death. He had been a writer, prosecutor, minister and diplomat. In his obituary in *The Times* on November 23, 1954, a figure of 5,000 deaths during the Great Terror and the purges was directly attributed to him in the name of the Soviet state.

Suspicions soon surfaced that Vyshinsky had been poisoned bringing on the heart attack. If he had been dealt with on the orders of Khrushchev, Serov was undoubtedly behind it.

The aftermath – Malenkov and Molotov

These bigger political beasts would prove implacable foes. Malenkov[245] had assumed the chairmanship of the Council of Ministers on Stalin's death and was expected to gain full control of the party, but Khrushchev had usurped him. That rivalry had intensified since 1949 when Stalin brought Khrushchev back from the Ukraine to reorganise the Moscow party organisation. Khrushchev dealt with Malenkov first, wrote Serov.

Khrushchev removed Malenkov in January 1955 from his post as Chairman of the Council of Ministers. Molotov's turn was soon to come.

Malenkov would be far from finished. Serov continues.

After the demotion of Malenkov it was Molotov's turn to be ousted from the Ministry of Foreign Affairs. I think that from the very beginning, Khrushchev used the case of Wallenberg against Molotov... Molotov understood the position very well and his attitude towards me was hostile, as he believed I was Khrushchev's man. At the session of the Presidium of the Communist Party of the Soviet Union in 1954, Molotov, together with Malenkov, spoke against my appointment as Chairman of the KGB. Both these two had wanted Shatalin,[246] the secretary of the Central Committee, to be the Chairman.

Serov explains that Khrushchev had left it to him to tackle Molotov. The following extract from what occurred in the Kremlin confirmed that the Foreign Ministry had no intention ever to come clean with the Swedes over the fate of Wallenberg.

I duly met Molotov in his office in the Kremlin. He very painfully reacted to my questions and said: 'Only idiots could hope to gain any profit from this case'.
Molotov went on to say that in no way should the Wallenberg case be used to re-establish confidential relations with the Swedish government. Angrily, he repeated to me that the issue was closed and would not be re-opened.
At the end of our meeting Molotov peered at me suspiciously and said: 'Why are you raising this matter now?'
I answered that that I was only fulfilling an order from the Central Committee.

---

[245] **Malenkov, Georgy**: See photograph *[Moscow-47]*.
[246] **Shatalin, Nikolai**: Upon Beria's arrest in 1953, he became first deputy in the ministry of internal affairs. Shatalin was ordered by Malenkov to announce the reasons behind Beria's arrest.

The backstory behind how Khrushchev, probably with Serov's help, did bring down Malenkov, Molotov, Kaganovich and other opponents within the Presidium, the inner body of the Politburo, is worth telling. It is an insight into Soviet political infighting.

The vultures were circling, sensing a finished corpse, as Khrushchev stood to address the 20th Congress of the CPSU in February 1956. The rapturous applause stunned the coterie of support for Molotov and Malenkov. Khrushchev weighed in against the old guard, soundly trashing Stalin's legacy and his carefully cultivated public image. He further took a swipe at the stooges who had aided the plotting and the role played by the security services in the terror. Molotov sat stony-faced, livid at the stooge accusations.

Under his watch, warned Khrushchev, mass arrests and executions were to be left in the Stalinist past. Why had Stalin ignored the warnings from Britain about a German invasion, Khrushchev roared? From the Ukraine under bombardment, he had warned Stalin by phone of the ferocity of the German assault and the urgent need to formulate a strong defence, advice contemptuously waved aside. Delegates were stunned at the masterly performance. With Serov watching his back, Khrushchev felt secure but the vultures still demanded a carcass.

In Moscow, the CIA station closely monitored the rival factions. 'Khrushchev's position was shaky', it reported to Washington, predicting that before the year was out the power battle would be conclusive. Khrushchev was under constant attack in the Politburo, accused of mishandling the uprising in Hungary.

As December ended, the CIA reported that the expected putsch had been postponed with Khrushchev actually bringing back Malenkov as an advisor. At the high-level meeting of satellite leaders in Budapest in the first week of January 1957, Malenkov accompanied him. Yet when Janos Kadar, Hungary's new post-revolution leader, visited Moscow on January 10, Malenkov was excluded from the talks: the truce with this nemesis at an end.

February marked the beginning of the showdown with Mikhail Pervukhin, the chairman of the state economic commission, presenting his growth targets at the three-day plenum. The CIA discounted the reported view that the plenum had been an orderly debate. Heated rows and accusations had dominated the proceedings, especially over Pervukhin's estimate that the rate of industrial output would fall to 7.1% during 1957, against 10.8% the previous year. Pervukhin placed the blame for the decline squarely on Khrushchev's reform of the industrial administrator system that had long preserved the inter-departmental barriers. Dismantling ministerial empires and dispatching industrial bureaucrats to all parts of the Soviet Union was indeed a major aim.

Malenkov and his supporters doggedly refused the proposals. Molotov had registered his own opposition by delivering a short note to his supporters at 3am on the eve of the plenum. These industrial administrators must not be deprived of their typical Moscow luxuries, Molotov had angrily argued. Pervukhin's forecast of falling output was allowed to stand.

After the plenum Khrushchev took the initiative. He sent congratulatory telegrams to agricultural workers and officials on their performance and he participated in the regional agricultural conferences. This propaganda exercise was widely reported in *Tass* and *Pravda*. Khrushchev went further. By the end of March, the first secretary of the party had prepared several theses on wide-ranging structural changes and he presented his plans to the Politburo. Elected chairman by the body to draft the required law, Khrushchev now felt the opposition had been outsmarted. Molotov and Malenkov had indeed been successfully sidelined, reported the CIA station to Washington.

The American news channel, CBS, interviewed Khrushchev shortly after a rousing speech in Leningrad in May, when he had boasted that his agricultural reforms would dramatically boost meat and dairy production. He even boasted that agricultural output per head in the Soviet Union would surpass comparative levels in the US. During the CBS interview, a group of Leningrad workers presented him with an achievement award. No Soviet leader since Stalin had received similar approbation.

This growing domestic and international acclaim deeply worried the managerial elite, who saw only further erosion of its established powerbase. Within a month of the CBS interview, the triumvirate of Malenkov, Molotov and Lazar Kaganovich launched the Anti-Party

Group: its aim to bring the leader down, reinstate Stalinism and the sprawling ministerial empires.

At the meeting of the Politburo on June 18, five members had joined the triumvirate including the influential Nikolay Bulganin and Dmitri Shepilov, the latter a surprise as he was closely identified with Khrushchev's foreign policy and was considered an ally. Voroshilov, the old Bolshevik, lent his support to the triumvirate but being senile his views were of little consequence.

By mid June, the triumvirate now enjoyed majority support within the Politburo. Khrushchev had been left very vulnerable with several of his supporters out of Moscow. Only two remained in the capital: Yekaterina Furtseva[247] and Leonid Brezhnev. The Anti-Party Group saw its chance.

Bulganin and Khrushchev had returned from talks in Finland on June 14 and were met at the airport by the triumvirate and other Anti-Party Group supporters, namely Anastas Mikoyan, Pervukhin and Maksim Saburov. Khrushchev called for an immediate full meeting of the Politburo to convene later that evening, which he deliberately delayed after he agreed to be interviewed in the Kremlin by a Japanese journalist. When it did begin, reported the CIA, 'the showdown began at once'. The first up was Malenkov who questioned whether the first secretary even had the right to preside. Khrushchev contemptuously brushed it aside. Malenkov now let rip, accusing Khrushchev of repeatedly violating the principles of collective leadership, interfering in the agricultural sector and ridiculously claiming that the Soviet Union would overtake the US in agricultural output per head by 1960.

Molotov weighed into Khrushchev's foreign policy, calling it 'Trotskyist' and 'Opportunist' with Bulganin, Voroshilov, Shepilov and Pervukhin joining in the affray. Pervukhin, unsurprisingly, was damning on the economic reform plans. The triumvirate put forward the motion to immediately remove Khrushchev as first secretary. As he vigorously defended his record, the leader would not have known that Bulganin had secretly placed guards around the Kremlin and the Politburo building. The intensity of the verbal kicking quickened, which several members of the Anti-Party Group felt was unnecessary.

By now, word had seeped out and 20 members of the Central

Committee, loyal to Khrushchev, rushed around armed with a petition, barging aside Bulganin's guards even though guns were raised. Although unable to gain access into the meeting, this rowdy league submitted its petition that any leadership decision taken by the Politburo had to be ratified by the Central Committee. The triumvirate was furious: Kaganovich being 'particularly insulting', stated the CIA. Khrushchev demanded that his supporters be allowed in to state their case, but was loudly overruled.

Zhukov, the wartime military hero, had urgently begun his own resistance against the triumvirate by summoning loyal provincial Central Committee members to immediately fly to Moscow: five ambassadors in the satellite countries were given similar instructions. Within the hour, Zhukov and others had gathered 70 members of the Central Committee to add to the 20 already at the Kremlin. Still championing his corner, that news was passed to Khrushchev who for the first time that evening detected that the triumvirate's opportunity to unseat him had passed. Subsequently, it was agreed that the Central Committee would eventually determine the leader's fate.

As the plenum of the Central Committee opened on June 22, of the 309 members present, a third clearly owed their careers to Khrushchev. There was only one item on the agenda, to re-affirm support for the leader of the party. Over the next eight days, the plenum 'turned into a full-scale rally of support for Khrushchev', reported the CIA, as the triumvirate and its own league were trounced. Of the 215 loyal members who requested permission to speak for the motion, 60 were allowed to do so, and the rest submitted written statements. Malenkov, Molotov, Kaganovich and Shepilov could only defend their positions but their support had ebbed away. Voroshilov did himself no favours by jumping up from his seat and waving hysterically in the direction of the Khrushchev supporters, shouting 'We will correct your brains!'

Zhukov struck the decisive blow on the final day, reaffirming his

---

[247] **Furtseva, Yekaterina Alexeyevna**: Arguably the most influential woman in Russian politics at the time. She died of heart failure in October 1974 but there were suspicions of suicide.

loyalty to Khrushchev and denouncing the plotters. At this point, Malenkov, Kaganovich and Shepilov felt forced to recant leaving only Molotov who stubbornly refused. Surprisingly, the four ringleaders were allowed to remain in the party. Khrushchev had won the day but it was close-run.

The Aftermath – Serov

During his Wallenberg investigation, lasting from December 1953 to March 1954, Serov had also been tasked by Khrushchev to prepare a secret brief to merge the MVD, the ministry of internal affairs, with the MGB, the ministry of state security. Colonel Dobrohotov, one of Serov's key officers he was using in the investigation, was more than up to the task with experience of both Secretariats. Khrushchev urgently wanted a new security service, untarnished by past horrors to compete with the huge resources that America was now committing to the CIA. Serov explains.

> *I must mention that the establishment of just one security agency had emerged unexpectedly. Earlier in the year, Kruglov, in the Presidium, had brought up the question on whether the Ministry of Internal Affairs should be restructured. At the time, Khrushchev had already tasked me with secretly preparing a proposal to set up the KGB.*
> *I entrusted the chief of the Secretariat, Dobrohotov, to prepare the proposal. I handed it to Shuisky, Khrushchev's assistant. I hadn't signed it.*

By not signing, does that infer that Serov couldn't risk any written association with Khrushchev's plan if the Presidium deigned to vote the merger down given the level of opposition towards the leader? Molotov and Malenkov did object as they did to Serov becoming the KGB's first chairman. Khrushchev merely waved their objections aside.

With members of the Anti-Party Group involved in the death of Wallenberg, Serov was under pressure in 1956 to dispense with any incriminating evidence.

The Wallenberg case was top secret within the MGB. When this issue was raised by Bulganin and Molotov at the Presidium of the Central Committee, Khrushchev, in 1956, had suggested to me to destroy all MGB and KGB documents on the case except those that might be needed for our explanations to the Swedes.

The case of Wallenberg for us had ended. It was of no main significance for the KGB. We had only fulfilled the orders of Khrushchev who had intrigued to get rid of Molotov.

In the West, people didn't realize that the noisy campaign to determine the fate of Wallenberg had been personally inspired by Khrushchev who was protecting his own interests. Khrushchev skilfully used the West for this purpose.

Khrushchev, after his victory in July 1957, had a new confidence even if the Anti-Party Group wasn't quite done. Malenkov would eventually be sent to Kazakhstan to manage a hydroelectric power station and Kaganovich was forced into the Urals to run a potassium producing plant. Mongolia was the chosen destination for Molotov. As the Soviet ambassador in Ulan Bator for three years, his speeches in the city's Lenin Club were respectful to Khrushchev but lacked any praise of his policies. The party ditched Molotov in 1962 and he died in 1986, of natural causes, his name living evermore with the Molotov cocktail incendiary, an association accorded to him by the mocking Finns in the Winter War with Russia after Molotov's pact with Ribbentrop. Serov was dumped as KGB chairman in 1958, after a vociferous campaign in the Politburo to unseat him over his poor management style but Khrushchev kept faith in his henchman moving him on to run the GRU, the prestigious counterintelligence arm of the military.

16

'The man who knew too much'

Molotov then raised the issue of liquidating Wallenberg as well as American, German, Japanese and other foreign citizens detained by us after the war.

Extract from Ivan Serov's memoir

NO ACCURATE RECORD is available on the number of foreigners held in Russian prisons and camps at the end of the war or in the years thereafter. A large release of Axis PoWs took place in the mid-1950s. As to the fate of 30,000 British and Commonwealth PoWs taken from German prison camps in Eastern Europe – mainly Poland – by the NKVD, Smersh and Red Army there has been only silence from successive British governments.[251] PoWs taken in the Korean War, mainly American, handed over to the Russians by China, joined the missing.

Not one British serviceman found his way home, and the Ministry of Defence should hang its head in shame. For those who didn't die in the mining camps, they were left to rot in the jails, the mental asylums, and the isolation centres. In the Arctic Circle where winter temperatures regularly hit minus 40 degrees centigrade, Komi was a major constituent of the Gulag with hundreds of camps. Situated near the village of Sed'vozh was Camp 225, nicknamed 'Britanka' by local inhabitants as British PoWs languished and were worked to their deaths. Recent research has indicated that in 1948 there were 480 inmates in Camp 225.

There had been a drip of releases of Americans in 1955 beginning with Wilfred Cumish, a US army private who had worked for the Military Intelligence Serial Detachment in Vienna and missing since March 1948. Intriguingly, a Frederick Charles Hopkins was on the list for release yet according to the US Department of State, the US military had no knowledge of him.

Parallels can be drawn between the liquidation of Raoul Wallenberg and Isaiah Oggins. Both died of 'heart failure' in 1947 with Molotov, the Soviet foreign minister, ordering their elimination. If Wallenberg had links to America's OSS, Oggins, born in the US of Russian parents, had been a key agent and recruiter for the NKVD. The US embassy in Moscow was later informed that Oggins had died in custody and buried in the Jewish cemetery in the city of Penza, some 625 km to the west of Moscow. There were immediate thoughts that in his final years of captivity he had been held in the Penza region or in the city with its two NKVD-run prisons: a pre-trial detention centre for up to 900 inmates, the other a transit jail for 1,800. Outside, there were eight labour camps with Nikolsk the largest. Lying 125 km northeast of Penza, Nikolsk had 2,000 prisoners assigned to logging and woodworking duties. Today, much of the area is given over to classy ski resorts for wealthy Russians.

There remain two operational files on Isaiah Oggins, one in the military procurator's office the other in the archive of Department S, and his story is as extraordinary as Wallenberg's.

Incarceration for Isaiah – known as Cy – had begun in arguably the coldest living place on earth: the nickel, copper, molybdenum and chrome mining camps of Norilsk. Throughout the Krasnoyarsk territory in the Arctic Circle there were 68 known camps, six prisons and two psychiatric prisons. In the Kola Peninsula lay the camps of Palatka, Karaul, Dudinka, Volochanka, Khatanga and the three camps to the south. In the city of Krasnoyarsk, two NKVD prisons housed 1,000 prisoners and two psychiatric prisons held hundreds more. Few survived.

In those mining camps, known as the Norillag system, for three months of the year the inmates never saw the sun rising as they endured back-breaking working conditions supervised by the

---

[251] *The Iron Cage: Are British prisoners of war abandoned in Soviet hands still alive in Siberia?* This excellently researched book by Nigel Cawthorne was published in 1993. The British government was singularly unhelpful to the author.

NKVD and the Soviet ministry of mining. Russian historians now believe that during the Stalin years more people died in the Norilsk camps than at Auschwitz. Andrei Vyshinsky, the state prosecutor, and Nikolay Yezhov, the head of the NKVD, particularly favoured Norilsk for enemies of the state.

Norilsk expanded post-war and in 1953 the inmates rebelled. Anxious government officials flew in from Moscow to negotiate as mining ground to a halt. There could only be one winner in the stalemate as Soviet bombers flew low over the camps setting them afire: survivors were dragged into the woods, executed and dumped into pits. Production restarted as the security services trucked in a new labour force.

With Mikhail Gorbachev opening up new channels of dialogue with Western leaders in the late 1980s, the US used the thaw to enquire about Americans still imprisoned in the Soviet Union. After deposing Gorbachev, Boris Yeltsin continued the collaboration and he instructed the KGB to undertake a thorough search in its archives. In charge was Colonel General Dmitri Volkogonov, the Deputy Director of Political Administration of the Soviet Armed Forces, and a military historian. At the first meeting of what became known as the US-Russia Joint Commission on Prisoners of War/Missing in Action, the Americans presented a list of a staggering 28,000 military and civilian personnel. One burning issue concerned the whereabouts of downed US pilots whose Lockheed P-38 Lightnings had been jumped by Soviet aircraft near Vienna on April 2, 1945. Washington was livid at the time and had threatened to end further military co-operation with its ally.

At the 17th and final gathering in November 2000 in the National Hotel, Moscow, both sides stood up and loudly applauded each other. Some 18,000 documents had been sifted. The Americans, however, were not prepared to give up on 39 individuals on whom Russian searches had supposedly yielded nothing. It was clear from the outset that missing spies, not just PoWs, would occupy much of the American focus. High on that list was Isaiah Oggins. US diplomats had been allowed to interview Oggins on two occasions in his Moscow prison cell in 1942 and demanded his release. Some years later, they were informed that Oggins had died in custody in 1948 but it was disbelieved.

Moscow had steadfastly refused to elaborate on the 'Kogan Ring', the cell of agents in Canada managed by Schloime Kogan, otherwise known as Sam Carr. He had recruited several British nuclear scientists seconded to McGill University in Montreal. The GRU defector, Ivor Gouzenko, in 1945, blew the ring alongside others, but the CIA and MI6 believed that more needed to be revealed on the full extent of Soviet atomic penetration in North America and Britain.

One spy that didn't figure in the US list was Alger Hiss, the former US State Department advisor, who during the war worked closely with James Byrnes, the secretary of state. At the Yalta Conference in 1945 when Stalin, Roosevelt and Churchill discussed the shape of post-war Europe, Hiss was part of Roosevelt's team. As the war ended and with Roosevelt dead, Hiss continued in post with Harry Truman and was selected to be the first secretary-general of the United Nations. As treachery rumours circulated within the intelligence community, that intended appointment was quietly abandoned.

Whittaker Chambers, a Soviet agent under investigation by the House for Un-American Activities Committee in August 1948, had named Hiss an equal fellow traveller. Hiss then stood trial, twice, denying all spying charges. In the first, Hiss only narrowly avoided a guilty verdict but in the second, he was sentenced to five years. Never tiring of expressing his innocence and on hearing of the Volkogonov investigations, Hiss wrote to the Russian enquiring on a private basis if any evidence on his spying activities actually existed in the Russian archives. The Americans had long contested that in its top-secret post-war *Venona* operation, which deciphered wartime Russian transmissions from the US, the reference to agent 'Ales' had referred to Hiss. A decryption of a cipher was never proof, argued Hiss, only a mathematical supposition.

Nothing had been located in the security archives Volkogonov reported back, which to Hiss represented full exoneration, not wasting the opportunity now to clear his name. Hiss had been a Soviet agent, Colonel Vladimir Barkovsky had told me, and a very good one, leaking the secrets of the White House and the US State

Department. The KGB was never going to provide the actual proof to Hiss, through Volkogonov, that his conviction in a US court was warranted.

Two arch-enemies meet in December 1993

As Lt. General Pavel Sudoplatov had spent 15 years in the Lubyanka and Vladimir, accused of crimes against the state, including responsibility for the notorious Laboratory X, Barkovsky had become one of the KGB's top spymasters. In his peak he had managed the STI – Scientific and Technology Intelligence – that had stolen countless Western secrets. On Sudoplatov's release in 1968, settling scores with past enemies was of little value with many of his contemporaries dead or executed. Yet there was mileage in restoring his sullied reputation.

Sudoplatov set about trashing reputations, and the respected Barkovsky became a target. Among the many 'special tasks' given to him by Stalin, claimed Sudoplatov, had been the wartime coordination of the highly successful operation to steal Allied nuclear secrets. Barkovsky was outraged: Sudoplatov's claim was utter nonsense, he responded. The operation had been jointly run by officers of the foreign intelligence directorate within the NKVD and the GRU, the Red Army's intelligence department.

With the collapse of communism, Barkovsky, in his eighties, still remained valuable to the KGB. Four days each week he travelled to Yaseneva, the intelligence headquarters, to continue the long-term project of writing up the history of the intelligence services using the operational files. With the KGB about to be replaced by the FSB, the new intelligence chiefs needed from its legendary spy chief an extensive brief on several secrets of the past. An enquiring Russian public needed answers. Barkovsky buried his pride and in the first week in December 1993, he called Sudoplatov. There was a Sudoplatov precondition to the meeting, which Barkovsky refused. Anatoli, one of Sudoplatov's two sons, and a former KGB officer, could not sit in.

As these two arch-enemies talked for four hours, Barkovsky would never know that Anatoli had expertly wired up the living room. Those revealing tapes still exist and amongst many episodes discussed was nuclear espionage. On one tape are the names of every Western asset who had helped the Russians steal the secrets of the atomic bomb. The circumstances behind the incarceration and execution of Isaiah Oggins also needed to be explored.

Who was 'the man who knew too much', as Sudoplatov and his officers had referred to Oggins when he was in their custody at Department S?

Born in the Willimantic, Connecticut, in 1898, Oggins had graduated from the prestigious University of Columbia, in New York, in 1920 with a BA in History and English. Strangely, the university alumni database does not record these subjects. In fact, his entire Columbia entry merits barely a line, omitting even a date of birth. There is one intriguing final entry: 'Last known address, Paris, France'. That detail had been phoned through to the alumni office in June 1982, but with no record of who had made the call.

As a student in New York, Oggins, like many students, flirted with communism, sympathetic with the Bolshevik revolution and the rejection of Tsarist power. The Socialist Party of America had attracted America's 'Left' but in 1919 there was a split as dissident factions pursued diverse radical objectives. Europe, too, sniffed the smell of insurrection, the cue to Russia to establish the Communist International, the Comintern, and bind recruits to the cause.

Moscow held its first Comintern congress attracting delegates from 19 countries, with the second in 1920 even better attended with 37. Lenin stridently demanded strict adherence abroad of his Twenty One Points that revolved around the promotion of revolution, and ordered that non-supportive members must be ejected from the party. A reactive US Attorney General jailed key leaders, which only resulted in uniting communist factions and the formation of the Communist Party of America in May 1921. The Comintern aggressively infiltrated labour unions and bankrolled strikes in the agriculture and textile sectors where wages were at poverty levels.

Membership grew, as did the agitation that spread into the industrial heartlands across the country with the administrations of Woodrow Wilson and Warren Harding refusing to recognise the

Bolshevik regime in Russia. The Comintern pumped more money into Leftist movements specifically targeting the young and educated. Among them was Isaiah Oggins who was developing into a very capable Comintern talent spotter. In New York, Oggins struck up a friendship with another young communist, Nerma Bermann. Her Russian family had emigrated to the US in June 1909, when she was aged 11.

That relationship with Nerma blossomed and in 1923, a year after Oggins graduated from Columbia, they married: the Russian Intelligence Services, even now, prefer couples as they work well undercover. During the mid-to-late 1920s, this husband and wife team targeted students in the best American universities with several in later years achieving high office in government agencies including the US State Department.

The order for the couple to relocate in Europe came in 1927, with the continent convulsing under political upheaval and post-WW1 industrial decay. Communist groups were banned and activists went into hiding: a fertile recruiting ground for the Soviets. In Britain, the previous year, the General Strike, the first in British industrial history, had brought the country to a standstill. The *Daily Mail* amongst other newspapers denounced striking workers as revolutionaries whose aim was to bring down the government. In Weimar Germany, the communists had taken to the streets with that very intention. Way to the east, in China, there was also turmoil as General Chiang Kai-shek's Nationalists fought with government forces and a British army division of 12,000 men was sent to defend British nationals in Shanghai.

Berlin and Paris were two assignments for Oggins and his wife, mainly reporting to Ignatius Reif.[252] Oggins recruited widely across Europe travelling under the name of 'Meerson' and using the codename 'Fritz'. He participated in establishing the extensive UK network. One agent never uncovered by MI5 was 'Islander', who is described in the Moscow archives as 'editor in chief of a major British journal'. He worked for many years at *The Economist* and supplied intelligence on British foreign policy. Reif and his fellow Paris *illegals* often met their British recruits in Geneva.

The name of Oggins appears in the NKVD operational files,

marked 'Students' and 'New Generations', files that specifically referred to recruitment amongst the British universities during the 1930s.

China the final assignment for Oggins

With the Soviet networks proliferating in China, Oggins was ordered to Manchuria and he arrived alone in the port city of Dairen in December 1936. He had travelled using a false US passport name and in the name of 'Meerson'. Nerma, highly capable in her own right, was instructed to remain in France and manage the NKVD safe houses.

The NKVD had established rezidentura in Peking, Shanghai, Tientsin, Guangdong, Guangzhou, Harbin and Dairen, all under the overall control of Aleksandr Panyushkin, the Russian ambassador.[253] Occupied by the Japanese since 1931, Manchuria was a dangerous assignment but the agent recruitment potential was high, given the large expat foreign community. The Razvedupra RKKA, the predecessor of the GRU, had its own extensive networks. On his arrival, Oggins checked in at the American consulate, as he was required to do being a US citizen. He then travelled to Harbin to meet his NKVD controller and head-of-station, the experienced Maxsim Steinberg, the former deputy head of NKVD counterintelligence in Moscow. Both men had previously worked together in Europe. For his *illegal* cover, Maxsim had found Oggins employment in Charles and Martin, a US-registered firm that sold Caproni Bergamaschi medium-range Italian bombers to Chinese nationalists.

---

[252] **Reif, Ignatius**: He used the name 'Max Volish' and the codename of 'Marr'. On his return to Moscow in May 1938, Reif worked as an assistant head of the Fifth Department of the NKVD First Directorate, the group responsible for foreign intelligence. In July that year he was arrested 'for participation in a counter-revolutionary terrorist organization' and subsequently executed at the Kommunarka mass execution site in southwest Moscow. He was posthumously rehabilitated in December 1956.

[253] **Panyushkin, Aleksandr**: Almost without exception by 1939 every Soviet consul general in China was an operative of the NKVD or GRU. He left China in 1944 and would later serve as Russian ambassador in the US.

The partnership between Oggins and Steinberg ended almost as soon as it had begun as three months in, Moscow Centre posted Steinberg to Lausanne, Switzerland, a key NKVD station with agents embedded within the League of Nations in Geneva. Steinberg was to be involved with Sudoplatov's operation to kill Leon Trotsky in Mexico by organising the US visa for Lt. General Leonid Eitingon, Sudoplatov's deputy, to co-ordinate the assassination.

Worldwide, this was an immensely worrying time for Jewish members of the Russian Intelligence Services whose ranks were being savagely purged on trumped-up charges. Operational agents were summoned back to Moscow on false pretences. London was purged and left with no NKVD presence and in Harbin, Oggins had every reason to be nervous.

In Switzerland, Steinberg had gone on the run, defecting after refusing his order to return to Moscow for training for a new assignment somewhere in Europe, probably Britain. Managing to get a message through to Harbin, Steinberg advised Oggins to leave China immediately by whatever means and go to ground in Europe with his wife. Any former colleague of Steinberg was now in great danger by association. Moscow Centre was in no mood to tolerate defectors after Walter Krivitsky fled in 1939.[254] His colleagues had been recalled, summarily tried and several executed. Krivitsky was later shot dead in a Washington hotel bedroom, paying the ultimate price of all defectors.

That dreaded order to Oggins to return to Moscow for re-assignment and training duly arrived in early 1939. A loyal agent for 16 years, Oggins still had faith in the service but he also trusted Steinberg's judgement. Choosing to believe his orders were genuine, Oggins began the long circuitous journey to Moscow that included passing through Europe, travelling on a false Czechoslovak passport. On arrival in Moscow, a room reservation had been made for him at the Moskva, a vast hotel adjacent to one of the entrances for Red Square.[255]

There he remained until his arrest on February 20, 1939 and for the next 11 months, he was held in Lefortovo: the trial took place on January 5, 1940. His relationship with Steinberg had, indeed, finished him. On the trumped up charge of supporting Trotsky in exile, Oggins was sentenced to eight years' hard labour in Norilsk.

News of the arrest had filtered back to Nerma in Paris who was now in grave danger. Taking advice, she fled to the US in August 1939 catching one of the last passenger liners to leave France as the 'Phoney War' ended and the Germans invaded. On arrival in the US, she was arrested by the FBI and immediately confessed to spying for the Soviets.

In Norilsk, Oggins tried as best he could to survive the work conditions and intense cold. He struck up a camaraderie with a group of Polish PoWs. In the camp the prisoners constructed a theatre and Oggins excelled as an actor, but in a freak accident he broke a leg on stage becoming an invalid as the bones refused to knit correctly given the primitive medical conditions. He worked as best he could but in constant pain. There was a real worry that his injury would lead to execution.

Germany's invasion of the Soviet Union, in June 1941, brought an unexpected opportunity for the American. Posters appeared in camp offering a full amnesty to the Poles if they agreed to fight in a new Polish army under its Polish PoW head, General Anders, who had occupied a cell in the Lubyanka for the past two years. Under Stalin's amnesty all previous 'crimes' committed by the Poles would be forgiven. Oggins' friends quickly applied and he, too, glimpsed a way out of the Norilsk hell. He carefully crafted a letter addressed to the US ambassador in Moscow, saying he was an American citizen and falsely imprisoned. Reluctantly one of the Poles agreed to pass over the letter if there was a chance he was ever in the Russian capital. Oggins included in the letter that he wanted news of his incarceration to be given to his 'sister' who lived in Brooklyn, New York: that was, in fact, Nerma's sister. The letter was dated September 16, 1941.

The Norilsk Poles duly entered the Anders Army and Oggins

---

[254] **Krivitsky, Walter**: He operated mainly in Europe with his last post The Hague. After his defection to the US, he wrote a book published in 1941, entitled *In Stalin's Secret Service,* a huge embarrassment to Moscow.

[255] Rooms were set aside for military and intelligence officers. As a courtesy, the management always left a bottle of Georgian brandy in the room.

could only hope his letter would reach friendly hands. In their new army camps, where the British had agreed to equip Stalin's new troops, they began their short training and within weeks the Poles, under British command, sailed in troopships from Krasnovodsk on the Caspian. For the remainder of the war they would serve in Persia [Iran], Iraq, Palestine and other theatres.

Surprisingly, that letter did reach the American embassy in February 1942. Staff had relocated from the embassy's grand building next door to the National Hotel, to Kuibyshev in the east given the threat of German occupation. Only a skeleton staff had remained, headed by Llewellyn Thompson the second secretary. On reading the letter, he sent it on to Kuibyshev for Lawrence Steinhardt, the ambassador, to assess. By the time that Admiral William Standley had taken over as ambassador in April, embassy staff had demanded prisoner access with Oggins. In the US, the FBI was aware that Oggins had been a Comintern recruit from his wife's confession.

Department S had Oggins transported to Butyrka, in Moscow. Sudoplatov left Oggins to the odious Dr Maironovsky from Laboratory X to do the breaking, and quickly. He needed to know the contents of the letter to the US ambassador. That letter certainly was revealing. Oggins had pleaded to the US to urgently engineer his freedom and in return he would name the American and European agents that he and other *illegals* had recruited. The networks would be blown.

In Washington anticipation grew and Roosevelt was kept in the loop. The Soviets were certainly rattled. An urgent cipher was transmitted to Moscow from the Russian embassy in Washington warning of the dire threat if Oggins was freed. Unexpectedly, Molotov acceded to American pressure for a supervised visit and on December 6, 1942, Thompson with his colleague, Francis Stevens, pitched up at Butyrka. From FBI photographs the two diplomats verified the prisoner as Oggins, but he was in poor shape and hobbled given the condition of his leg. The meeting was short. Two NKVD officers, fluent in English, sat in.

The biographical detail that Oggins was allowed to impart to the diplomats was cabled to Washington with a request for instruction on how to further proceed. A second meeting was permitted on

January 9, 1943, again supervised, but this time Stevens went to Butyrka alone. Stevens reported back that the physical and mental condition of Oggins had worsened. Requests were made for further visits, but all were refused. Sudoplatov returned Oggins, now a physical wreck, to Norilsk.

Washington applied more political pressure but the Russian Foreign Ministry remained steadfast. In the records of Department S is an *aide memoire* written by Eitingon, Sudoplatov's deputy, and his conclusion was damning: 'Isaiah Oggins can never be released as he is responsible for the recruiting of many of our agents in England and America'.

With the war at an end, the Americans again stepped up their efforts but with relationships souring they were rebuffed. Sudoplatov had been given a further remit by Stalin, heading up Department F whose officers arrested foreign PoWs in overrun German camps. The Moscow prisons were full to overflowing and the toll of executions was rising. Sudoplatov on his release from Vladimir in 1968 always tried to push the blame elsewhere but he was a brutal killer in his own right.

As Serov stated in his memoir, the decision was taken in 1947 to liquidate many foreigners in their jails and in camps such as Krasnogorsk. Wallenberg was one, Oggins another but the final list is endless. The Russians would never release Oggins, thus he met his end in the Lubyanka by lethal toxin, his organs already wracked with damage caused by the administered drugs during the many interrogations. A death certificate was issued with cardiac arrest given as cause of death, a version of events provided to Yeltsin by Volkogonov in 1992 who described the Oggins episode as a 'tragic tale worthy of Shakespeare's pen'.

Maxsim Steinberg, like Oggins before him, finally took the gamble and returned to Moscow in 1957 after expertly avoiding the KGB assassins for 19 years. The year before, Steinberg had discussed defection with MI5 and a new life in Britain. Serov ordered the immediate arrest of Steinberg and his wife, Elsa, on arrival and they were hauled away for painful interrogations. Strangely, execution was avoided but Steinberg was given a 15-year jail term and Elsa, 10 years. Eitingon, arrested in 1953 with Sudoplatov, accused of being implicated in the Beria plot to grab power, shared a cell with Steinberg in Vladimir for a short period. Steinberg was also a cellmate of Sudoplatov for 18 months and they barely spoke. Steinberg was released in 1966, two years before Sudoplatov.

'The man who knew too much' – a final twist?

Oggins, like Wallenberg, will remain an enigma. When Volkogonov began his investigation into the American missing in 1992, why did the Americans put Oggins high on the list only to later feign complete disinterest? Why in the alumni record for Oggins, at the University of Columbia, is so much detail missing? Who phoned through the information in June 1982 to the alumni office that Paris had been the last known address for Oggins, some 59 years after he graduated and 33 years after the Soviets had admitted his death to the Americans in 1948? If it had been a family member, why not provide more detail?

There remains the final conundrum. The Russians told the Americans that Oggins was buried in Penza, in the Jewish cemetery. Why there and so far from Moscow and the Lubyanka, where Maironovsky had administered his final injection? Faith was never a consideration for a special burial upon execution. Thousands of Jews are buried in the Butovo pits and at Kommunarka.

One Moscow source had an intriguing theory. Had Oggins somehow escaped his death sentence and had later been given his freedom but with the condition he didn't return to America? Paris had been one of his European assignments in the early 1930s. Had Oggins returned to the French capital to secretly live out the rest of his life?

[Moscow-1] Raoul Wallenberg's ashes lay under this mound in the grounds of the Donskoye crematorium, a short drive from the Lubyanka.

[Moscow-2] Col. General Viktor Semyonovich Abakumov was head of Smersh at the time of Wallenberg's arrest. In Gromyko's statement to the Swedish government in February 1957, blame for Wallenberg's death in captivity was placed on Abakumov, who by then had been executed. [PD]

[Moscow-3] The entrance to the nuclear reactor in the grounds of the Kurchatov Institute. During the Cold War, this facility was heavily guarded.

[Moscow-4] The head of the nuclear reactor with spent material nearby.

[*Moscow-5*] Colonel Vladimir Barkovsky outside the Kurchatov Institute in Moscow, one of our meeting places in Moscow. As he was one of the very few intelligence officers with unlimited access to NKVD, KGB and SVR operational files, he required official clearance to see me but that was never a problem.

[*Moscow-6*] Barkovsky outside his Moscow apartment block

[*Moscow -7*] My last meeting with Colonel Barkovsky in Moscow's National Hotel. Barkovsky arrived with his FSB minders, but they soon left and waited outside.

[*Moscow -8*] The fledgling Captain Vladimir Barkovsky, posted to wartime Britain as a political attaché in the London embassy. He was destined to become one of the greatest Soviet spymasters.

[*Moscow -9*] The firefight between the Soviet commandoes and German forces took place in the Nazi-occupied village of Krivaya Kosa [now Sedovo] on the Sea of Azov. Little has changed.

[Moscow -10] The schoolhouse in Krivaya Kosa where the 'atomic notebook' was found in a briefcase belonging to a Dutch SS officer, Major Van der Velde. The notebook that described German efforts to build an atomic bomb is regarded by the Russian Intelligence Services as the catalyst that restarted the Soviet nuclear programme.

[Moscow-11] Barkovsky was one of a very small team of NKVD officers tasked with obtaining nuclear secrets from Britain, the US and Canada – codenamed *Operation Enormoz*. They met only infrequently in later years to celebrate their achievements. *Left to right*: Colonel Anatoli Yatskov [New York 1941–46], Colonel Leonid Kvashnikov [New York 1943–45], Colonel Vladimir Barkovsky and Colonel Aleksandr Feklisov [New York 1941–46 and London 1947–50] – the last case officer for Klaus Fuchs.

Overleaf: [Moscow-12] Colonel Stanley Lekarev, KGB and SVR, enjoyed an intelligence career spanning nearly half a century. This photograph shows him in his Moscow apartment.

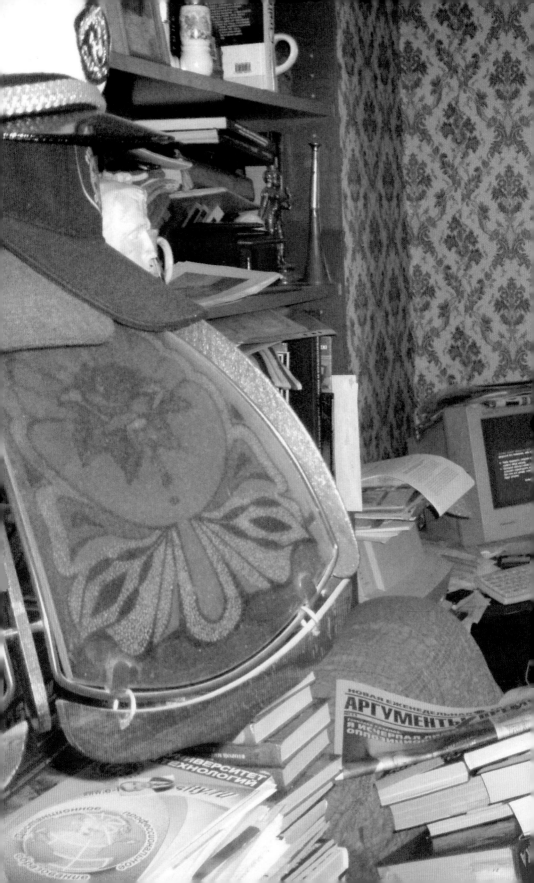

[Moscow -13] The Russian embassy's KGB photographer in London was killed by MI5. He was regularly used by Lekarev.

[Moscow-14] One of Lekarev's operations in London was to assess the sexual preferences of Edward Heath, then head of the Conservative Party and before he became prime minister. Lekarev used the renowned Russian Olympic gymnast team as part of the plan, with the gymnasts signing a photograph of the occasion.

[Moscow-15] Anatoli Sudoplatov and Stanley Lekarev in a photograph taken by the author outside one of our usual haunts in Moscow.

[Moscow-16] Lt. General Pavel Sudoplatov. A family photograph.

[Moscow-17] Colonel Yuri Kolesnikov, Robert Maxwell's final case officer.

[Moscow-18] Colonel Edward Sharapov is on left, with Anatoli Sudoplatov at our meeting in Moscow. Sharapov, KGB, the deputy director of the German desk in East Berlin, was on duty the night that the escaped MI6 spy, George Blake, arrived at a Berlin Wall checkpoint.

[Moscow-19] Colonel-General Ivan Serov, chairman of the KGB and director of the GRU. Serov probably was not in Moscow at the time of Wallenberg's liquidation as from 1945 until late in 1947, he was Chief of Civilian Administration in East Berlin, in Karlshorst. He returned to Moscow as deputy head of the MVD.

[Moscow-20] This photograph, from Serov's archive, encapsulates the beginnings of the Cold War. The Allied military commanders met in Berlin shortly before the final surrender. Serov is on the left alongside Eisenhower. Marshal Zhukov, in the middle, looks skywards. Montgomery on his right is typically dour.

[Moscow-21] How the *Daily Sketch* national newspaper portrayed Serov on his visit to Britain in March 1956. On that trip, Serov with his KGB colleague, Lt. General Oleg Gribanov, held secret meetings with Robert Maxwell and Victor Rothschild. [PD]

[Moscow-22] Colonel Oleg Penkovsky, GRU officer, after his arrest. The KGB established that a close relationship had existed between Penkovsky and Serov during the latter's time as KGB chairman. [PD]

[Moscow-23] Gestapo officer, Gustav Richter, was one of
Wallenberg's cellmates in the Lubyanka. During WW2,
he operated out of the German legation in Bucharest,
Rumania, and under Himmler's orders put forward a
plan to exterminate the Jewish community. One method
was to run packed transport trains aimlessly around the
country until most of the Jews were dead. The
photograph illustrates one such episode. [PD]

[Moscow-24] Lt. General Peter
Fedotov was a key source for
Serov in the Wallenberg
investigation. In December
1953, when head of MGB
counterintelligence, he disclosed
to Serov that a Wallenberg file
existed in the archives of the
defunct Committee of
Information [KI]. [PD]

[Moscow-25] Vyacheslav Molotov,
Soviet foreign minister, was
nicknamed 'stone-arse' by world
leaders. [PD]

[Moscow-26] Nikita Khrushchev, Soviet premier, instructed Serov in December 1953 to finally determine which individuals were to blame for Wallenberg's liquidation. [PD]

[Moscow-27] Colonel Vasily Dobrohotov was a key member of Serov's small investigation team. He had been head of the MVD and MGB Secretariats. His intelligence personnel record shows a gap in his file from December 1953 until March 1954 that neatly coincides with the Wallenberg investigation. Dobrohotov also prepared the blueprint for the formation of the KGB.

[*Moscow-28*] A typical Lubyanka cell.
Photograph taken in the early 1950s.

[*Moscow-29*] The entrance to Lubyanka-3.
The author used this entrance to visit the
KGB's internal operations museum.
Underground, there is a tunnel leading to
the execution chamber.

[*Moscow-30*] The notorious Butyrka prison in Moscow. Note the fire damage from the window in one of the cells.

[*Moscow-31*] Langfelder, after being split up with Wallenberg in the Lubyanka when they first arrived in Moscow on February 6, 1945, was taken to one of these older Butyrka cells.

[Moscow-32] The prisoner entrance to Lefortovo, Moscow, used by the security services. Both Wallenberg and Langfelder, his Budapest driver, were imprisoned here. In 1947, Wallenberg was returned to the internal prison in the Lubyanka from Lefortovo where he was liquidated.

[Moscow-33] Another view of Lefortovo.

[Moscow-34] A Lefortovo control tower.

[Moscow-35] Aleksandrovsk Central Prison. An older photograph. [PD]

[Moscow-36] Vladimir prison.

[Moscow-37] Vilmos Böhm worked in the Press Reading Bureau, within the British legation in Stockholm. [PD]

[Moscow-38] NKVD officer, Col. Zoya Rybkina, shored up trade relations between the Wallenberg family and the Soviet Union during WW2. She and her husband were posted to Stockholm in 1941 to counteract MI6's growing presence.

[Moscow-39] Major General Vasily Blokhin was for several decades a state executioner. He ran the Kommandatura and his name is on one of the death records recording Wallenberg's liquidation. Serov interviewed him. [PD]

[Moscow-40] One of the long trenches within the Butovo killing ground.

[*Moscow-41*] Another view of the Butovo killing ground which the Russian security services had long disguised as a staff shooting range.

[*Moscow-42*] Dr Grigori Maironovsky was the head of the notorious Laboratory X, the toxins laboratory. [PD]

[Moscow-43] The front gate of what was known as Scientific Research Laboratory No. 12, known as Laboratory X.

[Moscow-44] The killing room for Laboratory X scientists in Varsonof'evskiy Pereulok, a short walk from the Lubyanka-3 building, remains outside the public gaze. Hidden behind large rusting sliding gates and tall walls, FSB counterintelligence now has use of the building.

Right: [Moscow-45] Behind the gates of Varsonof'evskiy Pereulok is a large parking area and to the left a ramp descends to an underground garage. Above this ramp is a room with a small window, clearly seen in the photograph. This was the medical room, a 'Spetsialnie Laboratotornaya Kamera' cell strictly off limits to everyone without a special pass where first Dr Grigori Maironovsky, then Naumov, his Laboratory X successor, and Smiakov, Naumov's deputy, experimented on prisoners from the Lubyanka, Butyrka and Lefortovo. If the scientists liquidated Wallenberg, there is every probability he met his end here.

[Moscow-46] In August 1947, Andrei Vyshinsky, lawyer, prosecutor and foreign minister, delivered a note to the Swedish ambassador in Moscow, Söhlman, stating that Wallenberg was not on any Soviet territory nor did any Soviet authority know him. [PD]

[Moscow-47] Georgy Malenkov was a close collaborator of Stalin. Upon Stalin's death in March 1953, he became Chairman of the Council of Ministers, a post he held only until the appointment of Khrushchev as premier in the following September. [PD]

[Moscow-48] 'In memoriam of political oppression victims 1945–1953'.

17

Admission of guilt to a disbelieving world

Khrushchev felt that if we admitted our guilt into the liquidation of Wallenberg we could rebuild the Soviet Union's relations with Sweden and improve our relations with the West and the international banking community. In his mind, Khrushchev had also taken the view that Sweden might again act for us as a broker in forming secret ties with America and Britain.

Extract from Ivan Serov's memoir

SWEDEN TRIED a back-door approach in 1955, an attempt that was swiftly brought to Serov's attention. Through a conduit, the Swedish Foreign Office wanted to tap up Kliment Voroshilov, the Presidium chairman. A close early aide of Stalin, Voroshilov was in the Politburo in 1926 and Stalin made him Marshal of the Soviet Union in 1935. Scapegoats were necessary after the Germans encircled Leningrad and Voroshilov was one with his rank stripped. Back in favour in 1945, Stalin needed his former aide to establish the communist regime in Hungary, which he did until 1947. Given that link with Hungary, and his Presidium position, the Swedes hoped that Voroshilov might be prepared to assist.

Serov was briefed.

Our counterintelligence department told me, in 1955, that a social democrat from Sweden, a Jew, was to visit the USSR to meet Ilia Ehrenberg, one of our prominent writers. He wanted Ehrenberg to assist in arranging an audience with Voroshilov. The Swede had chosen Ehrenberg because he was also Jewish. Ehrenberg worked for the KGB and had been operationally developed by us.

Ehrenberg was no mere writer as Serov implies and there were strong suspicions he was a double agent. Abakumov had him arrested in 1949 but Stalin interceded. An ardent anti-fascist, Ehrenberg had endeared himself to Stalin who awarded the Jewish writer his celebrated peace prize. Ehrenberg coveted his international contacts with prominent Jews, among them Pablo Picasso.

Before Ehrenberg's meeting with the Swede, the writer was briefed by the chief of the KGB's political wing, Lt. General Fedor Kharitonov. For the first time, the instruction had been given to feed the line that Wallenberg had been held but was probably now dead, a victim of Beria and Abakumov. Aleksandr Panyushkin, the KGB's accomplished chief of foreign intelligence, and former Washington ambassador, was tasked to evaluate the outcome of Ehrenberg's hare.

> *He* [Ehrenberg] *should hint that the Soviet authorities did not rule out the fact that Wallenberg may have been imprisoned in the USSR and probably became the victim of Beria and Abakumov.*

Ehrenberg had done his job well, as a seasoned KGB operative should. Serov makes no further mention of Voroshilov, so we have to assume that the Presidium chairman was no longer part of this story, but what Ehrenberg had been instructed to impart had raised the stakes. Panyushkin did report back that the Swedes had offered a trade if Wallenberg could be found. As a counter, Sweden would absolve the Khrushchev leadership of any blame and place full culpability on the late Lavrenty Beria. There could be no trade of course, Wallenberg had been dead for seven years.

Serov set another hare loose two years later, in 1956, this time in Istanbul and Helsinki.

Major Pavel Yerzin, an experienced NKVD and KGB officer, who with Barkovsky and others had penetrated the wartime atomic secrets of Britain, met Swedish diplomats in Turkey to privately convey that the KGB still took Wallenberg's disappearance seriously and had begun its own investigation on whether Wallenberg might still be alive, 'lost' somewhere in the Gulag or held in some obscure institution. Helsinki was the second arm of this disinformation operation. The Finnish diplomat, Oke Frey, was on the KGB payroll and he carefully fed the same lie to his Swedish contacts. The manipulating Serov was in his element.

Khrushchev, mindful to the bigger political picture, saw advantages in an admission. As Serov confirms, the leader needed Sweden as a back-channel to rapprochement with the West. He had already illustrated his willingness to present an improved humanitarian face to the West by more releases of Axis PoWs and political prisoners. The USSR needed new alliances outside its own strategic area of influence, with substantial capital urgently required to rebuild its war-devastated industrial base. Sweden was vital in Khrushchev's vision, but fences needed mending.

Not for the first time, Sweden had brokered Soviet approaches to the West. During the Winter War with Finland in 1940, contact had been maintained with the diplomats in Stockholm, which proved of greater importance when Finland sided with Nazi Germany in 1941 and ended with the armistice signed in September 1944. With Finland out of the war, Soviet forces could concentrate their efforts in the push into Germany.

Khrushchev shows his hand

In early 1956, Sweden determinedly pushed for a high-level meeting in Moscow with Wallenberg top of the agenda. Tage Erlander, the Swedish premier, needed an audience with Khrushchev. Through channels, the KGB learnt that Erlander and his interior minister, Gunnar Hedlund, wanted to present testimony from interviews with newly released PoWs. In particular, Erlander wanted to impart the testimony of Gustav Richter, a Lubyanka cellmate of Wallenberg.

Dates were confirmed. Erlander and his aides would arrive in Moscow on April 3. Khrushchev turned to Serov to prepare answers to the inevitable questions that would be raised, with a strong caveat. Serov explains:

I think that this consideration put the case of Wallenberg at a very high level, otherwise no one else would have been bothered about it. The KGB was entrusted to prepare documents that would answer the questions that the Swedish government might ask. Our position on this

245

matter was always supervised and endorsed by Khrushchev. There was
to be a planned visit of the Swedish Prime Minister to Moscow, to
which the Soviet leadership attached great importance. The visit took
place in 1956, but no documents were handed over to the Swedish
delegation. Molotov and I were ordered by Khrushchev not to speed up
any responses before the parliamentary elections in Sweden had taken
place.

Serov's hand was probably behind the note to Sweden's acting chargé
d'affaires, Petri, in Moscow, on March 19. It was a real dampener just
weeks before Erlander's visit.

The Foreign Ministry considers it necessary to confirm that the
explanations previously given to representatives of the Swedish
Government by leading persons in the Soviet Government, that
Wallenberg is not in the Soviet Union's territory, are exhaustive
and final. The Foreign Ministry has nothing to add to the
above-mentioned explanations.

In a downbeat mood, the Erlander mission flew off to Moscow but
there was some hope that once the Russians viewed the PoW
evidence there might just be a softening in the intransigence.

According to reports, the Russian hosts were cordial. Erlander
presented his evidence that Wallenberg had been held captive within
the Soviet prison system, as had his driver Langfelder. Across the table
Khrushchev, Bulganin, and Molotov listened. Any confidence amongst
the Swedish delegation evaporated as the usual line was trotted out.

It was Khrushchev who broke the impasse. Both parties would
issue a joint communiqué stating that the Russian authorities would
undertake a new and extensive investigation into whether Wallenberg
might still be in the USSR and known only by a prisoner number.
Khrushchev promised to keep Erlander informed on progress. Sweden
believed Khrushchev's intervention to be a key turning point in
diplomatic relations.

On Erlander's return to Stockholm, his press conference on May
4 was laced with elation but tempered with caution as he declared
that for the first time the Russians were being true to their word. This

new-found enthusiasm was further bolstered by the foreign minister, Osten Undén, receiving a request from Moscow to supply more personal data and photographs. Within days that material was couriered.

It was a stalling move, of course, as Khrushchev had ordered Serov not to formulate any measure of response until Sweden's election that September. Rodionov, the Russian ambassador in Stockholm, fed the general deception by conveying to the Swedes that the promised investigation was proceeding apace. Erlander again briefed an impatient Swedish media. That September 1956 election came and went, with Erlander returned to power in a coalition, but from Moscow there was only silence. The Swedes petitioned deputy foreign minister, Zakharov, for news but in Stockholm there was a growing realisation that yet again they had been baulked.

Events in Hungary, with Khrushchev dispatching tanks onto the streets of Budapest in early November, took greater precedence: his patience and temper worn thin by the anti-Moscow leadership of Imre Nagy. Serov complemented the unfolding terror by sending in KGB snatch squads to arrest activists. At the UN, Russia was censored but other Security Council members, too, were in the dock. British and French aircraft had bombed Egyptian airfields on October 31, landing paratroopers on November 5, to guard the Suez Canal, only to embarrassingly pull them out in early December after mainly US opposition. Khrushchev's problems in Hungary hadn't prevented the Swedes ratcheting up the pressure. Söhlman, the ambassador, presented a further communiqué in November, seeking an urgent update on the promised internal investigation agreed to in May.

Ivan Serov must have been in two minds as he approved the final draft for Gromyko: sadly, he doesn't record what was the catalyst behind the statement on February 6, 1957, nor the worldwide condemnation and disbelief towards the Khrushchev regime that followed it. His investigation had been over for three years and the fate of the Swedish diplomat was of no consequence – a nuisance – yet now he was preparing the admission that Wallenberg had met his death in Soviet custody. It must be presumed that Khrushchev had maintained his intention to disclose the truth, even if the cause of death was a lie.

At least the year – 1947 – was correct, but Gromyko fed the line that Wallenberg had succumbed to a heart attack given an underlying cardiac condition. The Smoltsov document, the medical report that accompanied Gromyko's statement, was rightly ridiculed but Khrushchev could hardly come clean and admit that Wallenberg had been executed.

Almost certainly, the Swedish government sought advice from Britain and the US, who had independently chased leads on Wallenberg. Given the extent of the MI6 operation in Stockholm and the Russian networks, the British were well placed to explore the back-channels. One British agent was in the Politburo, a senior party leader from Leningrad tapped up by MI5 on a trade visit to London. General Leonid Raikhman, the KGB's top mole hunter, knew the British had a top-level source, but he could never uncover his man. How did the British advise the Swedes? Did MI6 admit that for some time it had known Wallenberg to be dead? Probably not.

Curiously, there was a further Soviet release within days of Gromyko's statement. Leopold Boissier, the president of the international committee of the Red Cross in Geneva, was handed a list of 15 foreigners who had died in Russian captivity. Boissier only disclosed one name on it: Max von Engelbrechten, who from 1940 until 1944 had been a German diplomat in Geneva and arrested by the NKVD in Berlin at the end of the war. No detail had been provided as to where or how he had died. The Red Cross has never disclosed the other 14 names despite pressure to do so. What had been the Soviet motive in releasing this list, was it to assuage more guilt?

The Swedish Left-wing newspaper, *Ny Dag*, had sent a reporter to Moscow to conduct an exclusive interview with Gromyko and it appeared in the February 18 edition. Gromyko had been unequivocal about Wallenberg's death in 1947 and that no further information would be forthcoming: all enquiries in Moscow were now terminated.

'The case of Wallenberg had to be regarded as one of the tragedies which occurred in the confusion prevailing at the end of the war', Gromyko had concluded.

The Swedish public was outraged at such obfuscation.

The following day, February 19, the Swedish Foreign Office formerly replied to the Russian Foreign Ministry. Unless corroborating evidence could be provided, it said, in its opinion Wallenberg remained alive and the Russian government needed to redouble its efforts to find him. That rejoinder had taken 13 days. Internally, the Swedish Foreign Office had a real dilemma. Unable to attest either way the veracity of Gromyko's admission, it felt it could only accede to the incredulous public outcry and doubt: the search had to continue.

18

Perpetuating the Wallenberg legend

K HRUSHCHEV HAD TOLD THE WORLD, even if the account had been doctored. No more statements would follow, until that momentous meeting in 1989 in Moscow, when the KGB vice chairman handed over to the Swedes some of Wallenberg's personal items. Khrushchev promoted Gromyko shortly after the Wallenberg announcement and he would be an internationally respected spokesman for the USSR, until his retirement in 1985. By its outright rejection of Gromyko's revelation the Swedish government was duty bound to follow all new leads, record every statement and present to the media its proactivity. Above all, the government had to offer a scintilla of hope.

Maj von Dardel, Wallenberg's mother, wrote to Simon Wiesenthal in April 1971[259] imploring the Nazi hunter to intervene in the search for her son. Wiesenthal duly obliged setting up vocal lobby groups worldwide, not least in the United States. In Sweden, Wiesenthal proposed the establishment of the 'World Committee for the Discovery of the Truth about Wallenberg' with Marcus Wallenberg in the chair but the family rejected that idea. Some years earlier, Wiesenthal had written to US senator, Henry Jackson, seeking US government support in re-examining the Wallenberg case evidenced by a number of 'sightings'. Wiesenthal had interviewed a former Russian medical doctor who was convinced he had examined Wallenberg in the 1960s in the KGB prison in Irkutsk. A further sighting in Irkutsk had been confirmed to Wiesenthal in 1967.

Global publicity was gained in 1981 when Wiesenthal convened the 'International Wallenberg Hearing' in Stockholm. The overwhelming consensus of the delegates and speakers agreed

Wallenberg to be alive and they condemned the medical statement that accompanied Gromyko's announcement as a fabrication. The CIA drank at the same well. To coincide with the event, it circulated an internal report entitled 'Wallenberg: A lingering tragedy of World War II'. The paper conjectured that the Swede could be alive.

The delegates were treated to a plethora of supposed sightings, encounters and cell-pipe knockings. One was as recent as 1980 in Kresti, the notorious prison in Leningrad. The Swedish Foreign Office had received a telegram from its office in New York.

'Wallenberg was being treated in the prison hospital under strict isolation. He is with a group of other foreigners, a fairly great number being of Polish origin. All his co-prisoners are of advanced age like him. A priest had the opportunity of talking to Raoul Wallenberg.'

If Wallenberg was alive in 1980 he was 68-years-old and after 37 years of incarceration in the brutal Soviet prison system, hospital stays would be frequent. Two years earlier there was a sighting in the Blagoveshchensk special psychiatric hospital, to the north west of Vladivostok. Other recent sightings had included the closed city of Gorky, a detention cell for foreigners in Potma, Moldova, and in the NKVD prison in Odessa. The Swedish Embassy in Vienna, in April 1974, had courteously received the Austrian doctor who claimed to have personally treated Wallenberg in the Chalmer-Ju labour camp in the northern Urals. He had moved to Russia in the 1930s to complete his medical studies and remained in the region to practice. During the summer of 1948, he was ordered to report to the labour camp and attend to an unnamed inmate.

André Schimkevitsch had filed another personal account. He was born in Paris in 1913 to Russian parents but they had separated and his father returned to Russia to live. He visited his father and was arrested, accused of espionage. In December 1947, reported Schimkevitsch, he had been moved to a new cell in the Lubyanka. His cellmate was Wallenberg and during the two days he shared with

---

[259] Pick, Hella, Simon Wiesenthal, *A Life in Search of Justice*, London, 1996, pp. 235-237

the Swede, they were forbidden to communicate with each other apart from introducing themselves. Schimkevitsch had been released in 1958 and he had returned to France.

Released Russian inmates in the Gulag added to the growing store of sightings. Avraham Shifrin, a former prisoner, published an extraordinary study in 1980 on the prisons and forced-labour camps of the Soviet Union.[260] Its publication riled the Moscow authorities. The study is meticulously researched with maps, diagrams, and photographs, including first-hand inmate accounts.

As part of this research, Shifrin and his fellow researchers constructed a chronological trail for Wallenberg sightings, beginning with Wrangel Island: a more remote location would be impossible to find in the Soviet Arctic, laying 140 km off the Siberian mainland between the Chukchi and East Siberian Seas. The authorities had categorically denied any camp existed but later excavations uncovered the foundations of rows of wooden buildings.[261]

Shifrin's next location for Wallenberg was in Zabaikale, in eastern Siberia, 4,530 km northeast of Moscow, and equally inhospitable. Stalin had ambitions to turn Zabaikale into a gigantic PoW detention centre, including 500,000 physically fit Japanese PoWs taken as the Red Army overran Manchuria. The Chinese territory had been occupied by Japan for 14 years. Stalin ordered the NKVD to recruit 35,000 guards to handle the volume. Several thousand British and French PoWs ended up in Zabaikale and they would complement the PoW labour force that would build the long-planned Baikal-Amur railway.

The notorious jail in Verkhneuralsk, in Chelyabinsk province, was Shifrin's next site for Wallenberg. Torture was the norm and there was no record of successful escapes. In the jail was the 'Tsar's punishment cell', in which few inmates survived. Maria Koppensteiner, Hitler's cousin, had been a prisoner with her husband, Schmidt. Smersh had rounded them up in the Spring of 1945 as the Red Army rolled into Austria. The NKVD had been ordered to arrest any Hitler relative. Although she had been only six when she met Hitler in 1906 at a family gathering, she wasn't spared and was jailed for a minimum of 25 years. Schmidt died in Lefortovo in July 1949 in the typical manner – a heart attack – and Maria was executed in Verkhneuralsk in August

1953. The posthumous pardon in 1998 to every Hitler relative executed in custody within the USSR came as quite a surprise.

According to Shifrin, there was no question, in his mind, that Wallenberg was finally transported to Vladimir. 'We can confirm that Wallenberg was in building No. 4, cell 23, and he may still be there today,' was his conclusion in 1980. Great efforts were made by the guards in Vladimir to maintain the secret identity of prisoners and when corpses were removed from the mortuary for transportation to medical institutes for dissection, each corpse was decapitated to prevent any recognition. Vladimir was regarded the strictest of all the political isolation facilities run by the security services.

The Swedish government produced its extensive White Paper in 1957, and another in 1965, detailing all the evidence it had accumulated that Wallenberg was alive. Erlander had visited Moscow again in 1964 with even more accounts of sightings and possible encounters to be confronted with courteous but forceful denials. With Khrushchev deposed in October 1964, Erlander tried again with Alexei Kosygin who on the surface appeared sympathetic.

One tantalising episode included in the second White Paper occurred in January 1961. Dr Nana Svartz, a Swedish scientist, had met with a Soviet physicist, Dr Aleksandr Myashnikov, at a Moscow conference. As per usual with meetings between Swedes and Russians, the subject of Wallenberg quickly entered the conversation. Myashnikov took Svartz aside to quietly report that the diplomat was alive, but as an inmate in a mental asylum not far from the capital. On her return, Svartz recanted the conversation and the Swedish government immediately used its channels to demand clarification. The Russians did precisely that, wheeling out Myashnikov who

---

[260] Shifrin A., *The First Guidebook to Prisons and Concentration Camps of the Soviet Union*, 1980. Second edition in English, published 1982.

[261] Wrangel Island: The Research Centre for Prisons, Psych-prisons and Forced-Labour Concentration Camps of the USSR, set up in Israel, interviewed several former inmates who said that there were three camps, one reserved for foreigners. The testimony of Efim Moshinsky in 1963, certified by a notary of the US embassy in Israel, stated that 'he knew for sure that until 1962 the Swedish diplomat Raoul Wallenberg was in the camps'. Supposedly Moshinsky and Wallenberg communicated by passing notes. That was a false claim but a large contingent of foreigners was imprisoned in Wrangel.

denied not only any conversation with Svartz but also any knowledge of Raoul Wallenberg.

One ugly incident in the early 1970s, although unrelated to Wallenberg, epitomised the mutual distrust between both countries. A KGB snatch-squad grabbed a Soviet defector in a busy Stockholm street and thrust a needle into his arm before attempting to bundle him into a car. The drug failed to work as the victim not only struggled but he began to cry uncontrollably. A bystander called the police and the KGB fled. The police interviewed the defector but despite the brutality of the attack he never admitted the likely nationality of his attackers given he had a wife and daughter still living in the USSR. Outraged, the Swedish government strongly objected but in Moscow there was only deep embarrassment within the KGB that its snatch operation had been bungled.

A bizarre episode in Moscow in 1992 caused a flurry of excitement within the Swedish Foreign Office. A veteran KGB officer, Sergei Stepanov, had walked into the Swedish embassy claiming news of Wallenberg. Stepanov – undoubtedly a false name – claimed the Swede was held in the Lubyanka until 1951 before being moved to Vladimir for two years and then held in the prison in the city of Yaroslavl, to the north east of Moscow. There was no surprise that Stepanov was never heard from again.

The story of Wallenberg's final fate gained new legs in 2010 when two long-standing researchers, Susanne Berger and Vadim Birstein, in on-going correspondence with FSB archivists, were handed documentation alluding to an unnamed prisoner in the Lubyanka, known only as Prisoner No.7. This man was interrogated six days after the July 17, 1947 date of death recorded by Gromyko in his statement to the Swedes in February 1957. As Serov doesn't confirm the day and month in 1947 when Wallenberg was liquidated, Prisoner No.7 might just be credible.

The Vladimir investigation

Given the high number of sightings in Vladimir prison over the years, in 1991 two researchers in the joint Swedish-Russian working group concentrated on identifying foreign prisoners: especially one, held in an isolation cell. This 'special prisoner' had been completely isolated from other inmates, and there was a belief that Wallenberg had been moved to an unknown location but was returned to Vladimir sometime in 1954.

Marvin Makinen, professor of biochemistry at the University of Chicago, and his Chicago colleague, Ari Kaplan, undertook the Vladimir investigation with the useful co-operation of Vadim Bakatin, the KGB chairman from August-December 1991, and head of one of its very short-lived successors, the Inter-Republican Security Service. Bakatin, a loyal supporter of Gorbachev in the attempted coup that year, had knowledge of the voluminous archives held within the ministry of the interior. Centred on the Korpus II block of Vladimir, the location of the isolation cells on the third floor and the area that held the special prisoners, the complexity of the phenomenal level of research is probably unparalleled in any prison investigation.[262]

In one week, a small team went through Vladimir's cell card files in the Kartoteka, the card registry, and found that there were 98,030 cell records relating from January 1947 until December 1972, the year of the last supposed sighting of Wallenberg in the prison. Given the limited time 2,000 cell records were chosen, relating mainly to foreign prisoners, yielding 8,049 individuals, some with names but the majority with prison numbers. Each record was photographed, translated, verified and archived using the specially constructed computer model. Every cell movement on the third floor of Korpus II was carefully analysed. The occupants of cell number 2-49 were of particular interest as was the identity of the foreigner prisoner held in solitary confinement in the cells opposite, 2-41 and 2-44.

A prisoner – Kirill Ivanovich Osmak – had died in 2-49 on May 16, 1960. Intriguingly, analysis confirmed that cells opposite remained empty from 243 to 717 days overlapping with the death of Osmak. The reason, presumed the researchers, was to conceal the identity of the foreign prisoner in 2-41 or 2-44 and to prevent cell-

---

[262] Entitled *Cell Occupancy Analysis of Korpus 2 of the Vladimir Prison – an examination of the Consistency of Eyewitness Sightings of Raoul Wallenberg with Prisoner Registration Cards from the Prison Kartoteka.*

tapping. The Russian authorities offered up for interview a former Vladimir prisoner and a jail worker. On studying a photograph of Wallenberg both agreed that the secret prisoner seen in Vladimir was the same man. Makinen and Kaplan believed that Wallenberg had been incarcerated in the Soviet Union at least into the 1960s, possibly the 1970s and further, even though Wallenberg's name never appeared on any record. Two Swedish judges, perusing the analysis concluded: 'In our view, and under Swedish law, the present enquiry must find that Wallenberg was probably alive and held at Vladimir, at least until the early 1950s, although there is no conclusive proof in this respect'.

The archive of the Swedish Foreign Office is a collective litany of sightings, many reported with the best of intentions. Any sightings recorded post-1947 were certainly false trails. The Swedes were forever in a bind over verification, illustrated from one very early sighting.

Adolphe Cohen, a released PoW, had shared his experience in a letter to the Swedish minister in Paris, a follow-up to a phone conversation. He claimed to have shared a cell with Wallenberg from December 1946 to March 18, 1947 in the Brygidki Cloister, the notorious prison in L'vov, in the Ukraine. Wallenberg, explained Cohen, had been angry that money and jewellery 'which had been given to him by some friends, for safety's sake' had been confiscated.

Cohen suggested in his letter that to confirm his Wallenberg claim, the Swedish authorities should smuggle fresh laundry into the jail. 'Laundry parcels are usually accepted, even for strictly isolated prisoners. Dirty laundry is taken from the prisoner and returned with a signed prisoner receipt. Having such irrefutable evidence in his own handwriting, the Russian authorities would then have to confirm his existence in prison in L'vov,' Cohen wrote. A postscript to the letter, however, did resonate. Wallenberg supposedly had related to Cohen that after his arrest in Budapest, a Russian intelligence officer told him that a Swiss diplomat had also been arrested. How had Cohen known about the Swiss diplomat? Could Cohen have heard through another source that two Swiss diplomats had been released after their arrest by the NKVD, or was there some truth that Wallenberg had been, or still was, in the

Ukraine? Was Cohen merely a fantasist?

In my trawl of the Swedish Foreign Office files, I wanted to locate at least one sighting or personal account that had fitted in with Ivan Serov's memoir.

I had long been drawn to Krasnogorsk, to Camp 27. This huge detention centre to the north west of Moscow held not only thousands of foreigners who were being sifted in 1945 before onward transportation to the jails or labour camps but prisoners who had been moved out of the Lubyanka because of cell overcrowding. Trying to uncover the name of Wallenberg's executioner, Serov stated that Krasnogorsk had been one of the killing grounds for the Laboratory X doctors. Had Wallenberg been in Krasnogorsk at any time during his two-year incarceration in the Soviet Union? His cellmate, Roedel, according to the Russians, had died of a 'heart attack' enroute to the camp in October 1947. Several released PoWs in their statements to the Swedish investigators had referred to 'K', outside Moscow. A tall Swede had been observed in Camp 27 and Wallenberg had been seen under an armed guard. Sadly, I couldn't locate any document that could accurately date the sightings.

Not mentioned in the memoir was the NKVD and Smersh holding centre in Gödöllö to the east of Budapest. There was no reason for Serov to mention this requisitioned high school as he dealt mainly with matters in Moscow.

Few inmates of Gödöllö remain alive but I did track down one in 2011, in Australia. I wanted to speak to Dr Jerzy Trau, who had written to the Swedish consul in Sydney in October 1978. A resident in Eastwood, New South Wales, Trau had previously spoken to the diplomat on the phone.

Escaping from the Vámosmikola concentration camp in Hungary, he had hidden in the ruins of Budapest before being caught by the Soviets after the city succumbed to the Red Army. With hundreds of other Hungarian and Polish Jews rounded up at the end of January 1945, Trau was taken to Gödöllö. For several days, wrote Trau, he and other prisoners were crammed into the school's cellar and sleeping next to him was a Swedish diplomat of about 30 years of age who wore a dark suit. They had shared many conversations in the short time they were together and the Swede had shown him his passport. Trau was later transferred out of Gödöllö to another camp, and the Swede had remained.

> 'I only learned about the search for Wallenberg several days ago from an article in the Australian Jewish Times. I no longer recall the name of the diplomat I met in 1945, but unless there was another Swedish diplomat of his age arrested at that time by the Russians in Hungary there is no possibility that he could be anyone else.'

Still residing in New South Wales, Dr Trau remains convinced that his former cellar mate in Gödöllö was Wallenberg. Almost certainly, Smersh, after lifting Wallenberg and Langfelder out of Pest would have held them in Gödöllö to await instruction from Moscow. Serov did confirm that Moscow hadn't determined what to do with Wallenberg and had even contemplated handing him back to the legation. Interrogation rooms at been set aside at Gödöllö and it was here that Wallenberg and Langfelder endured their first intensive Smersh grilling.

19

The Smoking Gun – final thoughts

*We had discovered that Wallenberg was cremated after his liquidation.
The ashes were buried in the grave of unknown remains for the years
1947-1951 in the Donskoye crematorium cemetery. Ashes of the three
foreigners were also buried there. As far as I can remember, Wallenberg's
driver was liquidated, as were the two cellmates of the driver. They had
to be killed because they knew the details on Wallenberg. Abakumov
believed that if these men would be freed and returned home, the
circumstances of Wallenberg's death would be made public.*

Extract from Ivan Serov's memoir

IVAN SEROV'S jumbled and uncategorised archive of files,
letters, documents and photographs was an astounding feast of
WW2 and Cold War secrets, but why in the new Russia hadn't this
revealing record, including the Wallenberg memoir, ever surfaced?
That could never be an option, Svetlana, his daughter, had admitted
to me with her father's name forever associated with several of
the worst excesses of both the Stalin regime and the KGB.
Serov writes:

> *In 1987, I received several phone calls at my dacha from both Russian
> and foreign journalists, all of them interested in the fate of one man –
> Raoul Wallenberg.*
>
> *I replied to all of them that I didn't want to talk about this matter and
> I knew nothing about this case. I was surprised how they had found
> my telephone number, which was not registered in any directory. I had*

259

my phone number immediately changed. However, because of the persistent nature of these requests I was convinced that the case of Wallenberg was of contemporary importance.

These are my recollections of the matter.

The existence of the Serov memoir – the smoking gun – posed a problem for me. If I published it, would the memoir be immediately trashed as a fake by those who persist in the belief that Wallenberg was alive after 1947, imprisoned somewhere in the Russian system and identified only by a prisoner number? Sceptics might further argue whether any memoir written by one of Russia's most notorious security chiefs could be deemed credible.

I had no reason to doubt the authenticity of the memoir. I had viewed the archive held in a Moscow apartment. It had long been rumoured in the Soviet security services that Serov had conducted an investigation into Wallenberg, yet nothing existed in the records. Nothing would ever exist. Khrushchev had ordered that the investigation be conducted in the utmost secrecy. He further suggested in 1956 that all pertinent documents should be destroyed and only retain whatever was necessary for any future explanation to the Swedes. The majority of documents were destroyed by Serov and his officers. The MVD personnel record for Colonel Dobrohotov, one of Serov's investigation officers, was doctored with an unaccountable three-month gap from December 11, 1953 until March 17, 1954. That missing period dovetailed perfectly with the timing of this investigation.

Serov had written his memoir on Wallenberg as communism within the Soviet Union was drawing its dying breath, and there were gaps in his account. It had been compiled from the documents and material in his possession and his memory, Svetlana had told me. I could only conjecture if Serov had some culpability in the decision to eliminate the Swede. In the memoir, there is no mention. His brief from Khrushchev was to determine who amongst the first secretary's political opponents, with Stalin, had ordered the killing and the name of the liquidator. Serov did admit to being mindful of the wartime surveillance on the Wallenberg family. A reminder:

I first heard of the name, Wallenberg, during wartime when I acted as the Special Representative of the Soviet High Command. At that time I had been informed that a member of the Wallenberg family had on several occasions visited the German-occupied Soviet territories, mainly the city of Pskov, where he had contacts with the fascist civil administration and the Abwehr, German military intelligence.

Had Serov been alerted to Wallenberg's execution in 1947? The timing is crucial and annoyingly the actual day and month is omitted in his memoir. Gromyko had accorded the diplomat's death as July 17 but that date cannot be deemed reliable. In the early months of 1947, Serov was still in Berlin serving as chief of civilian administration in the Soviet zone and building up Karlshorst, the Soviet intelligence centre. Serov was posted back to Moscow in the spring to become the first deputy minister of the MVD under Lavrenty Beria and in that role he certainly would be privy to the details of Wallenberg's death. Serov did disclose in his memoir that many foreign prisoners held throughout the Soviet prison system were executed that year.

Naming Wallenberg's killer would prove difficult. Each suspect was interviewed by either Serov or Colonel Kozyrev, his MVD investigator, but they all repudiated responsibility even refuting any knowledge of the diplomat prisoner. Blokhin, the NKVD's officially sanctioned state executioner, with his signature adorning a death certificate in the Wallenberg file, was the prime candidate but the toxicologists in Laboratory X could not be discounted. Serov was fully aware that the laboratory, headed by Colonel Zhelezov, had liquidated prisoners in the Lubyanka, Lefortovo, Butyrka, Vladimir and in the holding camp for foreigners in Krasnogorsk. Serov would often have sought recourse to the services of the disgraced head scientist, Dr Maironovsky, Dr Naimov, his successor at the time of Wallenberg's death, and Dr Smiakov, Naimov's deputy.

Upon Wallenberg's arrival in Moscow from Budapest, it is very likely that he would have encountered the methods of Maironovsky, who had admitted from his jail cell that Laboratory X maintained records of prisoners under its care. At the time of Serov's investigation, however, those records had disappeared. Dmitry

Sukhanov, a senior aide to Malenkov, one of the prime movers in the decision to execute Wallenberg, had removed all such incriminating records from the Lubyanka. That act does point to either Naimov or Smiakov being the killer.

The Swedish government rigorously pursued any avenue to discover what had happened to the nation's 'Lost Hero'. No effort had been spared in interviewing returning PoWs in the mid-1950s. In the Stockholm files are long lists of PoWs who were contacted but not everyone acquiesced to interview. That persistent Swedish Foreign Office investigator, Gunnar Lorentzon, often reverted to subterfuge. Posing as Johann Lorentz, a German businessman, he travelled into Soviet-occupied Austria, East Germany and other Eastern Bloc countries. He had some hairy moments and risked arrest with the KGB enforcing a blanket ban on any delving into the disappearance of Wallenberg. Tag Erlander, Sweden's prime minister, made tireless efforts to determine the truth with personal pleas in Moscow, first to Khrushchev and then to Kosygin.

I was given excellent assistance in my research from a senior official at the Swedish Foreign Office, and his staff, who still maintained a brief – somewhat lessening now – to monitor any new information on Wallenberg that came in. I never disclosed to him the existence of the Serov memoir but I did raise the question on whether the Swedish Foreign Office in 1957, after Gromyko's statement, might have believed that Wallenberg had indeed died in 1947. Some in the ministry and in other areas of government had surely looked beyond the usual Soviet disinformation fug at the time?

In the bitter pre-trial horse-trading between the Allies at Nuremberg, Raoul Wallenberg was a political pawn. What had been 'extracted' by Likhachev, the brutal Smersh interrogator, who Serov revealed always handled the high-profile cases?

From the reports of Dobrohotov and Fedotov, it became clear that Stalin and Molotov had planned to use evidence extracted from the interrogation of Wallenberg for secret negotiations with the Americans on issues not to be raised at the Nuremberg trials.

With the military tribunal of the top Nazis ending in October 1946, there remained one final window of opportunity for the Swedish government to save its man. Sadly, the Swedes deigned to refuse it.

At the ending of the Nuremberg trials Raoul Wallenberg had lost his validity and his usefulness to us. On the orders of Molotov and Abakumov, the Soviet Ministry of Foreign Affairs hinted to the Swedes that Wallenberg could be exchanged for the return of Soviet traitors who had escaped to Sweden. These proposals yielded no results.

The common image is of the Swedish government and the Wallenberg family working and acting together over Raoul, but had the family been privy to Molotov's *'hinting'* overture to the Swedish Foreign Office? That question quickly begs another. Had the government, and the family, exerted the strongest pressure in pursuing a release post-Nuremberg?

Was the concealment of Sweden's wartime activities and US corporate collaboration with the Nazis a greater priority?

Sweden's image of neutrality certainly had been tarnished. Senior members of its intelligence services and the military had handed over top-secret details of Allied military strength to Japanese intelligence officers working in Stockholm. The lucrative Stockholm-based trade in looted diamonds from Antwerp, run by a ring of German traders, had never been stopped. For all Swedish exports during the war to the British, including vital ball bearings, Sweden and the Wallenberg family demanded gold in payment, refusing Sterling. That action had really rankled in London especially as some German payments for Swedish ores and manufactures were made with looted funds from occupied Europe, laundered through the Swiss banking system.

The Wallenberg family had enjoyed a profitable war, its factories pumping output to both the Allied and Third Reich war machines. Post-war accusations of collaboration had put at stake the reputation of the growing industrial and banking dynasty. Stockholms Enskilda Banken, the Wallenberg bank, acting for the German Reichsbank in the United States, had conducted transactions with several Wall Street banks including Chase Manhattan and JP Morgan.

Does Khrushchev's commission to Serov in December 1953 to secretly investigate Wallenberg's death, indicate he wanted – then – to admit to Sweden that the diplomat was dead?

Khrushchev had only been in office for nine months. It was a pivotal time with the rebuilding of the war-ravaged economy faltering and starved of Western capital and technology. Lend-Lease had long been terminated and Stalin had refused to participate in the post-war Marshall Plan that gave US aid to Europe. America was in no mood to compromise with its former WW2 ally and in 1947, the US Senate Appropriations Committee had set the tone for the next 50 years by barring all high-tech exports to the USSR. Immediately caught up in the ban was an imminent $25mn shipment urgently required for a bombed Soviet oil refinery. Russia was energy rich but cash poor. Congress formalised the equally stringent Export Credit Act in 1949, again targeting Soviet oil and gas. Harry Truman's administration, the following year, further tightened the embargo with the Battle Act and punitive oil sanctions imposed on any third-party country that diverted US-made goods to the USSR. The Soviet Union was being frozen out.

Foreign economic assistance was urgently required, warned Khrushchev in the Politburo but Molotov, in particular, took the alternative view and demanded a return to the full rigours of Stalinism. Serov described how Khrushchev wanted to reactivate the secret 'back-channels' to Britain and the US that existed pre-war in Stockholm. For that to happen, the party secretary needed rapprochement with Sweden. Only an admission over the fate of Wallenberg would jumpstart a better political relationship with the West.

Serov provides no answer why Khrushchev didn't come clean to the Swedes once the investigation was over in March 1954. Perhaps it was Khrushchev's political vulnerability. Molotov and Malenkov remained dangerous, commanding support in the Politburo and the Central Committee. Both were directly implicated with Stalin on the decision to liquidate Wallenberg. Without Serov's unflagging support as chairman of the fledgling KGB, Khrushchev's position as first secretary looked tenuous.

The Swedish public will be angered and astonished by Serov's revelations. What has never been known until now, was the initial Soviet intention to hand the diplomat back in Hungary just days after he and Langfelder were lifted out of Budapest. The disclosure from a Soviet agent embedded in US Intelligence that Wallenberg's humanitarian role in Budapest provided the cover for clandestine activities had condemned him to interrogation and imprisonment in Moscow.

There was no homecoming for the Budapest hero, the decision not to exchange the Russian defectors and the killers from the Baltics had condemned Raoul Wallenberg to death, either by Blokhin's pistol or through a syringe administered by a Laboratory X poisoner. Might Wallenberg's jailers and interrogators have shared with him that fateful Stockholm decision not to negotiate? Did Mironov, the notorious Lubyanka prison director, personally tell Wallenberg? Mironov's name was on one of the death certificates located in the Committee of Information file.

In the years that followed, Sweden found it convenient to further trash Söderblom, the Moscow ambassador, for his abject failure in not pushing Stalin and Molotov. Serov had heightened the continuing intrigue as chairman of the KGB by setting hares running in the West that the KGB had embarked on a mission to determine what had happened to the diplomat. That was Serov at his best.

The enigma of Wallenberg perpetuated long after Serov was dumped as the GRU director in July 1962 after the GRU officer, Penkovsky, was uncovered by the KGB as an MI6 spy. Serov describes what he called an *'informal meeting'* with a KGB chairman who sought clarification over Wallenberg.

After I had retired on my pension I had an informal meeting with one of the Chairmen of the KGB. I don't wish to mention his name but he was fully aware about KGB operations in the past.

He asked me:

'Ivan Alexsandrovich, is there a possibility that Wallenberg may be found in places of imprisonment in the USSR, living under a false name?'

I responded that my officers had conducted a thorough review of the Wallenberg case and I had no doubts that Wallenberg, with three foreigners, had been liquidated in 1947.

In post–communist Russia the Donskoye is a quiet shelter from the hustle and urgency of a country bristling with oligarchs, some who grew fat on the corrupt proceeds of Yeltsin's dodgy public auctions of the country's vast energy and mineral wealth. Entering by the main gate, visitors approach the temple. To its left and down a short path is the largest memorial in the cemetery.

We had discovered that Wallenberg was cremated after his liquidation, wrote Serov. The ashes were buried in the grave of unknown remains for the years 1947-1951 in the Donskoye crematorium cemetery. Ashes of the three foreigners were also buried there.

The mound is marked with a memorial stone commemorating the victims of political oppression from 1945 until 1953, the year of Stalin's death[263]. In the middle of the memorial is a large stone figure kneeling in prayer. Around the mound are headstones, victims executed by the security services during this period through poison or the bullet. To the right is the headstone for 13 Jewish victims, members of a Jewish committee who Stalin had slaughtered by the MVD on August 12, 1952 during the dictator's final Jewish purge and just months from his own death. To the left of the Jewish headstone is one in Japanese commemorating the killing of one of its own. Further left is a headstone for a prime minister of Hungary. There are more than a dozen headstones.

Within hours of his execution, the body of Raoul Wallenberg was driven to the Donskoye and the Kommandatura detail had carefully observed and recorded the cremation of this special prisoner. His ashes were unceremoniously dumped into the open pit.

---

[263] See photograph *[Moscow-48]*.

The final enigma in the Wallenberg story?

Intriguingly, there is a much smaller marble memorial stone a few feet to the left and front of this mound, easy to miss under the snow. 'Common grave, No. 3, victims not identified, no enquiries, 1945-1989', it says.

Do Wallenberg's ashes lay under this stone?

20

Col. General Ivan Serov –
Chairman, KGB, March 1954 – December 1958
Director, GRU, January 1959 – July 1962
– His memoir in full

★ ★ ★

IN 1987, I RECEIVED SEVERAL PHONE CALLS at my dacha from both Russian and foreign journalists, all of them interested in the fate of one man – Raoul Wallenberg.

I replied to all of them that I didn't want to talk about this matter and I knew nothing about this case. I was surprised how they had found my telephone number, which was not registered in any directory. I had my phone number immediately changed. However, because of the persistent nature of these requests I was convinced that the case of Wallenberg was of contemporary importance.

These are my recollections of the matter.

I first heard of the name, Wallenberg, during wartime when I acted as the Special Representative of the Soviet High Command.[264] At that time I had been informed that a member of the Wallenberg family had on several occasions visited the German-occupied Soviet territories, mainly the city of Pskov,[265] where he had contacts with the fascist civil administration and the Abwehr, German military intelligence.

Many years passed and I forgot about Wallenberg until in late 1953 when his name came up in conversation with Fedotov, chief of the MGB's Counterintelligence Directorate.[266] Fedotov related to me that agents of several foreign intelligence services had brought up the matter of Wallenberg in Moscow.

I ordered Fedotov to provide me with more details on Wallenberg.

Fedotov related to me that Wallenberg had been the representative of the Swedish Red Cross in Budapest and had been closely connected with German and American intelligence services. In 1947, he and three other foreigners connected with him were liquidated on the orders of Abakumov.[267]

He told me that Wallenberg's registration card was still being held in the Counterintelligence Directorate but more importantly, Wallenberg had a file, which was held in the archive of the Committee of Information and had been there since Fedotov had been its deputy chairman.

I now asked Dobrohotov,[268] another MVD officer, to uncover the operational details of the Wallenberg case. He had recently transferred from the MGB Secretariat to the foreign intelligence department.

From what information I had collected, I briefed Nikita Khrushchev.[269] He became very interested in what I had to say, and ordered me to delve further, but forbade me from talking to Molotov[270] or anyone else in the Ministry of Foreign Affairs about the secret assignment that he had given me.

From my conversation with Khrushchev, I had the distinct impression that he wanted me to show clearly that Beria and Abakumov had been responsible for the liquidation of Wallenberg.

Khrushchev felt that if we admitted our guilt into the liquidation of Wallenberg, we could rebuild the Soviet Union's relations with

---

[264] Serov, deputy head of Smersh, was the most senior intelligence officer with Marshal Zhukov on the push into German-held territory and the advance on Berlin.

[265] In northwest Russia.

[266] **Fedotov, Lt. Gen. Peter**: NKVD, Committee of Information (KI), MGB and KGB.

[267] **Abakumov, Lt. Gen. Viktor Semyonovich**: Smersh chief. When Smersh was rolled into the NKGB in April 1946 he was appointed minister of state security and dismissed in 1951. He was jailed and released in March 1953 on Stalin's death, but arrested again over his role in the 'Leningrad Trials'. Executed on December 18, 1954.

[268] **Dobrohotov, Col. Vasily Ivanovich**: MVD, MGB and KGB Secretariat head. During the time of the Wallenberg investigation, Serov tasked him with preparing the blueprint for the establishment of the KGB.

[269] **Khrushchev, Nikita Sergeyevich**: Elected to the Central Committee in 1934, and the Politburo in 1939, he headed the communist party in the Ukraine. Upon Stalin's death in March 1953 and the later elimination of Beria, Khrushchev was part of the collective leadership as First Secretary of the party. It took until 1955 before he could consolidate his position. In February 1956, at the 20th Party Congress, he denounced Stalin and his policies. Leonid Brezhnev, and others, forced Khrushchev to retire as leader in 1964.

[270] **Molotov, Vyacheslav Mikhaylovich**: Soviet foreign minister and deputy to Stalin on the wartime Council of Ministers. Known as 'hard-arse' Molotov in the international community. A plotter, Khrushchev finally had him expelled from the party in 1962.

Sweden and improve our relations with the West and the international banking community. In his mind, Khrushchev had also taken the view that Sweden might again act for us as a broker in forming secret ties with America and Britain. In this latter respect, Khrushchev was specifically interested, probably because he had other considerations in mind, which I will refer to later.

I continued my investigation.

Dobrohotov now had more details for me regarding Wallenberg's special wartime mission in our territories occupied by the Germans. He informed me that at the time, we had received details about Wallenberg's mission from America and Sweden. The intelligence we had received from America had been of particular importance.

One of our sources working in American Intelligence during the war, a prominent agent for the NKVD, had related to us that Wallenberg was a US Intelligence agent with established contacts in the Gestapo.

Under the cover of negotiating the fate of the Jews in the occupied territories, there existed secret and informal channels of communication between German and American intelligence.

It was Wallenberg himself who contacted the Red Army Command. Smersh detained him in the beginning of 1945, after the liberation of Budapest. As well as him, some Swiss diplomats were arrested.

At first the plan was to hand Wallenberg back to the Swedes but the NKGB's First Directorate had received a memorandum on his ties with Hitler and the US Intelligence agencies.

Stalin ordered Abakumov to issue a warrant to arrest Wallenberg and bring him to Moscow for interrogation. Wallenberg's driver in Budapest was also to be interrogated in Moscow.

From the documents taken from Wallenberg, it followed that he maintained regular contact with high-level Nazis, including the notorious Adolf Eichmann who organised the massive elimination of the Jewish population throughout Europe. We also had reliable information that the Swedish Embassy in Budapest had provided diplomatic passports and other documents to officers of Hitler's secret services involved in covert operations.

Wallenberg was suspected of being involved in these activities as he had on a number of occasions visited German-occupied territories, especially the city of Pskov. We had therefore accused Wallenberg of being a double agent and a Nazi spy.

Dobrohotov had summarised what was available in the files of the Committee of Information and it was clear that Smersh was responsible for the investigation and interrogation of Wallenberg. The officer in charge of the investigation and interrogation was Likhachev (who was later shot). Likhachev, the deputy head of the Investigation Department of Smersh, always handled the high profile cases.[271]

As well as using Dobrohotov into my investigation over the death of Wallenberg, I ordered Colonel Kozyrev from the Investigation Department of the MVD to look into Likhachev's original investigation.[272] Kozyrev reported to me that no details of the original investigation remained but of what there was, no direct evidence implicated Wallenberg with espionage. However, during the interrogation Wallenberg did not deny that he maintained regular contacts with prominent Nazis and persons who had been confirmed by the MGB[273] as American Intelligence officers.

From the reports of Dobrohotov and Fedotov, it became clear that Stalin and Molotov had planned to use evidence extracted from the interrogation of Wallenberg for secret negotiations with the Americans on issues not to be raised at the Nuremberg trials. Fedotov had been responsible from the Soviet end for the preparation of these trials and he told me that the Americans had met our request not to raise the issue of the secret Ribbentrop-Molotov protocols. In exchange, we could not raise the issue of the financial ties that existed between the United States and Hitler's industrialists arranged with the help of the Wallenberg family, and the secret contacts that had taken place on negotiating a separate peace treaty with the Germans.

At the ending of the Nuremberg trials, Raoul Wallenberg had lost his validity and his usefulness to us. On the orders of Molotov and

---

[271] **Likhachev, Gen. M.T**: He was executed in December 1954 with Abakumov and other security chiefs.

[272] **Kozyrev, Col. Aleksandr Alexandrovich**: NKVD, MVD and KGB investigator. During WW2, he was a member of the NKVD team that covered up the NKVD execution of one Soviet camp holding Polish PoWs.

[273] MGB: a predecessor of the KGB, its dates of operation were 1946-1953.

Abakumov, the Soviet Ministry of Foreign Affairs hinted to the Swedes that Wallenberg could be exchanged for the return of Soviet traitors who had escaped to Sweden. These proposals yielded no results.

Abakumov had given the note to Molotov that Wallenberg should be liquidated. In my investigation, that note was given to me personally by Malin,[274] Khrushchev's assistant in his secretariat, with whom I was on good terms.

Molotov had raised the issue of liquidating Wallenberg as well as American,[275] German, Japanese and other foreign citizens detained by us after the war. Stalin endorsed Molotov's proposal, believing that there was now no reason to return Wallenberg to Sweden.

We could not establish in our investigation the precise details of Wallenberg's liquidation as well as the liquidation of three other foreigners who were connected to him. One was his driver, an Austrian or German, and the other two were cellmates of the driver.

The documents in the Wallenberg file included the report by the prison doctor, the statement signed by the head of the internal prison, Mironov,[276] and the commandant of the Kommandatura of the MGB, Blokhin.[277]

It confirmed Wallenberg's death in 1947.

My officers subsequently questioned Blokhin. He stated that neither he nor any of his officers had a connection with Wallenberg's liquidation. He didn't even recall the episode.

We then questioned members of the special department within the MGB that had dealt with toxins and the use of such poisons at that time, including its head, Zhelezov,[278] and his officers, Naumov[279] and Smiakov,[280] on the events of 1946–47. They had liquidated a number of foreign citizens in the Lubyanka, Vladimir prison and in the PoW camp in Krasnogorsk.[281] However, all three men were unaware of the names of their victims.

Abakumov was already being questioned by Colonel Kozyrev (his case was being investigated by the MVD, not by officers in the prosecutor's office), and he confirmed that Wallenberg had been liquidated on the direct orders of Stalin and Molotov, with whom he had consulted on a number of occasions regarding the detained Swedish diplomat. We were also able to establish that the arrest of

Wallenberg had been sanctioned by the Politburo.

I reported these new disclosures to Khrushchev. He listened to me attentively and then he said:

'Those scoundrels Stalin, Molotov and Vyshinsky[282] stirred this dirty soup and now we must drink and eat up this shit.'[283]

Khrushchev wanted me to go into detail on the involvement of Molotov and Vyshinsky in Wallenberg's liquidation and he instructed me not to charge Abakumov or Abakumov's associates with his death. Khrushchev also wanted me to speak to Molotov and tell him that people in the West had serious intentions to bring up the disappearance of Wallenberg.

I duly met Molotov in his office in the Kremlin. He very painfully reacted to my questions and said:

'Only idiots could hope to gain any profit from this case.'

Molotov went on to say that in no way should the Wallenberg case be used to re-establish confidential relations with the Swedish government. Angrily, he repeated to me that the issue was closed and would not be re-opened.

At the end of our meeting Molotov peered at me suspiciously and said:

---

[274] **Malin, Vladimir**: Key Khrushchev member of his secretariat, 1954-65.

[275] **Isaiah (Isaac) Oggins** was one. An American, he was an NKVD recruiter operating in the US and Europe. Later arrested by the NKVD, detained in Norilsk and executed in the Lubyanka in 1947.

[276] **Mironov, Colonel Aleksandr Nikolayevich**: Long career in the Lubyanka prison service. Known for his torture methods.

[277] **Blokhin, Maj. Gen. Vasily Mikhailovich**: Kommandatura chief who was a long-standing state executioner.

[278] **Zhelezov, Anatoli Alekseyevich**: Administrative head of Laboratory X.

[279] **Naumov, Dr Vasily**: Succeeded Grigori Maironovsky as head scientist at Laboratory X.

[280] **Smiakov, Dr**: Deputy to Naumov at Laboratory X.

[281] Camp No. 27, Krasnogorsk, was one of three camps in the area run by the NKVD from 1942, and known to hold foreign prisoners. It was closed down in 1950.

[282] **Vyshinsky, Andrei Yanuaryevich**: Lawyer who was the Soviet chief prosecutor in the trials during the Great Purge, 1934-38. WW2 member of the Central Committee. In August 1947, Vyshinsky delivered a note to the Swedish ambassador in Moscow, Söhlman, stating that Wallenberg was not on any Soviet territory nor did any Soviet authority know him. Foreign minister in 1949. Later spokesman at the United Nations.

[283] This is the direct translation from Serov's diary.

'Why are you raising this matter now?'

I answered that I was only fulfilling an order from the Central Committee.

I reported my conversation with Molotov to Khrushchev. He became very angry and said that the leadership would have to get rid of Molotov. Khrushchev ordered me to secretly use our agents to assess what answer to the Wallenberg issue would satisfy the Swedish authorities. At the same time, Khrushchev forbade me to channel any documents or written reports on Wallenberg to the Central Committee without his personal sanction. I think that was because until the end of 1954, Malenkov[284] headed the Special Commission[285] that reported into the Central Committee. Sukhanov, his advisor,[286] was also on the Special Commission. Khrushchev didn't trust Malenkov who in January 1955 was removed from his post as Chairman of the Council of Ministers on the initiative of Molotov and Khrushchev.

After the demotion of Malenkov, it was Molotov's turn to be ousted from the Ministry of Foreign Affairs. I think that from the very beginning, Khrushchev used the case of Wallenberg against Molotov.

Molotov understood the position very well and his attitude towards me was hostile, as he believed I was Khrushchev's man. At a session of the Presidium in 1954, Molotov, together with Malenkov, spoke against my appointment as Chairman of the KGB.[287] Both had wanted Shatalin,[288] the secretary of the Central Committee, to be the Chairman.

I must mention that the establishment of just one security agency had emerged unexpectedly. Earlier in the year, Kruglov,[289] in the Presidium, had brought up the question on whether the Ministry of Internal Affairs should be restructured. At the time, Khrushchev had already tasked me with secretly preparing a proposal to set up the KGB.

I entrusted the chief of the Secretariat, Dobrohotov, to prepare the proposal. I handed it to Shuisky,[290] Khrushchev's assistant. I hadn't signed it.

Meanwhile, the case of Wallenberg remained under my personal control.

Our counterintelligence department told me, in 1955, that a social democrat from Sweden, a Jew, was to visit the USSR to meet Ilia Ehrenberg,[291] one of our prominent writers. He wanted Ehrenberg to assist in arranging an audience with Voroshilov.[292] The Swede had chosen Ehrenberg because he was also Jewish. Ehrenberg worked for the KGB and had been operationally developed by us. In 1949, Abakumov had asked Stalin for permission to arrest Ehrenberg but Stalin refused.

Before this meeting between Ehrenberg and the Swede, Ehrenberg had been briefed by Kharitonov,[293] the chief of the Fourth Department (the secret political group in the KGB). Kharitonov agreed that the meeting should take place but advised Ehrenberg to avoid providing any specific answers to questions on Wallenberg's fate. However, he should hint that the Soviet authorities did not rule out the fact that Wallenberg may have been imprisoned in the USSR and probably became the victim of Beria and Abakumov.

---

[284] **Malenkov, Georgy Maksimilianovich**: Close collaborator of Stalin who served on the State Defence Committee, the GKO, during the war. Upon Stalin's death in March 1953, he became Chairman of the Council of Ministers, a post he held only until the appointment of Khrushchev in the following September.

[285] It dealt mainly with intelligence issues.

[286] **Sukhanov, Dmitry**: He removed all poisoning records of prisoners from the Lubyanka.

[287] Established by Khrushchev in March 1954 with the merger of the MGB and the MVD, the two state security agencies responsible for internal security and external intelligence.

[288] **Shatalin, Nikolai**: MVD.

[289] **Kruglov, Gen. Sergei Nikiforovich**: Wartime deputy to Beria. Post-war, both Kruglov and Serov were deputy heads of the MVD.

[290] **Shuisky, Grigory Trokhimovich**: Key aide and speechwriter who also worked with Khrushchev when he ran the communist party in the Ukraine.

[291] **Ehrenberg, Ilia**: Abakumov was convinced he was a double agent. Good friend of Picasso.

[292] **Voroshilov, Kliment Yefremovich**: Close aide of Stalin and elected to the Politburo in 1926. Marshal of the Soviet Union in WW2, he commanded Leningrad during the German siege but stripped of his rank by Stalin. Between 1945-47, he supervised the establishment of the communist regime in Hungary. In March 1953, he became Presidium chairman and later he was a member of the Anti-Party Group.

[293] **Kharitonov, Lt. Gen. Fedor Petrovich**: Head of Fourth Directorate 1954 to 1957. From 1957-60 he ran the KGB in Rumania.

I also ordered Panyushkin[294] to evaluate the reaction of the Swedes after the meeting with Ehrenberg had taken place. Representatives of the Swedish Foreign Office had said that the Swedish government would not accuse the present leadership of the USSR over the disappearance of Wallenberg, as it was a criminal act of Beria.

However, I believed that we had to undertake a probe into how the Wallenberg case was being perceived internationally. Khrushchev sanctioned that we should leak out to other countries the same story that we were telling the Swedes. Through our rezidencies in a number of countries[295] we informed the Swedes that we were ready to discuss the Wallenberg issue and his fate.

This task was also arranged in Finland where we had a strong operational organisation. One of my officers met with a Finnish diplomat. Apart from Finland, other talks on this matter were conducted by our officers and trusted agents.

Khrushchev talked to me several times about Wallenberg. I had realised that this matter was extremely important to him, as he wanted to use this case amongst others to get rid of several members of the Presidium who represented a danger to him.

I think that this consideration put the case of Wallenberg at a very high level, otherwise no one else would have been bothered about it. The KGB was entrusted to prepare documents that would answer the questions that the Swedish government might ask. Our position on this matter was always supervised and endorsed by Khrushchev. There was to be a planned visit of the Swedish Prime Minister to Moscow, to which the Soviet leadership attached great importance. The visit took place in 1956, but no documents were handed over to the Swedish delegation. Molotov and I were ordered by Khrushchev not to speed up any responses before the parliamentary elections in Sweden had taken place.

---

[294] **Panyushkin, Maj. Gen. Aleksandr Semyonovich**: NKVD. Ambassador to China 1939-1944, 1952-1953. Washington ambassador and head of station 1947-1952.

[295] This was mainly done through the KGB rezidency in Ankara, Turkey. Pavel Yerzin, who had been a wartime NKVD colleague of Vladimir Barkovsky and Anatoly Gorski in London, was tasked with talking to intelligence staff of the Swedish Embassy.

[296] The Anti-Party Group had unsuccessfully attempted to depose Khrushchev in June 1957. Molotov was subsequently posted to Mongolia as ambassador. Malenkov fared worse. He managed a hydroelectric power station in Kazakhstan and remained in the territory for the next 30 years.

At the plenary session of the Central Committee, Khrushchev purged the Anti-Party Group led by Molotov and Malenkov.[296] Only then did I realise why he had ordered me to raise the documents on this dirty affair.

After I had retired on my pension, I had an informal meeting with one of the Chairmen of the KGB. I don't wish to mention his name but he was fully aware about KGB operations in the past.

He asked me:

'Ivan Aleksandrovich, is there a possibility that Wallenberg may be found in places of imprisonment in the USSR, living under a false name?'

I responded that my officers had conducted a thorough review of the Wallenberg case and I had no doubts that Wallenberg, with three foreigners, had been liquidated in 1947.

We had discovered that Wallenberg was cremated after his liquidation. The ashes were buried in the grave of unknown remains for the years 1947-1951 in the Donskoye crematorium cemetery. Ashes of the three foreigners were also buried there. As far as I can remember, Wallenberg's driver was liquidated, as were the two cellmates of the driver. They had to be killed because they knew the details on Wallenberg. Abakumov believed that if these men would be freed and returned home, the circumstances of Wallenberg's death would be made public.

The Wallenberg case was top secret within the KGB. When Bulganin and Molotov brought up the issue in the Presidium in 1956, Khrushchev suggested to me that all MGB and KGB documents surrounding the case should be destroyed. Only some should be retained for any future explanations to the Swedes.

The case of Wallenberg for us had ended. It was of no main significance for the KGB. We had only fulfilled the orders of Khrushchev who had intrigued to get rid of Molotov.

In the West, people didn't realise that the noisy campaign to determine the fate of Wallenberg had been personally inspired by Khrushchev who was protecting his own interests. Khrushchev skilfully used the West for this purpose.

Appendix 1

THIS ILLUMINATIVE and unique report, written in German, not Swedish, was compiled by an unknown member of the Swedish Legation in Budapest during the chaos and violence of German occupation. Written in an Austrian dialect, it refers to the period March 20 to June 20, 1944. It is a first-hand account of the emptying of the Jewish population of Hungary, outside Budapest, between those dates when 350,000 were transported to the death camp by train. The document is in the files of the Swedish Foreign Office.

The trains from Hungary to Birkenau ended July 9, 1944 and the total number of those exterminated was in excess of 400,000. There was a variance of tenses in the original, which has been maintained into the English translation. The first part of the report details events and decrees exacted as the occupation began, including Budapest.

March 20, 1944: The German agency ordered the establishment of the *Zentralrat der Juden in Ungarn* [Central Council of Jews in Hungary] and appointed its members. It ordered that Jews couldn't change their place of residence, travel, or relocate. Budapest is included.

March 31: The Hungarian government issued the first anti-Jewish decrees, in force throughout the country. Jews were banned from keeping non-Jewish servants or domestics, regardless of age. Jewish state officials have been immediately dismissed. Actors, journalists and lawyers were banned from their businesses. All Jews have to sew a yellow star, 10 cm in diameter, on outer clothing. These decrees were issued on a strictly racial basis. Some Jews were exempted through previous war service and the award of medals.

April 6: This is the day the Jewish star has to be worn for the first time. Baptised Jews with Aryan spouses are exempted from having to wear the star and do not incur the associated consequences. Vehicles, telephones and radio sets, belonging to Jews, have been confiscated. Those exempted Jews with military records are prohibited from wearing their uniforms.

April 7: The ban on travel was enacted, whereupon Jews could only use vehicles and travel by train with police permission.

April 14: The decree ordering the revocation of trading licences for pharmacists was issued.

April 16: All possessions of the Jews are confiscated. Valuables and security papers have to be declared. From the suspended bank accounts, a monthly withdrawal of 1,000 pengő is granted.

April 21: Closure of all Jewish shops was ordered, and all items are confiscated. Aryans were put in charge of the shops.

April 22: The Central Council of Jews, set up by the German agencies, is replaced by the *Verband ungerländischer Juden* [Union of Hungarian Jews] under a government decree.

April 23: Food supply for Jews was restricted. The sugar rations for Jews was reduced from 1020 grammes to 300 grammes per month, with no exceptions. Pregnant, breast-feeding women and small children receive the same ration. Rations for non-Jews are much higher. Instead of fat, Jews receive 300 grammes of sesame oil per month. Those Jewish workers in industry receive no additional stamps. The meat ration for Jews consists of 100 grammes of beef or horsemeat each week. They are not allowed to buy pork or calf. Only pregnant women, babies and children below the age of three receive milk. Non-Jews receive higher allowances. Regardless of this decree, on Sundays, Jews do not receive their milk portions from the milk distribution centre.

April 25: Lay-offs of Jewish intellectual employees were ordered and need to be carried out by the end of May. Those deemed economically important are excluded.

April 27: The decree concerning residences and dwelling places for Jews was announced. Some Jewish residences had been used for bomb attacks in Budapest. The Central Council has to hand over 500 residences within 24 hours, with the dislodged Jews forced to leave their furniture, bedding and washing for new residents. Since these 500 residences were not ready at the set time, another 500 were added. Two members of the Jewish Council were jailed, forced to sit for 24 hours facing a wall, for refusing to hand over the keys to the 1,000 residences. Eventually the keys were handed over.

Another decree ordered the institution of ghettos in cities or towns of more than 10,000 people. All Jews are now stripped of their licences for firearms.

April 30: A decree concerning 'the protection of Hungarian cultural life from the works of Jewish writers' was issued, which ordered that their works has to be removed from lending and public libraries and pulped.

That same day, the inspection of those *Verdienste* [awards] earned during the last World War was ordered.

May 2: Jews banned from using public baths.

May 6: Jews are now stripped of all commercial and trading licences, including tobacconist and liquor licences, under *Judengesetze* [Jew laws]. Previous exemptions for licence holders with previous military service, war widows, orphans, as well as those now counted as Jews, have ended.

May 13: The categories that determined an exception from the

Judengesetze have been changed, since some decrees had used differing criteria. Under the new arrangements, only war invalidity concerning wounds in more than 75% of the body, anti-revolutionary action and military service in the last World War are exempt from all Jew-related decrees. Only baptised Jews with Aryan spouses are exempted from wearing the star, the ban on travel and the ban on employing Aryan servants.

May 20: The shops of some Jewish tradesmen in Budapest had to be closed, including barbers, inns, restaurants, hotels and garages. On the same day, Jews were banned from entering inns, restaurants, coffee-houses and entertainment facilities, except for a few designated venues.

Arrests of Jews had begun as early as March 19, before any decree on prohibiting travel. Jews found at the railway stations had been arrested and taken to the *Schubhaus* [the holding centre]. From there, they were taken to the camp at Kistarcsa [a town to the north-east of Budapest]. Some 2,000 were interned at Kistarcsa, intended to hold only 800. The men had to lie on bare ground, and in some huts there was not enough space even to lie down. Infested with lice within days, all were shaven and disinfected. The camp commander did try to do everything in his power to improve the situation, but the overcrowding prevented his efforts.

Children below the age of 15, their mothers, pregnant women, women of more than 35 and men of more than 65 years in age were released from Kistarcsa. The rest remained in custody, regardless of whether they had wished to flee by being at the railway stations, or just travelling to work or even just simply waiting for someone on the railway platform.

May 20: 250 prominent Jews were arrested, being first housed at the Rabbi Seminary building [in Budapest] and later at Kistarcsa. The Rabbi Seminary was an assembly camp for those on the Central Council of Jews lists for detention even though they had committed no criminal action. All journalists were on the lists and 300 lawyers.

The manhunt on the Budapest streets began. Jews were interned in many places.

The decree concerning the wearing of the yellow star leaves room for doubt, such as whether it had to be worn in the office and in other business premises. Those who were found in such places, without the star, were brought to the *Schubhaus* and fined. Later they were interned. All those who were caught during raids in the street were interned on the grounds that they hadn't, or incorrectly, worn the star.

Some German soldiers invaded shops and homes arresting those who resisted their extortion.

Politicians and personalities were arrested and kept under guard in several locations: the basement of the Astoria hotel, the Royal Hungarian Academy of Sciences, the prison of the court for the surrounding area of Budapest, and on the Schwabenberg. Later, camps were built on the island of Csepel. Currently there are five such camps. The internees are staying in those, as well as the other camps in Budapest, which had served as refugee camps previously.

As the Jewish hospital has now been taken over as a SS hospital, the patients are being treated at two hospitals elsewhere. Those that had been sent to the Jewish hospital, by doctors, were taken back to camp without any medical examination.

April 15: The internment of refugees began. Those who appeared before immigration authorities, for the monthly attestation of their residence permit, were simply arrested there and then, and taken to the camp. The arrest of foreigners in their homes began. English and American Jews were placed at a separate *Schubhaus*.

The decree on travelling clearly stated that there are no limitations regarding use of the *Vizinalbahn* [railway] and the tram. Trusting this decree, the Jews from the surrounding area of Budapest have safely commuted to work but there are now arrests. During the final days in March, internments began all over the country of Jews in public life, rabbis and personalities, justified on the general assumption that they were listening to foreign radio channels and undertaking Communist propaganda activity. The number of internments was around 2-3,000 and they were housed at the *Schubhaus* and at the camps in Garany, Csörgő, Nagykanizsa, Bacstopolya and Ujszentgyörgy.

The deportation of camp internees began at Kistarcsa on April 28, with 1,170 taken away. From the *Schubhaus*, 400 were shipped off, as were 214 refugees in the Rabbi Seminary building.

This transport consisted of men and women, aged 16 to 50.

On the same day, 2,000 people, aged between 16-60, were transported from Nagykanizsa camp. The entire camp of Bacstopolya, some 1,000, was taken away.

☆☆☆

The concentration of Hungarian Jews began on April 16, 1944 in the ghetto. In other holding areas, such as the brickworks or farmhouses, the Jews were barred even from water. Many suffered extreme physical abuse if they didn't hand over hidden valuables. In the transportations, there were 70 people in most train wagons with just one bucket of water. We cannot go into details describing the concentration conditions in all localities, although the data does exist. Instead, we will briefly provide an account of the short lifespan of some typical concentration centres.

Nyíregyháza
[city in north-east Hungary]

April 16: Jews from 36 surrounding communes were resettled in Nyíregyháza and Simapuszta [puszta refers to the Great Hungarian Plain], which is 12 km away. In the Nyíregyháza camp, 4,120 Jews from the city and 6,639 from the surrounding area, were packed together in 123 buildings over 9,665 square metres. According to the regulations, the internees could bring two sets of underwear and a food package weighing no more than 50 kg – enough for two weeks. Jews from the town of Nyírbátor [in eastern Hungary] could bring nothing with them. On Friday, April 21, at 11pm, they were arrested in their homes by foreign gendarmes, and at 1.30am, they were brutally deported to Simapuszta.

May 1:The situation has worsened noticeably. From the Nyíregyháza ghetto, some Jews were taken to Padospuszta, where conditions are just as bad and food is scarce.They demanded to have blankets, straw mattresses, or just straw, so that at least the old and sick are spared from sleeping on the bare ground.

May 5: Due to a new directive, the Jews who had been concentrated in the almost completed ghetto in Nyíregyháza were taken away to the inn of Baron Molnár, where they were jammed together in the tobacco barns.There is a single well, 150 metres from the camp, where people can go but only accompanied by a gendarme.The situation is very sad.

May 7: Gendarmes surrounded the Nyirjespuszta and Simapuszta camps at dawn. No one can get close.The people are starving, receiving only 100 grammes of bread and beans daily.They have no money and only the clothes they are wearing.

May 8:The expulsion from Nyíregyháza continues. Only members of the Jewish Council and *Frontkämpfer* [military veterans] remain. At Nyirjespuszta [north of Budapest], 5,665 are penned up in a very small area and the treatment they receive is similar to that of a concentration camp.The situation is getting even more unbearable, as the only well is now muddy.The shortage of water at Simapuszta is even worse.The camp at Harangodpuszta is being filled, starting today.

May 10:The resettlement to Harangodpuszta [in north-east Hungary] continues.The number held in the tobacco barns reaches 3,000 persons.There is dangerous overcrowding.The camp has no water, as the digging of a well was unsuccessful. Although the Jewish Agency allowed the inmates to bring necessary items, the gendarmerie confiscated everything at the camp entrance. In the camps of Simapuszta,Varjulápos and Nyirjes [north of Budapest], the daily food ration per head amounts to 100 grammes of bread, 100 grammes of potatoes and 10 grammes of oil.

May 15: On Monday, in the early hours, the first 3,200, among them old people, babies, pregnant women, were *Einwaggoniert* [put into railroad cars for transportation] in groups of 70. They were set for an 'unknown destination'.

May 22: In the morning, we are told by telephone that the number of deportees adds up to 9,600. The Nyirjes and Harangodpuszta concentration camps have been emptied. Some 760 remain at Simapuszta. At Nyíregyháza, however, only Jewish Council members are left.

May 23: The 760 Jews from Nyíregyháza, moved to Simapuszta are *Einwaggoniert*.

June 6: We hear from a telephone call with the police that all Jews from Nyíregyháza and the surrounding area have been transported, among them Chief Rabbi, Dr. Béla Bernstein.

Munkács
[then in north-east Budapest, now in the Ukraine]

April 30: The Jews of Munkács, numbering 15,000, were housed in 12 streets. The 20,000 Jews from Bereg County were concentrated at the Kallus and Sajovics brickworks. Since they could bring neither money nor food with them, the situation is alarming and disastrous.

May 1: German soldiers invaded the ghettos, which led to several deaths. There were announcements of three typhus cases. The situation is terrible because of medicine and food shortages. A doctor and an engineer committed suicide.

May 9: Two Jewish Council members were shot, the others badly abused.

May 14: The situation in the city's ghetto and the two brickworks has worsened significantly. Jewish functionaries and auxiliary policemen are banned from leaving the ghetto, which was permitted up to now. Gendarmes surround the camps and the deportations have begun. Families are not separated and are *Einwaggoniert*, accompanied by the worst atrocities. On Monday, another transport went off. The number of Jewish Council members was been reduced from 12 to six.

May 18: The bigger camp, holding 13,000, has been totally transported, beginning on Sunday. The rail transport, some 70-80 people per car, was despatched to Kassa. The transported could not carry anything with them. All were stripped of good clothing and each car had only one bucket of water. These tormented Jews wanted to break out of the car at Sátoraljaújhely and 30 of them were executed. The smaller camp, holding 7,000, is dissolved as well. In the early morning of May 17, these Munkács Jews in the ghetto were relocated to the now empty bigger camp, under brutal circumstances. Some men leapt at the policemen with knives. In doing so, five Jews perished. Even exempted categories, such as doctors, transferred by the internal affairs ministry, are in the camp.

May 30: We receive the following devastating message: Munkács, Huszt and Nagyszőlős are empty. The Jews have all been deported.

Nagyvárad
[now Oradea in Rumania]

May 3: At dawn, ghetto posters appeared and at 5am, a detective accompanied by a policeman was already taking away all the Jews' valuables. 15-20 minutes were granted for packing the most necessary clothes, bedding and food for 10 days. 16-18 persons were packed together in one room, the windows to the streets were blocked with wooden boards, and the ghetto was fenced in.

May 11: The guard of the fenced ghetto was tightened on the 11th. The commissioned police was replaced by gendarmerie, so that nobody could even get close to the ghetto. It is representative of the rigour, that those streets with one side belonging to the ghetto, such as Kertész, Szacsvay and Kapucinus alley, are guarded by gendarmerie who allow the Christian population only to walk on the pavement. The so-called richer Jews or those considered rich were arrested without exception. They are either under arrest at the police building or with the gendarmerie at the castle, where they have to endure infernal torments. That way they are forced to admit to alleged hidden treasures. The Jewish Council was arrested as well.

May 24: The "small ghetto" where Jews from the surrounding area had been concentrated has already been emptied out. The people, agonised half to death, were put into railroad cars of 70. The big ghetto was beleaguered even tighter and the torture continues.

May 25: The *Einwaggonierung* continues. Nagyvárad is *entjudet* [De-Jewed]

Kassa
[now in Slovakia]

April 28: The Jews from Kassa were assigned 11 streets for a ghetto. These were reduced to three on April 30. Eventually, the majority of the Kassa Jews was housed at the brickworks.

May 2: The fate of the 12,000 Jews housed at the brickworks is terrible. Women, children and the elderly – deprived of all their possessions – are inside the drying room and under a roof, but the space provides no shelter, as it has no sidewalls. Since these Jews were ordered to suddenly leave their homes, they brought no food and other essential items. Only 60% receive any food. Drinking water is brought in once daily by municipal water wagons.

May 8: From a reliable old friend, someone very prominent, we received the following letter:

'For a few hours I am outside the horror, in the public kitchen which needed me for some temporary work. I'm afraid I cannot take it for too long as we suffer very badly. We lie in the dust and have neither straw mattress nor blanket. We will freeze to death. The dwelling is sealed, I see no way out. Do not send me anything, we don't receive it anyway. We still have food for a few days. How it will go on – God only knows. There are about 15,000 people here. The public kitchen now gives us some soup-like liquid once a day, but we have to stand in line for a long time. But who will maintain this camp, because the community won't be able to? I haven't eaten for days, which will shorten my life here. We are so neglected and we do not look like human beings anymore. There is no opportunity for washing. We haven't taken off our clothes since we came here. My regards to you all. Pray for us, so we may die soon.'

May 15: The first eight barracks in the first camp were emptied, the last stage in the suffering of the Kassa Jews, with 4,800 *Einwaggoniert*. In front of the railcars in the open, all the men and boys were ordered by the gendarmes to undress, to check for concealed possessions. In the barracks, the women and girls, too, were checked thoroughly by the gendarmes, in a similar fashion. Many have died during *Einwaggonieren* with 70-80 people in each train car. In one car, many were badly beaten.

May 18: The concentration camp is sealed from the outside world by the gendarmerie and police. Not even Jewish Council members may get close to it.

May 20: At 6 pm, the Jewish Council members are arrested. Those Christians who came to their aid were *Einwaggoniert* as well and deported along with the Jews.

June 7: There are no Jews left in Kassa. The entire Jewish population of Hungary is now transported or in camps, with the exception of Budapest. Measures regarding Budapest are to be announced within the next days, and there is no doubt as to what fate awaits them. At present, the following cities and towns have become *entjudet* [Jew free] entirely: Munkács, Ungvár, Beregszász, Nagyszőlős, Huszt, Máramarossziget, Nagyvárad, Nagybánya, Beszterce, Kolozsvár, Marosvásárhely, Szatmárnémeti, Mátészalka,

Baja, Barcs, Bácstopolya, Újvidék, Szabadka, Zenta, Zombor, Muraköz, Gyöngyös, Sátoraljaújhely, Sárospatak, Szilágysomlyó, Szászrégen, Sepsiszentgyörgy, Técső, Aknaszlatina, Nagykároly, Felsővisó, Nagykanizsa, Kassa, Dés, Nyíregyháza and Kisvárda.

The Jewish population of Komárom, Győr, Dunaszerdahely, Miskolc and Pécs are now in ghettos, and will be transported within the next days.

[The author of this report now details the emptying by region and town, by number]

Subcarpathia:

Munkács	35,000
Ungvár	12,000
Beregszász	9,000
Nagyszőlős	8,000
Huszt	12,000
Máramarossziget	12,000
Felsővisó	3,500
Técső	3,000
Aknaszlatina	3,500
Iza	3,000
Total	106,000

Transylvania:

Nagybánya	14,000
Beszterce	12,000
Kolozsvár	18,000
Marosvásárhely	6,000
Nagyvárad	25,000
Dés	6,000
Szilágysomlyó	8,000
Szászrégen	6,000

Sepsiszentgyörgy	3,000
Total	94,000

Upper Hungary:

Kassa	15,000
Sátoraljaújhely,	
Sárospatak	15,000
Gyöngyös	5,000
Total	35,000

Upper Tisza area:

Nyíregyháza	18,000
Kisvárda	12,000
Mátészalka	12,000
Szatmárnémeti	25,000
Nagykároly	8,000
Total	75,000

South Hungary:

Nagykanizsa	7,000
Baja	8,000
Barcs	2,000
Bácstopolya,	
Újvidék, Szabadka,	
Zenta, Zombor,	
Muraköz	3,000
Total	25,000

From May 16 to June 10, a total of 335,000 Jews from Hungary were transported.

Appendix 2

**Russian intelligence offers that served in Sweden,
1921 to late 1980s.**

A listing of Soviet intelligence officers operating out of the
embassy or other Soviet entities, under the cover as commercial,
foreign or military attaché or ambassador. The term rezident refers
to head of station. Illegal refers to working undercover in the
community and not through the legation or embassy.

Compiled by the author from KGB sources.

1920s

1921-1923: **Kerzhentzev** (also known as Lebedev), Platon
Mikhailovich – Intelligence Directorate

1923-1925: **Shteinbrik** (also known as Shteibriuk), Otto Ottovich
– Intelligence Directorate rezident

1924-1927: **Dovgalevskii,** Valerii Savel'evich – Intelligence
Directorate rezident. Ambassador

1926-1927: **Arosev,** Aleksandr Yakovlievich – Intelligence
Directorate

1927-1930: **Dmitrievskii,** Sergei – OGPU

1927-1930: **Kopp,** Viktor Leont'evich – Intelligence Directorate
rezident. Ambassador

1928-1930: **Sobolev,** Aleksandr Aleksandrovich – Naval attaché
He had a nervous breakdown, refusing to return to
Russia

1930s

1930-1945: **Kollontay** (also known as Domontovich), Aleksandra
Mikhailovna – Ambassador

1930s [end]: **Mirnyi**, Semen Maksymovich – Intelligence
Directorate

1933-1934: **Burde**, Fritz Fridrikhovich – Intelligence Directorate.
Illegal

1934: **Bolotin**, Ilia Mironovich – Intelligence Directorate
rezident

1934-1937: **Artur**, Matveevich (codename *Gaib*) – OGPU rezident

1936: **Orlov**, Aleksandr Mikhailovich (real name Fel'dbin
Leiba Lazarevich) – NKVD. *Illegal*

1936-1938: **Ritter**, Artur Rudolfovich – GRU

1939-1944: **Pavlov**, Aleksandr – GRU

1939-1945: **Nikitushev**, Nikolai – GRU

1940s

1940-1941: **Chichaev**, Ivan Andreevich – OGPU rezident

1940-1941: **Fomenko**, Pavel Nikolayevich – GRU

1940-1941: **Starostin**, Viktor – GRU. Expelled

1940-1942: **Ivanov**, Konstantin – GRU

1940-1942: **Artem'ev**, Stefan – GRU rezident

1940-1943: **Graur**, Andrei Grigor'evich – NKVD. Expelled

1940-1944: **Guberman**, Roman – NKVD

1940-1944: **Gusev**, Petr Mikhailovich – GRU

1940-1945: **Panov**, Aleksei – NKVD

1940-1945: **Skotnikov**, Nikolai – GRU rezident

1940-1946: **Vasil'ev**, Nikolai Ivanovich – NKVD. Expelled

1940-1947: **Aleksandrov**, Andrei Mikhailovich – GRU

1941-1942: **Sidorenko**, Vasilii – GRU rezident

1941-1944: **Rybkin**, Boris Arkadevich (also known as Boris
Yartsev) – NKVD

1941-1944: **Voskresenskaya**, Zoya Ivanovna (also known as
Aleksandra Nikolayevna Yartseva, codenamed *Irina*) –
NKVD. Press attaché

1941-1944: **Klimov**, Dmitrii Petrovich – GRU

1942- : **Onyukhov**, Mikhail – NKVD. Expelled

1942-1944: **Spichkin**, Igor – NKVD

1942-1944: **Erofev**, Vladimir Ivanovich – GRU

1942-1945: **Kossov**, Mikhail Borisovich – NKVD. Tass

correspondent. Returned to Sweden for second spell
with KGB, 1971–1973

1942–1947: **Vinogradov**, Konstantin Fedorovich – GRU

1943–1945: **Roschin**, Vasilii Petrovich (real name Tischenko) –
NKVD rezident

1943–1945: **Slepenkov**, Zakhar – GRU

1943–1945: **Ognivtsev**, Arkadii Leonidovich – NKVD

1943–1945: **Slavin**, Grigorii Ivanovich. – NKVD

1943–1947: **Ivashchenko**, Vladimir Gavrilovich – NKVD

1943–1947: **Makushin**, Fedor Semonovich – GRU

1944–   : **Sinitsin**, Elisei Tikhonovich – NKVD rezident

1944–1948: **Zavarukhin**, Petr – GRU

1944–1951: **Anisimov**, Viktor – GRU

1944–1945: **Baturin**, Aleksandr – GRU

1944–1948: **Lemekhov**, Dmitrii Aleksandrovich – GRU

1945–1947: **Degtyarov**, Kusan Illarionovich – NKVD

1945–1948: **Vasil'ev**, Aleksandr Nikolaevich – GRU

1945–1949: **Simson**, Ernast Rudol'fovich – NKVD

1945–1950: **Aleshkin**, Aleksandr Vasil'evich – GRU

1945–1951: **Petropavlovskii**, Vladimir Aleksandrovich – NKVD

1946–   : **Korshunov**, Mikhail – GRU

1946–1947: **Podoprigora**, Gennadii – GRU

1946–1947: **Bakurskii**, Aleksei Dmitrevich – GRU

1946–1948: **Golovin**, Leonid Leonidovich – GRU

1946–1951: **Samokhin**, Yurii Stepanovich – NKVD

1946–1951: **Kiselev**, Anatoly – GRU

1947–   : **Mikhailov**, Georgii – GRU. Expelled

1947–1950: **Larinchev**, Dmitrii – GRU

1947–   : **Granovsky** – NKVD

1947–1953: **Kaplin**, Anatolii Stepanovich – NKVD

1948–1950: **Denisov**, Ivan Aleksandrovich – GRU

1948–1951: **Chernyi**, Stepan – GRU

1948–1951: **Frolov**, Porfirii Vasil'evich – GRU

1948–1952: **Utemov**, Adolf – KGB.

1948–1952: **Egorov**, Viktor Mikhailovich. KGB. Expelled

1948–1953: **Yakovlev**, Nikolai Fedorovich – GRU

1948–1953: **Erin**, Arkadii Alekseevich – GRU

1949-1951: **Orlov**, Nikolai Petrovich – GRU
1949-1952: **Presnyakov**, Fedor Ferorovich – KGB
1949-1952: **Farafonov**, Georgii Nikolaievich. KGB. Returned
1958-1963
1949-1954: **Novikov**, Pavel Filipovich – KGB

1950s

1950-1953: **Grachev**, Nikolai Matveevich – GRU
1950-1953: **Shestakov**, Vladimir Vasil'evich – KGB
1950-1954: **Chumak**, Ivan Vasil'evich – GRU
1950-1954: **Tarabrin**, Evgenii Anatol'evich – KGB.
1950-1956: **Mokretsov**, Il'ya Alekseevich – KGB. Returned
1959-1964
1950-1957: **Belousov**, Viktor Vasil'evich – KGB. Expelled
1951-1954: **Pan'zhevskii**, Aleksei Afanas'evich – KGB
1951-1955: **Konobeev**, Vladimir Petrovich – GRU
1951-1956: **Lisovskii**, Ivan. KGB.
1951-1956: **Miroshnikov**, Petr Sergeevich – KGB. Expelled
1952-1953: **Viilo**, V Adol'f Aleksandrovich – GRU
1952-1954: **Zakrevskii**, Gennadii Aleksadrovich – GRU
1952-1955: **Markin**, Vasilii Petrovich – GRU
1952-1956: **Fil'kov**, Mikhail Kuzmich – GRU
1952-1957: **Istomin**, Sergei Mikhalovich – KGB
1953-1954: **Gavrilov**, Nikolai Fedorovich – GRU
1953-1956: **Lykov**, Stepan Mikhailovich – GRU rezident
1953-1957: **Belokhvostikov**, Nikolai – KGB. Expelled
1953-1957: **Golanov**, Vladimir Evgen'evich – KGB. Later,
1960-1966, 1970-1971
1953-   : **Vil'yu**, Adol'f – KGB. Expelled
1953-1957: **Klyuzo**, V. Serafim Timofeevich – GRU. Rezident
1963-1964
1954-1956: **Sokolov**, Nikolai Ilyevich – GRU
1954-1957: **Lepeshkin**, Leonid Ilyevich – KGB
1954-1957: **Kabalin**, Vladimir Nikolayevich – GRU
1954-1957: **Konev**, Boris Aleksandrovich – GRU
1954-1958: **Morozov**, Nikolai Mikhailovich – KGB
1954-1958: **Shchedrin**, Vilen Ivanovich – GRU

1954-1958: **Evdokimov**, Sergei Vasil'evich – GRU
1955-1956: **Luk'yanov**, Sergei Grigor'evich – KGB
1955-1957: **Davidov**, Dmitrii Dmitryevich – KGB
1955-1959: **Chegvintsev**, Grigory Nikiforovich – GRU
1955-1961: **Tret'yakov**, Konstantin Georgievich – KGB
1956-1957: **Lobanov**, Anatolii Aleksandrovich – KGB
1956-1958: **Darenskii**, Dmitrii Afanas'evich – GRU
1956-1959: **Ruskikh**, Vladimir Mikhailovich – KGB
1956-1959: **Ryazanov**, Aleksandr Afanas'evich – GRU
1956-1960: **Koval**, Nikolai Danilovich – KGB. Returned
1963-1966
1956-1962: **Studenikin**, Ivan Yakovlevich – GRU
1957-1958: **Klimenko**, Anatolii Filipovich – GRU
1957-1959: **Kolk**, Avgust Savlovich – KGB
1957-1960: **Borisov**, Ivan Dmitrevich – KGB rezident
1957-1960: **Ognev**, Aleksandr Tikhonovich – KGB
1957-1960: **Yushchenko**, Semon Ivanovich – KGB
1957-1960: **Rimyans**, Leonid Vladislavovich – KGB
1957-1961: **Shumakov**, Aleksei Georgevich – KGB
1957-1962: **Mel'khishev**, Petr Pavlovich – GRU.
Ran Swedish spy, Stig Vennerstrom
1958-   : **Fedyanin**, Vladimir Petrovich – KGB
1958-1961: **Lapin'sh**, Gunnar Petrovich – KGB
1958-1963: **Konovalov**, Leonid Nikolayevich – GRU
1958-1963: **Lukashin**, Ivan Sergeevich – KGB
1958-1963: **Kolesov**, Dmitrii Ivanovich – GRU
1959-1962: **Abramov**, Vladimir Mikhailovich – GRU
1959-1962: **Smirnov**, Viktor Nikolayevich. – KGB.
1959-1962: **Kirienkov**, Vladimir Mikhailovich – KGB
1959-1962: **Naidenkov**, Vsevolod Andrevich – KGB
1959-1962: **Teplov**, Mark Ivanovich – KGB
1959-1964: **Chervyakov**, Vladimir Ivanovich – GRU

1960s
1960-   : **Levchenko**, Nikolai Ivanovich. – KGB
1960-1963: **Sergeev**, Yurii Pavlovich – GRU
1960-1963: **Astashkov**, Naum Petrovich – KGB

1960–1963: **Toompu**, Adol'f Yanovich – KGB
1960–1966: **Vybornov**, Aleksandr Dmitrevich – KGB
1960–1965: **Zhitkov**, Anatolii Anatol'evich – KGB
1961–1964: **Statskevich**, Nikolai Viktorovich – KGB. Rezident
1971–1973
1961–1964: **Smirnov**, Viktor Petrovich – KGB
1961–1965: **Veshkin**, Aleksandr Vladimirovich – KGB
1961–1965: **Sushkov**, Nikolai – KGB
1961–1965: **Sokolov**, Mark Nikolaievich – KGB. Returned 1970
1961–1966: **Goloshubov**, Yurii Il'ich – KGB
1962–   : **Farmakovskii**, Vadim Vadimovich – GRU
1962–1963: **Grichakov**, Aleksei Mikhailovich – KGB
1962–1964: **Khabalov**, Nikolai Andrianovich – KGB
1962–1965: **Malyshev**, Konstantin Yakovlevich – KGB
1962–1966: **Chernov**, Sergei Fedorovich – KGB
1962–1966: **Sheshin**, Valentin Valentinovic – GRU
1962–1966: **Toom**, Pavel Mikhailovich – KGB
1962–1966: **Yakovlev**, Aleksandr Mikhailovich – KGB
1962–1967: **Sotskov**, Lev Filippovich – KGB. Rezident 1969–1971
1962–1969: **Sinitsin**, Igor Eliseevich – KGB
1962–1972: **Lopatin**, Aleksandr Georgevich – KGB
1963–   : **Baranovskii**, Georgii Pavlovich – KGB. Expelled
1963–   : **Nikol'skii**, Vitali Aleksandrovich – GRU. Expelled
1963–   : **Seregin**, Aleksandr Ivanovich – KGB
1963–1966: **Deryugin**, Yurii Ivanovich – KGB
1963–1966: **Selanskii**, Valentin Ivanovich – KGB
1963–1967: **Nikolaev**, Pavel Ivanovich – KGB
1963–1969: **Makusskii**, Ignet Nikandrovich – GRU
1964–1966: **Shirokov**, Evgenii Aleksadrovich – KGB
1964–1966: **Churilin**, Anatolii Khrisanfovich – KGB. Returned
1972
1964–1969: **Parfenov**, Kapiton Ivanovich – KGB rezident
1964–1967: **Zakenfeld**, Yanus Yanovich – KGB
1964–1970: **Gergel**, Evgenii Ivanovich – KGB. Rezident from
1969
1965–   : **Smirnov**, Petr Vasilevich (Petrov Sergei) – KGB
1965–1967: **Veber**, Val'demar Pavlovich – KGB

1965-1969: **Maksimov**, Vladimir Borisovich – KGB

1965-1970: **Mednis**, Vladimir Augustovich – KGB

1966-   : **Popov**, Gennadii Fedorovich – KGB

1966-1967: **Ogurtsov**, Anatolii Andreevich – KGB

1967-   : **Erofeev**, Valerii Nikolaievich – KGB

1967-1969: **Ivanov**, Viktor Vasileyevich – GRU

1968-1972: **Poselyanov**, Nikolai Fedorovich – KGB

1968-1972: **Ryabovol**, Leonid Aleksandrovich – KGB

1969-1971: **Shebanov**, Yurii Konstantinovich – KGB

1969-1973: **Maslovskii**, Georgii Borisovich – KGB rezident

1970s, selected officers only, not complete

1970-   : **Fedoseev**, Georgii – GRU military attaché.
He wanted to defect, but was discovered by the GRU
and recalled to Moscow under false pretences
Executed

1970-   : **Shumilov**, Evgenii – KGB

1970-1971: **Svetanko**, Dmitrii Andreevich – KGB

1970-1972: **Antipin**, Veniamin Vasilyevich – KGB

1971-1975: **Statskevich**, Nikolai Viktorovich – KGB rezident

1971-   : **Yakovlev**, Mikhail – Ambassador

1971-   : **Baranov**, Ivan Konstantinovich – KGB

1971-   : **Kuzminich**, Nikolai Ivanovich – KGB

1971-   : **Egorov**, Anatolii Grigoryevich – GRU

1971-   : **Gusev**, Lev – KGB

1971-   : **Polyakov**, Yurii – KGB

1971-   : **Shalaev**, Nikolai Vasil'evich – GRU

1971-   : **Zubko,** Marat Vasil'evich – KGB

1971-   : **Chekalkin**, Igor Aleksandrovich – KGB

1972-1973: **Mochaliov**, Georgii Aleksandrovich – KGB

1975-1978: **Shapkin**, Lev Nikolayevich – KGB

1978-1982: **Koretskii**, Vladimir Petrovich– KGB rezident

1979-1983: **Rapota**, Grigorii Alekseevich – KGB. Expelled

1982-1987: **Selivestrov**, Nikolai Sergeeevich – KGB rezident

1987   : **Nikiforov**, Igor Leonidovich – KGB rezident

1995-   : **Smirnov**, Mikhail – GRU. Expelled

Appendix 3

Chronology: The search by the Swedish Foreign Office

**This is the written Swedish Foreign Office chronology
from its archives. It may differ from the research
conducted by the author in Moscow.**

1944

Shortly after German forces occupy Hungary the Swedish
assistance to Hungary's Jews begins.

July 9: Swedish mission in Budapest strengthened because of the
increased burden of relief work. Raoul Wallenberg arrives in
Budapest as Legation Secretary, holding a Swedish diplomatic
passport and entitled to diplomatic immunity. Working in C
Division, he takes charge of relief work for the city's Jews,
reporting to Chief of Mission, Danielsson.

October: Relief work intensifies after the Szálasi government
takes power.

December 23: The last direct communication from the Swedish
Legation in Budapest is received by the SFO in Stockholm.

December 24: Russian Red Army final offensive on Budapest
begins.

1945

January 15: The Pest side of the Danube falls to the Red Army.
Wallenberg and other members of the Swedish Legation are on
the Pest side. Others are in Buda where the German army is
making its final stand.

January 16: Söderblom, the Swedish ambassador in Moscow, is informed by Dekanozov, the Soviet Deputy Foreign Minister, that Wallenberg was in Pest and had been encountered in the part of the city captured by the Soviet troops near Benczur Street. Wallenberg had informed the Russians that the other members of the Swedish mission were in Buda, still held by the Germans. Dekanozov related that measures to protect Wallenberg and his safe houses have been taken by the Soviet military authorities. After this communication, the SFO now believes that Wallenberg is safe but there are now fears for the safety of Danielsson and other members of the Legation.

Jan 17: Wallenberg, with his driver, Vilmos Langfelder, leave Pest in the company of three Russian military persons.

February: Mrs Alexandra Kollontay, the Soviet ambassador in Stockholm, assures Mrs Maj von Dardel, Wallenberg's mother, that her son was alive in the Soviet Union and being well treated.

February 9: Stockholm urgently cables its mission in Moscow to ascertain from the Russians the fate of its staff in Budapest.

February 13: Söderblom tells the Swedish Foreign Office [SFO] that he had been in touch with the Russian Foreign Office [RFO] many times to discover the whereabouts of the Swedish delegation members.

February 17: SFO cables Söderblom that if communication could be established with Wallenberg, then instructions would be given to him once Danielsson was found.

February 17: SFO sends further cable to Söderblom to state to the Russian authorities that it was very concerned over the fate of its Budapest delegation.

February 17: SFO cables its Consulate in Vienna to say that Wallenberg had been safe for a month, but on the other members of the Budapest delegation it had no news whatsoever.

February 19: Söderblom responds to Stockholm to say that he had again asked about the Budapest delegation.

February 19: The SFO receives a vague dispatch from the Russians that Danielsson and others are safe.

March 8: SFO cables its ambassador in Moscow that Wallenberg would soon be expected in the Russian capital, but when was he due to arrive?

March 10: The Swedish mission in Bucharest, Rumania, cables Stockholm that according to reports, Danielsson had been arrested by the Soviets on February 20.

March 11: As a result of the March 10 cable, the SFO instructed Söderblom in Russia to make enquires over the whereabouts of Danielsson.

March 12: Söderblom cables Stockholm that he has asked Dekanozov to expedite enquiries, as no confirmed information had been received over the whereabouts of Danielsson.

March 12: Söderblom cables Stockholm that the Swedish mission in Bucharest, in its telegram of March 7, had stated that Wallenberg had been missing since January 17 when he had stated his intention of leaving Budapest by car.

March 15: The SFO is informed that a radio station in Hungary, Kossuth Radio, had reported on March 8 that the Gestapo had probably murdered Wallenberg, missing since January 17.

March 17: Söderblom instructed to make the strongest enquiries of the RFO with regard to the fate of Danielsson, Anger and Wallenberg.

March 21: Söderblom was cabled by SFO that Mrs Alexandra Kollontay, the Soviet ambassador in Sweden, had also promised to help in expediting enquiries for the missing diplomats.

March 23: A cable arrives from Moscow stating that most of the Swedish Legation personnel are in Bucharest, Rumania, staying at the Athene Palace Hotel. Wallenberg is not amongst them. The SFO and the Swedish ambassador in Moscow now asked the Soviet authorities for information on the whereabouts of Wallenberg.

March 27: SFO cables Söderblom to make the most urgent enquiries of the RFO about Wallenberg who remains missing.

April 21: SFO cables its mission in Moscow to urgently contact Dekanozov in person, and in reference to his message of January 16. Dekanozov had said that Wallenberg and his property was now under Russian protection in Budapest.

April 25: Söderblom responded to the SFO that he has again reminded Dekanozov to make urgent enquiries.

April 26: Söderblom cables the SFO to say that he had contacted Dekanozov on countless occasions, verbally and in writing.

April 28: Marcus Wallenberg requests the assistance of Mrs Kollontay, the Soviet ambassador in Stockholm, to try to put pressure on the Russian Foreign Office.

May 19: Söderblom again cables the SFO to say that two days earlier, he had been in touch with Dekanozov.

June 5: Sweden's military attaché in Moscow makes an appeal to the Russian authorities for news.

July 6: To the consternation of the SFO, it is dismayed at the Söderblom cable which suggests that no action is called for at the present time because of the rumour that Wallenberg was undercover and still in Budapest.

July 12: Sahlin, in the SFO, instructs Söderblom that his 'impassivity' is wrong and that the RFO should be vigorously pursued.

August 14: Söderblom ignores this SFO instruction and 'considers that in the present situation it was hardly appropriate to pursue the matter from Moscow'.

October 31: The SFO again tells Söderblom to actively pursue the matter of the disappearance of Wallenberg.

November 3: Söderblom finally relents to the instructions from Stockholm and sends a note to the RFO.

November 30: Söderblom again contacts the RFO and receives a response from Abramov that the Russian military authorities have been contacted and ordered to investigate what had happened to Wallenberg. A reply had yet to be received.

1946

January 3: Söderblom cables the SFO to say that he had had detailed conversations with Abramov at the RFO and Mrs Kollontay, the Soviet ambassador in Stockholm.

March 10: Söderblom informs the SFO that he has written to the RFO with a new appeal and has provided the Russians with some information, especially the names of the three Russian military people who were reported to have been with Wallenberg on January 17, 1945, the day he disappeared in Budapest.

April 30: Söderblom informs the SFO that is still actively pursuing the Russians over Wallenberg.

June 15: Söderblom tells the SFO that he has taken up the matter of Wallenberg with Stalin.

July 24: Söderblom again reminds the RFO that he is waiting for a response to his recent enquiries.

November 28: The SFO instructs its mission in Moscow to take a new tack with the RFO.

December 12: A note is handed to Sysojev at the RFO by Swedish Chargé d'affaires Barch-Holst.

December 13: Barch-Holst follows up with Losovski.

1947

January 13: Barch-Holst takes up the Wallenberg matter with Novikov at the RFO.

January 30: Hägglöf talks to Novikov who replied that despite the most extensive investigations carried out by a number of Russian agencies, including the Russian security services, no trace has yet been found of Wallenberg.

April 9: Sweden's Foreign Minister, Undén, meets the Russian ambassador in Stockholm who promises to write to Moscow about Wallenberg.

May 27: The SFO informed Söhlman, the [new] Swedish ambassador in Moscow, to make a renewed request to the RFO.

June 12: Söhlman requests a prompt reply from Malik of the RFO.

July 16: Söhlman reminded Vetrov about Wallenberg

August 18: A note is delivered to Swedish ambassador, Söhlman, from the Soviet deputy foreign minister, Vyshinsky, that after careful investigation Wallenberg was not in the Soviet Union and that he was unknown to the Soviet authorities.

1947: The Minister of Foreign Affairs, Undén, asks an unfortunate question of the Wallenberg Committee. The 'Dagens Nyheter' publication continues to remind its readers of Undén's poor record in his negotiations with the Russians. He had asked the committee, 'Do you think Vyshinsky is lying?'

Aug 1947 – 1951

No new facts on the disappearance of Wallenberg are received in the SFO. Further Swedish requests to Moscow are rebuffed by Moscow, who continues to state that Wallenberg is not known to the Russian authorities. Theories abound that Wallenberg may have been killed in the Soviet bombardment of Budapest, imprisoned in Hungary or Russia, liquidated, or just lost: a fate that befell hundreds of thousands after the ending of World War II.

End 1951-1952

European PoWs begin to drift home after imprisonment in Russian jails or the Gulag. The SFO receives many statements that Wallenberg had been sighted or heard of in the Lubyanka and Lefortovo jails. The statement from Claudio de Mohr, an Italian, appeared credible to the SFO.

February 11: The Swedish Foreign Minister presented a note to Rodionov, the Russian ambassador in Sweden, that the Claudio de Mohr testimony, with others, confirmed that Wallenberg was alive and he should immediately be returned to Sweden. This note was titled 'The Government of the Soviet Union must take the necessary measures for the prompt return of Wallenberg to Sweden'.

April 16: The Russian Embassy in Stockholm responds in a very brief note that it has nothing new to add to the August 18, 1947 statement by Vyshinsky that Wallenberg was unknown to the Soviet authorities.

May 23: The Foreign Minister presents another note to Rodionov. It was also presented to Soviet Deputy Foreign Minister, Zorin, in Moscow on May 26. In this note, Foreign Minister Undén states that 'the Swedish authorities, upon receipt of the reply given by the Government of the Soviet Union in August 1947, did not wish, in view of conditions after the war, to preclude the possibility that Wallenberg could be in the Soviet Union even though his whereabouts and identity could not be established'.

November 17: Swedish Foreign Minister, Undén, meets Russian Foreign Minister, Vyshinsky, in New York.

February 1952–March 1956

The SFO exchanges 15 written and 34 verbal communications with the Russian Foreign Ministry, the Russian ambassador in Stockholm or via the Swedish ambassador in Moscow, over the disappearance of Wallenberg and demanding his safe return. The SFO has undertaken an extensive programme of interviews, in many countries, of returning refugees and PoWs from Russia with regard to sightings. There were a number of sightings of Wallenberg in Lefortovo jail. There has been great difficulty in finding people prepared to talk with many worried about their personal safety.

1953

August 5: Lundberg, the Swedish Cabinet Secretary, received a verbal communication, accompanied by a written text, from Rodionov saying that all attempts to connect the question of Wallenberg's fate to an alleged stay in the Soviet Union were entirely without foundation. He said that 'over a period of several years the question of Raoul Wallenberg has been exploited in the most shameful manner for hostile purposes in relation to the Soviet Union'.

1954

September 29: Söhlman, the Swedish ambassador, presents a comprehensive memorandum in Moscow to Deputy Foreign Minister, Zorin. Included are statements from returning European PoWs who believe that they may have seen Wallenberg in the Soviet Union. Many statements were from returning Austrians.

1955

September: Following the visit to Moscow by West German Chancellor, Conrad Adenauer, the remaining German PoWs were returned. The SFO used this German release to again press Moscow for more information on the fate of Wallenberg. Interviews with some of these PoWs took place.

November 2: Undèn makes a statement in the Riksdag debate on the disappearance of Wallenberg, citing these statements made by returning German PoWs.

September-October: The SFO was in contact with Gustav Richter, an Austrian, who had claimed that he had been a cellmate of Wallenberg in the Lubyanka in 1945. This statement was given in Autumn 1955 and tape-recorded in German. There would be further communication.

November 8: Undèn has a verbal communication, accompanied by a written text, with Rodionov, citing the statements of returning German and Austrian PoWs.

1956

February 26: Acting Charge d'Affaires in Moscow, Petri, is instructed to remind the Soviet authorities in Moscow that it needs an urgent answer on the fate or whereabouts of Wallenberg.

March 10: Note presented by the Swedish Foreign Minister to Rodionov, the Russian ambassador, which include statements by Supreme Court Judges, Eklund and Lind, regarding Wallenberg's imprisonment in the Soviet Union. The judges had viewed the statements made by the PoWs that Wallenberg had been seen in the Soviet Union and were of the opinion, according to Swedish law, that 'there is no doubt that Raoul Wallenberg, after he was placed under effective Russian custody in the middle of January 1945, was later a prisoner in the Soviet Union'. This investigation had also concluded that Langfelder was also a prisoner in Moscow, but not kept with Wallenberg. On the basis of these PoW statements, the Swedish Government considered 'that all the necessary requisites exist in order to trace Raoul Wallenberg and send him back to Sweden'.

March 19: Note received from Gribanov, the Assistant Chief of the Scandinavian Division of the RFO, to acting Chargé d'affaires, Petri, in Moscow. It categorically stated that 'the Foreign Ministry considers it necessary to confirm that the explanations previously given to representatives of the Swedish Government by leading persons in the Soviet Government, that Wallenberg is not in the Soviet Union's territory, are exhaustive and final. The Foreign Ministry has nothing to add to the above-mentioned explanation.'

April 3: This is a key turning point in the relations between Sweden and Russia over the fate of Wallenberg. A joint Swedish-Soviet communiqué is issued in connection with the visit to Moscow of Swedish Prime Minister, Erlander, and Foreign Minister, Hedlund. Erlander and Hedlund make a detailed account of Swedish and world opinion on Wallenberg's disappearance directly to Bulganin, Khrushchev and Molotov. At the close of the conversation, the Russians promise an extensive investigation of Wallenberg's fate, whereupon the result of the investigation would be communicated to the Swedish government.

May 4: The Russians ask the SFO for more personal data and photographs of Wallenberg.

May 12: The SFO provides this requested material on Wallenberg to the Soviet authorities.

July 14: Ambassador Rodionov informs the SFO that a reply regarding the investigations by the Soviet Union authorities would be delivered to Sweden as soon as possible.

July 14: The Swedish Foreign Ministry issues a Press Bulletin on the recent discussion with the Soviets.

September 27: Memorandum presented by Acting Chargé d'affaires, Petri, to Deputy Foreign Minister, Zacharov, in Moscow.

November 17: Memorandum presented by Sweden's ambassador in Moscow, Söhlman, to Deputy Foreign Minister, Gromyko.

1957

February 6: Deputy Foreign Minister, Gromyko, has responded to the Swedish Government's request for the release of Wallenberg, given the witness statements the SFO had compiled. Gromyko stated in a memorandum to the Swedish ambassador in Moscow, Rolf Söhlman, that on the basis of a document found in the Lubyanka Wallenberg had died in the Lubyanka, 'presumably as a result of a heart attack' in 1947, according to a hand-written note addressed to the head of Russian State Security, Abakumov, by Colonel Smoltsov, of the Medical Corps and the chief of the sanitary department of the Lubyanka prison. Smoltsov's note was dated July 17, 1947.

Responsibility for Wallenberg's detention in prison, and for the incorrect information previously provided to the Swedish authorities, has been blamed on the Russian Security Services. The Soviet Government expresses its sincere regrets about what happened. Full blame is placed on Abakumov who had been executed for other crimes.

February 7: The Swedish Government's responds to the note from Gromyko.

February 7: Arne Lundberg, from the SFO, provides a commentary in the Swedish radio programme. 'Dagens Eko', on events leading up to and after Wallenberg's disappearance, the actions of the SFO, and to Gromyko's statement.

February 18: The Swedish communist newspaper, *Ny Dag*, carries an interview it had done in Moscow with Gromyko. He said that no new material about the death of Wallenberg in 1947 could be anticipated and that the Russian enquiry was now closed. No other documentary material had been located other than that submitted to the Swedish government. 'The case of Wallenberg had to be regarded as one of the tragedies which occurred in the confusion prevailing at the end of the war', said Gromyko.

February 19: Ambassador Söhlman, hands the Swedish Government's sharp response to Gromyko's statement to Russian Deputy Foreign Minister, Zacharov. He further asks for more clarification on Gromyko's statement, given it throws doubt on the veracity of previous Russian statements. However, the Swedish press is angry that the Swedish government has not unequivocally demanded a further complete and exhaustive report from the Soviet authorities.

March 10: The SFO prepares a White Paper on the disappearance of Raoul Wallenberg, which is edited by Gunnar Lorentzon, a Second Secretary in the Commercial Division. It comprises 104 pages but in the opinion of many, the report adds no new

significant information. Lorentzon had personally interviewed the
PoWs released from the Soviet Union, whose testimony and
personal description of life in the camps and Soviet jails were
included in the report. There were 19 witnesses used in the
White Paper, who provided information on the imprisonment of
Wallenberg and Langfelder. Lorentzon's key responsibility within
the SFO was with matters concerning the European Free Trade
Area [EFTA], of which Sweden was a member. He used this job
as cover to gain more information on the whereabouts of
Wallenberg, which included trips to Israel to interview Israeli
immigrants. In Lorentzon's opinion, the Russians had still not
produced conclusive evidence that Wallenberg was dead, and that
until this evidence was forthcoming, the Swedish government
would actively pursue the matter. Lorentzon reported directly to
the Foreign Minister, Nyström, on anything new.

April: The Soviets reply to the Swedes that, unfortunately, it had
no more information that that previously supplied, and could add
nothing more.

1989

October 17: Visit to Moscow by Nina Lagergren, Wallenberg's
half-sister, Guy von Dardel, Wallenberg's half brother, Sonia
Sonnefeld, the secretary of the Raoul Wallenberg Association and
Per Anger, Wallenberg's Budapest colleague. The Russian
delegation included Vladimir Pirozhkov, the deputy head of the
KGG and Valentin Nikiforov, the deputy Foreign Minister.
Wallenberg's passport returned with other personal items,
including money, a daybook and a permit to carry a pistol [he
always carried a pistol in Budapest]. Members of the Swedish
delegation said that they still believed that Raoul Wallenberg was
still living in a Soviet prison, under another name, and that the
Soviet authorities were either unwilling or unable to locate him.

2000–2001

April: The International Raoul Wallenberg Foundation asked the Russian authorities and the Vatican to release all files concerning missing persons, including Raoul Wallenberg. This action was supported by the UN Secretary General, Kofi Annan, whose wife is Raoul Wallenberg's niece. The Magnusson Report is published. This was the final report of the joint Swedish/Russian study group.

2003

Official enquiry into the disappearance of Raoul Wallenberg published, which was highly critical of the actions of the SFO.

Appendix 4

★★★

The Gromyko statement given to the Swedish
ambassador in Moscow on February 6, 1957

Page ___1___ of ___

Encl. No. ___1___

Desp. No. __964__

From __Stockholm__

UNCLASSIFIED UNCLASSIFIED

(Classification)

MEMORANDUM SUBMITTED FEBRUARY 6, 1957, BY SOVIET VICE FOREIGN
MINISTER ANDREI GROMYKO TO SWEDISH AMBASSADOR IN MOSCOW ROLF
SOHLMAN IN THE RAOUL WALLENBERG CASE

(Translation of text as released by the Swedish Foreign Office
to the press February 7, 1957)

In pursuance of the Swedish Government's request, the Soviet
Government instructed the pertinent Soviet authorities to peruse
the material concerning Raoul Wallenberg which had been received
from Swedish quarters at the Swedish-Soviet negotiations in Moscow
in March - April 1956 and also in May 1956. In the course of
perusal and testing of the said material, the Soviet authorities
have made a careful search of the archives which refer to the
accounting for prisoners and to investigation questions ("Sledstvenye
Dela"), for the purpose of finding possible information on Wallenberg.
Similarly, many persons have been questioned who could have had
anything to do with the circumstances mentioned in the material
received from Sweden.

As a result of these measures, however, it has not been possible to find any information whatsoever concerning Wallenberg's
sojourn in the Soviet Union. It has transpired that none of those
heard knew any person by the name of Wallenberg. In this connection,
the competent Soviet authorities have undertaken a search page by
page of the archive documents from all wards in certain prisons.
As a result of such search of archive documents from the health
service in the Ljublanka Prison, a document has been found which
there is good reason to consider as referring to Raoul Wallenberg.

This document has the form of a hand-written report, addressed
to the former Minister of the State Security in the Soviet Union,
Abakumov, and written by the head of the health service at the
said prison, A.L. Smoltsov, reading as follows:

"I report that the prisoner Wallenberg, who is well known to
you, died suddenly in his cell this night, probably as the result
of a heart attack. Pursuant to instructions given by you that I
personally have Wallenberg under my care, I request approval to
make an autopsy with a view to establishing the cause of death.
"July 17, 1947.
"Smoltsov,
"Chief of the Prison's Sanitary
Ward,
"Colonel in the Medical Service."

On this report, the following notation is found, in Smolssov's
handwriting: "I have personally notified the Minister and it has
been ordered that the body be cremated without autopsy. July 17.
Smoltsov."

UNCLASSIFIED UNCLASSIFIED

UNCLASSIFIED

The Gromyko statement (front)

312

(Classification)

UNCLASSIFIED

UNCLASSIFIED

It has not been possible to find any other information whatsoever having the character of document or testimony, all the more since the aforementioned A. L. Smoltsov died on May 7, 1953. On the strength of what has been cited above, the conclusion should be drawn that Wallenberg died in July 1947.

Raoul Wallenberg was apparently arrested along with other persons in the area for military operations by Soviet troops. At the same time, it may be considered indisputable that Wallenberg's subsequent detention in prison as well as the incorrect information about him supplied by certain former leaders of the security organs to the Soviet Union's Foreign f Ministry over a period of years comprised the result of Abakumov's criminal activities. In connection with gross crimes committed by him, it will be recalled that Abakumov, who had engaged in activities implying violation of the laws of the Soviet Union and who had sought to inflict upon the Soviet Union all kinds of damage, was executed in accordance with verdict handed down by the Supreme Court of the Soviet Union.

The Soviet Government presents its sincere regrets because of what has occurred and expresses its profound sympathy to the Swedish Government as well as to Raoul Wallenberg's relatives.

Translation: NMöller

UNCLASSIFIED

The Gromyko statement (back)

Appendix 5

★★★

Wallenberg's registration cards

Wallenberg's registration card at the Lubyanka

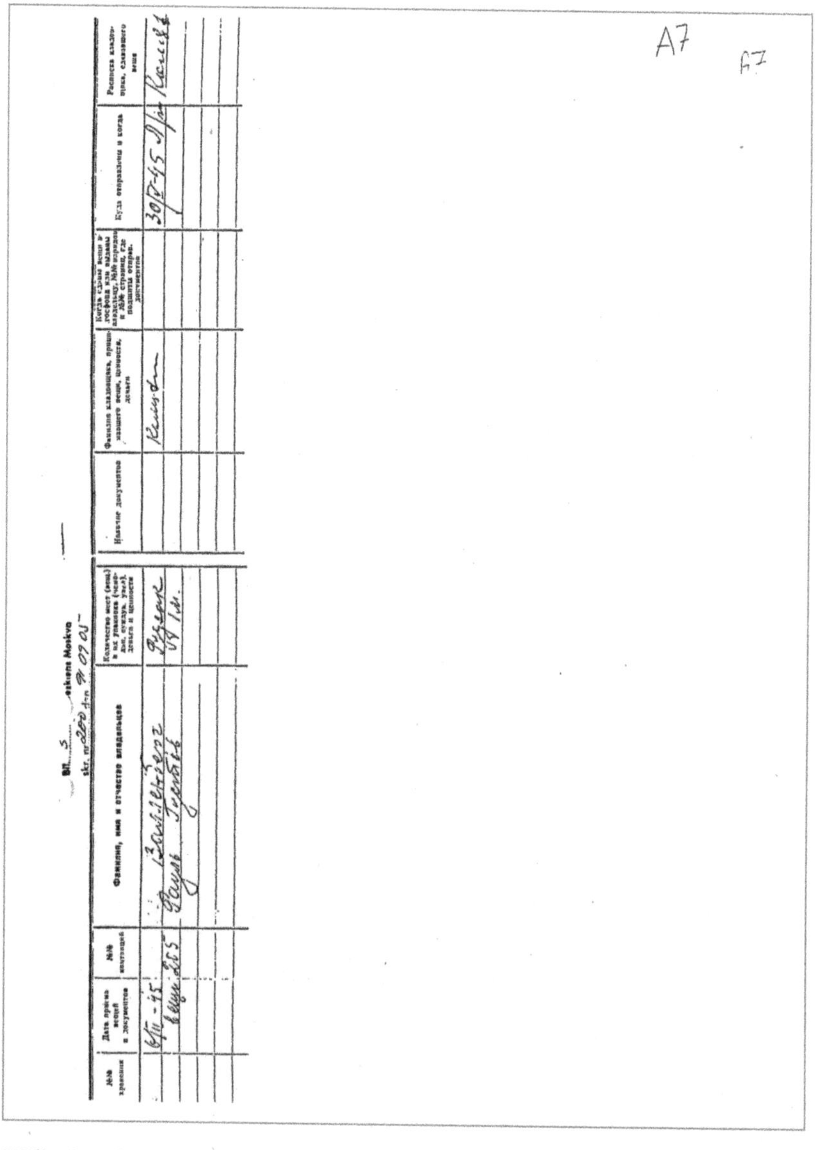

Wallenberg's registration card at Lefortovo

Appendix 6

★ ★ ★

ПРЕДСЕДАТЕЛЮ КОМИТЕТА ГОСБЕЗОПАСНОСТИ
ПРИ СОВЕТЕ МИНИСТРОВ СССР
Генералу армии тов. СЕРОВУ И.А.

25 февраля 1957 г.

Во исполнение поручения Инстанции о привлечении видных представителей деловых кругов Запада к пропаганде достижений советской науки и культуры в связи с предстоящим празднованием 40-годовщины Великой Октябрьской Социалистической Революции, докладываем на ваше рассмотрение:

В проводимых нами мероприятиях принимает участие влиятельный предприниматель из Англии Р.Максвел, связанный с одним из руководителей Лейбористской партии Г.Вильсоном.

В ходе поддержания делового конспиративного контакта с Максвелом нами установлены его широкие коммерческие возможности. В связи с этим считаем целесообразным удовлетворить просьбу Максвела выступить в качестве зарубежного продюссера документальных фильмов "Большой Балет" и "Лебединое озеро", намеченных к прокату в 1957-58 гг. в США, Англии и других странах.

Принимая во внимание важность дальнейшей работы с Максвелом, учитывая возможность значительного экономического эффекта от его издательской деятельности, представляется необходимым, чтобы Минвнешторг и Минкультуры СССР получили по вопросу сотрудничества с ним соответствующие указания Инстанции, дополнительные средства и квоты.

ПЕРВЫЙ ЗАМЕСТИТЕЛЬ ПРЕДСЕДАТЕЛЯ КОМИТЕТА
ГОСБЕЗОПАСНОСТИ ПРИ СОВЕТЕ МИНИСТРОВ СССР
-Генерал-майор   /К.ЛУНЕВ/

НАЧАЛЬНИК 2 ГЛАВНОГО УПРАВЛЕНИЯ
- Генерал-лейтенант   /О.ГРИБАНОВ/

Исполнитель: Н.Бородин

Robert Maxwell – the first KGB secret document. It relates to how the KGB was making payments to Maxwell's companies, and is dated February 25, 1957.

Robert Maxwell – the first KGB secret document

The English translation from the Russian. Serov had signed it.

Top secret
To chairman of KGB, State Security Committee of the Council of Ministers of the USSR
To Army General Comrade Serov, I.A
Date 25 February 1957

Following the request of the Organisation concerning attracting prominent representatives from the West for positive propaganda of Soviet science and achievements in connection with the future celebration of the 40th anniversary of the Great October Socialist Revolution, the following is for your consideration:

We have undertaken measures assuring the involvement of influential business representatives from England, R.Maxwell, who is connected with one of the Labour Party leaders, Harold Wilson.

Aiming to maintain business and conspiratorial contacts with Maxwell we have identified his broad commercial possibilities. In connection with this we feel it feasible to meet Maxwell's request to become a foreign producer of documentary films 'The Bolshoi Ballet' and 'Swan Lake', planned to be shown between 1957 and 1958 in the United States, Europe and in other countries.

Given the importance of further work with Maxwell and considering the feasibility of significant economic benefits of his publishing activity, we feel it necessary that the Ministry of Foreign Trade Bank and Ministry of Culture of the USSR receive respected guidelines of the Organisation regarding the opportunities for cooperation with him, in addition to additional funding and quotas.

Signed: First Deputy Chairman of the KGB
Major General K. Lunyov
And the Head of the 2nd Chief Department
Lt. General O. Gribanov

Prepared by N. Borodin. The document
says 'agreed' with Serov's signature.

285

Министру финансов СССР
тов. ГАРБУЗОВУ В. Ф.

24.06.80   1071-Ц

Уважаемый Василий Федорович!

В соответствии с Вашим указанием совзагранбанки в _Швейцарии_ приостановили финансирование сделок по контрактам компаний _Р. Максвелла_ ввиду неполучения платежей по выделенным в 1979 г. льготным кредитам.

Во исполнение поручения Инстанции о содействии по нашей линии _Р. Максвеллу_ в утверждении влияния в ведущих изданиях _США и Великобритании_, полагали бы целесообразным учесть эту задолженность перед совзагранбанками в сумме _8 млн. долл. США_ в счет выделенных нам в 1979/80 гг. СМ СССР лимитов на проведение _спецмероприятий за рубежом_.

В связи с вышеизложенным также сообщаем, что согласно полученной нами достоверной информации, погашение предоставленных кредитов будет, как и ранее, проведено "Нэшнл Вестминстер Банк" не позднее 1 октября с.г.

Прошу Ваших указаний о незамедлительном возобновлении операции совзагранбанков с этими фирмами.

Первый заместитель Председателя   С.ЦВИГУН

Верно:
Нач. Секретариата—пом. 1-го зам. пред.

Поздоровский Г.А.

Отпечатано в 4 экз.:
1. Адресату.
2. Секретариат КГБ СССР.
3. 2 Гл. Упр. /т. Григоренко Г.Ф./.

Исп.: Волков А.А.
Тел. 224-45-04

15-ЛМ
25.01.80г.

Robert Maxwell – the second KGB document

Robert Maxwell – the second KGB document,
this one dated June 24, 1980

Like the first document on Robert Maxwell only a senior KGB officer, in this case, A.A.Volkov, has completed the document by writing in the highly sensitive information and then underlining it. In the document Volkov includes his telephone number in KGB headquarters. The use of the term 'Authority' in KGB documents can often be misleading. It usually relates to the head of the KGB but in some instances it can refer to the Russian Premier. Semyon Tsvigun was the First Deputy Chairman of the KGB and the brother-in-law of Leonid Brezhnev. His death in January 1982 was sudden. It was officially reported that he had committed suicide by taking cyanide, but that was never independently confirmed. One theory was that he was executed after being implemented in a corruption scandal that involved the Kremlin. The reference to 'soft credits' relates to credit extended on generous or subsidised terms.

The English translation from the Russian:

Top secret
Copy No 2
285
June 24, 1980   1071-Ts
For the attention of the Minister of Finance of the USSR
Comrade Garbuzov, V.F.

Dear Vasily Federovich!

In accordance with your instruction the Soviet foreign banks in Switzerland have suspended the financing of the transactions relating to contracts of R.Maxwell's companies due to non payment, for soft credits extended to them in 1979.

In implementing the order from the highest Authority on assistance to R.Maxwell, in our line of business, which is to strengthen influence in leading American and British publications, it would be deemed expedient to treat this debt to the Soviet foreign banks amounting to $8 million on account of the limits allocated to us for 1979/1980 by the USSR Council of Ministers for carrying out special measures abroad.

In connection with the above we also inform you that in accordance with reliable information received by us, repayment of these credits should be made, as in the past, by the National Westminster Bank, not later than October 1 this year.

We ask for your instructions on the immediate resumption of the operations of the Soviet foreign banks with these companies.

First Deputy Chairman
S.Tsvigun

Correct:
Head of the Secretary – assistant to first Deputy Chairman
Pozdoroski, J.A.

[Pozdoroski has signed the document]

Typed in four copies:
1. Addressee
2. Secretariat of KGB USSR
3. 2nd Chief Directorate (to Comrade Grigorenko, G.F)

Implemented by Volkov A.A.
Telephone: 224-49-04

15-DM
23.6.80g

Photograph of a cell in the internal jail of the Lubyanka taken in 1950.

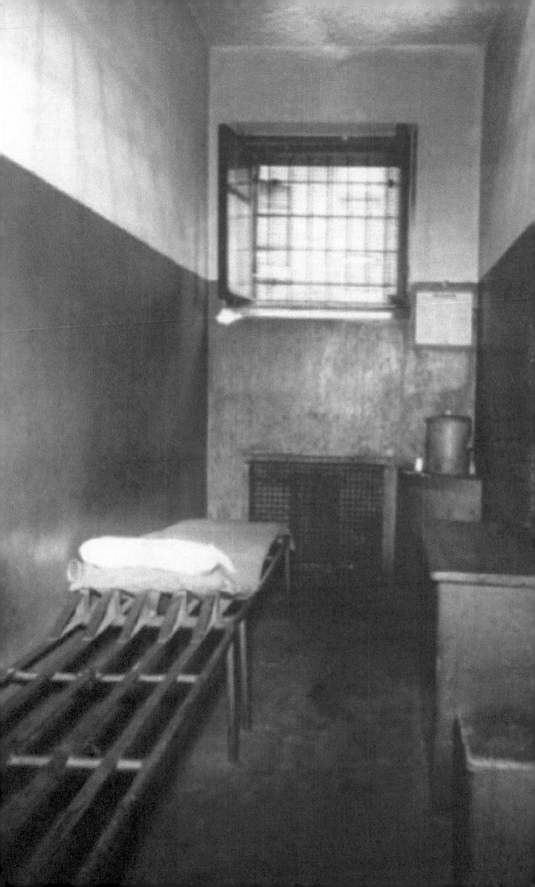

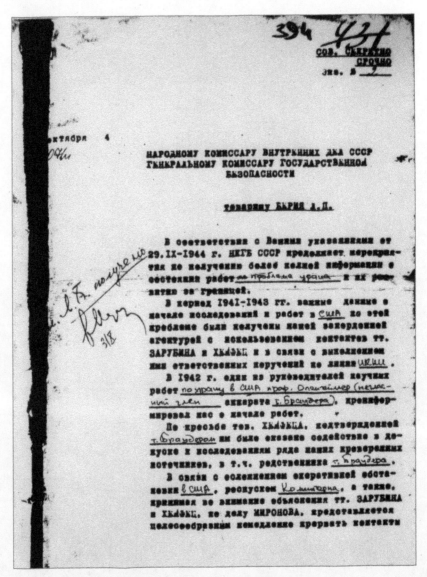

The Oppenheimer document (front)

Professor Robert Oppenheimer: the NKVD document

The English translation from the Russian: again, the sensitive parts of the document have been written in by hand, to shield the names and content from the Lubyanka typing clerks.

394 [431 is crossed out]

Top secret
Urgent
Copies – 9

To the People's Commissar of Internal Affairs of the USSR and General Commissar of State Security

Comrade Beria LP.

In accordance with your instructions of September 29, 1944 the NKGB continues its work to obtain fuller information on the state of progress on the uranium problem and its development abroad.

In the period 1941–1943, important data on the beginnings of research and work in the USA, concerning this problem was received by our overseas agents network using contacts of Comrades Zarubin and Kheifets, and in connection with their implementation of important tasks to do with uranium.

In 1942 one of the leaders of scientific work on uranium in the USA, Professor Oppenheimer [secret member of Comrade Browder's network] informed us about the beginning of the work.

At the request of Comrade Kheifets, confirmed by Comrade Browder, he provided assistance in gaining access to research of several reliable sources we have, including a relative of Comrade Browder.

Due to complications in the operational situation in the USA, the dissolution of the Comintern, and taking into account the clarifications of Comrades Zarubin and Kheifets in the case of Mironov, it seems expedient to break immediately the contacts of the leadership and the activists of the Communist Party of the US

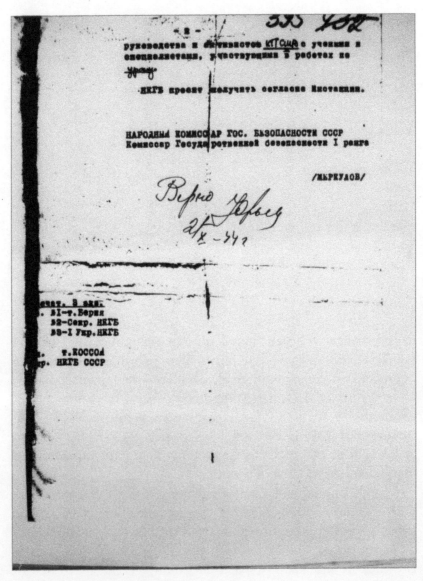

The Oppenheimer document (back)

with scientists and specialists participating in the work on uranium. NKGB asks to obtain the consent of the top leadership.

Signed: Merkulov,
Commissar of State Security of the USSR First Rank

October 2, 1944

Typed in 3 copies
1. Comrade Beria
2. Secretariat of the NKGB
3. First NKGB Directorate

Prepared by: Comrade Kossov, NKGB USSR

Character index

A

Abakumov, Col. Gen. Victor: Security head, Smersh, MGB.
5-6, 10-11, 106, 108, 110, 113-114, 118, 120, 127, 133, 149,
181, 196, 208, 216, 219-220, 244, 259, 263, 269-273, 275,
277, 308-309

Afonin, Maj. Gen.: Red Army officer, Hungary.
118

Aldercreutz, Col.: Swedish military general staff.
159

Anger, Per: Swedish legation deputy head, Budapest.
3, 70, 74, 76-77, 137, 139, 172, 300, 310

Antonescu, Ion: Marshal, Rumania.
96

Antonescu, Mihai: Rumanian foreign minister.
97, 120

Arafat, Yasser: Palestine Liberation Organisation.
210

'Archie': Codename given to author's high-level Moscow source.
24-25, 28, 140

Artuzov, Gen. Arthur: OGPU chief.
169-170

B

Bagirov: Soviet Praesidium, Azerbaijan premier.
41

Baky, László: Ministry of the Interior, Budapest.

C

H

L

13-14

Pronin, Col. Gen.: Moscow Military District.
40

R

Rodionov: Russian ambassador, Stockholm.
247, 307

Raikhman, Lt. Gen. Leonid: NKVD, Moscow.
115, 248

Rakovsky, Christian: Founder of Pravda.
221

Reiff, Ignatius: NKVD, Paris.
236-237

Rensinghoff, Bernhard: German PoW.
100

Ribbentrop, von: German foreign minister.
58, 138

Richter, Maj. Gustav: Austrian PoW.
96-99, 100-104, 120, 122-124, 131-132, 245, 306

Roberts, Frank: British Foreign Office, London.
162-164, 176-177

Roedel, Wilhelm [Willy]: PoW, cellmate of Wallenberg.
5, 99-100, 124, 130-131, 218, 257

Rogov, Col. Gen. Aleksandr: GRU, Moscow.
50-51

Ronchi: Italian PoW.
90

Roosevelt, Theodore: US president
138, 141, 144, 233, 240

Roschin (aka Tischenko), Colonel Vasily: NKVD, head of station, Stockholm.
83, 169-172, 174-175, 177, 180

Rösel, Dr Rudolf: German press corps deputy head, Stockholm.
167

Rosenblatt, Maj. von: German military attaché, Stockholm.
158

Rosstel: PoW.

212

Yeltsin, Boris: Russian premier.
21, 195, 232, 241, 266

Yerzin, Maj. Pavel: NKVD foreign intelligence, Istanbul.
244, 276

Yezhov, Nikolay: NKVD chief, Moscow.
199, 203-205, 232

Young, Gordon: British journalist, Stockholm.
174

Z

Zakharov: Soviet deputy foreign minister, Moscow.
247

Zakharov, Maj. Gen. N.: KGB, Moscow.
34

Zenkov, Capt. Nikolai: Smersh, Budapest.
119-121, 124

Zhdanov, Andrey: Politburo.
133

Zhelezov, Anatoli: Administrative head, Laboratory X, Moscow.
198, 212, 214-215, 217, 261, 272-273

Zhukov, Marshal Georgii: Commander, Red Army.
33, 40-41, 177, 227, 269

Zinoviev, Grigory: Soviet communist party leader.
199, 220

Zorin, Valerian: Soviet deputy foreign minister.
92, 305-306

Names **in bold** are names mentioned by Ivan Serov in his Wallenberg memoir

The Author

NIGEL BANCE has enjoyed a long and successful career in journalism, research and publishing, including *The Economist*, *Daily Mail*, *Euromoney* and the *Petroleum Economist*. He contributed to many other titles, such as *The Daily Telegraph*, *The Times* and the *Petroleum Review*. In 2005, in Moscow, he was presented with a prestigious award by a Russian defense and security institute for extensive research into Soviet nuclear intelligence during WW2 and the Cold War. Some of his past work has been published in Russian. He has BA and MA degrees in History from the University of London.

In recent years he has written regularly on security issues in the global oil and gas industry, in particular the growing threat of kidnapping and piracy.